AF548238

Martin Steigerwald
Simon Neumann
Nico Barbat (ed.)

AMIGAOS 3.2

REFERENCE MANUAL

AmigaOS 3.2 Reference Manual
Original title (2024): AmigaOS 3.2 – Das Handbuch

Martin Steigerwald
Simon Neumann
Nico Barbat (ed.)

With text contributions by Anton Preinsack, Sascha van Wahnem, Frank Greshake and Daniel Reimann.

Editorial support: Marcus Gerards, Olaf Barthel, Camilla Boemann, Thomas Klein, Rainer Müller, Mikhail Malyshev, Ignacio Gully

Edited and typeset by Nico Barbat
Proofread by Simon Busby and Per-Olof Yliniemi
Cover image by Paul Kitching
Printed by PRINTMER, Krakow, Poland

1st edition, 2024

Barbat & Neumann GbR, Simrockstr. 43, 53619 Rheinbreitbach, Germany

Bibliographic information of the German National Library
The German National Library indexes this publication in the German National Biography; detailed bibliographic data is available on the internet at http://dnb.d-nb.de.

ISBN: 978-3-9826022-6-4
This book is also available as a digital edition (PDF, EPUB).

For all Amiga developers – yesterday's pioneers, today's innovators and tomorrow's visionaries – whose dedication, creativity and tireless work on software and hardware continue to keep the legacy alive. Thank you for making the impossible possible and the possible even better.

For Jürgen Haage.
Without your vision and passion,
Amiga would not be what it is today.

Foreword

As a member of the development team of AmigaOS 3.2, I would like to share my enthusiasm for our work with you. It has been an inspiring experience to create AmigaOS 3.2. Our motivation has always been to give something back to the enthusiastic community – the people who have kept the magic of this extraordinary computer alive for almost four decades. If you are reading this, you are a valuable part of that community, and it is important to us that we express our sincere gratitude.

Our commitment is not limited to the development of AmigaOS 3.2 and 3.3; we also endeavour to develop tools and write developer documentation to make it easier for other developers to create software of any kind for the AmigaOS. Our goal is to further strengthen the active developer community – a task that requires a lot of work and time.

Knowing these challenges, there is little room for direct dialogue with users. This is why it is a special pleasure for us to see that this book has been written for the large and loyal German Amiga community. We would like to assure you that we, the team behind AmigaOS 3.2, have carefully reviewed this book and provided the authors with valuable insights and explanations during its production.

By purchasing and reading this book, you are not only helping to keep the Amiga spirit alive, but also giving us developers motivation to continue our work on AmigaOS. AmigaOS 3.3 will be released next – and your commitment gives us the strength to pave the way for the Amiga into the future.

Camilla Boemann on behalf of the entire AmigaOS development team

Contents

About this book

This **AmigaOS 3.2 Reference Manual** serves as a guide to the latest version, 3.2, of the Amiga operating system. It was written in close cooperation with the developers of AmigaOS 3.2 with a clear focus on practical usability and comprehensibility. From basic knowledge and advanced functions to specialized know-how for experienced users, it offers a well-founded insight into all aspects of the system. The aim is to provide readers with an easy introduction and lead them step by step towards more advanced topics.

This work is not intended as a replacement for, but a practical further development of, the Amiga manuals of the 1980s and 1990s. It sees itself in the tradition of the "AmigaOS 3.9 – User's Manual" by Haage&Partner, which was published in 2000.

Spread across eight chapters, the book uses a color scheme based on the original Workbench palette:

› **Orange** marks basics and basic knowledge:
chapters 1 to 4 (Installation of AmigaOS 3.2 and ROMs, Basics, Preferences and Programs)

› **Red** is aimed at experienced users:
chapters 5 and 6 (Shell and Power Users, e.g. start scripts, shortcuts, AmigaGuide, ARexx programming)

› **Blue** includes general knowledge:
chapters 7 and 8 (Next Steps and Quick Reference, e.g. data transfer, internet, hardware and software, error codes, FAQ)

Special attention has been paid to a high level of comprehensibility and readability to make the content accessible. Some technical terms need to be used where unavoidable. To help you understand these terms, please use the glossary and index.

The margin column on all pages contains key terms for the adjacent paragraphs, making it easier to find the information you are looking for.

The design of the book uses a number of visual highlights to help you keep track:

› *Italics* for names and paths
› **Bold** for key terms
› `Monospace` (fixed-width) font for shortcuts and commands (command arguments are capitalized)

Keyboard shortcuts are clearly marked in square brackets to assist in understanding and usage. `[R-Amiga]` stands for the right Amiga key, `[L-Amiga]` marks the left Amiga key. For example, `[Ctrl]+[L-Amiga]+[R-Amiga]` will cause the system to reboot (reset). In this book, the left mouse button is also referred to as the Select button and the right mouse button is called the Menu button.

You will be well equipped to take full advantage of AmigaOS 3.2 and the next steps with this manual at your side.

Now it's time to get ready: insert the disk and get started!

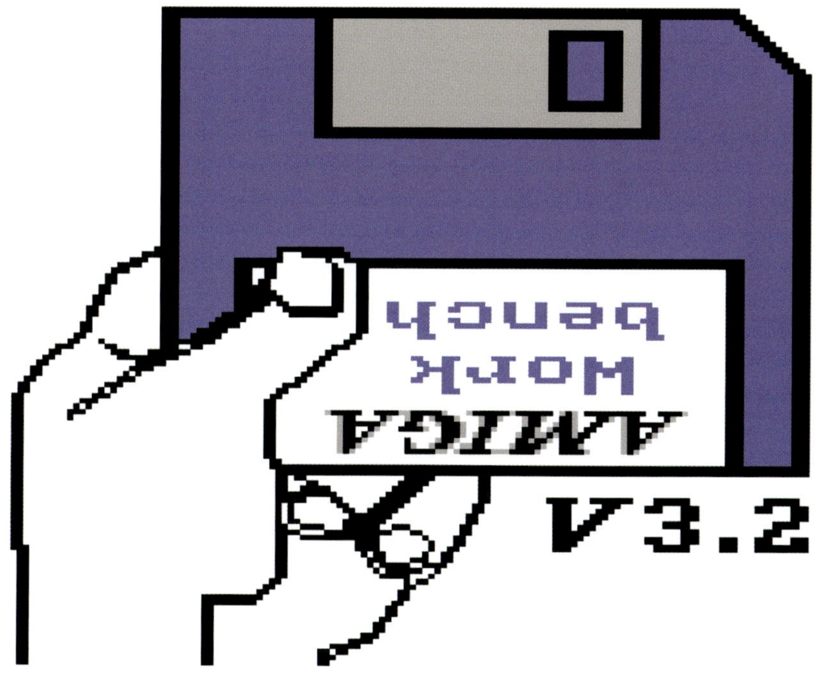

Versions in comparison

Over the past 30 years, six major versions of AmigaOS have been released. The following compact overview shows the key data related to the major milestones: 3.1, 3.9 and 3.2.

	AMIGAOS 3.1
Manufacturer/developer	Commodore
Year of publication	1994
Medium	Disk
Packaging	Cardboard box
Documentation	books
Core system	
ROM module	●
Extended boot menu	✗
Generic CPU libraries	✗
PowerPC as coprocessor	✗
Workbench features	
GUI system	ClassAct
Workbench prefs	✗
Reaction prefs	✗
Datatypes update	●
DefaultIcons system	✗
GlowIcons	✗
Integrated search	✗
Drive functionality	
Storage media over 4 GB	✗
ADF management	✗
CD-ROM support	●
FAT32 support	✗
Software equipment	
TCP-IP stack	✗
Browser	✗
Multimedia tools (MP3, video, CD)	✗
Integrated unpacker	✗
Quick launch bar (dock)	✗
Power user	
Command Line Interface	Shell
Shell extension	✗
ARexx: Workbench interface	✗
ARexx: MultiView/TextEdit interface	✗

AMIGAOS 3.9	AMIGAOS 3.2
Haage&Partner	Hyperion Entertainment
2000	2021
CD	CD/ADF
CD case (OS3.5: cardboard box)	DVD case
HTML	AmigaGuide
✗	●
✗	●
✗	●
● [1]	✗
ReAction	ReAction
●	● [4]
●	●
●	●
●	●
●	●
●	●
●	●
✗	●
●	●
✗	●
● [2]	✗
● [3]	✗
●	✗
●	✗
●	✗
ViNCEd	Shell
●	●
●	●
✗	●

* **1** WarpUp, **2** Genesis, **3** AWeb, **4** extended

Installation

1

There are many paths to a successful first installation of AmigaOS 3.2, whether on a classic Amiga or emulated system. Here, you will discover what steps are necessary, from the installation of the Kickstart ROMs on the various classic models, to the preparation of the WinUAE emulator and installation from floppy disk, ADF or CD-ROM. We even cover the THEA500 Mini, on which it is also possible to make AmigaOS 3.2 work. And this is how it is done...

Registration and support

If you are using AmigaOS 3.2 for the first time, you should register it. This has two important benefits.

Registering your copy of AmigaOS 3.2 entitles you to free support from the manufacturer and access to free updates.

A registration number is required to activate AmigaOS 3.2. This can be found on a sticker on the packaging foil.

TIP **Keep your registration number safe**
Remove the sticker with the registration number from the packaging foil before discarding it and stick it on the inside of the CD case. If you have already discarded it by accident, please contact Hyperion Entertainment directly with the receipt from the purchase of the product.

Registration

To register your version of AmigaOS 3.2 online, visit the website www.hyperion-entertainment.com using a web browser of your choice. The Hyperion Entertainment website will open in English. Proceed as follows:

You must register as a user on the site by selecting *Create an account* from the menu on the left. In the following form, enter your name, your preferred username, your e-mail address and your desired password. After clicking on the *Register* button, you will receive an e-mail to your e-mail address, in which you must click on a confirmation link. Once you have done this, you can log in with your username and password in the left-hand column of the website under *Username* and *Password*.

After logging in, a *user menu* appears in the left-hand column with the items *Your Details*, *Logout* and *Product registration*. Click on *Product registration*. A page with the title *Your current registered products* and a link *Register a product* will appear. If you click on this link, you will be taken to a page with a selection menu (drop-down menu). Select the product you have purchased – for example, *AmigaOS 3.2 (disk version)*. You will now be shown three text fields in which you must enter the three parts of the *registration number* (*Serial Number*). Once you

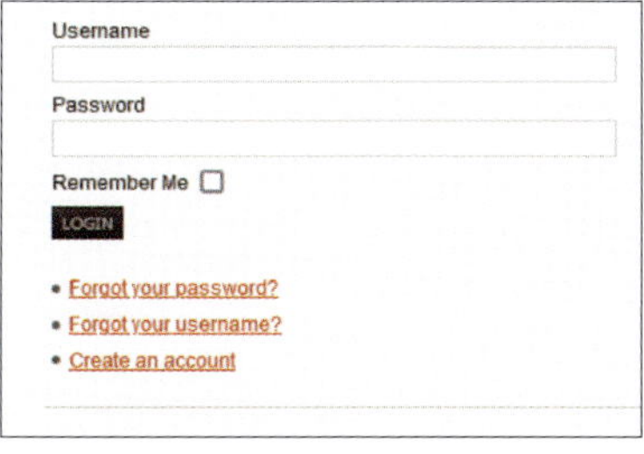

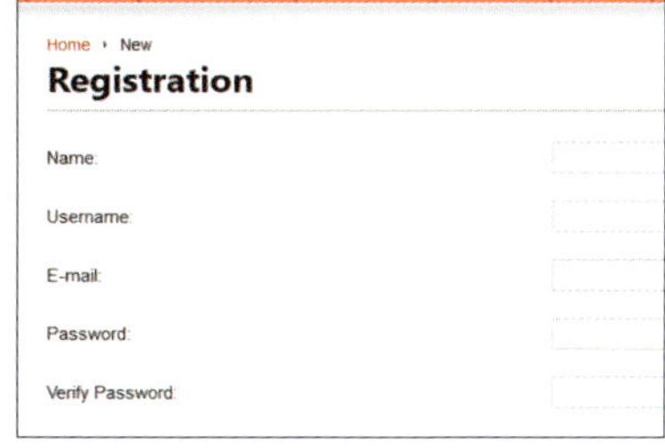

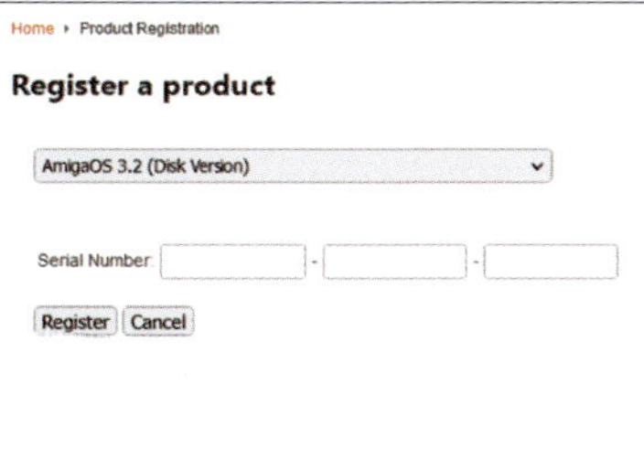

Registration of AmigaOS 3.2: create an account on the support website, log in, enter the version of the product and registration number

have entered the number, click on the *Register* button and your AmigaOS 3.2 should finally be registered.

To check whether this is really the case, switch to the *Product registration* area – the registered AmigaOS 3.2 version should now appear here.

Updates

You might want to download the first updates immediately after your registration. Click on the *Downloads* link at the top of the page. A link labelled *AmigaOS 3.2* will appear, which you can click on directly. Here you will find all of the available updates for AmigaOS 3.2. As of July 2024, updates to versions 3.2.1 and 3.2.2, as well as the hotfix 3.2.2.1, are offered.

Download all of the updates and install them after the basic installation of your AmigaOS 3.2 system, as explained in the following sections.

Assistance and support

Once you are registered, you will be able to make use of the manufacturer's support services if required. There are two ways to do that:

1. Contact via e-mail in English describing the problem: support@hyperion-entertainment.com
2. Use the English support forum at: https://forum.hyperion-entertainment.com/

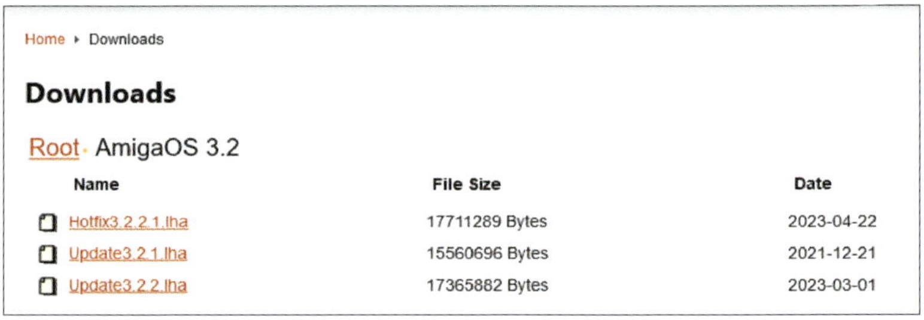

Home ▸ Downloads

Downloads

Root · AmigaOS 3.2

Name	File Size	Date
Hotfix3.2.2.1.lha	17711289 Bytes	2023-04-22
Update3.2.1.lha	15560696 Bytes	2021-12-21
Update3.2.2.lha	17365882 Bytes	2023-03-01

All relevant update files can be found in the downloads area (currently 3.2.1, 3.2.2 and 3.2.2.1).

If you are not comfortable communicating in English, you can try an online translation tool such as www.deepl.com or translate.google.com to automatically translate phrases or entire sentences.

You can also contact these two independent service points at any time:

1. Write an e-mail to your trusted Amiga dealer: almost all Amiga dealers who stock AmigaOS 3.2 also have experience with the new Amiga system and are usually very helpful with customer enquiries.

2. Start a discussion in an independent Amiga forum: there are several Amiga and AmigaOS discussion forums on the internet in countries such as the UK and the US, France, Sweden, the Czech Republic, Poland and many more. There are many experts and even developers of AmigaOS 3.2 happy to discuss problems and answer questions.

Installation of Kickstart ROMs

Installing appropriate Kickstart ROMs on the Amiga is not essential, but will improve performance.

Advantages of Kickstart ROMs

It is possible to run AmigaOS 3.2 without new Kickstart ROMs. The minimum system requirement is Kickstart 3.1, but 3.1.4 would also be compatible.

However, the newer physical Kickstart ROM chips offer three key operational advantages:

Firstly, boot times are shortened because Kickstart does not have to be loaded into the RAM during the first cold boot process. The typical reset after the first boot process, which is familiar from AmigaOS 3.9, is no longer necessary.

Secondly, memory consumption is lower because Kickstart can be loaded directly from the ROM chip, rather than having to be copied into the main memory. Without the built-in ROM chips, 512KB of memory would be taken. (Note that without physical ROM chips, the total RAM required is 2.5 MB instead of 2 MB. As a result, on an A1200 without a memory expansion, you would not be able to use the new AmigaOS 3.2 without built-in Kickstart ROMs).

Thirdly, if you are using a 3.1.4 or later ROM, you can set up hard disk partitions of any size throughout, and you do not need to provide a boot partition of less than 4 GB.

Preparing the ROM installation

Suitable Kickstart ROMs are available from Amiga dealers individually or as a bundle with the operating system itself.

Before installing the Kickstart ROMs, check the following to ensure a smooth installation:

1. **Time:** Allow sufficient time for installation. Inexperienced users may need up to an hour or more to open the case and remove the ROMs, depending on the Amiga model.
2. **Lighting:** Illuminate your workplace well. Bright rooms with plenty of daylight and additional lamps for reading or working, such as those from a hardware store, are ideal.
3. **Antistatic:** Use a stable, antistatic base material. An antistatic mat on a work table or an antistatic wrist strap is ideal. If you do not have such items, touch an earthed metal object, such as a metal radiator, immediately prior to the installation.

4. **Documentation:** Take photos with a camera or a smartphone of all the steps involved in opening the case. This will make it easier to reassemble.

Recurring steps

Procedure for changing the ROM

The steps involved in changing the Kickstart ROM (or ROMs) differ to a greater or lesser extent from model to model. In the following sections, you will learn which steps are required for each Amiga and what you need to pay attention to. From opening the case and the protective plates, to locating the ROM(s) and levering out and inserting the chips, to finally closing the case and testing the operation, the procedures are identical. Here, we explain what you need to bear in mind: how bent chips are straightened, how chips are levered out and inserted, and how the function of the Amiga is tested after installation.

Required tools

Prepare suitable tools. It is helpful to use an *extractor* (see photo 1), a *plastic rod* or a *slotted screwdriver* to lever out the components. The 11 original Amiga models were supplied with different types of screws. Have suitable Phillips and Torx screwdrivers to hand for opening and closing the housing.

Straightening bent pins

Eliminate any static charge before touching the ROMs (touch a radiator or use an antistatic strap). With new ROM components, check that all the pins are straight and are located above the contacts of the ROM socket. Often the pins protrude outwards and need to be bent slightly inwards (see photo 2). To do this, place the chip on its side on the table so that the pins on one side are parallel to the table surface. Gently press the chip onto the table so that the pins slowly bend inwards (see photo 3). Repeat the process with the pin strip on the opposite side of the chip. All pins should now be positioned vertically to form a 90 degree angle to the chip (see photo 4).

Removing ROM chips from the socket

You should remove installed ROM chips very carefully using a special lifter, a plastic stick or, if necessary, an insulated slotted screwdriver (e.g. a current tester).

To do this, carefully press the appropriate tool under the chip from one side between the module and the socket (see photo 5), and slowly and gently lever it out of the socket. Pull out the lever

Photo tutorial: Straighten the Kickstart ROMs

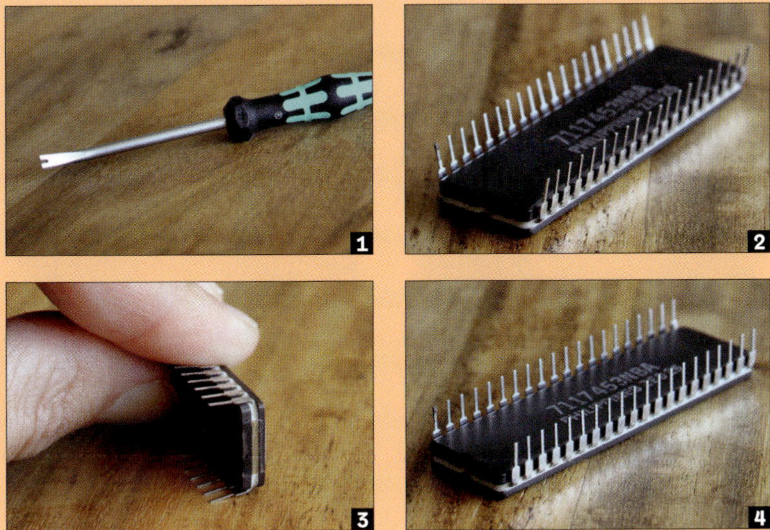

A lever tool will help you remove the old Kickstart ROMs properly (1). If the pins of the new chips are bent (2), carefully straighten them (3, 4).

Photo tutorial: Lever out, remove and insert chips

Using a lever motion, carefully lift the chip from both sides until it can be easily detached (5 to 7). Put the new chip in the socket with the pins in the correct position, then gently and evenly press it into the socket (8).

tool and repeat the process at the other end of the ROM module (see photo 6). Lift the chip evenly so that it does not jam, bend or break the legs.

Be patient during this procedure, as you may have to repeat the process several times before the component has completely detached from the socket. Unless you're a Jedi Knight, never use force, as this can damage not only the chip, but also the socket and the entire hardware. Be careful not to slip so you don't damage the motherboard with the tool.

Store the removed ROM chip in an antistatic ESD foil or in a small box with foam.

Insert ROM chips into the socket

Once you have removed the ROM chip(s) from the motherboard, you can replace them with the new 3.2 ROM(s), as described in the following installation instructions for each model. Unpack the new 3.2 ROM chip and take a look at it.

Check on which side of the chip the small notch is located. Align the module using the notch, and place the module carefully on the socket. If the pins do not fit properly when placed on the socket, bend them slightly as shown in photos 2 to 4.

Caution: Incorrect installation of the ROM chip(s) can lead to damage to the module or even to the motherboard. Please double and triple check that the orientation and position of the chip(s) is correct. The new ROM must be in the same position and have the same orientation as the old ROM.

Once you are sure that the chip is in the right place and correctly aligned, slowly press it into the socket, applying equal pressure on both sides with your thumbs. The chip should slide into the socket without much force and be inserted flat (see photo 8).

Check after installation

Having reassembled the Amiga, it's time to perform your first test. Reconnect the power cable from the power supply unit to the Amiga and switch on the computer. The Boingball and Kickstart 3.2 should appear after a short time. In this case, the installation was successful.

If a black, white or other color screen appears after powering up, turn off the Amiga. Disconnect it from the power supply and open it again. Check that you have correctly inserted the ROM chips. If not, remove the ROM carefully and reinsert it properly.

Different ROMs in Amiga models

The Amiga has been produced in various models and revisions over the years. There are significant differences in the number, compatibility and capacity of the ROM components, which you should be aware of.

The ROMs are divided into three groups: the first comprises the Amiga 500, Amiga 600, Amiga 2000 and Amiga CDTV models, with a single ROM of 512 KB capacity; the second includes the Amiga 3000D, Amiga 3000T, Amiga 1200, Amiga 4000D and Amiga 4000T models, each with two ROMs of 512 KB capacity; and the third group is one machine, the CD32, with a 1 MB module.

In addition, older Amiga 500s (prior to revision 6) and Amiga 2000s (prior to revision 4.1) cannot cope with EPROM chips. However, AmigaOS 3.2 ROMs are usually supplied on EPROMs, so a modification is required. As an alternative, a so-called ROM adapter can be used.

The Amiga 1000 was manufactured without a fixed Kickstart ROM, so the contents of the ROM had to be read from a floppy disk into memory before each boot. ROM adapters for the A1000 do exist, however, which allow Kickstart ROMs to be retrofitted to the original Amiga.

For details on how to change the Kickstart ROM on each model, and for technical specifications, please refer to the following sections.

Flash ROM and MapROM

Flash ROMs: EPROM alternative 1

In addition to EPROMs, compatible Flash ROM components are also available in a range of capacities. The advantage to using Flash ROMs is that up to four Kickstart ROMs can be stored on a single chip, and users can swap between them. They can also be erased and reprogrammed very easily. As a result, these components are more expensive than EPROMs. If you need a lot of different Kickstart ROMs and the ability to switch between them, this solution is a better choice than buying a conventional double switcher with twice as many EPROM chips.

You can see what such a Flash ROM module looks like in the *ROM-replacement in an Amiga 600* section on page 26.

MapROM: EPROM alternative 2

Another alternative to EPROMs, or components in general, is the extended MapRom function. In this case, the Kickstart data is stored in flash memory on an accelerator card using a special utility program, and is then loaded directly into the Fast RAM. This feature, found on ACA accelerator cards for example, is even faster than the ordinary MapRom function, which copies the Kickstart from the ROM chip to the Fast RAM so that it can be used more quickly.

Replacing the ROM in an A500/500+

Revisions

The Amiga 500 and 500+ were produced in different board revisions, and installing the Kickstart 3.2 ROMs will be slightly different depending on the revision, as these ROMs are typically supplied by Amiga dealers on an EPROM chip.

Unfortunately, older board revisions cannot handle these kind of components, so an extra step is required. This step is not required for the newer revisions, 6a and 8a. With the older revisions 3 or 5, however, two ROM connection pins must first be connected via an additional cable. We do not recommend doing this yourself and suggest using a ROM adapter (see photo below) in those specific Amiga revisions. After installing such an adapter, the ROM modules can be used in exactly the same way as with newer board revisions.

On the A500's motherboard, the ROM is located directly between the long 68000 CPU and the square Fat Agnus chip.

ROM replacement in an Amiga 500(+)

1. Switch off the Amiga 500/500+, and disconnect the device from the **power supply**.
2. To **open the case**, you will need to remove **three screws** from the front and back of the bottom panel. Make a note of the screw locations and cable connections – if necessary, with photographs – as this will come in handy for reassembly.
3. Once the six screws have been loosened, the **case cover** can be removed to reveal the keyboard, the shielding plate, the floppy drive and the hard drive (if applicable). Remove the keyboard cable, slide the keyboard out of the mount and place it in a suitable location.
4. You will see the exposed **shielding plate** in front of you. Remove the four screws from the shielding plate, and bend all the locking lugs on the plate upwards. You can now carefully remove the plate.
   Caution: The plate can be sharp – take care not cut yourself.
5. Now the **motherboard** of the A500 is lying open in front of you. The first thing you need to do is identify the computer's Kickstart ROM, which is located on the left side of the Amiga between the elongated, vertically positioned 68000 processor and the square, socketed Fat Agnus chip. The ROM socket is labeled *ROM/U6* and the notch (marking pin 1) points towards the rear of the case. Take a photo to be on the safe side. Ground yourself again before moving to the next step.
6. Now, **remove** the built-in ROM chip using a suitable tool as described in section *Recurring steps* (1.2.1) under *Removing ROM chips from the socket*.
7. The **ROM socket** is now exposed. The A500+ / A500 Rev. 8a socket is slightly different from the Rev. 3 to 6a sockets. Instead of 40 pins, the new revisions come with 42 pins. The two additional poles must not be used! Ensure that the ROM is positioned at the lower end of the socket (front side of the case) and that the notch is facing the back side of the case. Carefully insert the new ROM into the socket as described in section *Recurring steps* (1.2.1) under *Insert ROM chips into the socket*.
8. Using the photos you've taken, and these instructions, check again to make sure the chip is **correctly positioned and aligned**.
9. Finally, fully **reassemble** the Amiga 500. Then, perform the **operational check** as described in the section *Recurring steps* (1.2.1) under *Check after installation*.

Replacing the ROM in an A600

Revisions

Although the Amiga 600, like the Amiga 500, was manufactured in different board revisions, they do not differ with regard to the ROMs. As such, these instructions apply to all revisions of the Amiga 600.

Note that in some Amiga 600s, however, the Kickstart ROM is permanently soldered to the motherboard (see step 5). In this case, you should entrust the ROM replacement to a specialized repair service.

On the A600 motherboard, the ROM is located to the right of the PCMCIA port. Here, you can see a Flash ROM variant (see page 23 for details).

ROM replacement in an Amiga 600

1. Switch off the Amiga 600 and disconnect the device from the **power supply**.
2. To **open the case**, turn the machine upside down. On the underside, remove two screws at the back, three screws at the front and one screw on the side. Make a note of the screw locations and cable connections – with photographs if necessary – as this will come in handy for reassembly.
3. Once the screws have been removed, carefully **remove the top cover**, including the keyboard. When separating the upper and lower parts of the case, pay attention to the plastic tabs on the sides, especially the one on the right-hand side near the disk drive. Remove the keyboard cable by gently pulling up the catch on the keyboard socket on the

motherboard. You can now remove the case top completely. The shielding plate, disk drive and hard drive (if applicable) are now revealed.

4. Remove the **two screws** from the **shielding plate**. Bend the locking lugs of the plate upwards, then carefully remove it. **Caution:** The plate can be sharp – take care not cut yourself.
5. The Amiga 600 **motherboard** is now before you. The first thing you need to do is identify the computer's Kickstart ROM. This is located in the bottom left-hand corner under the processor (68000), to the right of the PCMCIA slot. The 42-pin ROM socket is labeled *ROM/U6*, and the notch (marking pin 1) is facing the PCMCIA slot. The peculiarity is that the socket has 42 pins, whereas most ROM chips, such as the *EPROM 27C400*, only have 40. Make sure you leave the two pins on the left side empty. The correct alignment is marked by a small arrow below the socket. Ground yourself again before moving to the next step.
   Caution: Some Amiga 600 models do not have a socket at this position, and the ROM module is soldered directly to the board. If this is the case, please get in touch with your Amiga dealer or a specialist repair shop. The component will need to be removed from the motherboard, and a socket soldered in its place.
6. Now **remove** the built-in ROM chip using a suitable tool, as described in the *Recurring steps* (1.2.1) section under *Removing ROM chips from the socket*.
7. The **ROM socket** is now exposed. There are always 42 poles in the A600 socket – the two additional poles on the left-hand side must not be used. Ensure the ROM is positioned at the right-hand end of the socket and the notch is facing the PCMCIA slot. Carefully insert **the new ROM** into the socket, as described in the *Recurring steps (1.2.1)* section under *Insert ROM chips into the socket*.
8. Use the photos you have created, and these instructions, to check again if the chip is in the right position and **correctly aligned**.
9. Finally, fully **reassemble** the Amiga 600, then perform the **operational check** as described in the *Recurring steps* (1.2.1) section under *Check after installation*.

Replacing the ROM in an A2000

Revisions

The Amiga 2000 was manufactured in various board revisions, just like the A500. The installation of the 3.2 ROM is slightly different for the rare revision 4 (a model made in Braunschweig, Germany) than for other revisions, as the ROM is often supplied by Amiga dealers as an EPROM version. This early revision cannot handle these chips, so an additional step is required. This step is not necessary for the newer revisions 4.1 to 6.5. With revision 4, however, two of the ROM's connection pins must be connected via an additional cable. We do not recommend doing this yourself and suggest using a ROM adapter (see photo below) with those specific Amiga revisions. After installing such an adapter, the ROM modules can then be used in exactly the same way as with newer board revisions.

On the A2000's motherboard, the Kickstart ROM is below the processor, beside the square Agnus chip (8375 VBB).

ROM replacement in an Amiga 2000

1. Switch off the Amiga 2000 and disconnect the device from the **power supply**.
2. To **open the case**, remove two screws at the side and one screw at the top-center of the rear. Take care not to damage the cable connecting the power supply unit to the motherboard and the disk drive cable under the power supply unit when opening. Make a note of the screw locations and cable connections, as this will come in handy for reassembly.

3. Once the screws have been removed, carefully **pull the case cover** forward and disconnect the cables from the motherboard. It is a good idea to take a picture of this.
4. The **ROM chip** is located under the drive cage of the Amiga 2000, which you will need to remove. Remove the two screws at the front of the cage and the two screws at the rear of the power supply unit. You can then lift the entire cage, including the power supply, out of the case.
5. With the A2000's **motherboard** exposed, locate the **Kickstart ROM** directly to the right of the 68000 processor, the largest elongated chip on the board, and below the socketed, square Fat Agnus chip. The notch of the component points in the direction of Fat Agnus. Ground yourself again before moving to the next step.
6. Now, **remove** the built-in ROM chip using a suitable tool, as described in *Recurring steps* (1.2.1) section under *Removing ROM chips from the socket*.
7. The **ROM socket** is now exposed. Carefully insert **the new ROM** into the socket, as described in *Recurring steps (1.2.1)* section under *Insert ROM chips in the socket*.
8. Check again that the chip is in the **correct position** and orientation.
9. Finally, fully **reassemble** the Amiga 2000, then perform the **operational check** as described in the *Recurring Steps* (1.2.1) section under *Check after installation*.

Replacing the ROM in a CDTV

Revisions

The CDTV is also special when it comes to replacing the ROM chip. There are different BootROMs, which increase the work required when changing – this applies to unmodified models released before 1992. Further, installing the *experimental* 3.2 ROMs in a CDTV requires replacing its BootROMs with the newer versions 2.7, 2.30 or 2.35.

ROM replacement in an Amiga CDTV

1. Switch off the CDTV and disconnect the device from the **power supply**.
2. To **open the case**, two screws on the side and two screws on the back must be removed. Make a note of the screw locations and cable connections, as this will come in handy for reassembly.

Almost cosy: on the Amiga CDTV motherboard, the Kickstart ROM is right alongside the Gary custom chip (5719).

3. The **case cover** can now be removed to reveal the **motherboard** and the power supply unit. Locate the Kickstart ROM roughly in the center of the motherboard between the Gary chip 5719 and two white plugs. The ROM socket is labeled *U13*; the notch (marking pin 1) points in the direction of the power supply unit. Ground yourself again before moving to the next step.
4. Now, **remove** the built-in ROM chip using a suitable tool, as described in *Recurring steps* (1.2.1) section under *Removing ROM chips from the socket*.
5. The **ROM socket** is now exposed. Carefully insert **the new ROM** into the socket, as described in *Recurring steps (1.2.1)* section under *Insert ROM chips in the socket*.
6. Check again that the chip is in the **correct position** and orientation.
7. Finally, fully **reassemble** the Amiga CDTV, then perform the **operational check**, as described in the *Recurring steps* (1.2.1) section under *Check after installation*.

Replacing the ROM in an A3000D

Revisions

There are two models of Amiga 3000: the common but rare desktop model (3000D) and the even rarer tower (3000T). The two machines not only differ in terms of design, they also have different motherboards inside, which means that the procedure for replacing the ROM chips is different.

Unlike the A500, A600, A2000 and CDTV, both versions of the Amiga 3000 carry not one but two ROM chips, each with a capacity of 512 KB.

As a special feature, the A3000D motherboard can hold four ROMs. ROM slots U180 and U181, located next to the Super DMAC chip, are typically populated.

ROM replacement in an Amiga 3000D (desktop)

1. Switch off the Amiga 3000D and disconnect the device from the **power supply**.
2. To **open the case**, you must remove two screws on each side and one screw in the center at the back. Make sure not to damage the cable connecting the power supply unit to the motherboard or the floppy cable under the power supply unit when opening the case. Make a note of the screw locations and cable connections – this will come in handy for reassembly.
3. Once the screws have been removed, carefully pull the upper **metal shell**, including the front panel, out towards the front. Disconnect the cables from the motherboard.
4. The **ROM chips** are located in the right-hand corner under the power supply unit, right next to the mouse and joystick

connectors. To do this, loosen the screws on the power supply unit/drive mount at the front and rear of the housing. To be able to lift off the mount, you'll need to remove the daughter board with all the expansion cards. Remove the screws at the front and rear of the case directly on the metal part of the daughterboard. Pay attention to the two S-shaped plastic parts and the paper insulation layer that separate the metal wall from the daughterboard – these parts are very fragile and difficult to replace. It may also be necessary to disconnect other cables.

5. The motherboard of the Amiga 3000D is now sufficiently exposed to provide you access to the ROM chips. Locate the **Kickstart ROM sockets** between the mouse and joystick interfaces and the large, square, socketed Super DMAC chip – the notches of the chips point in the direction of the socketed chip. At this point you will see the Amiga 3000D's special feature – there are not just two ROM slots, but four! Most 3000D models carry the ROM chips in the pair of sockets labeled *U180/ ROM 0* or *U181/ROM 1*, and these sockets are compatible with EPROMs. If the ROM chip is located in either of the other pair of sockets labeled *U182/ ROM 0* or *U183/ROM 1*, these are not compatible with conventional chips such as the *27C400*, and the chips you need are hard to come by. As such, it is best to use the *U180/ U181* sockets. If these are not available, you should consult a qualified technician to carry out the installation. Ground yourself again before moving to the next step.
6. Now, **remove** the built-in ROM chips using a suitable tool, as described in *Recurring steps* (1.2.1) section under *Removing ROM chips from the socket*.
7. The **ROM sockets** are now exposed. Make sure to insert the *LOW chip* into the socket labeled *U180/ROM 0* and the *HI chip* into the socket labeled *U181/ROM 1*. Carefully insert **the new ROMs** into the sockets, as described in *Recurring steps (1.2.1)* section under *Insert ROM chips in the socket*.
8. Check again that the chips are in the **correct position** and orientation.
9. Finally, fully **reassemble** the Amiga 3000D – note that the device will not start without its daughterboard plugged in. Then, perform the **operational check** as described in the *Recurring Steps* (1.2.1) section under *Check after installation*.

Replacing the ROM in an A3000T

Revisions

Like the desktop version of the Amiga 3000, the Amiga 3000 Tower (A3000T) uses two ROM chips, each with a capacity of 512 KB. The advantage of the A3000T is that, due to its size and design, it can be easily disassembled and modified, and ROM replacement is therefore fast.

The two Kickstart ROMs of the Amiga 3000T are located between the large Super DMAC chip and the edge of the motherboard, near the barrel battery and the MC68882.

ROM replacement in an Amiga 3000T (tower)

1. Switch off the Amiga 3000T and disconnect the device from the **power supply**.
2. To **open the case**, remove the two screws from the right-hand side panel (as seen from behind) and pull the panel backwards. Make a note of the screw locations and the cable connections detached in the next steps, as this will come in handy for reassembly.
3. Since the Amiga 3000T offers a lot of space and is not as compact as the 3000D, it is not necessary to dismantle any other parts. The **motherboard** of the 3000T is immediately exposed and accessible.
4. Identify the **Kickstart ROM sockets** in the computer, located between the large, square, socketed Super DMAC chip and the edge of the motherboard near the barrel battery or the battery holder for the clock. (If a barrel battery is still installed on your A3000T, it is essential to have it replaced by

a qualified engineer as soon as possible, as it runs the risk of leaking.) The notches on the chips point in the direction of the interfaces leading to the outside. Ground yourself again before moving to the next step.

5. Now, **remove** the built-in ROM chips using a suitable tool, as described in the *Recurring steps* (1.2.1) section under *Removing ROM chips from the socket*.
6. The **ROM sockets** are now exposed. Make sure to insert the *LOW chip* into the socket labeled *U180/ROM 0* and the *HI chip* into the socket labeled *U181/Rom 1*. Carefully insert **the new ROMs** into the sockets, as described in the *Recurring steps (1.2.1)* section under *Insert ROM chips in the socket*.
7. Check again that the chips are in the **correct position** and orientation.
8. Finally, fully **reassemble** the Amiga 3000T, then perform the **operational check** as described in the *Recurring Steps* (1.2.1) section under *Check after installation*.

Replacing the ROM in an A1200

Revisions

Like many Amigas, the Amiga 1200 desktop computer was produced in different board revisions, but they do not differ in terms of Kickstart ROMs. As such, these instructions apply to all revisions of the Amiga 1200, and their replacement is fairly quick and easy.

ROM replacement in an Amiga 1200

1. Switch off the Amiga 1200 and disconnect the device from the **power supply**.
2. To **open the case**, three screws at the front and one screw on each side must be removed on the underside. Make a note of the screw locations and cable connections, as this will come in handy for reassembly.
3. Once the screws have been removed, the **top shell** of the case can be removed – when separating the top shell, pay particular attention to the plastic tabs on the edge of the case. The keyboard, shielding plate, floppy drive and, if applicable, hard drive will be revealed. Remove the keyboard cable by pulling the connector flap on the motherboard slightly upwards and slide the keyboard backwards out of its position.
4. You do not need to remove the **shielding plate** to replace the ROMs, but the process is much easier without it.

The two Kickstart ROMs in the Amiga 1200 are located between the small 68EC020 processor and the clock port.

To remove the shielding plate, pull out the three screws on the plate and bend all the locking lugs on the plate upwards. Once this is done, carefully remove the plate.
Caution: The plate can be sharp – take care not cut yourself.

5. The motherboard of the Amiga 1200 will now be exposed. **Locate** the Kickstart ROMs at the bottom edge of the mainboard between the small processor and the clock port. The ROM sockets are labeled *U6A* and *U6B*, and the notch (marking pin 1) points in the direction of the PCMCIA port. Note that the socket has 42 pins, but most ROM chips, such as the EPROM *27C400*, only have 40 pins. Leave the two pins on the left empty. The correct orientation is marked by an arrow. Ground yourself again before moving to the next step.
6. Now, **remove** the built-in ROM chips using a suitable tool, as described in the *Recurring steps* (1.2.1) section under *Removing ROM chips from the socket*.
7. The **ROM sockets** are now exposed. Make sure the *LOW chip* is placed into the socket marked *U6B* and the *HI chip* into the socket marked *U6A*. Carefully insert **the new ROMs** into the sockets, as described in the *Recurring steps (1.2.1)* section under *Insert ROM chips in the socket*.
8. Check again that the chips are in the **correct position** and orientation.

9. Finally, fully **reassemble** the Amiga 1200, then perform the **operational check** as described in the *Recurring Steps* (1.2.1) section under *Check after installation*.

Replacing the ROM in an A4000D

Revisions

The Amiga 4000 comes in two models: desktop (4000D) and tower (4000T). The two models have different motherboards, and therefore the ROM chips need to be swapped out differently. In addition, unlike the A3000, the data on the ROM chips is not identical. This means that there is a separate Kickstart version for the tower model – make sure you order the correct ROM version for your Amiga model.

The ROM chips in the Amiga 4000D are located just below the processor card that is to be removed, between the Ramsey and Fat Gary custom chips.

ROM replacement in an Amiga 4000D (desktop)

1. Switch off the Amiga 4000D and disconnect the device from the **power supply**.
2. To **open the case**, you must remove three screws on the rear side of the case. To make it easier to install the Kickstart ROMs, remove the front panel too by carefully detaching the plastic clips. Make sure to not damage the cable connecting the power supply unit to the motherboard or the floppy drive cable under the power supply unit when opening the case.

Make a note of the screw locations and cable connections, as this will come in handy for reassembly.

3. Once the screws have been removed, carefully lift off the **upper metal shell**. Before you disconnect any further cables from the motherboard, take a photo for reference.
4. In revision 2/B, the **ROM chips** are located in the right-hand corner under the 5.25" drive cage directly next to the CPU slot of the A4000D. This needs to be completely removed, including all cables. To do this, remove the screws on the drive mount at the front of the case. The processor card will appear underneath, as the A4000D in Rev. 2/B was always supplied with a processor card. As the ROM chips are located directly under the processor card, this card must also be completely removed. The notches of the chips point in the direction of the rear of the case. If you need additional space to work, it may be useful to remove the daughterboard including all expansion cards. Ground yourself again before moving on to the next step.
   Caution: On the very rare CR Rev. D revision board, the processor is soldered onto the board and the ROMs are not located directly to the left of the processor slot, but in the bottom corner next to each other. The notch of the chips point in the direction of the left side of the case.
5. Now, **remove** the built-in ROM chips using a suitable tool, as described in the *Recurring steps* (1.2.1) section under *Removing ROM chips from the socket*.
6. The **ROM sockets** are now exposed. Make sure you insert the *LOW chip* into the socket marked *U176* on the left and the *HI chip* into the socket marked *U175* on the right. Carefully insert **the new ROMs** into the sockets as described in the *Recurring steps (1.2.1)* section under *Insert ROM chips in the socket*.
7. Check again that the chips are in the **correct position** and orientation.
8. Finally, fully **reassemble** the Amiga 4000D, then perform the **operational check** as described in the *Recurring Steps* (1.2.1) section under *Check after installation*.

Replacing the ROM in an A4000T

Revisions

As with the desktop A4000, the tower A4000 also uses two ROM chips, each with a capacity of 512 KB. The advantage of the A4000T is that it is easier to dismantle due to its design, and so the ROM replacement takes less time.
Caution: The Amiga 4000 tower has its own Kickstart version – make sure you order the correct version for your Amiga model.

The two Kickstart ROMs of the Amiga 4000T are located near the Fat Gary and Ramsey custom chips.

ROM replacement in an Amiga 4000T (tower)

1. Switch off the Amiga 4000T and disconnect the device from the **power supply**.
2. To **remove the cover**, place the 4000T on its right side when viewed from the front and remove the five screws on the back of the metal case. Make a note of the screw locations and cable connections, as this will come in handy for reassembly.
3. Once the screws have been removed, carefully pull the **metal shell** backwards. Before disconnecting the cables from the board, take a photo of the connectors.
4. The ROM chips are located under the **hard drive cage** in the center of the A4000T, which must be removed. To do this, carefully remove the front panel to access the four screws at the front of the cage. The interface board at the rear and two further screws on the cage must also be removed. The drive cage is hooked in at the rear end. Carefully lift it out of the mounting notch and pull it forwards out of the opening.

5. The motherboard of the Amiga 4000T is now exposed, but the **processor card** in the front right-hand corner, and the IDE cable are still in the way. Carefully remove them both. Now, **locate the Kickstart ROMs** between the Gary chip and the IDE connector. The notches of the chips point in the direction of the rear of the case. Ground yourself again before moving on to the next step.
6. Now, **remove** the built-in ROM chips using a suitable tool, as described in the *Recurring steps* (1.2.1) section under *Removing ROM chips from the socket*.
6. The **ROM sockets** are now exposed. The *LOW chip* must be inserted into the socket labeled *U176 A/B* on the left, and the *HI chip* into the socket labeled *U175 A/B* on the right. Carefully insert **the new ROMs** into the sockets, as described in the *Recurring steps (1.2.1)* section under *Insert ROM chips in the socket*.
7. Check again that the chips are in the **correct position** and orientation.
8. Finally fully **reassemble** the Amiga 4000T, then perform the **operational check** as described in the *Recurring Steps* (1.2.1) section under *Check after installation*.

Replacing the ROM in a CD32

Revisions

The various revisions of the CD32 do not differ with regard to ROMs. As such, the following instructions apply to all CD32 revisions. Unlike all other Amigas, 1 MB ROMs were used in the 32-bit console instead of the usual 512 KB ROMs. Please note that the 3.2 ROM for the CD32 is labeled as *experimental* – no guarantee is given that it will function.

ROM replacement in an Amiga CD32

1. Switch off the Amiga CD32 and disconnect the device from the **power supply**.
2. To **open the case**, turn the console upside down and remove one screw on each side and three screws on the front. You will also need to remove the screw for the expansion slot on the back of the unit. Make a note of the screw locations and cable connections, as this will come in handy for reassembly.
3. Once the screws have been loosened, carefully lift off the **top shell**. Disconnect the flat ribbon cable for the CD drive and the cable to the control panel from the bottom of the

case so that you can remove the top of the case completely. When disconnecting the top shell, be particularly careful with the flat ribbon cable as it is very short. Before disconnecting any other plugs or cables from the motherboard, take photos of all the connections for reference.

4. The **shielding plate** of the CD32 will be in front of you. Remove the three screws from the shielding plate and bend all the locking lugs on the plate upwards. Then, carefully remove the shielding plate.
   Caution: The plate can be sharp – take care not to cut yourself.

The Kickstart ROM is hidden on the far right of the CD32 motherboard, directly next to the four memory chips and below the 68EC020 processor.

5. The **motherboard** of the CD32 is now revealed. Locate the console's Kickstart ROM in the bottom right corner under the processor (68EC020), to the right of the four memory chips. The 42-pin ROM socket is labeled *U6A*, and the notch (marking pin 1) points towards the edge of the board. Note that the socket has 42 pins and the ROM chip also has 42 pins (for example, the *27C800* EPROM).

Please note: Some CD32 machines do not provide a socket in this position on the motherboard and the ROM module is soldered directly to the motherboard. If this is the case, please contact your Amiga dealer or a specialized repair company. The module will need to be removed from the motherboard, and a socket soldered in its position.

6. Now, **remove** the built-in ROM chip using a suitable tool, as described in the *Recurring steps* (1.2.1) section under *Removing ROM chips from the socket.*
7. The ROM socket is now exposed in front of you. Make sure to correctly align the ROM chip with the notch pointing towards the edge of the motherboard. Carefully insert **the new ROM** into the socket, as described in the *Recurring steps (1.2.1)* section under *Insert ROM chips into the socket.*
7. Check again that the chip is in the **correct position** and orientation.
8. Finally fully **reassemble** the Amiga CD32, then perform the **operational check** as described in the *Recurring Steps* (1.2.1) section under *Check after installation.*

After the ROM has been changed

Next steps

Once you have successfully completed the replacement of the Kickstart ROM chip(s) in your Amiga, you can move on to the software side: installing AmigaOS 3.2 via floppy disk or ADF image (section 1.4), or via CD-ROM (section 1.5).

Setting up WinUAE

AmigaOS 3.2 can be used on Windows PCs and other third-party systems with no issues thanks to emulation software like UAE. This section shows how to prepare your system for installation.

Due to its widespread use, we will demonstrate how to install and set up WinUAE on a Windows 11 PC in order to get a virtual Amiga with OS 3.2.X up and running. Given the complexity of the software, we will focus on the most important settings for simulating an Amiga 1200 with the greatest possible compatibility.

What is WinUAE anyway?

WinUAE is a software developed for Windows PCs to emulate Amiga hardware, i.e. to reproduce it and make it usable. WinUAE, which evolved from its predecessor UAE, is the widely used quasi-standard among Amiga emulators and also forms a virtual construction kit for configurations of Amigas that never actually existed, such as an Amiga 600 with Zorro III cards, 128 MB memory and high resolutions. However, the most common use of WinUAE is probably the software-side emulation of an Amiga 500 with a 68000 CPU, OCS chipset, Kickstart 1.3 ROM and 1 MB RAM as a classic gaming machine. The current use case is the emulation of an Amiga 1200 with a 68060 processor, AGA chipset and Kickstart 3.2 ROM as a powerful working environment. Like all Amiga emulators, WinUAE reads virtual floppy disks in ADF format and also, if required, Amiga-native data storage devices such as hard disks. WinUAE is open source and has been maintained for many years by the Finnish developer Toni Wilen.

TIP **How much power does the PC need?**
Emulation is power-hungry. Accordingly, a PC used for emulation should be reasonably powerful and Direct3D capable. WinUAE can run on Windows XP SP3 (32-bit), but for real Amiga fun with emulation we recommend Windows 11 (32/64-bit), an i3-generation Intel processor and at least 8 GB of memory.

Step 1: Downloading WinUAE

Visit the website www.winuae.net with a web browser on your PC (e.g. Firefox or Chrome) and navigate to the *Download* section via the top menu. The latest version of WinUAE is available as an installer and a ZIP archive. You will also find additional material such as PowerPC core plug-ins or drive sounds for emulating the Amiga-typical clicking sound of the floppy drive. Click on the link to download the 32-bit or 64-bit hardware architecture version of the installer (depending on your PC hardware; if you are unsure, use the 32-bit version). The setup file will then be downloaded automatically. WinUAE 5.3.0 is the latest version as of August 2024 and is used for this step-by-step guide.

Step 2: Starting the WinUAE installer

From within the web browser, press `[Ctrl]+[J]` to navigate to the download directory (alternatively, use *Windows Explorer*). You will find the setup file *InstallWinUAE*5300*.msi* (for 32-bit PCs) or *InstallWinUAE5300_x64.msi* (for 64-bit PCs). Double-click the relevant file to start the installation of the emulator. Click *Next* in the welcome screen.

Step 3: Components of the WinUAE-installation

The default installation of WinUAE installs the *WinUAE* executable, some documentation, the required configuration data (*Configuration files*) and various Amiga-related files (*Amiga Files*). If there are individual components you do not want to install, click on the hard disk icon next to *Component* and click

Entire feature will be unavailable – an *X* will appear on the icon. WinUAE is typically installed on your hard disk in the folder *C:\Program Files\WinUAE*. To change the location, select the *WinUAE* component and click the *Browse* button – a requester window will appear in which you can select the location and confirm by pressing *OK*. Click *Next*, and then click *Install* in the following dialog box. The emulator will then be installed on the hard disk. Click *Finish* to close the setup window.

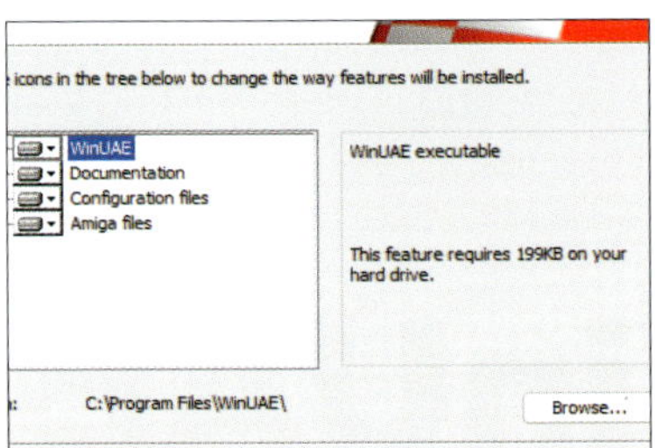

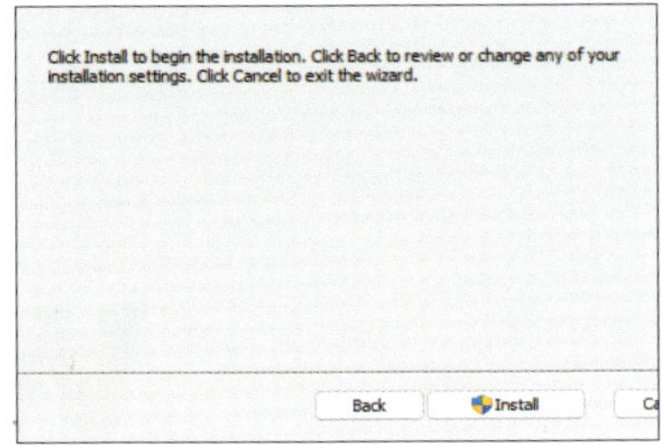

Step 4: Storage locations

The emulator is now located in the folder that you specified during installation. If you are unsure where to navigate to, in Windows 11, click the *Start* button in the taskbar and type *WinUAE* in the search box at the top. The result is usually *C:\Program Files\WinUAE*. It contains the main program, the language files, the documentation, the original configuration data for the host system (needed later) and relevant Amiga programs. WinUAE also stores additional files in *C:\Users\Public\Documents\Amiga Files\WinUAE* – among other things, the ROM file and the ROM key file that are required to run the virtual Amiga plus config-files *(Configurations)*, system *savestates* and screenshots *(screen recordings)* are stored here. You can change all storage locations in WinUAE under *Settings > Directories*.

Step 5: Language files

WinUAE runs in English by default, but other language extension can be installed manually. These include French, German and Spanish, among other languages. The Service Website for this book (https://lookbehindyou.de/en/amigaos32book) lists some of the languages available and provides the latest links to download. We will try to keep this list up to date.

If you wish to use a language other than English in WinUAE, please download the appropriate localization file for your language. You will need to rename the downloaded file – for example, rename the German language file to *WinUAE_german.dll*. Select the file using Windows Explorer and press F2 to do so. Depending on your Windows system settings, you may need to click on *Yes* in a dialog that opens to confirm that the renaming should take place. Confirm the administrator rights in the subsequent dialog with *Continue*. Finally, copy the file to the WinUAE program folder – in our case, *C:\Program Files\WinUAE* (move it with the mouse or select the file, press `[Ctrl]+[X]`, open the program folder and press `[Ctrl]+[V]`).

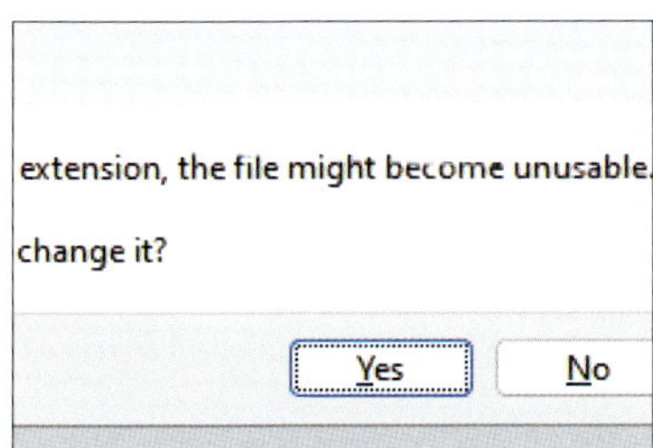

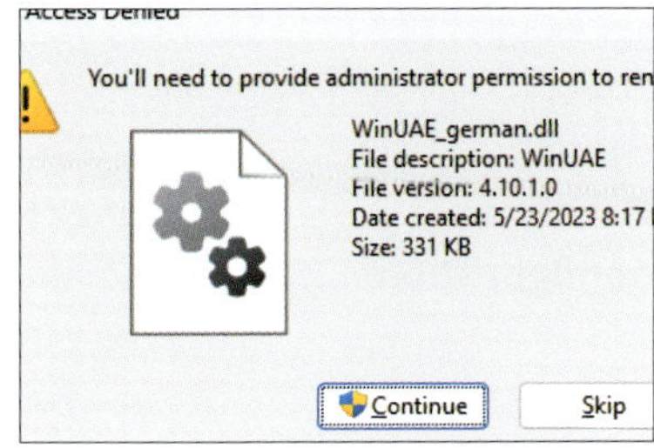

TIP **Alternative emulators**

There are many alternatives to WinUAE for various platforms, including Windows, Mac, Linux, Android, iOS and Raspberry Pi. Examples include FS-UAE, AmiBerry and Denise. The commercial product Amiga Forever, made by Cloanto, includes a preinstalled UAE environment, data transfer tools, games and a full set of ROM files from version 1.0 to 3.1.

Step 6: WinUAE overview

Execute WinUAE from the *Start* menu, or in Windows Explorer from the program folder (e.g. *C:\Program Files\WinUAE\ > winuae64.exe*). WinUAE starts in a window with numerous tabs and settings options. This can be confusing at first glance, but it is logically structured. On the left-hand side of the window you will find a list of settings divided into two categories: *Hardware* (the emulated Amiga) and *Host* (the emulating platform). These two categories contain various sections for settings such as *CPU*, *Chipset* or *Display*. Clicking on these sections opens the appropriate settings in the window's main area. In the following sections, we will explain step by step which settings changes have to be made in order to set up a basic configuration. WinUAE can be closed at any time by clicking on *Exit* at the bottom left of the window.

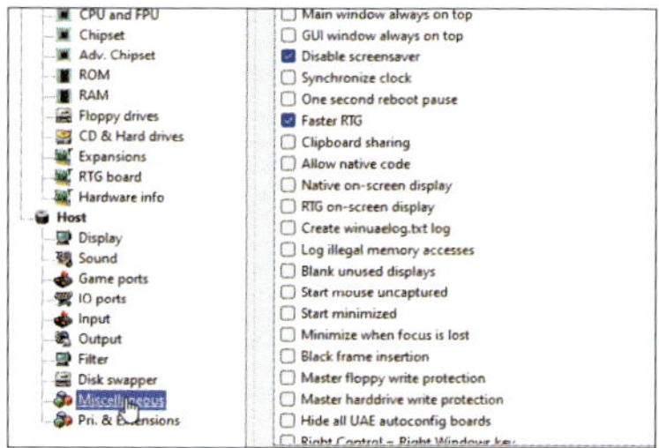

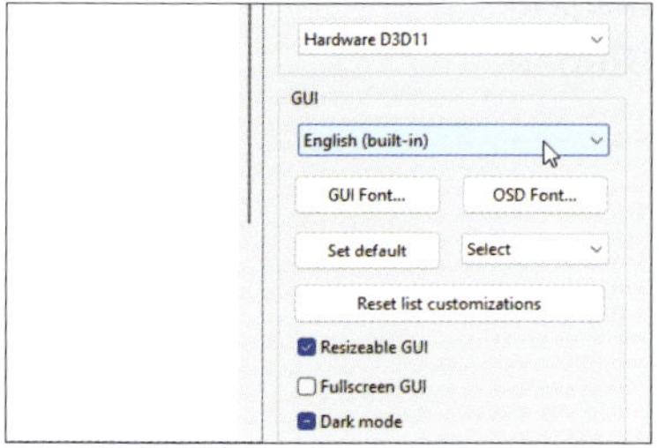

If elements in WinUAE are displayed in English after the first start (left image), switch to Miscellaneous on the left, under Host. Change the selection from English to your preferred language. It will change without restarting.

Step 7: Create a configuration

The *Configuration* section stores the settings in central configuration files. Enter a name, e.g. *My virtual Amiga*, and a description, e.g. *Configuration for AmigaOS 3.2.X*, and click the *Save* button. In the *Configurations* folder, there will now be a new configuration file: *My virtual Amiga.uae*. If you are going to make important changes in WinUAE in the future, you should save these changes by selecting the relevant configuration in the *Configurations* section and clicking on the *Save* button.

Step 8: Processor

The virtual Amiga 1200 we build should be powerful, but as compatible as possible. We are going to begin with the *CPU and FPU* section and transplant a 68030 processor into our virtual Amiga. Furthermore, we will enable the *more compatible* option, as well as *JIT*. This *just-in-time emulator* gives the computer faster legs. We leave the standard JIT setting as it is shown at the bottom right. The FPU (*floating point unit*, a mathematical coprocessor) can normally be omitted (option: *none*). Set the CPU emulation speed to the *fastest possible*.

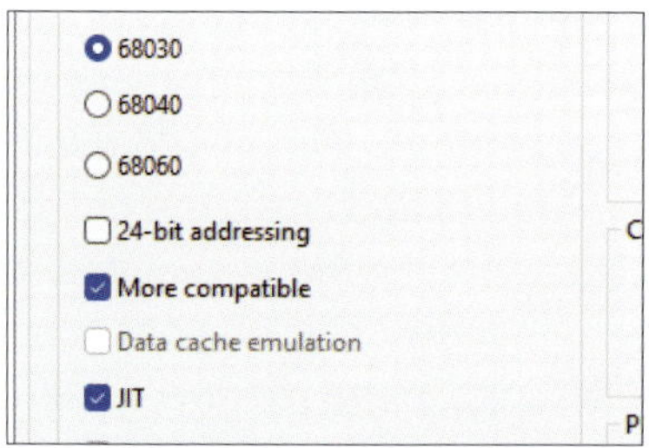

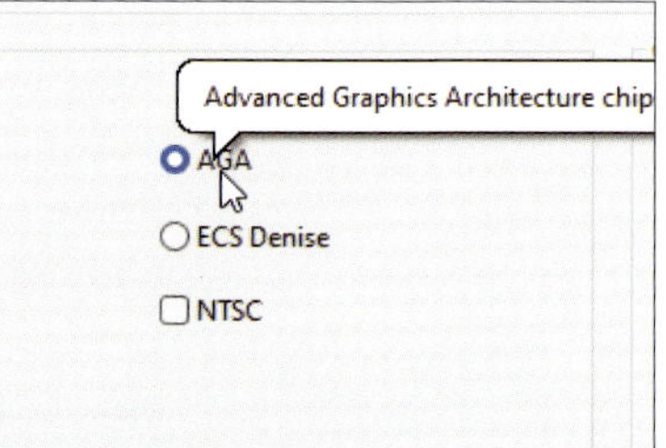

You can define the emulated processor under CPU (left). Under Chipset, you can choose between OCS, ECS, AGA or variants (right).

Step 9: Chipset

The AGA chipset was installed in the original Amiga 1200, so our virtual Amiga should also support *AGA* – this can be set in the *Chipset* section. We should also increase the collision level to *full* and tick the option *Keyboard connected* in the top right.

In the *Adv. Chipset* section, activate the *Compatible Settings*. Advanced users can later make detailed chipset settings to customize the emulation.

Step 10: ROM

Read Only Memory is read-only, data-proof memory integrated into the original Amiga in the form of one or two ROM chips. System-relevant information is permanently stored in this memory, without which no Amiga, whether genuine or emulated, would function. In emulation mode, the system is fooled into believing it has hardware ROM. Therefore, we need a file in which the important details are bundled: the ROM file. AmigaOS 3.2 provides this ROM file. You should copy the file from the ROM directory of the 3.2 CD into the WinUAE data directory (see step 4) in the hardware version that you want to emulate (the ROM files are named according to the original Amiga model, e.g. *kicka3000.rom* for an Amiga 3000). Version 3.2 of AmigaOS contains ROM files with revision 47.96, while version 3.2.2 features revision 47.111 – that sounds like a nice smelling fragrance and is similarly splendid. Select the ROM file you require – in our case, this is the *A1200.47.111.rom* for the emulation of the A1200. In the *ROM* section, click on the button with the three dots under *ROM main file*, and select and open the file *A1200.47.111.rom* in the requester window, which will then be displayed in the ROM field.

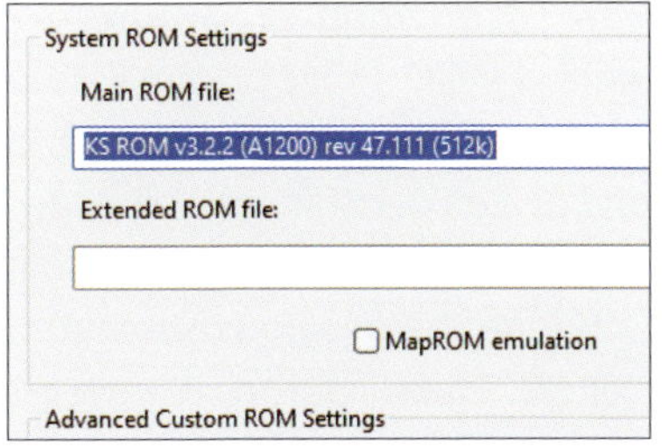

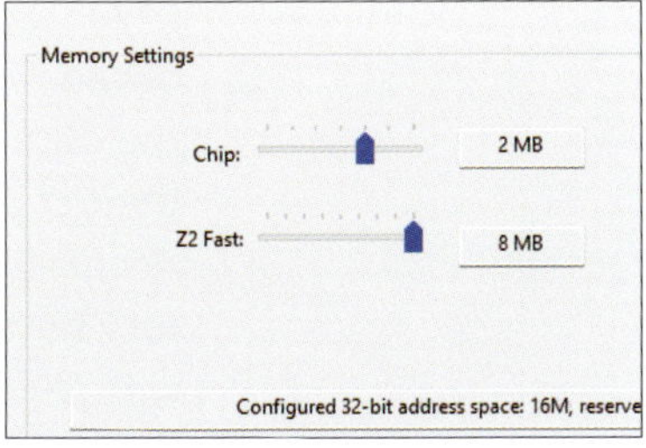

They just sound similar: the emulated Kickstart ROM is embedded in the ROM section (left), while memory is defined in the RAM section (right).

**Step 11:
RAM**

The winner takes it all: none of the original Amiga models have as much RAM as an emulated Amiga – theoretically over 2 GB of memory (remember: the Amiga 1000 originally had 256 KB!). So we must first grant the virtual Amiga 2 MB of Chip RAM in the *RAM* section using the slider at the top (see the screenshot on page 47). The list under *Advanced Memory Settings* contains the entry *Processor Slot Fast RAM* – select it and move the slider to its right to 64 MB. Perfect for a high-performance system!

**Step 12:
Floppy drives**

Floppy drives do not affect emulation performance (only a small amount of RAM is used), so just activate all four floppies (DF0, DF1, DF2, DF3) in the *Floppy drives* section with the default option 3.5" DD. Click the triple-dot button next to the drive to open the file requester. This allows you to insert ADF files into the virtual drive (ADF files are disk files that were originally developed for emulation). The virtual disk can be ejected clicking the *Eject* button. Leave the drive speed at *100% (compatible)*.

**Step 13:
CD & Hard drives**

WinUAE supports a variety of different storage mediums.
For example, the emulated AmigaOS can integrate entire PC drives such as CD drives, hard drives (SSD, IDE, SCSI) and network drives, and even directories on the PC as drives on the Workbench. With little extra effort, Amiga-native hard drives and memory cards (SD or CF), which can replace the hard drive on the Amiga via an IDE adapter, can also be integrated. *Hard disk files* – called *hardfiles* or *HDF*s for short – are of particular interest because they bundle all the data of a hard disk into a single file. We will now create two virtual drives:

The first should be an image of the 3.2 CD for the installation of AmigaOS 3.2. Use *Windows Explorer* to create a directory called *AmigaOS 3.2 CD-ROM* on the PC hard drive. Copy all of the data from the 3.2 CD into this new folder. In WinUAE, go to the *CD & Hard drives* section and click on the *Add Directory or Archive* button. In the new requester, click on the *Select directory* button, choose the previously created directory and confirm with *Select folder*. The directory is now displayed in the *Path* field. In the *Device name* box, use the name *AmigaOS3.2CD*, and add a suitable volume label below, e.g. *AmigaOS 3.2 CD-ROM*. Remove the tick next to *Bootable* and confirm with *OK*. The virtual CD is now displayed in the device list.

Now create the second volume, which will become the main hard disk in the Amiga, as a *hardfile*. The *Add hardfile* button

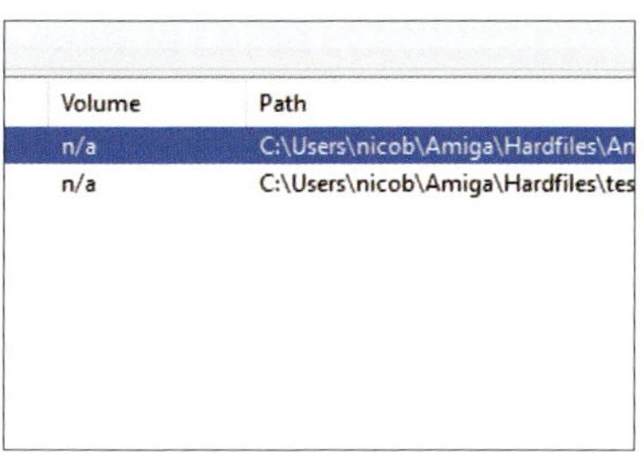

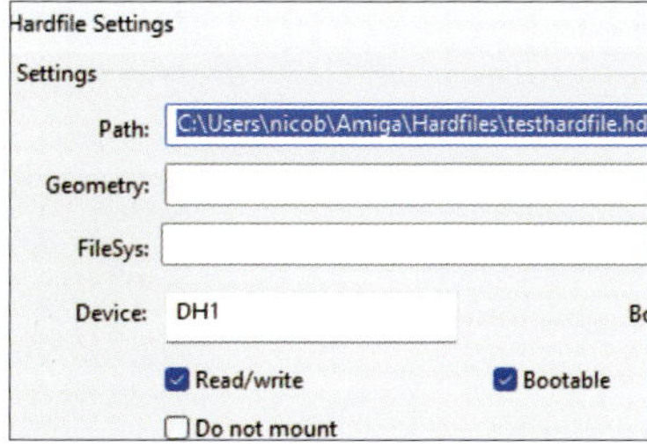

Hardfiles, which store multiple files as a single file, and pure directories on the Windows drive, are the most popular hard disk formats among WinUAE users.

takes you to the setup dialog. Under *New hard disk image file* in the lower area of the window, define the capacity of the virtual hard disk by typing in a suitable number into the *MB* field. 120 megabytes is more than sufficient for a simple system hard disk, so enter *120* into the field and click the *Create* button. In the opening file requester window, enter *System* as the name for the hard disk and *save* it. Make sure that the *Bootable* option is ticked (the boot priority is then automatically set to 0) and assign a name in the *Device* field, e.g. *DHO* or *System*. Click *OK* to complete the setup – the hard drive setting is now completed.

Step 14: RTG graphics card

WinUAE allows you to simulate a graphics card and uses the graphics card module *UAE* as a Z2 or Z3 variant. For the first installation, select the *UAE (Zorro III)* model in the *RTG graphics card* section under *Card* (see screenshot below).

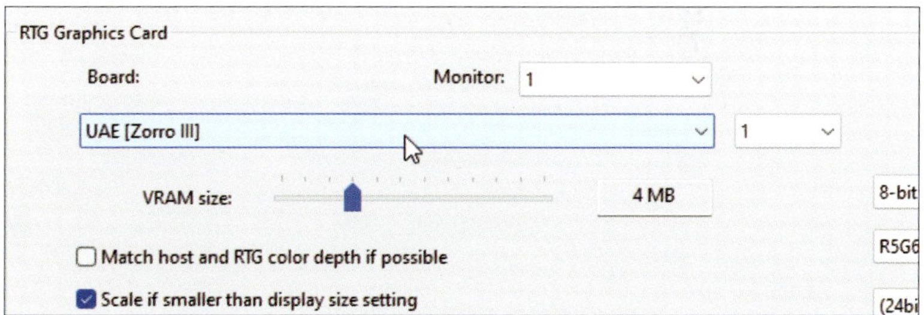

Once you have installed AmigaOS 3.2 on the emulated Amiga, you will be able to select high resolutions in the *ScreenMode* prefs (see screenshot on page 50). The screen modes are listed with the prefix *UAE:*. It is a good idea to set the same resolution for the Workbench as for the emulation. A recommended resolution for many emulation environments is *UAE: 1280 x 1024 16*

bit, which corresponds to twice the *Hires Laced* resolution of the Amiga *(640×512)*.

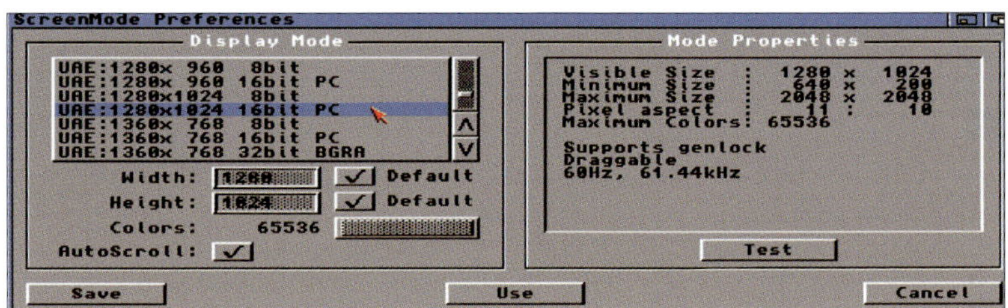

Step 15: Display

After the graphics card has been "set up", you can now synchronize the system display, i.e. the monitor, in the *Display* section. As mentioned in step 14, it is recommended to synchronize the Workbench resolution with the emulation resolution. Select the resolution 1280 x 1024 for the test system under *Fullscreen*, and enter 1280 and 1024 in the two value fields under *Windowed*. Activate the *Windows resize* option. In the *Settings* area, choose *Windowed* from the *Native* select list and from the RTG select list, if the emulation is to be run in a Windows window on the Windows desktop. You might also want to select *Full-Window* if the display is to be full screen in the native PC resolution with correct scaling. Tick the options *Blacker than black* and *Hires (normal)* for the resolution. The line mode on the right should initially be set to *Single*. Many users find it pleasing to have *horizontal* and *vertical alignment* activated in the *Centering* area.

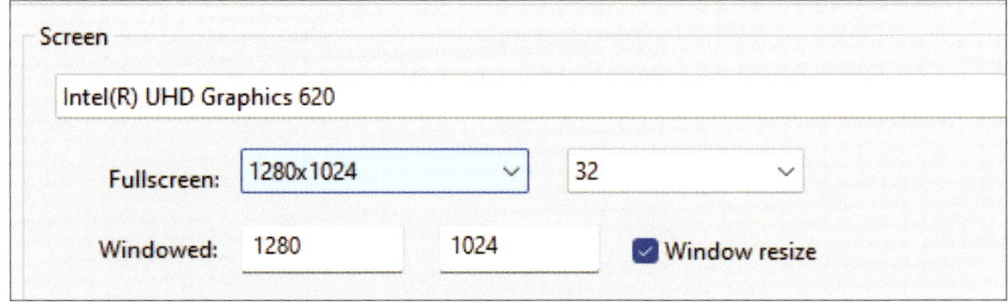

Step 16: Final settings

Let's take a quick tour of the remaining settings before booting the system.

In the *Sound* section, the preselected *Default Audio Device* is left as is so that the sound is output via the activated speaker of the PC. For sound emulation, the *Enabled* option is selected, *Stereo* is selected as the channel mode, and 44.100 is selected as the frequency. If you want to hear the original clicking and rattling of the floppy disk drive during operation, select *A500 (WinUAE built in)* below – if not, switch to *No sound*. In the *Game ports* section, *Windows mouse* should be in port 1, and you may choose your USB gamepad or a keyboard setup in port 2.

In the *Extensions* section, tick the box next to *bsdsocket. library* – this gives the virtual Amiga itself access to the internet, for example to use a web browser or an e-mail client.

Step 17: The first time with WinUAE

Ready? Go back to the *Configurations* section, click on your current configuration *(My virtual Amiga)* and save the settings by clicking on the *Save* button. Choose the ADF disk *Install32.adf* as your DF0 drive in the *Floppy drives* section. Now you're ready to go: click *Start* in the bottom of the WinUAE settings dialog to open a new window. A short time later, the installation environment for AmigaOS 3.2 will appear showing the Workbench with its install disk, the virtual *AmigaOS3.2 CD-ROM* and the unformatted *System hard disk*. The next steps for the installation and use of AmigaOS 3.2 are the same as if performed on native hardware.

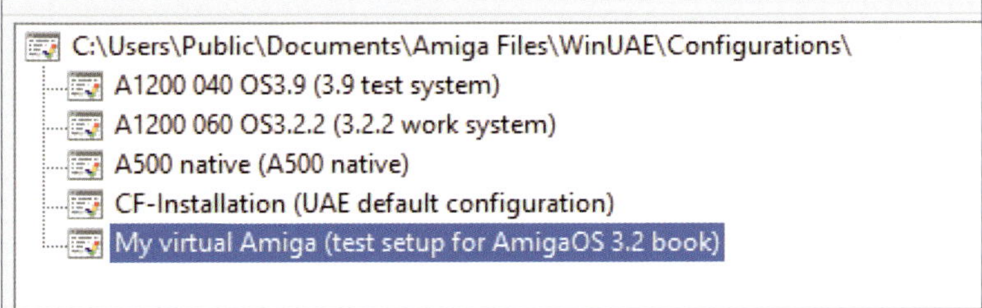

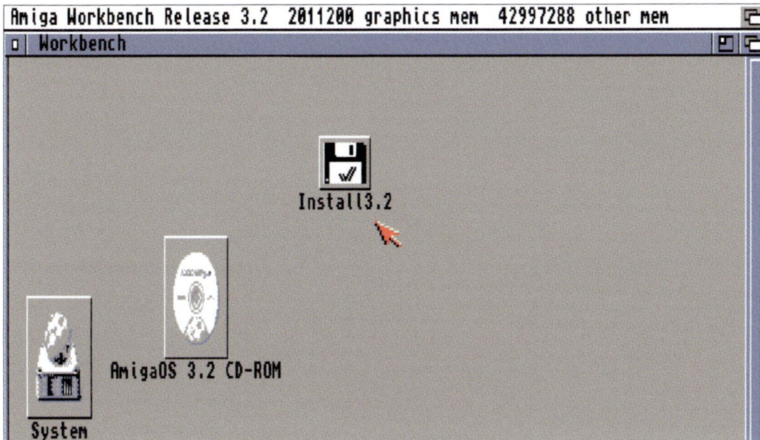

The first time you start the installer, the Workbench will look a bit grainy. Don't worry, it won't stay that way!

TIP **Where is the Amiga button?**
On PC keyboards there is usually a *Windows key* and a *Function (Fn)* key to the left and right of the two *Alt* keys. In order not to impair the functioning of Windows, and to prevent unwanted processes, the two Amiga keys in WinUAE have been assigned to other keys on the keyboard: by default, the `[L-Amiga]` key is located on the `[Insert]` key, while `[R-Amiga]` is often located on `[POS 1]` or `[HOME]`.

Step 18: Settings, restart and more

You can adjust many settings in WinUAE while the emulation is running – just press *F12* to open the WinUAE dialog. You can return to the emulation by clicking *OK* (accept changes) or *Cancel* (discard changes). *Restart* restarts the entire WinUAE environment including the emulation, while *Quit* closes WinUAE completely. Clicking on *Reset*, on the other hand, corresponds to a reset of the emulated Amiga – in other words: `[Ctrl] + [L-Amiga] + [R-Amiga]`. Have fun with your new virtual Amiga!

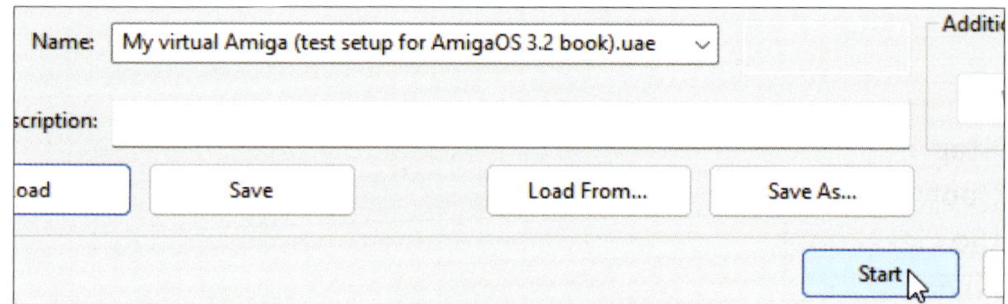

Shortcuts for WinUAE users

Shortcut	Function
[F12]	opens WinUAE settings
[Ctrl] + [F12]	switches back and forth between full screen and window display
[Alt] + [Tab]	switches to the next open Windows application
[Pause]	freezes the emulation
[Print]	takes a screenshot of the Workbench
[Print] + [End]	takes a screenshot of the Windows desktop including the Workbench window

Installation from disk or ADF

Whether on a real or an emulated Amiga, the installation of AmigaOS 3.2 onto a volume can be done using physical floppies or virtual ADF floppies.

The basic installation of AmigaOS 3.2 on native or emulated Amigas usually works without complication, but varies due to different hardware configurations. The procedure is the same whether you use real or virtual disks.

TIP **ADF: Virtual disks**
Since AmigaOS 3.2, ADF files have been supported natively. This file format, which has been tried and tested in the emulator world for many years, behaves like a virtual floppy disk. In AmigaOS 3.2, ADF images can be mounted by double-clicking on the ADF icon and then fully utilized. More than one ADF disk can be mounted at the same time.

Step 1: Booting into the installation environment

Installation requires having a suitable preformatted hard disk or memory card (CompactFlash or SD card) in the Amiga. The preparation of the drive is explained in detail in chapter 4.4 in the *HDToolBox* section.

If you want to install from physical disks, insert the *Install* disk into the disk drive and start or reset the Amiga. The Amiga will then boot into the Workbench. Open the *Install3.2* disk by clicking on the disk icon.

If you wish to install using ADF images, the ADF data must be stored on a medium that can be read and recognized by the Amiga – it does not matter whether the ADF images are on the original CD-ROM, a memory card (CF or SD card) or a USB stick integrated into the system via the Gotek drive (for more information on the necessary data exchange, see section 7.4). Boot the system executable in the usual way to get to the Workbench (for example, 3.1 or 3.9). Change to the drive and mount the ADF file *Install3.2.adf* by double-clicking on it (on the *AmigaOS 3.2.2 CD*, all ADF data is located in the *ADF* directory). The virtual disk is mounted and displayed – click the icon.

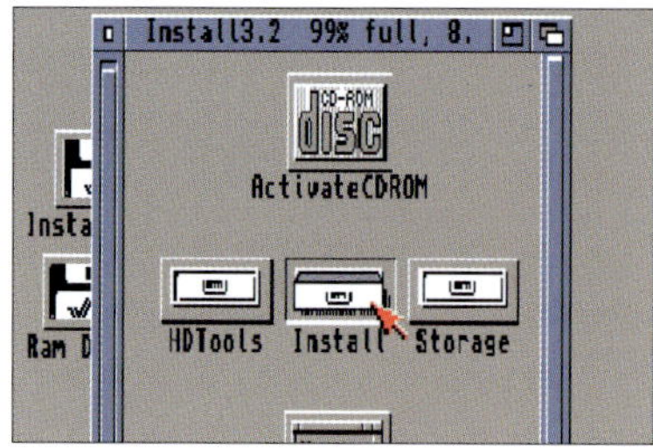

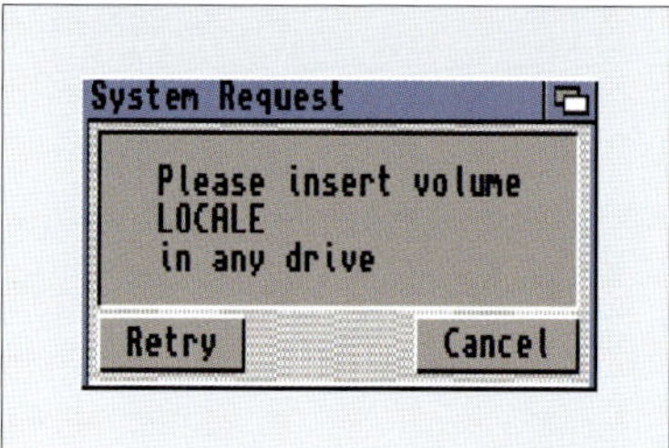

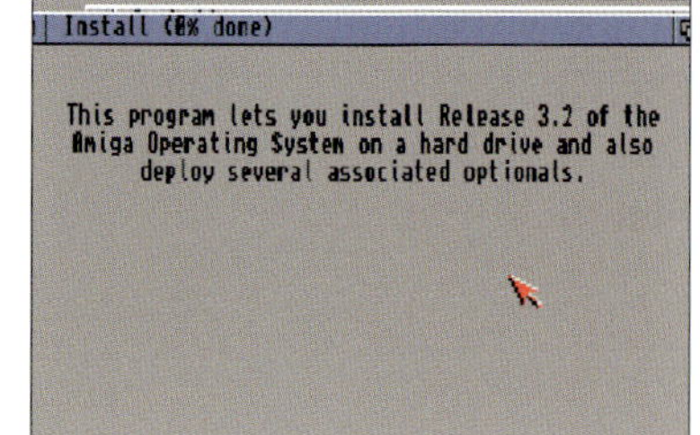

On the way to installation (steps 1 and 2)

TIP **Lost? Help and abort!**

The installer provides explanations for most options, which can be accessed by clicking the *Help...* button. You can also cancel the installation at any time (click *Abort Install*), although this is strongly discouraged – only do this in an emergency if the installation cannot be continued properly.

Step 2: Starting the installer

Open the *Install* folder, in which the installation executables are displayed in 15 languages. Click on *English* to start the installation process in English, or select a different language for your system. If you are installing in a other language than English, the installer will ask you to insert the locale disk from time to time during the installation. You will then need to insert the *Locale* disk or the *Locale.adf*. If you are installing in English, the Locale disk is not required. Either way, the installation dialog will open. Click *Proceed*.

TIP **Install3.2 disk**

If possible, leave the *Install3.2* disk inserted in a second drive or leave the ADF *Install3.2.adf* mounted, as the installer will access this disk several times. If this is not possible, insert *Install3. 2* into the floppy drive or remount the ADF if you are prompted to do so during the installation.

Step 3: Selecting the installer options

The installer offers four options: install the full 3.2 version, install or update only individual languages, install the GlowIcons (if not done in a previous update), or install accelerator support libraries. The first step is to ensure that the operating system is properly installed on the computer. Select *Install Release 3.2*, and click *Proceed*.

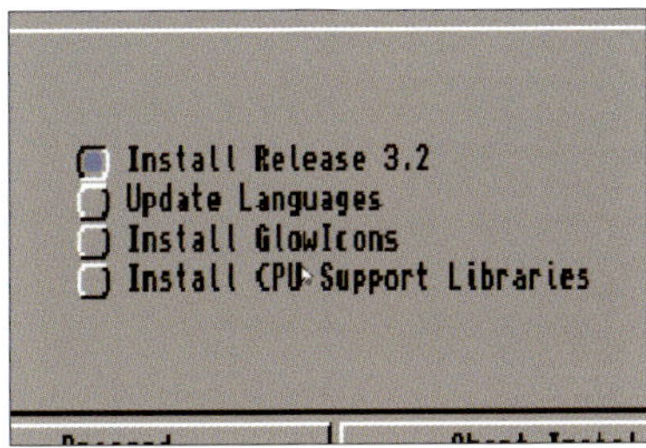

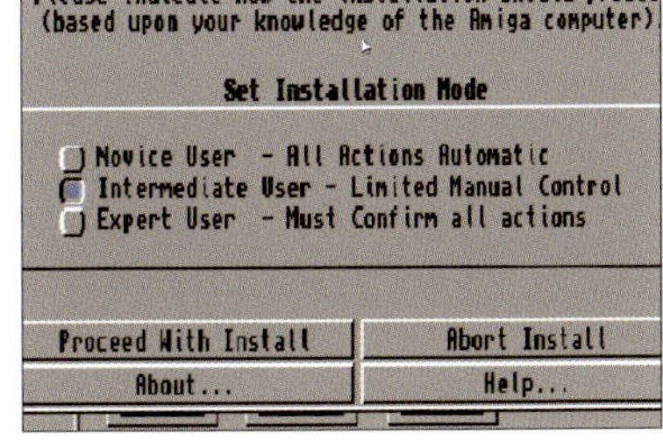

Step 4: Selecting your knowledge level

Now it's up to you: how familiar are you with AmigaOS? What options do you want to set during the installation? The installer prompts you for the installation mode. If you are unsure, select *Novice User* to perform all actions automatically – we recommend the *Intermediate User* option to semi-automate the installation. Then click on *Proceed with Install*.

Step 5: Logging errors

You can use the installation program to deploy the operating system to the hardware or to simulate the installation for debugging purposes. In the latter case, a log, which can be printed or saved to a file, will help you to find any stumbling blocks. If this is your first installation, select *Install for Real* and *None* for logging actions, then click *Proceed*.

INFO **Installation without Kickstart ROM 3.2**
If you install OS 3.2 without a suitable Kickstart ROM, the necessary modules will be installed from the supplied *Module* disk. The installer will attempt to determine which Amiga model is being used, and will ask to confirm.

Step 6:
Here we go!

Are you ready? Are your fingers a little sweaty? The installer will ask you again if you really want to install the operating system, and will tell you the name of the partition on your hard drive where the operating system will be installed (*System:*, in the below example). Don't be afraid: click *Yes* to get started.

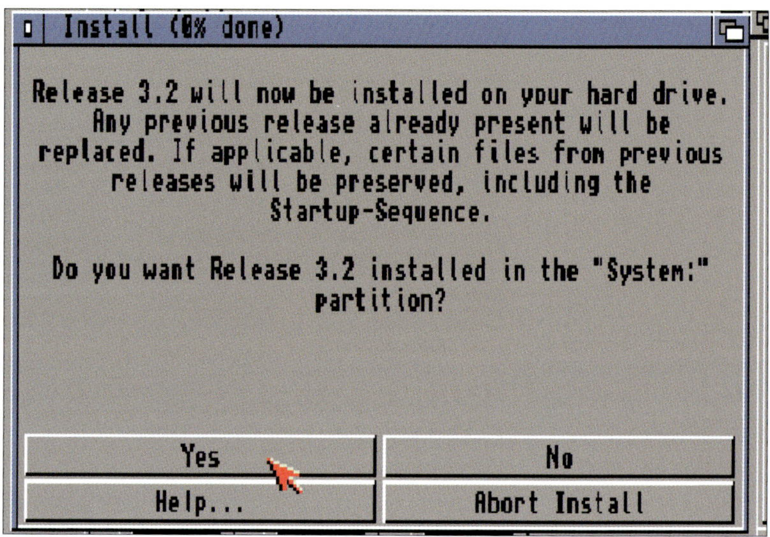

Step 7:
Languages

AmigaOS is talented at languages and currently supports a total of 15, which can be toggled in the settings dialogs during operation. Activate the languages you want to install in the selection dialog (in this case: *English*). Click *Proceed* to move to the next step.

Step 8:
Printer drivers

The system supports printers made by Epson, Hewlett Packard (HP) and NEC (Pinwriter series). The drivers for these printers can be installed, as well as for PostScript output. PCL-HP printers, for example, are now fully supported by the *TurboPrint* printer driver package. The Epson driver, on the other hand, is currently only suitable for old matrix printers. If you want to preinstall AmigaOS printer drivers, tick the corresponding types. Click *Proceed*.

Step 9: Keyboard layout

AmigaOS 3.2 allows you to assign 19 different language settings to the keyboard. This is useful if you need a special keyboard layout or if you occasionally write texts in different languages that contain unfamiliar characters. Select the keyboard mappings (so-called *keymaps*) that the system should support (in this case: *British* and *American*) and click *Proceed*.

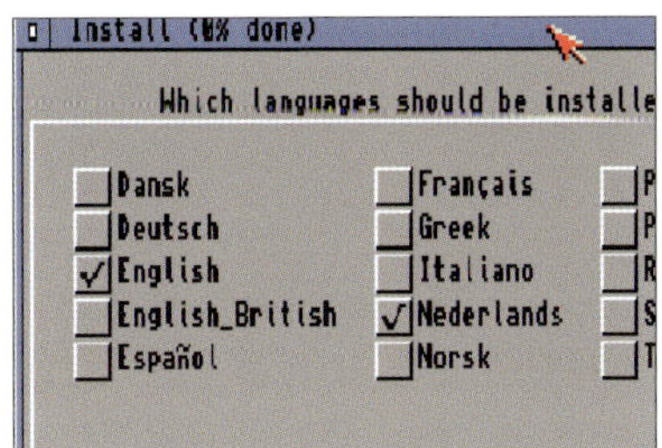

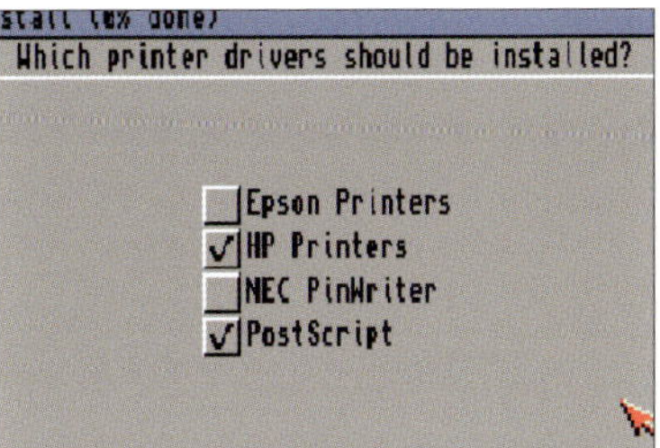

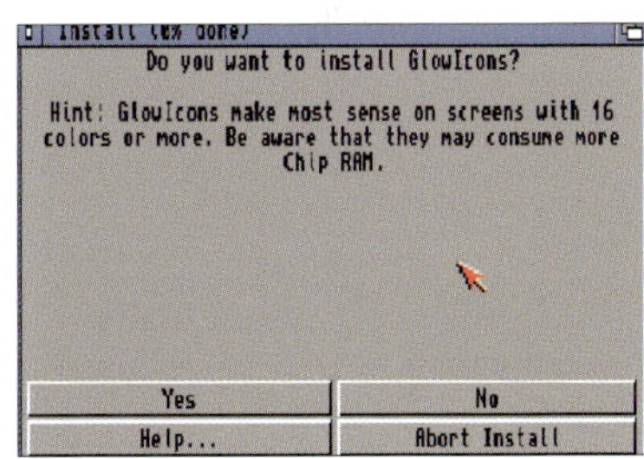

Important options prior to the copying process (steps 7 to 10): languages, printers, keyboard layout and GlowIcons

Step 10: Icon style

The Workbench icons can be displayed in the default style or the more colorful GlowIcons style supported by AmigaOS 3.2.X. The integration of GlowIcons requires slightly more Chip RAM and some additional free memory on the system volume. They are recommended for AGA Amigas or devices with RTG graphics cards. If you want to install GlowIcons, confirm by clicking *Yes* or decline by clicking *No*.

Step 11: Start copying

The data will start being copied to the installation partition as soon as you have inserted the *Workbench 3.2* disk or mounted the ADF *Workbench3.2.adf*. Once the disk is detected, the installation will proceed automatically. If not, please click *Proceed*. The system displays a progress bar showing which files are being installed in the current process. The percentage progress is roughly displayed at the top of the window.

Step 12: DiskDoctor installation

Despite what its name suggests, DiskDoctor is not designed to heal entire floppy disks. However, the tool is capable of recovering files from defective floppy disks or hard disks that have been formatted with the OFS or FFS file system. In this step, the Doc is required – insert the *DiskDoctor* disk or ADF, and confirm its installation by clicking on *Proceed*.

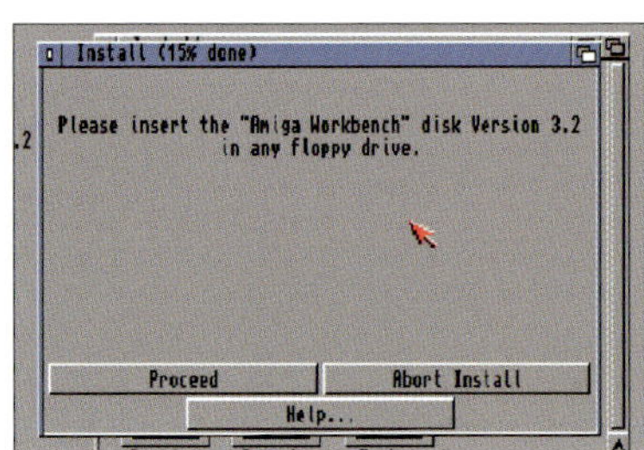

The installer requests the Workbench, DiskDoctor, Locale, Extras, Classes, Fonts, Storage, Backdrops and, if applicable, GlowIcons disks or ADFs, and copies all data to the system volume (steps 11 to 19).

Step 13: Languages installation

All required language files will now be copied. First, insert the *Locale* disk or ADF when prompted, and continue via *Proceed*. You will then be asked to insert the appropriate language disk, e.g. Locale-EN for English or Locale-DE for German. Insert the relevant disk or ADF, and click *Proceed* to continue, if the process does not continue automatically.

Step 14: Extras installation

The *Extras* disk contains important programs from the Prefs, Tools and System directories. When prompted, insert the *Extras3.2* disk or ADF, and click *Proceed* if necessary.

Step 15: Classes installation

The *Classes* disk provides important data from the *Devs folder*, for example for the detection and use of devices such as drives or audio equipment. When prompted, insert the *Classes3.2* disk or ADF, and click *Proceed* if necessary.

Step 16: Fonts installation

Fonts are the typefaces that appear in various locations on the Workbench and in programs – in other words, they are essential components of the operating system. When prompted, insert the *Fonts3.2* disk or ADF, and click *Proceed* if necessary.

Step 17: Storage installation

The *Storage* disk holds important data such as the *Datatypes* for supporting extended file formats (such as PNG), *DOSDrivers* (e.g. CrossDOS for reading PC floppy disks), *Monitors* (for integration of screen types), *Printers* (for controlling printers) and *Keymaps* (keyboard assignments). This step only installs the data that is relevant to the installation or that you have selected. When prompted, insert the *Storage3.2* disk or ADF, and click *Proceed* if necessary.

Step 18: Backdrops installation

The *Backdrops* disk contains a variety of background images for the Workbench and for folders, each available in different resolutions. The selection can be done later. The installation is required and cannot be skipped. When prompted, insert the *Backdrops3.2* disk or the ADF, and click *Proceed* if necessary.

Step 19: GlowIcons installation

If you have decided to use the GlowIcons system in step 10, it will now be installed (if not, this step will be skipped). When prompted, insert the *GlowIcons3.2* disk or ADF, and click Proceed if necessary.

Step 20: Libraries for faster processors

The system will detect a faster 68030, 68040 or 68060 processor installed in the Amiga. If you have such a CPU onboard or via an accelerator board, the installer will show a text explaining that so-called generic replacement libraries are supplied with

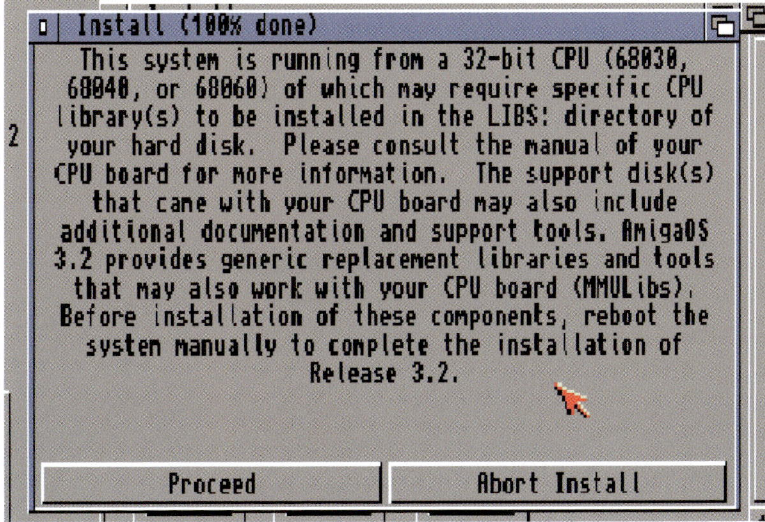

AmigaOS 3.2 comes with CPU libraries for 68k processors, which have to be installed subsequently.

AmigaOS 3.2. These originate from the *MMULibs* package developed by Thomas Richter and are constantly being updated. Any available accelerator boards can thus be integrated smoothly into the system. These libraries can be installed at a later time. Read more about installing the CPU libraries in section 1.6.

The installer tells you that the system should be restarted before further installation. Click *Proceed*.

Step 21: Installation completed

The installation is mostly finished. That was quick, wasn't it? Remove any inserted disks from the disk drive and click *Next*. Now reset the computer if it does not shut down and restart automatically (shortcut `[Ctrl]+[L-Amiga]+[R-Amiga]`). After rebooting, the Amiga comes up with a fresh AmigaOS 3.2 interface.

The next steps are to install the CPU libraries if a 68030, 68040 or 68060 processor is built into the system, and to install any existing AmigaOS 3.2 updates. Read how to do this in sections 1.6 and 1.7.

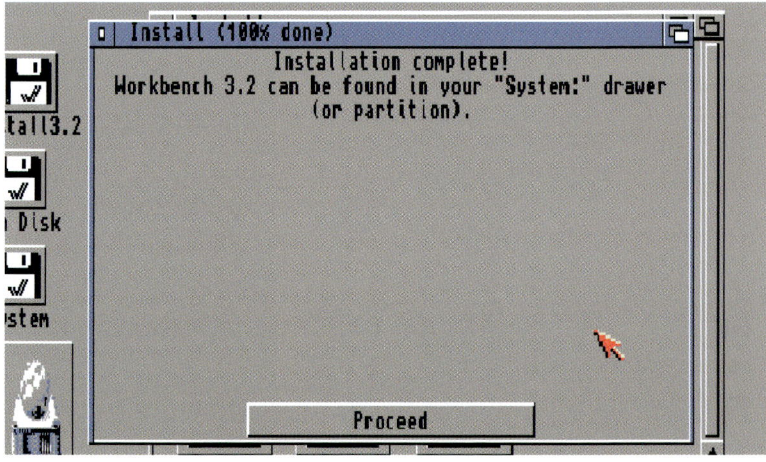

Done: once the installation has been completed successfully, the system will boot into the new AmigaOS 3.2.

Installation from CD-ROM

You can easily install the operating system from an AmigaOS 3.2 CD if an external or internal CD-ROM drive is connected to your Amiga. New to AmigaOS 3.2 is the so-called AmigaOS Preinstallation Environment.

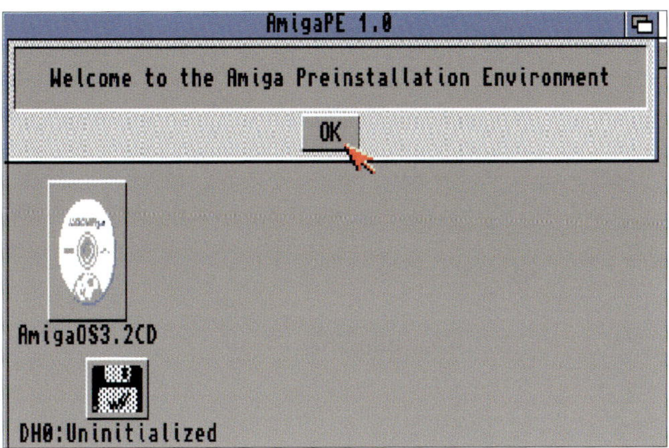

VARIANT 1 — INSTALLING FROM CD WITH A BOOTABLE CD DRIVE

Step 1: Booting from CD to AmigaPE

The *AmigaOS Preinstallation Environment – AmigaPE* for short – is a new feature in AmigaOS 3.2. When the system is booted from the AmigaOS3.2CD, this slimmed down installation environment is opened. So if you own a bootable CD drive, start your Amiga, insert the CD and you can boot directly into AmigaPE.

Step 2: Preparing the hard drive

From the *Amiga Preinstallation Environment*, you can prepare a hard disk or a compatible memory card for the installation of the operating system. Double-click to open the contents of the *AmigaOS3.2CD* and open the Install directory. Double-click on *Format* to start the formatting tool.

Step 3: Selecting the device

The formatting tool will list all the accessible drives in the system – in addition to the CD-ROM and floppy drives, this will include one or more connected hard disks or memory cards (CF/SD). From this list, select the volume on which you would like to install the operating system afterwards, and then click *Continue*.

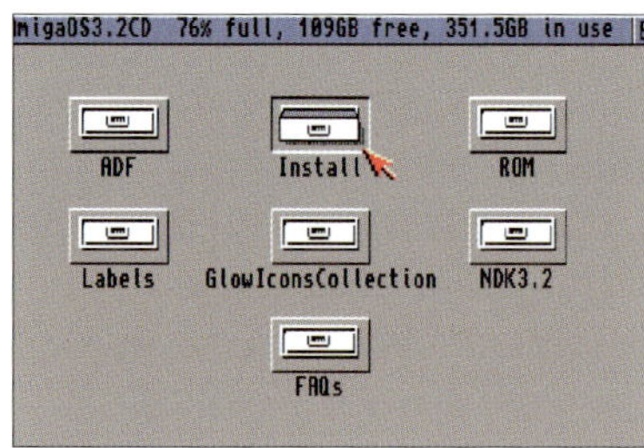

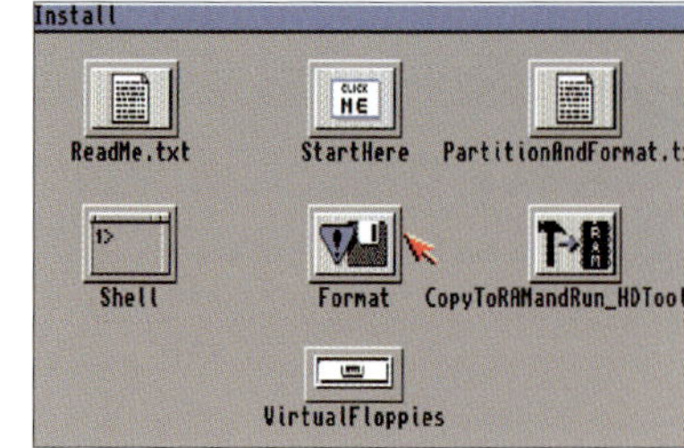

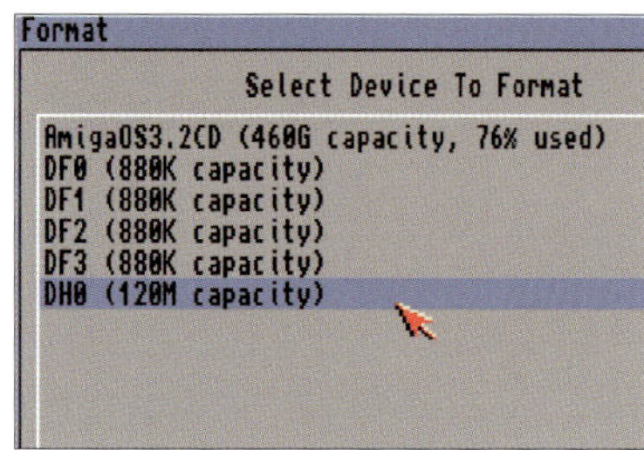

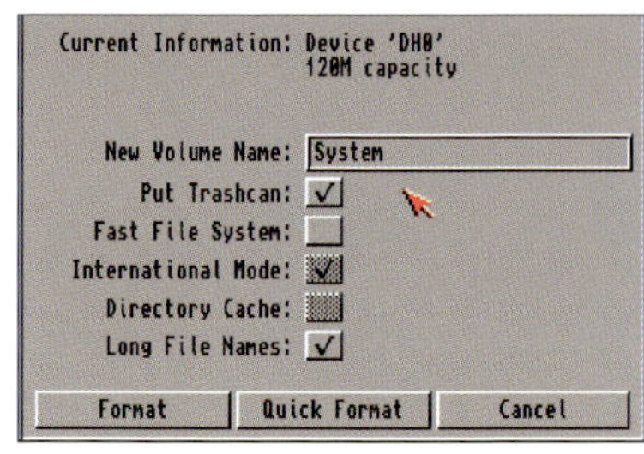

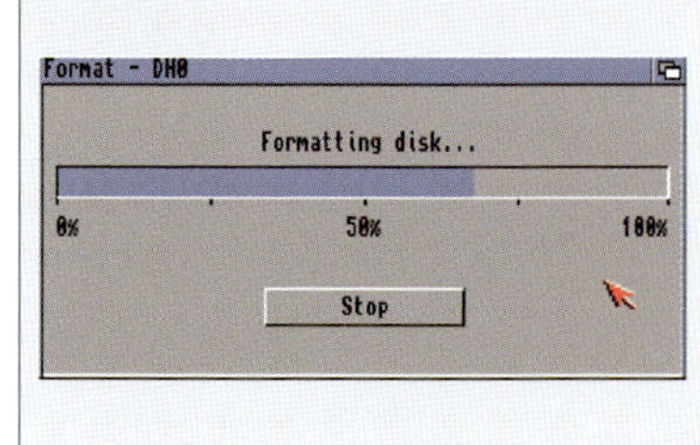

Before the AmigaOS data can be stored on the hard disk or memory card, the device must be prepared (steps 2 to 5).

Step 4:
Naming the volume

In the requester, you can enter a name for the volume. For example, change the default name *Empty* to *System* or *Workbench*. Enable the *Long File Names* and *Put Trashcan* options by activating their checkboxes.

Step 5:
Double-checking the device

When you start the formatting process by clicking *Format*, you will be warned twice. Make sure that you are formatting the intended drive or partition. You can still cancel the process at this point. If you are sure, confirm by clicking *Format*. You will then see a progress bar as the disk is formatted.

Step 6:
Starting the installation

When the formatting of the device is complete, a new *Install3.2* disk icon will appear on the Workbench. Double-click the *Starthere* icon in the main installation directory on the CD. This will mount the *Install3.2* and *Locale* ADFs from the CD. Then click on the *Install3.2* icon and on the *Install* folder.

Step 7: Installation program

Clicking on the desired language, e.g. *English*, opens the installation program. The procedure is identical to the installation via floppy disk or ADF, except that the floppy disks do not need to be changed – so please jump back to section 1.4 and follow the instructions from step 2 onwards. Once completed, the operating system is ready to be run on the selected device.

Mount the ADFs on the Install CD using StartHere on the CD, then initiate the installation (steps 6 and 7).

VARIANT 2 — INSTALLING FROM CD WITH A BOOTABLE FLOPPY DISK

Step 1: Booting via floppy disk

If the AmigaOS3.2CD does not boot automatically, you will need to initiate the installer using a floppy disk. Insert the *Install 3.2* disk into the drive and boot the Amiga. Click on the *Install3.2* disk icon. A bootable partition that is suitable for the installation must be created and formatted on a hard disk or memory card. If this is not yet available and ready for use, a device must be prepared as described in Variant 1.

Step 2: Customizing the CD drive

Depending on the CD drive or drive controller, you may have to adjust the tool types of the icon manually. On the *Install3.2* disk, open the *Storage* directory, then the *DOSDrivers* directory. Highlight the *CD0:* file, choose *Icon > Information* from the menu, and in the requester switch to the *Icon* tab. You will see two entries in the text input box: *device=scsi.device* and *unit=2*. Depending on your configuration, you will need to change the device and the unit. However, never use unit value 0. You can find the relevant information in the instructions for your controller. For example, if you are operating a SCSI CD drive on a GVP controller, you would have to enter *gvpscsi.device* and the ID of the drive with which you are operating it in the SCSI chain. See also section 4.4 for an overview of selected devices.

Step 3:
Activating the CD

Once the CD drive has been customized, double-click on *CDO* to mount the drive. Close the window. Insert the *AmigaOS3.2CD* into the CD drive. Then click on *ActivateCDROM*. A window opens with a script that activates the CD – confirm by pressing the Enter key. The window will close automatically after the CD has been activated. Double-click the *StartHere* icon in the main directory of the Install CD. This will mount the *Install3.2* and *Locale* ADFs from the CD.

Step 4:
Starting the installation

On the *Install3.2* disk open the *Install* folder, and double-click on the installer in the desired language, e.g. *English*. The installer will be started. This is similar to installing via disk or ADF – the only difference is that you don't have to take on the role of a disk jockey. Please go back to section 1.4 and follow the instructions from step 2 or 6. Once the installation is complete, the operating system will be on the disk you specified and will be ready to run.

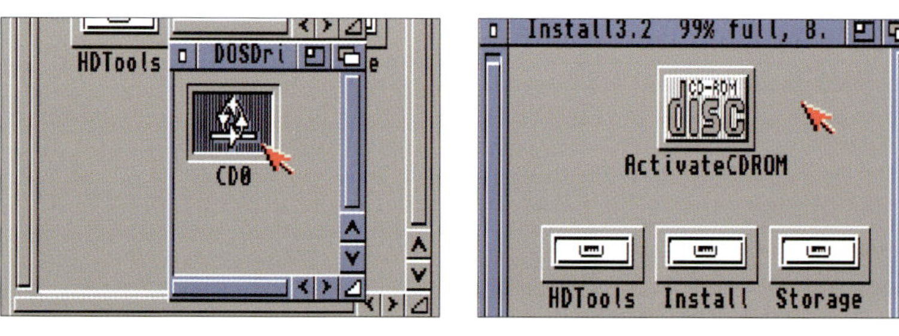

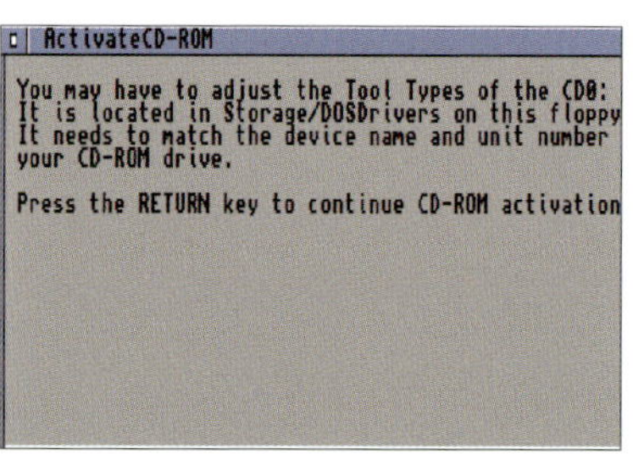

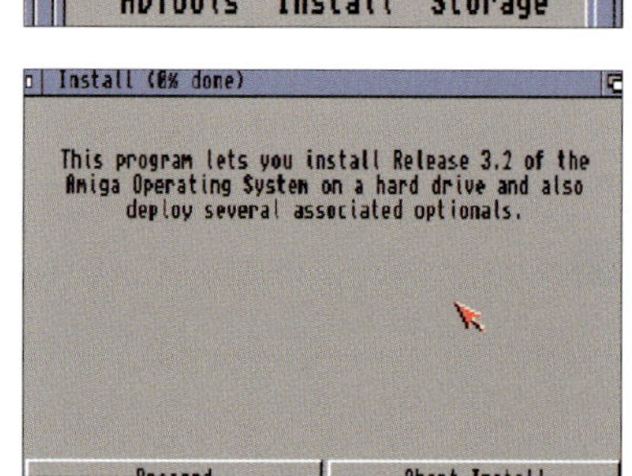

After starting from the boot floppy disk: mount CD0, activate the CD-ROM and start the installation (steps 1 to 4).

Installation of CPU libraries

Certain CPU libraries must be installed separately in order for the system to correctly support a 68030, 68040 or 68060 processor.

Step 1:
Error message?

The CPU libraries are copied to the system after the initial installation of the operating system. If the Amiga does not find any libraries compatible with the installed processor during the boot process, an error message may be displayed indicating missing libraries and thus inadequate support of the CPU (see screenshot). You should therefore install these CPU libraries before working productively with the system.

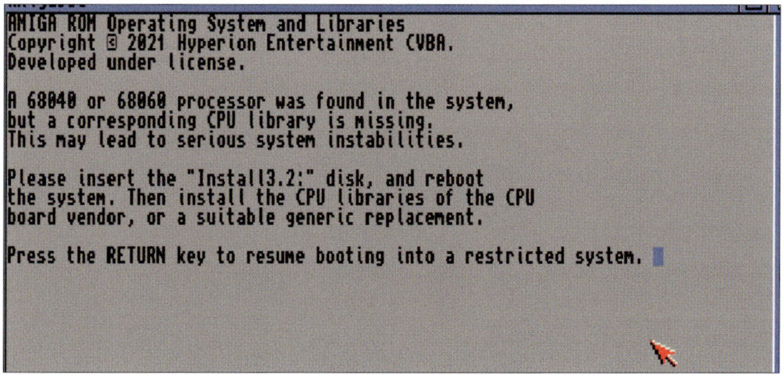

```
AMIGA ROM Operating System and Libraries
Copyright © 2021 Hyperion Entertainment CVBA.
Developed under license.

A 68040 or 68060 processor was found in the system,
but a corresponding CPU library is missing.
This may lead to serious system instabilities.

Please insert the "Install3.2:" disk, and reboot
the system. Then install the CPU libraries of the CPU
board vendor, or a suitable generic replacement.

Press the RETURN key to resume booting into a restricted system.
```

Step 2:
Starting the installer

Reset the Amiga and boot into the Workbench from the previously inserted *Install3.2* disk or the *AmigaOS3.2CD*. As before, open the installer by double-clicking on the *Install3.2* icon, then on the *Install* directory and on the preferred installer language version, e.g. *English*. This time, however, instead of selecting *Install Release 3.2*, choose the fourth item in the list: *Install CPU Support Libraries*. Then click *Proceed*.

Step 3:
MMULibs versions

The installer will now transfer the supplied version of *MMULibs* to the Workbench and perform the required ROM mapping. The current version in AmigaOS 3.2.2 is MMULibs 46.21. Confirm the partition where the AmigaOS 3.2 Workbench is located by clicking *Yes* (or change the partition setting by clicking *No* and selecting the correct partition). If necessary, insert the *MMULibs* disk or ADF, and click *Proceed*.

Step 4: Specification of the CPU card

You must determine which 68k CPU card is installed in your Amiga. Tick the appropriate option for the accelerator you have (for example the Blizzard or CyberStorm from phase5; the G-Force 030 or A1230-040 from Great Valley Products (GVP); or the ACA1234 or ACA500plus from iComp). If you are unsure or are using an emulated system, select *Other*. Click *Proceed*. The system will then copy the necessary *mmu.library* to the *Libs* directory on the system partition and complete the installation. The Amiga must be restarted to activate the CPU card – eject all disks and click *Proceed*.

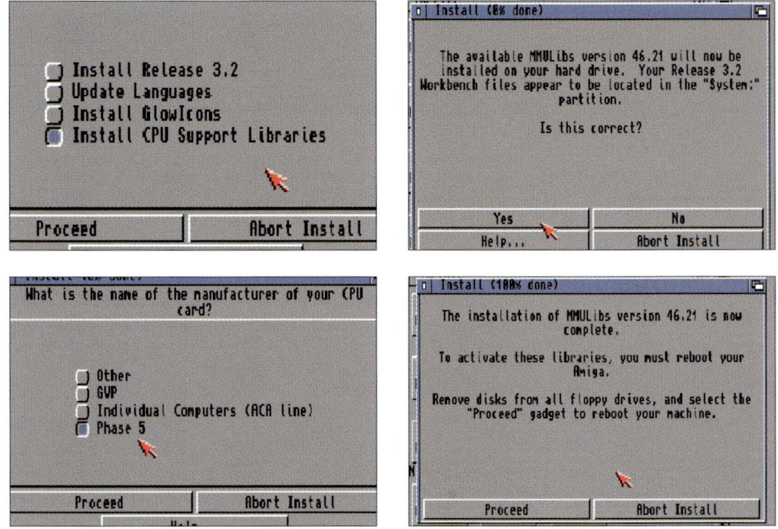

Installing the CPU libraries: start the installer, confirm the MMULibs version, select the CPU model, reboot to finish (steps 2 to 4).

TIP **Manufacturer libraries or OS3.2 libraries?**

You can use the libraries supplied by the manufacturer of the accelerator card or the libraries supplied with AmigaOS 3.2. The original libraries from the manufacturers are better adapted to the accelerator board, but are not optimized for OS3.2 and will not be developed further. The *MMULibs libraries* from Thomas Richter included in OS3.2 are generic, but are constantly being updated. We recommend that you install the libraries from the OS3.2 package. If you experience problems, please send a bug report to the developer and test the vendor's library.

Installation of updates

Updates to the operating system must be downloaded and installed manually after registering the software. The steps are largely identical for the various updates. The latest release at the time of writing is 3.2.2.1.

Step 1: Download of update files

Before you can access the updates, you must register as a purchaser of AmigaOS 3.2 with Hyperion Software, as described in section 1.1 on *Registration and support*. Once you have done this, visit www.hyperion-entertainment.com and log in on the left-hand side. Click on *Downloads* in the menu on the left and select *AmigaOS 3.2*. Here you will find three update packages: *Update3.2.1.lha*, *Update3.2.2.lha* and *Hotfix3.2.2.1.lha*. You will only need the hotfix for the update – download the package with your Amiga (note that this file is 17 MB in size). If your Amiga does not have internet access, you can download the package using another computer and transfer the data to your Amiga using a CF card, USB stick or over a network (see section 7.4). Alternatively, dealers also offer update services.

Unpack the downloaded LhA archive into a temporary directory of your hard disk or into the Amiga's RAM Disk (if it's ig enough), open the update folder, e.g. *Hotfix3.2.2.1*, followed by the *ADF* folder and the *Hotfix* folder. The package also contains all other 3.2.2 updates in the *ADF > Update* folder.

Step 2: Start the installer

Mount the ADF *Update3.2.2.1* by double-clicking on the ADF symbol. This opens the virtual *Update3.2.2.1* disk on the Workbench. Close all windows, open the virtual disk, then the *Install* folder and then the installer in the desired language, e.g. *English*, to initiate the installation process.

Step 3: Quick run-through

The installer will tell you that you are ready to update to the new version. Click on *Proceed*, and then choose *Intermediate User* and *Proceed With Install*. Select *Install for Real* without an activated protocol (*None*), and finally *Proceed*. When prompted to confirm that updating is now being performed, click *Yes*. Shortly afterwards, the latest version of AmigaOS will be installed on your computer.

Reboot your Amiga and celebrate – you can finally get started! Move on to chapter 2!

Installation on THEA500 Mini

Small but powerful, the THEA500 Mini was released in 2022 and has won the hearts of many (former) Amiga fans. AmigaOS 3.2 can even be installed on this new miniaturized edition with a little effort.

Introduction

The THEA500 Mini, the official name of the new edition of the Amiga 500, was developed by Retro Games Ltd. and taps into nostalgic memories for former Amiga users. Since its launch, this small computer has rekindled the enthusiasm of many former Amiga owners. The idea behind the new development: unbox it, supply it with power via USB-C, connect it to the TV via HDMI and get started with 20 preinstalled games, with no fuss. But the A500 Mini is not just for games – even AmigaOS 3.2 can be installed on it. However, this requires a deep dive into this bag of tricks, as Frank Greshake shows in this installation guide. The installation is time-consuming, but worthwhile.

Hardware

Technically speaking, the A500 Mini runs an emulation of the Amiga system via UAE. The device itself works with an *All Winner H6 ARM* processor *(Cortex A53)* with 512 MB DDR3 RAM and an *ARM Mali-T720 MP2* graphics unit. The emulation system is stored in a 256 MB flash memory.

Requirements

The Mini uses the *Amiberry emulator* in the old but stable version 3.3 for its Amiga emulation (the current version is 5.6.6).

As of *firmware* version 1.1.1 of the A500 Mini, it is possible to integrate ADF files (see 2.11) and WHDLoad directories from a connected USB stick. However, the system itself is still closed – installation of third-party software is not intended. To prevent such an installation, Amiberry is only accessible via a workaround.

The backdoor for accessing the Amiberry graphical user interface is a so-called *exploit* (a technical vulnerability) in WHDLoad, a software solution for running games from the hard disk that were originally intended to be played on floppy disks. It also pushes the door wide open for extensions on the Mini...

TIP **Service website**
All web links and summaries of data such as scripts can be found on the service website for this book: https://lookbehindyou.de/en/amigaos32book.

Step 0: Before it starts

If you follow these instructions, please take a few precautions. In addition to patience, you will need the two main players, the *A500 Mini* and the *AmigaOS3.2 CD*, as well as a *USB stick*, a *USB keyboard* and a *PC* or *Mac* with an *Amiga emulator* (e.g. *WinUAE*) set up. You can find out how to prepare WinUAE in chapter 1.3.

You should also have tools set up that allow you to open ZIP archives and LhA archives. If you use Windows, we recommend *WinRAR* (https://winrar.de/downld.php); for Mac users, *The Unarchiver* (https://theunarchiver.com) is an option.

Step 1: Setup of your USB stick

The Mini is supplied with data via a USB stick, which must first be prepared. Ideally, the stick should have a maximum size of 32 GB to avoid additional work. It is important that the USB stick has a *Master Boot Record* (MBR) and is formatted in *FAT32* with standard cluster size. This is how it works under Windows:

Insert the USB stick into a USB port on the PC. Press the `[Windows]+[R]` keys and enter `cmd` into the input field to open the Windows command prompt (alternatively, use the `[Windows]+[X]` shortcut in Windows 11 and select *Terminal* to start the *PowerShell*).

Inside the Shell, type the command `diskpart`. Once the program has started, type `list disk`. The USB stick should be displayed in the list. On our test system, a Windows PC with a hard drive with only one partition and no other connected drives, the USB stick was listed as *Disk 1*.

Caution: Identify your USB stick with absolute certainty, e.g. based on its size or using Windows' Disk Management utility, otherwise there is a risk of data loss!

By entering the command `select disk 1` (the number corresponds to the unit of your USB stick, see above), *diskpart* changes the active disk.

If you are absolutely sure that you have selected the correct disk, enter the command `clean`. This will write a new partitioning structure to the USB stick, making all data on the USB stick permanently unreadable!

The USB stick must have a *Master Boot Record* (MBR). To do this, enter the command `convert mbr` and wait for confirmation that the conversion was successful.

Finally, create a single partition on the USB stick. This step is achieved with the `create partition primary` command. Exit *diskpart* and the Shell using the `exit` command.

Step 2: Formatting your USB stick

In Windows Explorer, the USB stick will appear in the list on the left. Right-click on its entry and select *Format* from the menu. In the dialog that appears, set the *file system* to *FAT32* and the *size of the allocation units* (this corresponds to the cluster size) to *Standard*. Assign a unique name such as *Mini32*. Click on the *Start* button to initiate the quick format process. After completion, the USB stick is finally ready to be used inside the Mini.

Step 3: Downloads

You will need three archives from the manufacturer's website:

- *THEA500 WHDLoad Package V1.0.1*
  https://retrogames.biz/support/thea500-mini/whdload/
- *Bonus USB Games Pack*
  https://retrogames.biz/support/thea500-mini/bonus-games/
- *A500 Mini Firmware 1.2.1*
  https://retrogames.biz/support/thea500-mini/upgrade/

Use *Windows Explorer* or *Finder* on Mac to create a folder on the hard disk, e.g. with the name *AmigaMini*, in which you store those three files and all other data for the project.

Step 4:
Firmware update

To update the firmware of the A500 Mini, copy the downloaded file *theA500-mini-upgrade-v1.2.1.a5u* into the root directory of your USB stick. Start the Mini, insert the USB stick into a USB port on the rear of the Mini, and tap the *Menu* button on the gamepad to access the settings.

If you switch to the *Advanced settings* area and then to *System information* (both with button A), the Mini will report that it has detected the firmware on the USB stick. Update the system by pressing button A. When the update is complete, the Mini will restart.

Step 5:
File modification

On the PC, unpack the archive *THEA500-Bonus-USB-Games-1.0.0.zip* into the *AmigaMini* directory. There you will now find the directory *THEA500-Games* containing three files. Unpack the archive *Citadel_v1.3.lha* into the same directory. You will now see the *Citadel* directory with the associated *info file* for the icon. Switch to the *Citadel* directory and delete the file called *Disk.1* (this will prevent the archive from opening on the Mini).

Move the *Citadel* directory and the *Citadel.info* file to a directory that you can access with the emulator such as WinUAE (to be set up in *WinUAE* via *CD & Hard drives > Add directory or archive*). Start the emulated Amiga with WinUAE on your PC. If you have not already done so, install *LhA* and LhA*GUI*, and *Directory Opus* (downloaded from http://aminet.net/util/arc/lha.run, http://aminet.net/util/arc/LhA-GUI.lha and http://aminet.net/util/dopus/DOpus416JRbin.lha, respectively). Use these tools to pack the *Citadel* folder and the *Citadel.info* file back into an LhA archive, e.g. with the name *Boot.lha*.

As an alternative, you can of course use a real Amiga for this step, or the Windows-based file manager *Total Commander* (see section 7.4 on *data transfer*) using the extension *LHA for Win*.

Step 6:
Folder structure

For the sake of clarity, this USB stick will be used exclusively for AmigaOS in these instructions. Use Windows Explorer to create a folder called *AmigaOS3.2* with two subfolders called *ROM* and *Transfer*.

Step 7:
THEA500 and Boot.lha

Unzip the *THEA500 WHDLoad package* on the PC and copy the *THEA500* folder from it to the root directory of the USB stick. Copy the previously created LhA archive *Boot.lha* into the *AmigaOS3.2* directory (this time, do not unpacked the LhA file!).

Step 8: Testing in the A500 Mini

Start the A500 Mini and wait until the selection carousel appears. Then insert the prepared USB stick. In the carousel, use the gamepad to select the USB stick (blue symbol).

Switch to *AmigaOS3.2* in the file selection and select the created *boot* archive with the A button. Run it with the *Home* button on the gamepad.

The A500 Mini will now attempt to run the archive but will display an error message due to the missing *Disk.1* file and return to the selection carousel. Under certain circumstances, an almost forgotten acquaintance, *Guru Meditation*, may appear. Remove the USB stick and switch off the device.

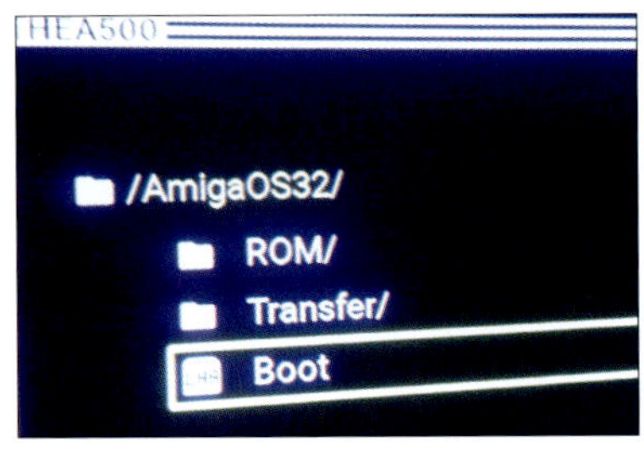

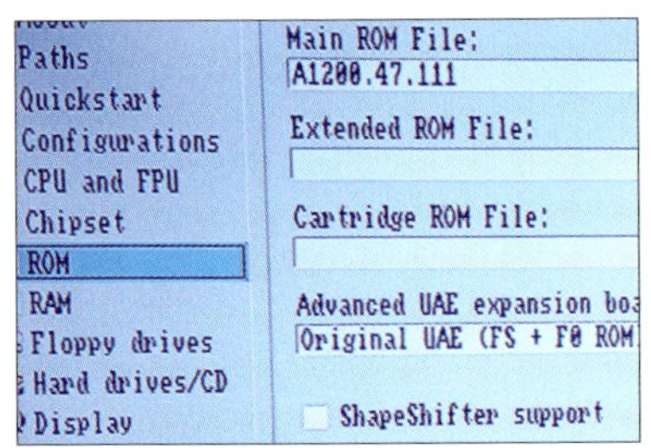

AmigaOS 3.2 on the THEA500 Mini: the Amiberry emulator interface can be accessed via a workaround.

Step 9: Boot_ol.uae modification

On the USB stick you will now find a new file with the name *Boot_ol.uae* in the *AmigaOS3.2* directory in the *Boot.lha* archive. This UAE configuration file was created by the Mini. Open the file with a text editor such as *Notepad++* or *TextEdit*. Insert the following four lines right at the start of *Boot_ol.uae*:

```
amiberry.open_gui=F12
amiberry.save_state_on_exit=true
amiberry.ignore_gui=false
use_gui=yes
```

Save the file again (make sure the suffix does not change). Right-click on the file in Windows Explorer and select *Properties* in the context menu. In the window that appears, tick the *Read-only* option and confirm by clicking the *OK* button. This will prevent the A500 Mini from overwriting the file and corrupting it.

Step 10: Amiberry's user interface

As a test, insert the USB stick into the A500 Mini, switch to USB mode and navigate to *Boot.lha* in the *AmigaOS3.2* folder. Press the A button and then the *Home* button to start the media.

Tada! A moment later, the Amiberry user interface appears. This will allow you to make changes to the host system in future. We do not recommend using a gamepad to control the user interface, and mouse control is near to impossible – a USB keyboard and frequent use of the [TAB] key is more convenient.

Step 11: Hardfiles

Various kinds of installation media can be used for the installation of AmigaOS 3.2 in the Amiberry environment. In addition to a large WHDLoad image, directories on a USB stick or hardfile images (HDF) are also an option. In this example, the latter two are used. We recommend using an emulator to create a hardfile, as described in chapter 1.3 on *WinUAE*.

On the Amiga, you can use the *TSgui* tool for this step (see section 7.6). *TSgui* even allows you to export an existing disk as an HDF to make the following steps easier (see step 12).

Step 12: OS3.2 installation

It is wise to prepare AmigaOS 3.2 from scratch for use in the A500 Mini. There are two ways in which this can be done. We will only briefly explain them here, with references to other sections of the book:

1) Create a RAM drive on an Amiga (with at least 10 MB free RAM) (chapter 2.10) and install AmigaOS 3.2 (3.2.2.1) on this RAD drive (chapter 1.4 and 1.5). Then use *TSgui* (section 7.6) to create a hardfile of the RAM drive called *DH0* containing the installed operating system.

2) Set up WinUAE or a different Amiga emulator of your choice on your PC (chapter 1.3) and install the current AmigaOS on a hardfile (chapters 1.4 and 1.5).

Whether you use an Amiga or Windows PC, create a second, formatted hardfile called *DH1*. On this virtual hard disk you can easily store data such as software archives, graphics or modules you want to use on the A500 Mini later on.

Step 13: Data on your USB stick

On the PC, move the hardfiles *DH0* and *DH1* to the *AmigaOS3.2 directory* on the USB stick. You can also place files in the *Transfer* directory for quick exchange between Amiga and PC.

Copy the appropriate Kickstart ROM, such as *A1200.47.111.rom* for AmigaOS 3.2.2.1, into the *ROM directory* on the USB stick.

**Step 14:
Amiberry setup**

Switch the A500 Mini on and start the *Boot.lha* (see step 10). Using the Amiberry user interface, add the HDF images and the *Transfer* directory to the system. You can change this in the *Hard drives/CD* section (using *Add Hardfiles* and *Add Directories*).

You make changes to the system in a similar way to that described in chapter 1.3 on WinUAE. The key specifications for this particular example are: 68020 (CPU), AGA (chipset), A1200.47.111.rom (ROM), 8 MB (RAM), hardfiles as above, 720 x 284 pixels (display).

**Step 15:
Save the configuration**

Though you can save your configuration under *Paths*, it will not be reloaded the next time you reboot. As such, a workaround is required: once you have completed the configuration, boot the virtual Amiga using the *Start* button in the bottom right. As soon as the Workbench is loaded, press the *Home* button on the gamepad to access the selection carousel. If the Workbench is set up with the standard graphics mode (and only then!), you can create a *savegame* using the *down* button of the control pad. This savegame represents the configuration file, which must be called up after each restart.

**Step 16:
Booting with your configuration**

Select the USB stick, navigate to the *Boot.lha* and press the *A* button, but *not* the *Home button* this time. Instead, use the *B* button to return to the selection carousel, press *down* on the control pad and use button *A* to load the savegame you have just created. The Mini boots into AmigaOS 3.2 via Amiberry!

TIP **Optimize resolution**

The standard resolution of the emulated Workbench will appear out of proportion. Amiberry's RTG option can help. However, you will no longer be able to make a *savegame*. In order to use RTG, you must install the UAE monitor in AmigaOS (keyword: Picasso96) and allocate it memory (RAM section in the configuration). If the *savegame* was created with the standard resolution, it can be started with the RTG option switched on.

Step 17: Refining the configuration

You will notice that not all parameters set in Amiberry are transferred in the *savegame* file. Therefore it is advisable to edit the configuration file *Boot_ol.uae* manually to define as many parameters as possible before loading the *savegame*.

The *savegame* is located on the USB stick in a hidden folder called *a500states*. To display this folder, you will need to select *View > Show > Hidden items* in Windows 11 Explorer, or the key combination `[Shift]+[Command]+[.]` on a Mac with Finder. In the hidden folder – in another subfolder – you will find the savegame you are looking for under the filename *slot-0.uae*. The label of the disk under which the savegame was saved is hidden in *slot-0.png*. Copy *slot-0.uae* with the new name *Boot_ul.uae* into the AmigaOS3.2 folder.

Edit the configuration file with a text editor and adapt it to your requirements. You can download a prepared configuration file from this book's service website at https://lookbehindyou.de/en/amigaos32book.

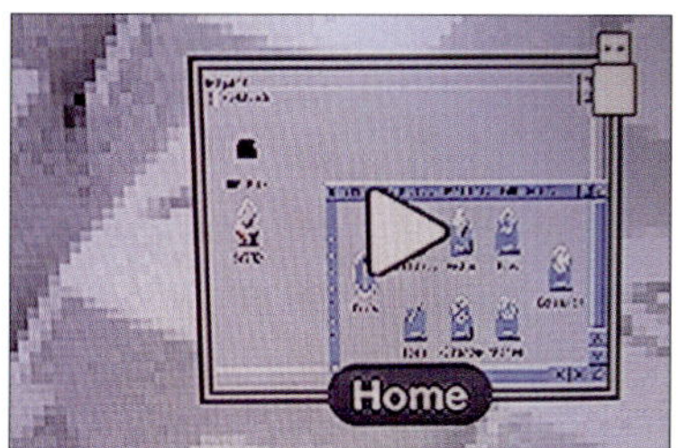

Proof: AmigaOS 3.2 on the THEA500 Mini (left image). Fine-tuning the configuration file is a good idea (right image)

Basics

2

In AmigaOS 3.2, as in all previous versions, the desktop environment is the Workbench. In this chapter, we will guide you through the most important Workbench elements, such as windows, icons and menus. We will explain its basic operation and discuss special features such as RAM and RAD, devices and ADF. A large section is devoted to file systems, which play an important role in the use of AmigaOS.

Workbench in detail

Icons, gadgets, buttons, fields – the Workbench is full of different elements. This is what they are called.

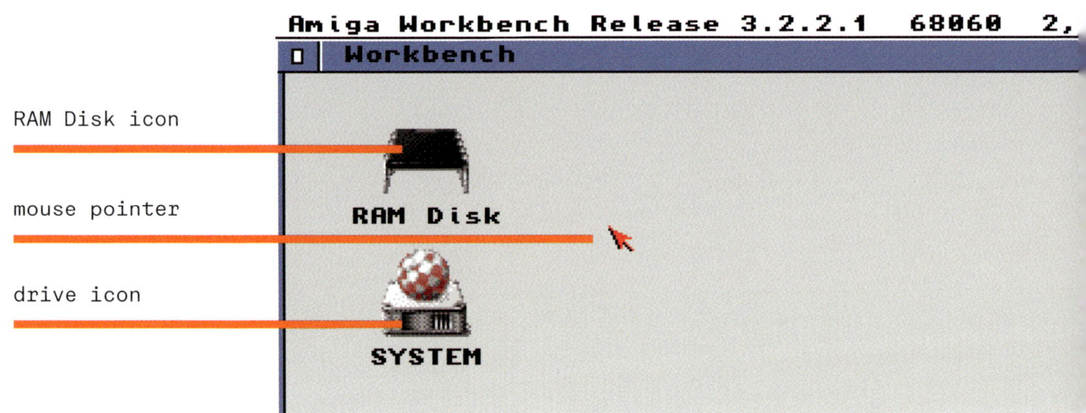

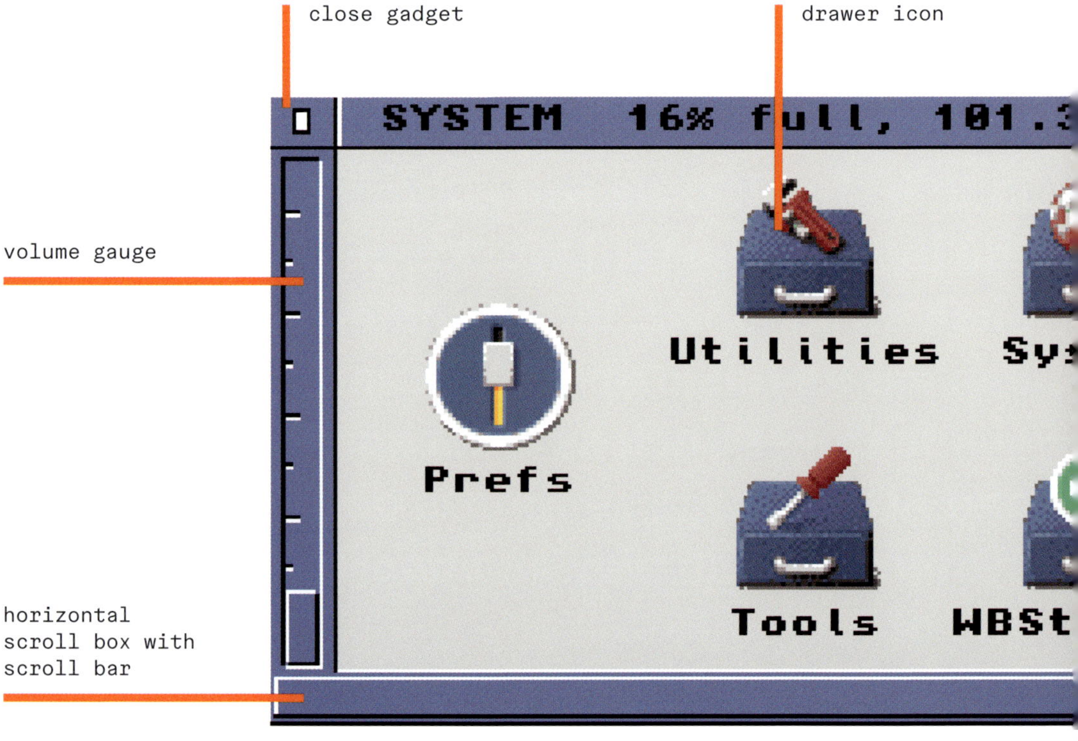

close gadget

drawer icon

volume gauge

horizontal scroll box with scroll bar

SYSTEM 16% full, 101.

Utilities

Prefs

Tools

WBSt

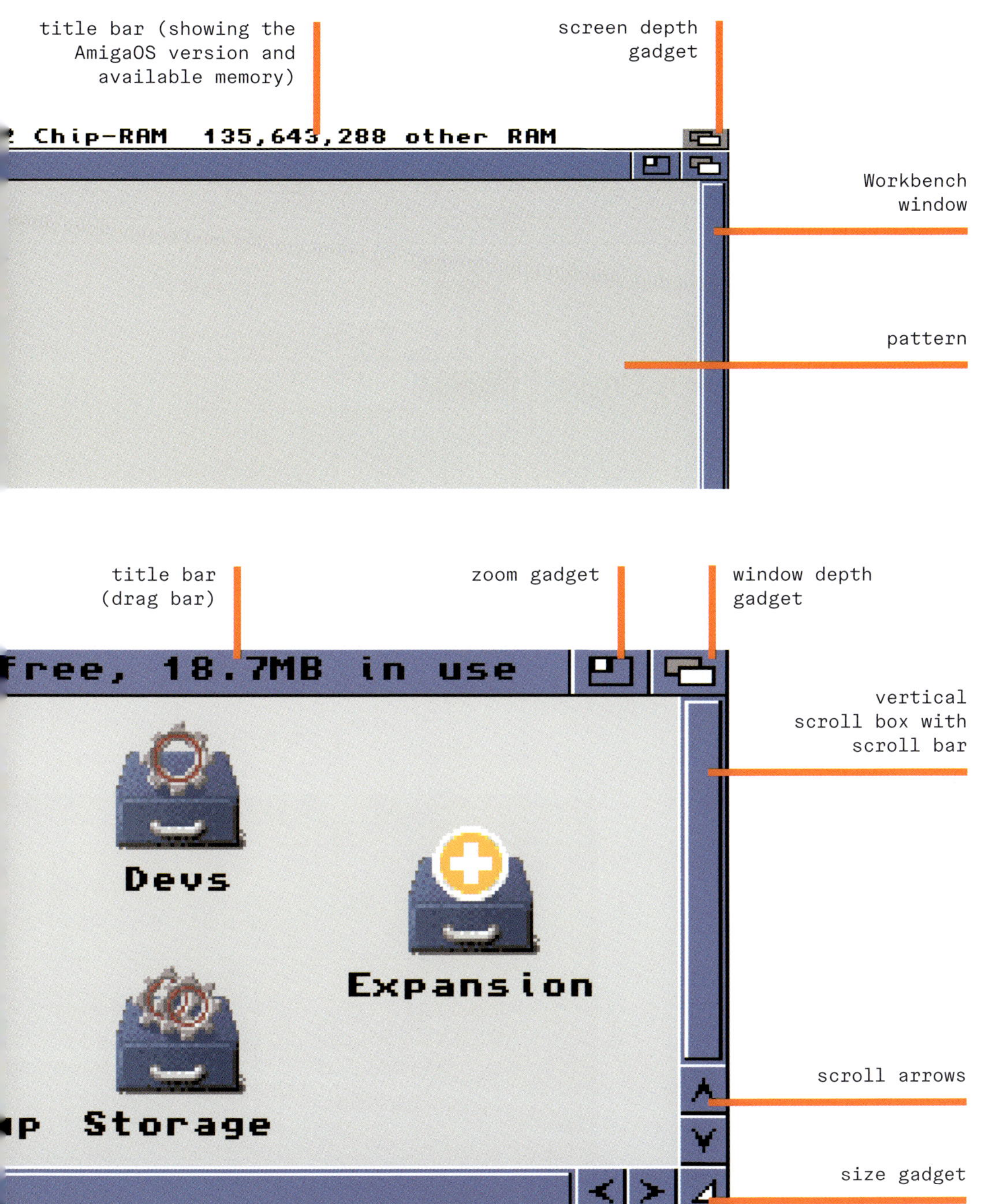
title bar (showing the AmigaOS version and available memory)
screen depth gadget
Chip-RAM 135,643,288 other RAM
Workbench window
pattern
title bar (drag bar)
zoom gadget
window depth gadget
free, 18.7MB in use
vertical scroll box with scroll bar
Devs
Expansion
Storage
scroll arrows
size gadget

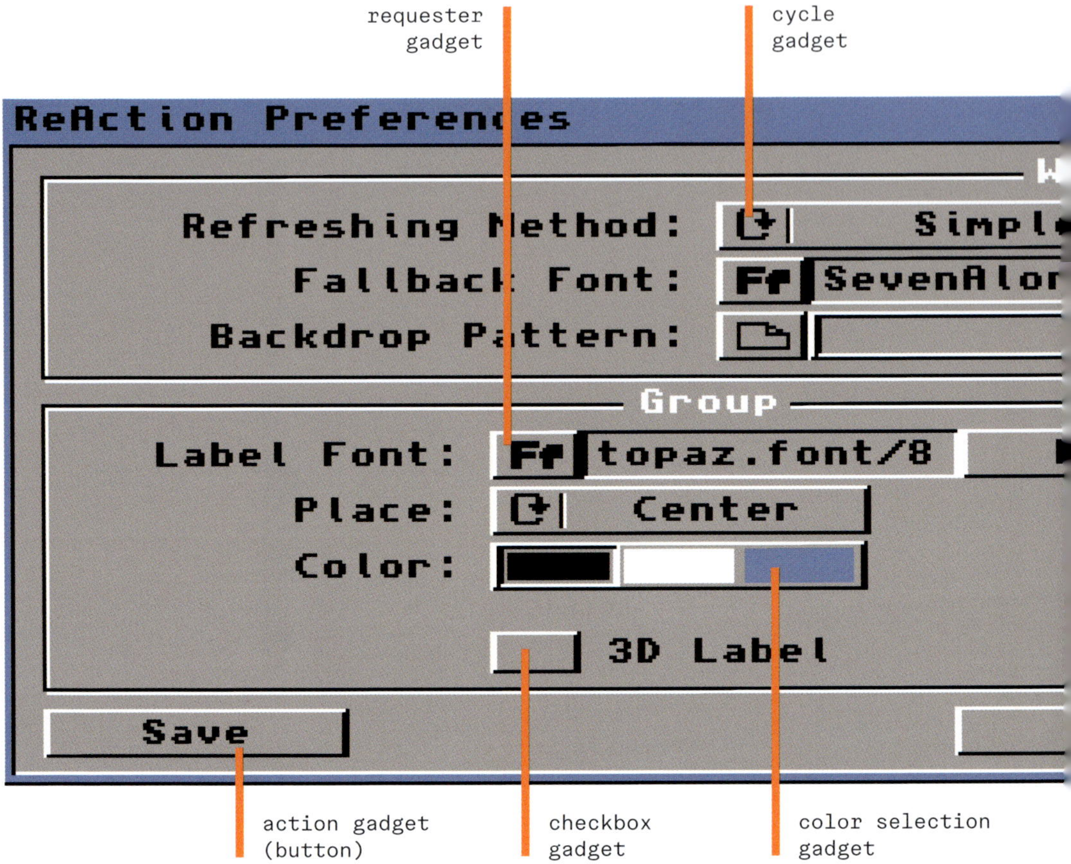

requester gadget
cycle gadget
ReAction Preferences
Refreshing Method:
Simpl
Fallback Font:
SevenAlor
Backdrop Pattern:
Group
Label Font:
topaz.font/8
Place:
Center
Color:
3D Label
Save
action gadget (button)
checkbox gadget
color selection gadget

radio button
Serial Preferences
Baud Ra
Input Buffer Si
Handshaking
XON/XOFF
RTS/CTS
None
Parity
None
Even
Odd
Mark
Space
Save

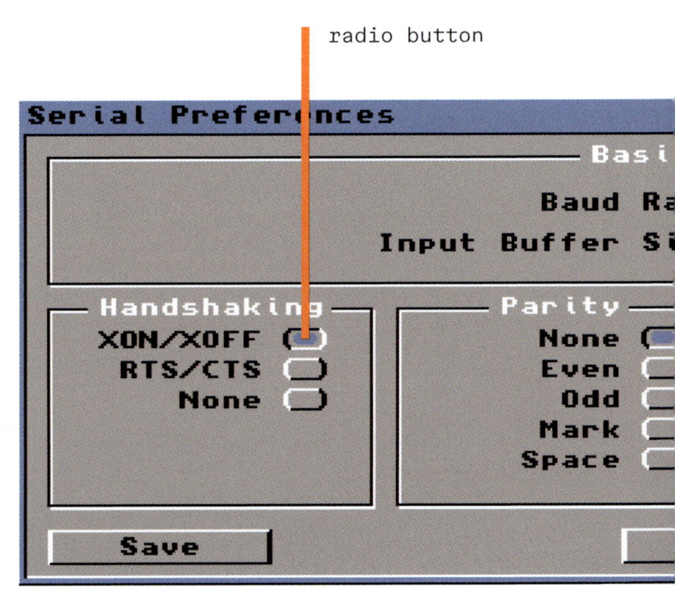

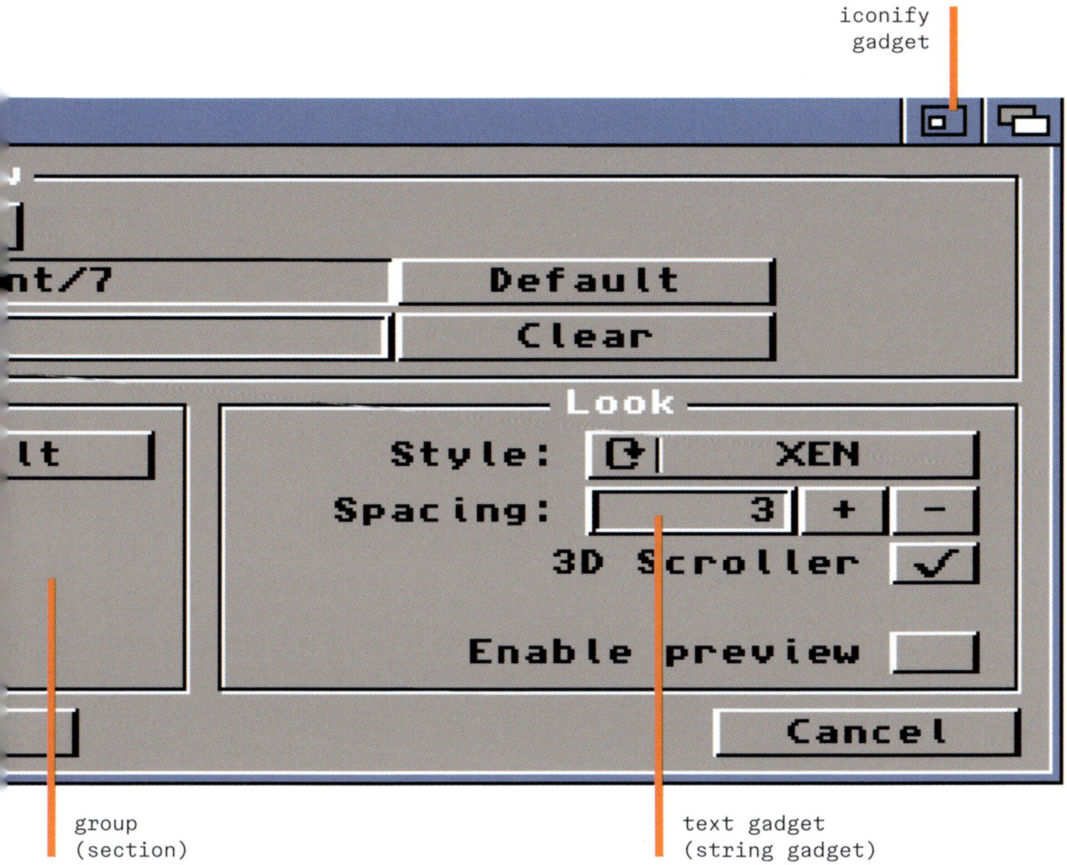

iconify gadget

nt/7

Default

Clear

lt

Look

Style: XEN

Spacing: 3 + −

3D Scroller ✓

Enable preview

Cancel

group (section)

text gadget (string gadget)

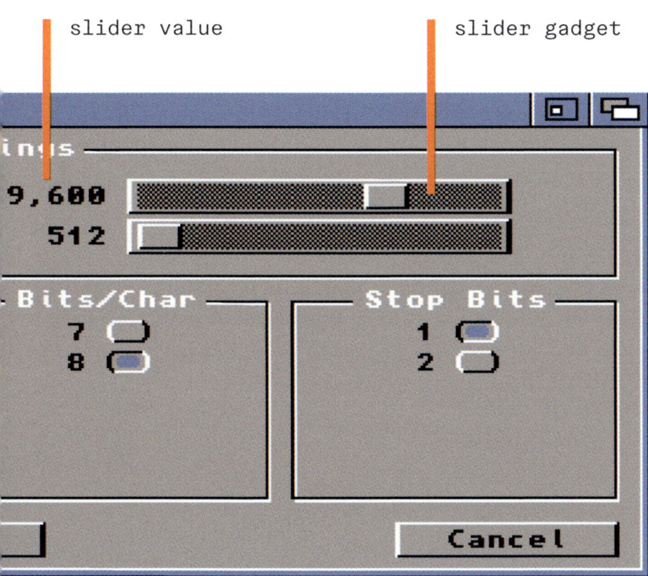

Workbench structure

The Workbench is the graphical user interface (GUI) of AmigaOS. At first glance, it consists of a window that fills the entire screen and a menu at the top, and icons inside the window to work with.

Workbench screen

After booting AmigaOS 3.2, the Workbench loads on the screen. The desktop is the actual working area of the operating system that you, the user, can interact with in a variety of ways.

The look of the Workbench in AmigaOS 3.2 has been kept in the same classic style you will be familiar with from previous versions of the Amiga operating system. The screen is essentially made up of two parts: the title or menu bar is at the top, while the Workbench window takes up the majority of the screen. You can also opt to view the user interface without a window.

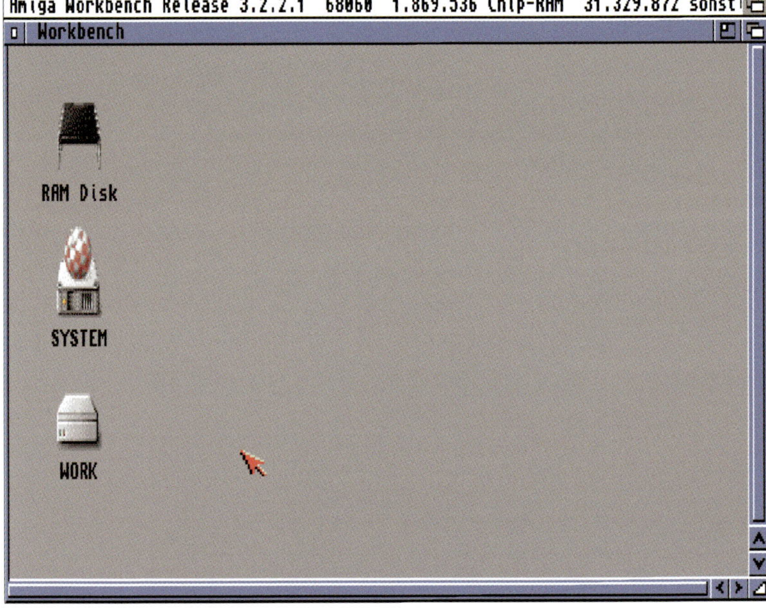

The default Workbench look after installing AmigaOS 3.2: with its blue standard window, grey background and white top menu bar (windows with additional disks), displayed in LoRes or HiRes screen resolution.

Menu bar (title bar)

As its name suggests, the menu bar contains a selection menu. This menu provides AmigaOS 3.2 functions and commands that can be selected and started directly. These functions are explained in detail on page 90 and throughout the book.

If you left-click into the Workbench screen, some system information is displayed in the menu bar. By default, the first value is the Workbench version loaded. Release 3.2 should be specified here. AmigaOS 3.2 loads this information automatically, but it can be changed (more on this later).

RAM display and RAM types

The amount of memory available to use is shown in the title bar. This information does not refer to the total capacity of the hardware-based memory installed in the Amiga, only the amount of memory actually available, i.e. minus the amount of memory already used by the operating system and any loaded software and data.

AmigaOS makes a distinction between different types of random access memory (RAM, the working memory). Chip RAM, or graphics RAM, is memory that is directly accessible by the Amiga's custom chips. It is used in two ways: first and foremost, it is used to store graphics and audio data that can be directly accessed and processed by the custom chips. If no Fast RAM or other memory is installed in the Amiga, program data can also be stored here and used directly by the processor. Because of this dual use, this memory is slightly slower, but it is essential to the operation of the Amiga and the AmigaOS. Chip RAM is limited by the technology of the Amiga to a maximum of 2 megabytes (MB).

Fast RAM is pure working memory that can only be accessed by the processor (CPU). The custom chips cannot access this memory directly; it can in fact only be addressed by the CPU. Fast RAM is therefore significantly faster than Chip RAM (depending on the accelerator card or memory expansion installed). The processor uses Fast RAM to load and process software data. AmigaOS combines the available memory. For example, the Fast RAM on a built-in accelerator card is added to the memory on the motherboard.

The fastest memory in the system (usually on an accelerator card) is always prioritized first, and the slowest memory (usually on Zorro cards) is last in the line. In theory, the Amiga can hold up to 3.5 gigabytes of memory – AmigaOS is not able to handle more at the moment.

Foreground and background

On the far right of the menu bar, you will see the tiny *foreground/background gadget*. You can use this to switch between programs if multiple have been started on the Workbench. This only works if launched applications use their own screens.

There is another way to access other applications running in the background: move the mouse pointer to the menu bar and hold down the left mouse button. You will then be able to move the menu bar, and thus the whole screen, up or down to get a view of an application that is running in the background. This feature is available for graphics output via the custom chips, but is not always available for output via ReTargetable Graphics (RTG) with a graphics card.

A small yet subtle difference: the Workbench in background display mode without window frames. This display mode is very popular with purists.

Workbench windows

The Workbench window is your actual workspace. By default, it contains two icons: the RAM Disk and the system drive, if it has already been set up. This window is used to perform all operating functions and to open other windows, programs or directories.

The Workbench screen can be displayed in two ways: as the default *window*, or as a *background*. The differences between them are enormous. Take a look at the window display: any icons or windows opened in this Workbench window may be larger than the actual screen resolution. There are sliders at the right and bottom edges of this window. When you open a window that is larger than your screen resolution, you can use the sliders to move the window contents back and forth, allowing you to work in a much larger area than what is actually visible.

You can use this feature even when no application is running. To do so, move the mouse pointer over the arrow icons at the bottom of the window. There are four arrows: two for horizontal scrolling and two for vertical scrolling. If you hold down the left mouse button, the contents of the window will move in the opposite direction – and the icons will move out of sight. You can use the other arrow to scroll the contents of the window backwards. If elements are outside the visible area of the window, you can tell by looking at the bars at the bottom or right of the window, which no longer cover the entire scrolling field.

An icon that allows you to change the size of the Workbench window itself is located between these arrows. If you place the mouse pointer on it and hold down the left mouse button, you can change the size of the window continuously.

The background display can be activated via the menu item *Workbench > Backdrop*. This removes the Workbench window. All contents are now displayed directly on the Workbench screen. Any icons that were positioned in the invisible area of the screen will show up right away. The downside of this is that it reduces the size of the Workbench workspace to the set screen resolution. Although this has the advantage that all activities and icons are channeled into the visible area of the screen, it also limits the area in which you can operate.

You can switch between window mode and background mode at any time. Whichever works most efficiently for you is entirely up to your personal preference.

Workbench icons and symbols

Icons, sometimes called pictograms, are central elements on the Workbench for identifying programs, directories and files with a visual symbol.

The Workbench and its windows contain a large number of icons. These graphical symbols represent files, whether they are an executable program, a directory or a project file.

Dealing with icons

By default, the Workbench will have two or more icons, depending on how it has been started, e.g. the Workbench icon and the RAM Disk icon when booting from a floppy. These are called drive icons. As a test, move the mouse pointer to the RAM Disk icon and click on it once with the left mouse button. You will see that the icon changes its appearance – it is now *selected*. If you hold down the left mouse button while the mouse pointer is on the icon, you can "grab" and move it, and drop it anywhere by releasing the mouse button. Use this function to arrange icons within a window.

AmigaOS has always saved its icons as a separate file on the disk. These symbol files can be identified by their *.info* file extension, but they are only visible in a file manager such as *DirOpus*. In addition to the actual image and alternative image, further information such as position, attributes or default program is stored in these info files. Conversely, this means that every file and directory you work with regularly should have a suitable icon in the form of a supplementary info file for the Workbench to display and process it correctly.

Thanks to the automatically loaded info tool *RAWBInfo* (see section 4.38), you can get an insight into all the relevant information about an icon and its associated file. You can access this view when the icon is selected using the menu *Icon > Information* or via the keyboard shortcut `[R-Amiga]+[I]`. Details on using the info display can be found in the *RAWBInfo* section in the *Programs* chapter.

AmigaOS and Workbench distinguish between five different types of icon:

Drive icons

Drive icons belong to storage media such as floppy disks, hard drive partitions or CD drives. Drive icons are only located in the main window of the Workbench. In contrast to all other *.info files*, which must always have exactly the same name as the assigned program or drawer, this file is always called *disk.info* and is located on the top level of the disk or partition.

Drawer icons

Drawers are directories on a drive that can be accessed and opened directly on the Workbench. These directories contain files of all kinds and other drawers that can be sorted and displayed according to various criteria. The *Prefs* drawer, for example, contains programs that can be used to change Workbench settings. Drawers and their icons can be nested within each other.

Program icons

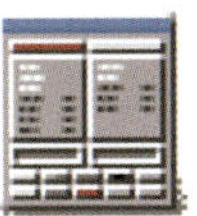

Program icons can be used to execute programs by double-clicking. Depending on the application or game, a program icon can look very different and customized, as can be seen here in the example of the *Directory Opus 5* icon. Tools, utilities and commodities in the Workbench system folder are also programs that are identifiable by their own icon symbols.

Project icons

Projects are files of various types that can be processed by programs. Typical examples of project files are text documents, music, graphics or archives. Project icons can be used to specify which programs should be used to open the file. Depending on their file type, projects have icons in different designs to visually identify the type.

Default icons

In AmigaOS you can define default icons for file types. If a file has a specific extension such as *.iff*, the system identifies the file type and triggers an action when the icon is double-clicked, e.g. opening an image file with *MultiView*. AmigaOS can also identify file types using other methods of analysis.

Using the Workbench

The AmigaOS 3.2 Workbench is very intuitive to use. It can be controlled with both the mouse and the keyboard.

Mouse control

One of the strengths of AmigaOS right from the start was its intuitive control using the mouse. All methods of input are dedicated to and optimized for this tiny little digital rodent. This starts with the installation of the operating system. It continues through all areas of the graphical user interface.

Not only can you place the mouse pointer anywhere on the Workbench, you can also use the buttons to perform actions such as starting programs or opening windows. When the mouse pointer is positioned over an icon for a program or directory, you can open it by double-clicking on it with the left mouse button. Use the right mouse button to activate and operate the pop-down menu in the Workbench title bar.

In this context, the left mouse button is called *the selection button* and the right mouse button is called *the menu button*.

Keyboard control

If you do not have a mouse available, you can also control AmigaOS 3.2 and the Workbench using a keyboard. Further, keyboard control is useful as a supplement to the mouse and speeds up many everyday tasks. Press and hold either of the `[Amiga]` keys on the keyboard, then use the arrow keys (up, down, left, right) to move the mouse pointer in the desired direction on the screen. The mouse pointer will move slowly in the selected direction. Simultaneously pressing one of the two `[Amiga]` keys and one of the two `[Shift]` keys will make the mouse pointer jump around the screen in larger movements. This allows you to comfortably cover short and long distances on the Workbench using the keyboard.

Programs on the Workbench or functions from the menu can also be selected using the keyboard. To do this, move the mouse pointer to the desired icon as described above, hold down one of the `[Amiga]` keys and press the left Alt key `[L-Alt]` twice at short intervals to simulate a double-click of the left mouse button. The combination of holding down the `[Amiga]` key and pressing the right Alt key `[R-Alt]` corresponds to a right-click with the mouse. If you want to navigate and control the menu bar, hold down both keys and move the cursor through the menu structure.

Numerous keyboard shortcuts are implemented in AmigaOS to speed up and simplify its use. You can find a complete overview in the *Shortcuts* section in the *Quick Reference* chapter.

Multiple selection of icons

You can select multiple icons on the Workbench at the same time. This can come in handy in situations where you want to open, copy, delete or move several objects (files as well as drawers) at once. Both the mouse and the keyboard can be used for multiple selection.

For example, open the Workbench directory, which contains various icons. Hold down the left mouse button and move over the icons to select all elements in an area. As soon as you press the mouse button, a dashed line appears. All icons within this line or within the drawn rectangle are selected when you release the left mouse button. The selection can be cleared by clicking the left mouse button outside the selected area.

If you want to select specific icons rather than an entire area, hold down the `[Ctrl]` key and left-click the icons you want to select. These icons are at your disposal and do not necessarily have to be in a line. Pressing the left mouse button again deselects.

To understand how several icons can be opened at the same time, try the following: in the active Workbench window, three drawers are to be opened at the same time. To do this, hold down the `[Ctrl]` key and click on three drawer icons with the left mouse button. They will now be displayed as selected. Then hold down the right mouse button, select *Icons > Open* from the menu and release the right mouse button. This opens all three windows at once, one on top of the other.

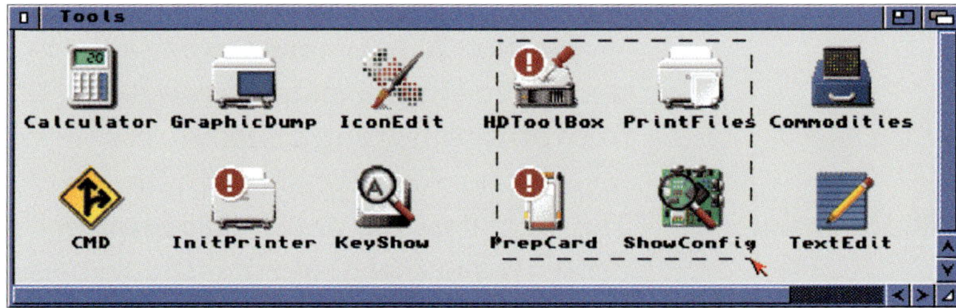

Click and hold the left mouse button to select multiple icons in a window.

Workbench menu

The Workbench menu is the hub for interacting with windows, icons and other elements of the Workbench.

The Workbench menu has always been integrated into the title bar of the Workbench. Hold down the menu button (right mouse button) to open the menu and you will see four items: *Workbench*, *Window*, *Icons* and *Tools*. As soon as the mouse pointer is positioned over one of the menu items, a corresponding sub-menu with its own structure will be opened. Release the menu button to trigger a function under the mouse pointer.

Workbench menu

You can change the Workbench display mode, either as a window or as a background, using the *Backdrop* function, which is described in more detail on page 84.

You can run a command not only from the command line interface (see chapter *Shell*), but also from the menu using the function of the same name: *Execute command*. A window will open up with an input field.

A new feature in AmigaOS 3.2 is the *Open volume* item, which allows you to view all mounted drives and partitions in a submenu, sorted by name. Selecting a device from the list will open it.

The interface is refreshed using the *Redraw all* function. The screen flickers instantly. Click *Update all* to reload the Workbench, any active windows and their contents. *Last message* calls up the last Workbench information message, which is displayed on the title bar. *About* displays the versions of AmigaOS, Workbench and Kickstart in an info window.

Use the *Quit* command to close the interface if all programs are closed. This function does not trigger a reset, as is known from other operating systems.

Window menu

The functions *New drawer*, *Open parent, Close*, *Update*, *Select contents* and *Clear selection* should be self-explanatory and always refer to the active window: create a new drawer, open an existing drawer, close the active drawer, select the contents inside a drawer and clear the current selection.

You can arrange elements in any window using the function *Clean up by* and the options *column*, *name*, *date*, *size* and *type* in its submenu. *Resize to fit* adjusts the window size to the content up to the maximum visible screen size. *Snapshot* fixes the position and size *of the window* or of *all* elements.

The *Show* function is also important for everyday use: it determines whether only files with a linked *.info* file are displayed (*only icons* option) or all files, including those without an .info file (*all files* option).In this context, use the *View by* function to specify whether content is displayed using *icons* or as a list sorted by *name*, *date*, *size* or *type*. You can change the *sort order* of contents to be *forward* (ascending) or *backward* (descending).

The *Find* item is linked to the search function of the *Find* command (see page 224) – a new input window will open.

Icons menu

In this menu you can *open* files and folders (equivalent to double-clicking), *copy*, *rename* and *delete* them. *Snapshot* fixes the position of selected icons, *UnSnapshot* releases them again.

The *RAWBInfo* requester opens when you click *Information*. There you can set protection bits and change tool types (see page 250), for example. *Format disk* is linked to the *format tool* (see page 226). *Empty trash* deletes the contents of the trashcan.

Some nice features are *Leave out* and *Put back*, which place icons from folders directly on the Workbench or move them back to the folder. This speeds up working with files.

Another new feature in AmigaOS 3.2 is the *Eject disk* function. It ejects removable media, such as ADFs or CDs, provided the drives have no open files or directories. This process is not yet reliable with all types of hard disk controller.

TIP **New in AmigaOS 3.2: Create icons automatically**

If you display the contents of a drawer as a list, all files without icons are assigned matching *DefIcons*. When *snapshotting* such an icon, the Workbench creates a copy of the DefIcon used for the file in the folder. This allows you to conveniently create icons for files that do not yet have their own *.info* file.

Tools menu

ResetWB restores the Workbench user interface to its original state. *Auto-arrange Icons* organizes the icons and fixes the size of the window. *Help* calls up the help (see section 4.17).

Devs and Storage

The Devs and Storage directories store data that is relevant to the system for the use of file types and keyboard mappings, and for other purposes.

The two directories Devs and Storage in the System folder of the operating system have an identical structure and contain a range of data that has a major impact on the use and flexible expansion of the operating system. The data is divided into five directories:

Contents of Devs and Storage

DataTypes provide a standardized interface for processing a wide range of file formats. Applications can access these data types to open and process files without having to worry about the details of the respective file format. For common file formats such as Ascii and AmigaGuide texts or IFF and JPG images, AmigaOS 3.2 provides support out of the box. DataTypes for other formats can be downloaded and installed later (e.g. at www.aminet.net/util/dtype). See page 94 for further details on DataTypes.

DOSDrivers are special drivers that are used to seamlessly integrate various devices and file systems into the AmigaDOS

The Devs and Storage directories both contain DataTypes, DOSDrivers, Keymaps, Monitors and Printers.

system. These include, for example, CD-ROM drives, as well as third-party systems such as PC-DOS floppy disks, which can then be processed by the Amiga. See section 2.12 for details.

Keymaps are configuration files that determine the keyboard's language mapping. A keymap defines which character or action is assigned to a specific key. The preinstalled American English keymap, for example, is labeled *la*, the British English keymap is called *gb*, Swedish *s*, French *f* and so on. See section 3.6 on *Input* for an overview.

Monitors contains configuration files for supported monitors and resolutions. The *PAL driver* comes as the default one on European systems. See section 3.15 for details.

The **Printers** drawer contains the printer drivers needed to run a printer on the Amiga. See sections 3.11 to 3.13 for details.

As mentioned, both the *Devs* and *Storage* contain five directories with the same names. However, their content is not identical.

Devs drawer

The *Devs* drawer is read at system startup so the drivers and scripts it contains are automatically integrated into the Workbench. This means, for example, that you can only select a keyboard layout in the Keyboard preferences that has its own configuration file in the *Devs/Keymaps* drawer. If a system item such as a DOS driver is to be loaded automatically by the system, you must copy or move the appropriate driver from *Storage/DOSDrivers* to *Devs/DOSDrivers*.

Storage drawer

As the name suggests, the *Storage* drawer is used by AmigaOS to hold various system files that are only to be used when they are actually needed. This means that the data contained in *Storage* is not integrated into the system when AmigaOS 3.2 is started, so that it cannot be used, and also does not occupy any RAM. If you need drivers or scripts, you must remove them from the *Storage* drawer and copy or move them to the *Devs* drawer of the same name.

A practical example: you want to be able to frequently read and write PC-formatted disks with your internal floppy disk drive. Open both the *Devs/DOSDrivers* and the *Storage/DOSDrivers* drawers and drag the *PC0 icon* from the *Storage* part to the *DOSDrivers* directory on the *Devs* part. The PC drive driver will now load automatically when the system is restarted, so PC disks can be used straight away when inserted.

DataTypes

AmigaOS learns how certain file formats can be interpreted and processed by the system and by programs with the help of the DataTypes feature.

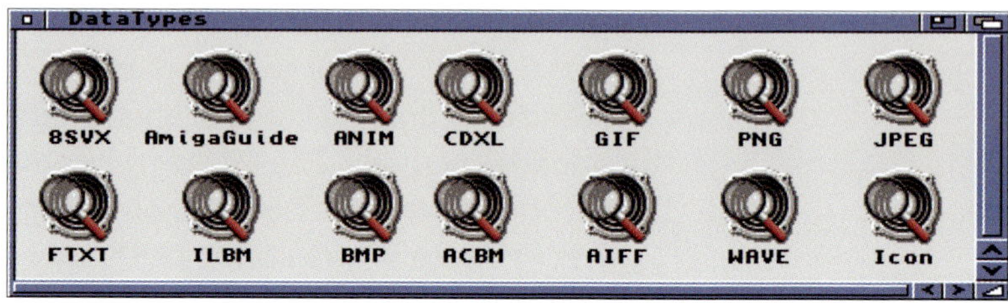

The DataTypes drawer contains important file type descriptions that are required for opening and processing files.

Function

The innovative DataTypes system was a flagship feature of AmigaOS when it was introduced. Not only can *MultiView* (see page 221) uses this standardized interface, but theoretically any Amiga software can access it. Depending on the type, the file formats can not only be read, but also written. AmigaOS comes with several DataTypes as a standard – including image, text and animation formats (see screenshot). The active DataTypes can be found in the system directories *Devs/DataTypes* and *Classes/Datatype*. To save system resources, move unused DataTypes to the system drawer *Storage/Datatypes*. Read more about *Devs* and *Storage* on the previous page.

DataTypes extension

The flexible extensibility of the system to adding new file types is remarkable. Many alien DataTypes are available for download from the Aminet and other software sources. Among others, the relatively new *WebP* image format is of interest. This is used on many websites, so it's worth making the system understand this file format using a special DataType (download: www.aminet.net/package/util/dtype/WarpWebPdt). There are separate versions for a variety of 68k processors. When installing, ensure that you choose the correct version for your CPU to get the best performance. Using this DataType, web browsers such as IBrowse or AWeb are now able to load the widely spread WebP image format and display websites properly.

Expansion

Drivers for some hardware extensions are located in this directory, which receives little attention from most users.

Function

The *Expansion* drawer stores important expansion modules and configuration data. These are primarily a few drivers for hardware that is not automatically configured during a cold start. This directory is usually automatically filled by the installation routines of expansion hardware. You will be informed of this step during the installation of said hardware and in its product manual.

The drivers are loaded during the boot process by the `BindDrivers` command invoked in the *startup-sequence*. To avoid system instability, you should not manually copy any installation packages into the *Expansion* drawer and refrain from making any other changes.

Expansion is located in the top drawer of the system drive.

WBStartup

Programs in the WBStartup directory are automatically loaded when the system starts.

Function

The *WBStartup* drawer has been designed to allow tools to be executed directly and conveniently when the Workbench is booted, once the boot process has completed the *startup-sequence* and the user-startup (see page 332). Once AmigaOS 3.2 has been installed, you will find six useful system tools in this drawer, which are called *Commodities*. Each of those applications will be explained in the Commodities section starting on page 236.

Default contents of the WBStartup drawer

Inappropriate and suitable content

You can add system extensions to the *WBStartup* drawer. However, avoid software that cannot run on the Workbench, such as programs that use their own screen. Integration of such software may result in you not being able to access the Workbench. In this case, you will need to make changes to the system manually using an *Emergency Disk* or the *Early Start* function (see page 337).

RAM and RAD: Data in memory

AmigaOS provides free memory to store files and directories. The RAM Disk (RAM) or the RAM Drive (RAD) can be used for this purpose.

RAM and RAD differences

RAM, short for *Random-Access Memory*, is the main memory of the computer. To store files and directories in this memory, AmigaOS gives the user two convenient options:

1. The **RAM Disk (RAM)** is automatically available after booting AmigaOS. All content stored on this virtual disk will be lost when the Amiga is restarted.
2. A **RAM Drive (RAD)** is only available after you have mounted it. Its data is usually retained until the Amiga is turned off. This means it usually survives a warm restart.

A RAM Disk (left) and a RAM Drive (right) on the Workbench

RAM Disk (RAM)

The RAM Disk is probably familiar to every AmigaOS user. It is available by default under the name *Ram Disk* on the Workbench or from the Shell and can be used just like a classic data medium. Its device name is `RAM:`. Its size is dynamic and goes up to the maximum size of the available free main memory. This means that, aside from some administrative information, it only ever occupies as much memory as the size of the files and directories stored on it.

The drive name for the RAM Disk has not always been *Ram Disk*. In the past, a name without spaces was used. However, the AmigaOS developers wanted to help other developers fix installer scripts and other programs that cannot handle spaces in file and directory names. Nevertheless, there are still many installer scripts, especially from older software, that exit with an error when using spaces. If you want to avoid this, add a line such as `Relabel RAM: RAM` to your user-startup sequence in *S/user-startup* on your system drive (see section 6.1 about startup-scripts for more information).

RAM drive (RAD)

The device driver *ramdrive.device* provides one or more persistent RAM drives. By default, AmigaOS does not provide such a drive after booting. However, there is a suitable mount list on the system drive in *Storage/DOSDrivers* named *RAD*. By simply double-clicking the icon or executing the command `Mount RAD:` you will create a *RAD Drive* the size of a DD floppy disk. AmigaOS used to occupy the often scarcely available Chip RAM for this purpose. Provided the turbo card correctly integrates its memory into the system, this is no longer the case in AmigaOS 3.2.

Multiple RADs

If you want to use several RAD drives, simply copy the DOS driver file *RAD* including the icon: the easiest way to do this is on the Workbench with `[Amiga]+[C]` or simply use the menu *Icons > Copy*. In the icon information that shows via `[Amiga]+[I]` or *Icon > Information*, switch to the *Icon* tab. Now change the unit number. To do this, adjust the line `unit=0` accordingly. Each RAD drive needs a unique number. If there is enough main memory, increase the size of the RAD drive by adjusting the value in the line `HIGHCYL=79`. The standard size is 80 cylinders from 0 to 79, which is the size of a standard DD disk. With `highcyl=159` you'll get twice the space.

A RAD drive is formatted with the *Old File System* after it is mounted. If necessary, format it with the *Fast File System* to save slightly more data with the same main memory consumption (see 2.12, *file systems*).

Bootable RADs

RAD drives survive a warm restart of the Amiga via the keyboard shortcut `[Ctrl]+[L-Amiga]+[R-Amiga]`. They are also bootable. This means that on an Amiga that boots from floppy disks and has sufficient main memory, the boot floppy can be copied to the *RAM drive* in order to boot from it. As a starting point, you can copy the *AmigaOS 3.2 Workbench disk* to the RAD drive. Depending on the processor installed, you will also need the appropriate CPU library. For a RAD drive with the capacity of a DD disk, you may need to free up space for it beforehand by deleting unnecessary files from the RAD drive. If there is sufficient main memory available, simply use a higher value for `HIGHCYL` in the icon settings, e.g. 179. Then copy the files to the RAD drive using `Copy Workbench3.2: BOOTRAD: ALL CLONE`. The CPU libraries can be found on the *MMULibs* disk. If there is enough space, copy all contents with `Copy MMULibs: BootRAD: ALL CLONE`. Otherwise, only copy what you need for the CPU you are using. Your Amiga will now boot up much faster than with floppies – but only until the next reboot.

The boot priority of a RAM drive is usually 0. A bootable partition on a hard disk or other disks also has a boot priority of 0 by default. This means that AmigaOS may attempt to boot from a RAM drive after it has been mounted. However, if the RAD does not contain the operating system files, you will only receive an empty Shell window. So if you normally boot from another data medium but would still like to use a RAM drive, it makes sense to set the boot priority of your regular partition in *HDToolBox* to at least 1 or to lower the boot priority of the RAM drives to -1, for example. To do this, simply enter *bootpri=-1* in a new line in the corresponding mount list or enter this line as an icon feature. If you do this by mistake, restart the Amiga while holding down the left and right mouse buttons. Then simply select the correct boot drive in the *Amiga Early Startup Control* boot menu under *Boot Options*. Then click on *Use* and finally on *Boot*.

If you want to remove a RAD drive without restarting your Amiga, use the `RemRAD` command. Enter the device name of the RAD drive as the only parameter. For a drive that still uses AmigaDOS, the `FORCE` option must also be specified. The command instructs the *ramdrive.device* driver to delete all files. The driver sets the drive to *busy* (*in use*). The drive only disappears completely after a warm restart.

ADF: Virtual disks

WinUAE has made the "Amiga Disk Format" popular. Now ADF has finally found its way into AmigaOS.

Function

ADF stands for *Amiga Disk Format* and has become very popular in the past 20 years due to the spread of Amiga emulators such as WinUAE and FS-UAE. ADF files are virtual *disk images* that make digital Amiga disks usable. They are also an important method of preserving old software, as physical disks often become unusable due to aging. Since AmigaOS version 3.2, ADF disks can finally be read directly in the Amiga operating system on classic Amiga hardware.

Both the content and structure of a physical Amiga disk are stored in the ADF file. This includes the file system and names, directory structures and the actual data content of the disk. ADF files are always the same size due to the 1:1 mapping of a physical disk, namely 880 KB. Disks with a high recording density, so-called HD disks, hold 1760 KB – also in ADF format.

Using ADF on the Workbench

ADF is automatically embedded in AmigaOS 3.2. Double-click on an ADF file in a directory to mount the ADF, i.e. make it readable for the system. This opens a new virtual disk, which you can use the same as any other medium directly in the Workbench user interface.

The technical background of ADF support in AmigaOS 3.2 is the new command `DAControl` (inside the *C* drawer) in combination with the new driver *trackfile.device* (inside the *Devs* drawer). `DAControl` is responsible for mounting, loading, ejecting and creating ADFs. The command can also be executed in the Shell and has various arguments such as `MOUNT`, `EJECT`, `WRITEPROTECTED` or `BOOTABLE` – details on this can be found in the section about `DAControl` in the *Shell* chapter.

TIP **DA0:**
Virtual ADF disks are set up in the operating system with device names DA0:, DA1: , etc., in the order in which they are mounted.

File systems in detail

The active management and associated reading and writing of data on a disk is handled by a file system.

Overview

A file system reads and writes files to and from a disk, such as a hard disk, a SSD, a floppy disk, a USB stick, a memory card, an ADF file, an HDF file or the system's main memory. It decides how to store files and directories on such a medium, which is usually organized in blocks. This means that the user does not have to decide and remember which blocks contain the data of a file.

The default file system of AmigaOS 3.2 is the *Fast File System*. Alternatives are the *Smart File System* or the *Professional File System*. Compatibility with Windows and other systems that support the *FAT file system*, such as Linux and Mac OS X, is ensured by the *CrossDOS file system*. The *CD File System* is responsible for accessing CDs and DVDs.

But which file system should you choose for your own system? That's a difficult question:

The standard **Fast File System (FFS)** has been continuously improved and thoroughly tested by the AmigaOS development team. With *DiskDoctor*, which was virtually rewritten in AmigaOS 3.1.4, it has a good tool at its side for recovering data from damaged file systems. However, the Fast File System was not originally written for large file systems and large files. It does not scale well. For example, files larger than 2 gigabytes are problematic, even if they are rarely found on most systems. Partitions larger than 4 gigabytes are possible with appropriate support from the driver or with Direct SCSI. However, the file system was not originally intended for this. With a suitable block size such as 4 or 8 KB, a Fast File System also works well on a partition with, for example, 50 GB, as long as it essentially contains files larger than 50 MB.

The **Smart File System (SFS)** supports files with a size of 4 GB minus 2 bytes and partitions up to 128 GB. It has a data recovery tool on board in the form of the *SFSsalv* program. With the incompatible DOS type SFS\2, it even supports partitions and files larger than this limit. However, only a few program such as AmiDVD, LhA and DvPlayer can cope with files larger than 4 GB (see also the FAQ for SFS, download at www.aminet.net/package/disk/misc/SFS). In addition, you will be using SFS without a safety net: There is currently no data recovery tool for the DOS type SFS\2. Although a data recovery tool does not replace backup copies, it is helpful if the last backup copy was made a while ago.

The **Professional File System (PFS)** supports larger file systems up to 104 GB. Data recovery tools are available with the *PFSDoctor* and *DiskValid* programs. However, the file size is also limited to 2 GB.

Note: The developer of ApolloBoot, Willem Drijver, has observed that PFS takes longer to write data than other file systems. Therefore, when using PFS, it is better to wait a bit after a write operation before switching your Amiga off. (Even with other file systems, it is advisable to wait a few seconds to ensure the write process is really completed.)

With small files, SFS and PFS sometimes have performance advantages, as they work with a block size of 512 bytes and can save small files in a very space-saving manner. However, the Fast File System is the only Amiga file system supplied with AmigaOS – apart from CrossDOS and CD File System. In this respect, only this file system is officially supported. Less experienced users in particular should favor FFS.

TIP **File system recommendations**

Use the Fast File System wherever possible to be on the safe side. It is very actively maintained and considered future-proof. The Professional File System is also maintained on an ongoing basis, but is more for experienced users. The Smart File System, on the other hand, is no longer actively developed for OS 3.x. Regardless of which file system you use, it is important to create regular backups with suitable backup software. In the emulation environment, or when using CF and SD cards as well as USB sticks, backup copies can also be created under Linux and Windows.

Devices, drives and disks

AmigaOS provides storage media through so-called *devices*. These have names such as *DH0:* (for a partition on a hard disk or another large medium) or *DF0:* (for a floppy inserted in the first floppy drive). However, *RAM:* and *RAD:* are suitable for storing data in main memory. The following is a selection of typical device names:

Device name	**Function**
CC0:	PCMCIA card (Amiga 600 and 1200)
CD0:, CD1:	First, second etc. CD/DVD/Blu-ray drive
DA0:, DA1: etc.	First, second etc. drive for a disk saved as an ADF file
DF0:, DF1:, DF2:, DF3:	First to fourth floppy disk drive (Amiga format)
DH0:, DH1: and similar	Typical names for a partition on a hard drive or other large storage device
PC0:, PC1:	First and second floppy disk drive (PC format)
RAD:	Simulates a data drive in main memory
RAM:	The RAM Disk, whose data is only stored in the system's main memory

In addition to the device names, there are also the names of the actual data drives, also known as *volumes* on the Amiga. For example, *DH0* can take the name *System*, and *DH1* can take the typical name *Work*, and so on. For devices or drives that support changing the medium, such as floppy disk, CD and DVD drives and card readers, the device name always remains the same, while the name of the drive changes depending on the media inserted.

Partitions

You can divide large storage devices into areas known as *partitions*. This is done with *HDToolBox* or any other partitioning program. These partitions can be given any name. Typical names are *DH0*, *DH1*, etc. Indeed, it is also possible to use names such as *HD0*, *HD1* or *DAT* for a partition with data or *MUSIC* for a partition with music files. The name can be up to 30 characters long. For details, see section 4.4 about *HDToolBox*.

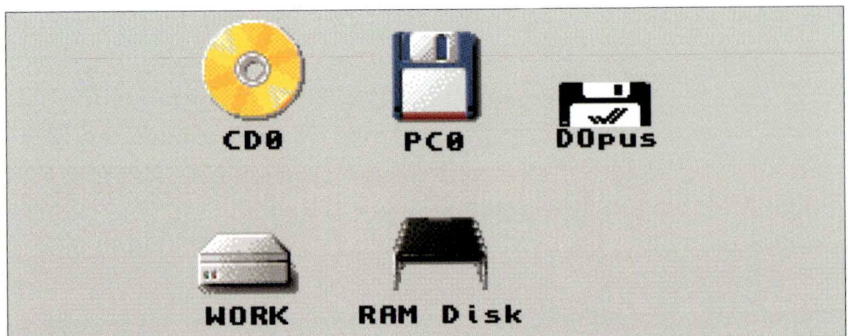

A selection of typical device names: CD0, PC0, DF0, DH1, RAM

Fast File System (FFS)

The first AmigaOS file system was the *Old* or *Original File System (OFS)*. It used 24 bytes per sector for checksums, which reduced its usable size from 512 to 488 bytes. It was mainly suitable for floppy disks. The maximum length of file or directory name was 31 characters.

The *Fast File System (FFS)* no longer uses checksums. As a result, it offers 878 KiB of free space on a double density disk with 880 KiB raw capacity instead of 836.8 KiB. It is faster than OFS and more capable of handling large amounts of data. AmigaOS developers have extended it over the years to include the important capabilities of handling umlauts (mutated vowels such as ä or œ) and accented characters in file and directory names (international mode), optimising directory entries for faster access (directory cache) or storing directory and file names up to 107 characters long (long name). Longer file names cannot be combined with directory caching. Other accesses are also slower on file systems with an activated directory cache.

The *Original File System* and *Fast File System* both work with a bitmap. They mark this as invalid during the write process, write the data, update the bitmap and then remark it as valid. If the write process is abruptly interrupted, the file system must be validated. Depending on the type of drive and the number and size of the files and directories, this may take several minutes.

AmigaOS 3.2 contains an improved version of the *Fast File System*. This works smarter, faster and with multiple threads.

The DOS type determines which functions are actually used:

DOS type	Hexadecimal	Properties
DOS\00	0x444F5300	OFS
DOS\01	0x444F5301	FFS
DOS\02	0x444F5302	OFS with international mode
DOS\03	0x444F5303	FFS with international mode
DOS\04	0x444F5304	OFS with directory cache and international mode
DOS\05	0x444F5305	FFS with directory cache and international mode
DOS\06	0x444F5306	OFS with long file names and international mode
DOS\07	0x444F5307	FFS with long file names and international mode

For compatibility with earlier AmigaOS versions and support for umlauts and characters with accents, DOS type DOS\03 is recommended. For file systems that can only be accessed by AmigaOS 3.2 and higher or AmigaOS 4 and higher, the long name mode with DOS type DOS\07 is also suitable. Apart from in special cases, it should not make much sense to use the directory cache mode.

The Fast File System supports different block sizes. Depending on the size, 1024 or 2048 bytes is recommended for a good balance between management and space consumption, and 4096 or even 8192 bytes for large files. The FAQ for the Smart File System even recommends 16384 bytes for a Fast File System that only stores files larger than 1 GB. Large block sizes speed up the reading and writing of files. However, they slow down the reading of directory information. In addition, FFS uses more space for administrative information with larger block sizes. So it is important to have a good balance here. For new, larger hard disks that use 4 KB blocks internally and larger partitions, a block size of at least 4096 bytes makes sense.

AmigaOS uses buffers in the main memory for fast access to file systems. Unlike Smart File System and Professional File System, however, the Fast File System in AmigaOS versions up to 3.2.2 does not necessarily use this memory for buffering metadata, but mainly for juggling several blocks, insofar as this is necessary. Therefore, increasing buffers for Fast File System is of little use. A number of 30 to 100 buffers depending on the block size is sufficient. The Fast File System in AmigaOS 4 and higher works differently because developer Olaf Barthel has implemented the concept of buffers differently. Higher values are therefore definitely worthwhile.

A storage medium can be formatted with OFS or FFS using the *Format* tool (see the *Partitioning with HDToolBox* section in the *Programs* chapter as well as the *Shell* chapter). This writes the appropriate data structures for the respective variant of the file system to the volume. You can divide hard disks and other large volumes into several partitions beforehand using HDToolBox.

To recover files from a medium with a corrupt OFS or FFS, AmigaOS provides the appropriate tool: *DiskDoctor* (see chapter 5 about the *Shell*). The developers have rewritten this tool for AmigaOS 3.1.4.

CD File System

The *CD File System* in *L:CDFileSystem* supports the ISO9660 file systems commonly used for compact discs (CDs) with long file names in accordance with the *Rock Ridge Interchange Protocol* (RRIP).

AmigaOS 3.2 contains prepared mount lists in *Storage/DOSDrivers* in the system drive. The DOS driver *CD0* uses the DOS type *CD\01* (hexadecimal: 0×43443031) for the standard file systems and extensions mentioned above. You specify the device driver and the unit using the icon features *Device* and *Unit*. The *scsi.device* is preassigned with unit 2.

A double-click or the command `mount CD0:` activates the DOS driver. If you want to use the optical drive by default, copy *CD0* to *Devs/DOSDrivers*. If you use several optical drives, copy the DOS driver according to your needs.

CrossDOS

With the help of *CrossDOS*, AmigaOS can access FAT-formatted volumes. CrossDOS consists of the CrossDOS file system driver, which is located in *L:CrossDOSFileSystem*, and the commodity *CrossDOS* for filtering and converting texts in files and file names. The *mfm.device* driver, which is also supplied, allows access to PC disks. The CrossDOS included from AmigaOS 2.1 onwards was previously a third-party product that was available for AmigaOS 1.2 and 1.3. As of version 3.1.4 of AmigaOS, CrossDOS also supports FAT32 and long file names.

There are two preconfigured mount lists for the first and second floppy drive in *Storage/DOSDrivers* inside the system drive. The DOS drivers *PC0* and *PC1* use DOS type MSD\00 (hexadecimal: 0x4D534400). You specify the unit using the icon settings for *Unit*. The default values are 0 or 1. If required, overwrite the device driver *mfm.* defined in the mount list with the DEVICE icon settings. Double-click on one of the DOS drivers to activate it. If you want to use PC floppy disks permanently, copy the corresponding DOS drivers to *Devs/DOSDrivers*.

Using *HDToolBox* or an appropriately adapted mount list, it is also possible to mount other volumes with FAT32, including a FAT32 partition on a hard drive or other large media.

You can use the *CrossDOS* commodity to activate the filtering and/or translation of text for a specific CrossDOS drive. MS-DOS uses both *Carriage Return (CR)* and *Line Feed (LF)* to mark the end of a line. AmigaOS, however, only uses *Line Feed (LF)*. Filtering text automatically adjusts the end of the line. The character encoding also differs. The translation of text offers an option to automatically adjust the character encoding. The *ASCII-7* option reduces the text to pure ASCII characters, while *INTL* supports umlauts. *MAC* is suitable for Apple MAC text files on PC disks and *DANSK* for Danish text files, for example.

The AmigaOS 3.2 reference documentation does not yet contain detailed instructions for CrossDOS. Partially outdated information can be found on the AmigaOS 4 Wiki (https://wiki.amigaos.net/wiki/AmigaOS_Manual:_Workbench_CrossDOS) or in the documentation for AmigaOS version 2.1 to 3.1. Further details on the use of CrossDOS can also be found in section 4.26 on *CrossDOS* in the *Programs* chapter of this book.

Smart File System (SFS)

The *Smart File System (SFS)* is an AmigaOS file system originally developed by John Hendrikx, later by Jörg Strohmayer. It is not included with AmigaOS. Release 1.277 for AmigaOS 3 dates from 2007, but runs stably on AmigaOS 3.2. There is a more recent version for AmigaOS 4 available in the Enhancer package.

Compared to the Fast File System, the Smart File System has clear performance advantages, especially with many files, large files and large file systems, which can be partially offset by using a block size of 1024 or 2048 bytes for the Fast File System. The Smart File System reads blocks in advance (read ahead) and uses a cache for writing (copy back cache). It therefore already runs quickly with 512 bytes per block. Larger block sizes tend to have disadvantages.

The Smart File System requires less space for metadata than the Fast File System. It therefore requires less space for a directory with the same set of files and subdirectories. By default, SFS supports file and directory names up to 107 characters long.

SFS also uses a special procedure to ensure that a transaction is either completely saved or does not exist. To do this, it first collects changes for a short while in main memory and then writes them in compressed form to a free memory area on the disk. This so-called *transaction failure block* is either completely written or not. Only then does it write the changes to the actual affected blocks in the file system. If the write process is abruptly canceled, SFS finds the transaction failure block and makes the changes. If the transaction failure block has not yet been written, the changes are lost. In this way, the file system creates consistency without the need for a lengthy validation process if writing is canceled.

Another useful function is a hidden directory called *.recycled*, which by default contains the latest 350 deleted files and directories. If necessary, you can simply copy a file from there to another location to restore it.

However, SFS also comes with limitations. The original Smart File System only supports files up to a maximum size of 4 GB minus 2 bytes and file systems with a maximum size of 128 GB. The version extended by Jörg Strohmayer supports files larger than 4 GB minus 2 bytes and file systems larger than 128 GB via the DOS type SFS\02 (0x53465302). File systems of this type are incompatible with older versions of the Smart File System by John Hendrikx. The tools for checking the Smart File System and for restoring files also do not work. It is therefore recommended to use this DOS type only for file systems that contain files larger than 4 GB. Of course not all programs support such large files.

AmigaOS 3.2 does not include the Smart File System by default. You can download it from Aminet if you wish (https://aminet.net/package/disk/misc/SFS). Unpack the archive. From the *SmartFilesystem* directory created by unpacking, just copy the commands `SFSformat`, `SFScheck` and `SFScheck` to *C:* with `Copy CLONE`, Workbench or a file manager. Also copy the commands `SFSconfig`, `SFSdefrag`, `SFSobject` and `SFSquary` from the *AmigaOS3.x* directory to *C:*, and copy the *SmartFilesystem* file system driver from the *AmigaOS3.x/L* directory to *L:*.

A Smart File System volume can only be formatted with the `SFSformat` command. It is not possible with the *Format* program delivered with AmigaOS 3.2. The program writes the appropriate data structures for the respective variant of the file system to the drive. You can divide hard disks and other large drives into several partitions beforehand using HDToolBox. With the `RECYCLED` option, there is no directory for deleted files. With `CASESENSITIVE`, a file system is created that distinguishes between upper and lower case, which is not typical for the Amiga. The DOS type is SFS/00 (0x53465300). For the incompatible SFS2 format mentioned above, it is SFS\02 (0x53465302). The manual recommends at least 100 buffers as the number of file system buffers, or even more.

You can check the structure of an SFS file system with the `SFScheck` command. Use `SFSobject` to hide a file or directory or make it undeletable if required. For example, `SFSobject Data HIDE` hides the *data* directory. Use `UNHIDE` to make it visible again. `UNDELABLE` prevents the accidental deletion of a file or directory. If an attempt is made to delete a file protected in this way, an error message appears stating that the object is in use. Use `DELABLE` to make the object deletable again. Use `SFSquery` and `SFSconfig` to query the configuration of an SFS file system. Use `SFSconfig` to change some parameters if necessary. As these changes are lost on a restart, write the appropriate command in the user start sequence *S:User-Startup* if required.

File systems are often no longer able to write files to the volume in blocks, especially when there is little free space, and they fragment. `SFSdefrag` is a simple tool for defragmenting files. After being called with the device name, the program opens a window with the block allocation and starts to copy blocks. With `SHOWRESULTS` the program displays a summary at the end, with `NOWINDOW` it runs without the window. Defragmenting files can fragment the free memory space. It is therefore advisable to defragment only when actually required. Instead, it is better to leave enough free space so that the file system does not fragment the files, or fragments them only slightly. It is generally not a good idea to let file systems fill up.

The *SFSSalv* tool, also included in the Aminet archive for the Smart File System, rescues files from corrupt SFS file systems. However, the version from the Aminet archive did not start under AmigaOS 3.2 even after installing the *gtlayout.library*.

Professional File System (PFS)

Yet another file system that can be used with AmigaOS 3.2 is the *Professional File System (PFS)* by Michiel Pelt. It was last updated and customized by Toni Wilen, the main developer of WinUAE, as *PFS 3 All in One*. It is recommended to use this newer version 19.2, as the *SCSI Direct support* important for AmigaOS 3.1.4 and 3.2 works correctly in this version.

Like the Smart File System, the Professional File System has performance advantages over the Fast File System, especially with many files, large files and large file systems. In addition, PFS, like SFS, takes up less space for metadata and is therefore particularly economical with the block size of 512 bytes recommended for PFS – especially when compared to FFS with a block size of 1024 or 2048 bytes, in order to compensate for at least some of the performance disadvantages of FFS.

The Professional File System also uses a special procedure to ensure that a transaction is either completely saved or does not exist. This procedure is called *PFS3 Atomic Commit*. Furthermore, PFS also has a hidden directory for the latest files deleted. This contains a maximum of 62 files by default. A maximum of 992 files are optionally possible. PFS also has a function for files that never exceed a certain size despite the constant appending of data. These are the so-called *rollover files*. If the size is exceeded, PFS forgets data from the beginning of the file. This is suitable for log files, among other things.

The Professional File System is not included in AmigaOS 3.2. To use it, first install the instructions and tools from the latest archive by Michiel Pelt (download: www.aminet.net/package/disk/misc/PFS3_53), which contains the outdated version 18.5 from 20 November 1999, using the installer. Deselect all file system drivers except perhaps the *FloppyPFS*, as it makes more sense to use the newer *All in One* version 19.2 from 2 October 2018 (download: www.aminet.net/package/disk/misc/pfs3aio). Copy the *All In One* version to *L:*. The file *pfs3aio* is usually sufficient. The *custom version* is only required for certain broken hard disk controllers.

A volume can be formatted using the `Format` program of AmigaOS 3.2 or with the `PFSFormat` command. The instructions recommend using PFSFormat, especially for large partitions. The number of *delete directory blocks*, each of which can hold up to 31 entries, can be specified. The maximum filename length can also be specified. The default is 31 characters.

```
PFSFormat DRIVE PFS: Name PFS QUICK DELDIRBLOCKS
```

`10 FILENAMESIZE 107` formats a partition with a maximum of 310 entries for deleted files and the maximum filename length of AmigaDOS. For PFS3 All In One with direct SCSI access, the DOS type PDS/03 (0x50445303) is used. The manual recommends 70 and 500 as the number of file system buffers.

You can check the structure of a PFS file system with the `DiskValid` command. The `ANALYSE` option provides additional information such as the number of files and directories. With `FIX`, the command attempts to repair a corrupt PFS file system on the spot.

An alternative to *DiskValid* is the *PFSDoctor* program, which has a graphical user interface. If you start DiskValid for a PFS file system while the current directory is on it, the command will no longer unlock the file system correctly. In this case, only a system restart will help. It is therefore recommended to switch to the RAM disk with `CD RAM:` beforehand. Repairing a file system on the spot harbours the risk of a faulty repair. Alternatively, use `PFSSalv` to recover files from a corrupt PFS file system to another file system (download: www.aminet.net/package/disk/salv/pfssalv2).

There are a number of other tools: the `SetFnSize` command displays the set maximum filename length or increases it subsequently. For example, `SetFnSize DAT: 107` sets 107 characters as the maximum length for a PFS partition with the name *DAT:*. Use `SetDelDir` to determine or change the size of the directory for deleted files. You can create rollover files with `MakeRollover` and change their size or position with `SetRollover`. There is an alternative command for displaying directory contents, `PFS3LS`, which also recognizes PFS3 extras such as rollover files. It uses options based on the Unix/Linux command `ls`.

PFS attempts to defragment files during copying processes. When `ANALYSED`, *DiskValid* also shows a list of fragmented files. Tools such as *PFS2DefragTry* or *PFS-Defrag* attempt to rectify this situation by copying affected files (download: www.aminet.net/package/disk/optim/PFS2DefragTry or www.aminet.net/package/disk/misc/PFS-Defrag10). However, this can fragment the free storage space and is not always successful, especially with very full file systems. It is therefore advisable to only use these tools when actually required. In general, it makes more sense to leave enough free space than to defragment, rather than letting file systems fill up.

Preferences

3

The Preferences, or Prefs for short, allow you to control important system settings. You can change visual settings such as the screen resolution (ScreenMode), the color palette (Palette) and backgrounds (WBPattern), as well as input settings such as languages used (Locale) and keyboard layouts (Input). There are also settings for printing, the serial port, sound, time and more. Software such as MUI or Picasso96 can also store its own settings in the Prefs directory. This section explains the key system settings to help you tailor the Workbench to your needs.

Preferences at a glance

Preferences are settings that allow you to make significant changes to the Workbench.

Function

The *Preferences*, known as *Prefs* for short, are usually located in the central *Prefs* directory of the same name on the main level of the system partition. These settings are an important part of the Workbench. They have an impact on various areas of the graphical user interface. For example, you can define the screen display including colors, specify languages and keyboard layouts, or simply change the time and date of the system.

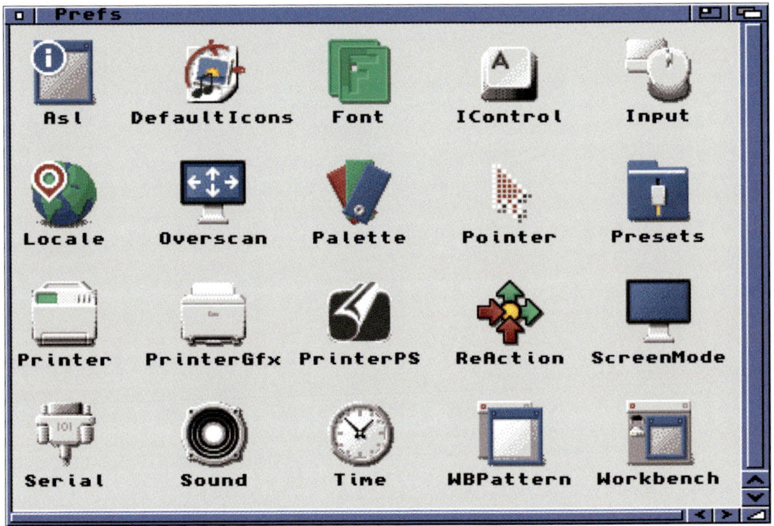

19 Preferences at a glance: the central Prefs directory contains all the control programs for customising the Workbench.

Prefs at a glance

After installing AmigaOS 3.2, the *Prefs* directory on the system partition contains 19 Prefs editor icons, as well as the additional *Presets* drawer where the presets are stored. On the next page you will find a list of the Prefs editors and their functions, which are explained in detail in this chapter.

Prefs	Function
ASL	ASL preferences for the behavior of the ASL file requester
DefaultIcons	Default icon preferences for the appearance and behavior of default icons for files without their own icon
Font	Character set preferences for character sets for Workbench icon texts, standard system texts and other texts
IControl	IControl preferences for the appearance and behavior of screens and windows, e.g. screen dragging and mouse wheel interaction
Input	Input preferences for the behavior of the mouse and keyboard, e.g. keyboard layout and mouse speed
Locale	Locale preferences for languages, country and time zone
Overscan	Margin preferences for defining the display area for text and graphics
Palette	Color preferences for setting up the colors of various elements of the Workbench
Pointer	Mouse pointer preferences for changing the size, shape and color of the mouse pointer
Printer	Printer preferences for configuring the printer driver and other options such as paper format
PrinterGfx	Graphic print preferences for adjusting the graphic output on the printer
PrinterPS	PostScript preferences for controlling the output on PostScript-capable printers
ReAction	Preferences for user interface elements in ReAction, e.g. changing the scrollbars in windows
ScreenMode	Screen display preferences for setting the screen resolution and color depth
Serial	Serial preferences for changes to the serial interface
Sound	Sound preferences for setting up the acoustic signal in the event of system errors
Time	Preferences for changing the date and time of the system
WBPattern	Workbench pattern preferences for selecting and creating background patterns for Workbench windows and screens
Workbench	Workbench preferences for basic adjustments to the behavior of the Workbench, e.g. title bar content or hidden devices

Presets drawer

The *Presets* drawer is where settings that have been made with specific preferences are stored.

Each of the Prefs editors has a menu with the items *Project*, *Edit* and *Settings*. You can save and load settings via *Project*. This allows you to quickly switch between different configurations without having to restart the system.

These settings files are usually saved in the *Presets* directory located in *SYS:Prefs/Presets*. However, they can be stored in any directory of your choice.

If you click *Save as* in the *Project* menu to save the changes done in a Prefs window, these settings are saved in the path *SYS:Prefs/Env-Archive/Sys/name.prefs*. *SYS:* stands for the name of the drive that contains the file, and *name* stands for the name of the specific setting. At system startup, the presets saved in the *Env-Archive* drawer are recognized by *IPrefs* and loaded during the boot sequence (see section 3.20 on *EnvArc*).

TIP **Presets icons**

You can specify that icons are created for saved presets by enabling the icon function for any Prefs editor in *Settings > Create Icons?*. If a preset owns an icon, you can call up the settings directly by clicking the icon.

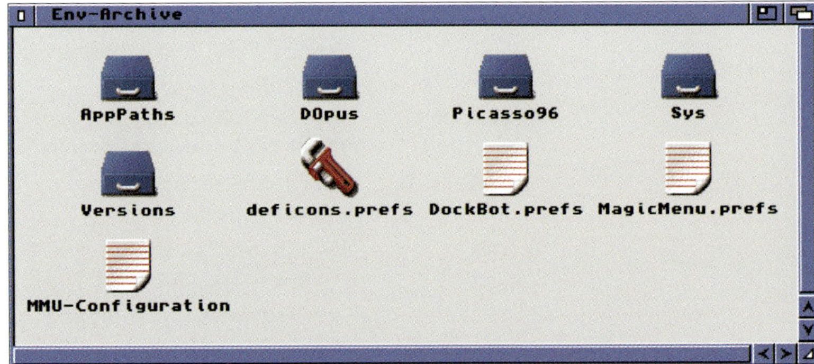

Depending on your settings and installed software the Env-Archive drawer is filled with preset files.

Prefs menus

With the exception of *Time*, each Prefs editor has the identical menu structure with the menu items *Project*, *Edit* and *Settings*.

In the **Project** menu, you can save the settings you have made to a file via *Save as* (see also the *Presets* section) or load previously created presets into the Prefs editor via *Open*. Use *Quit* to close the Prefs editor without saving changes. This function corresponds to the *Cancel* button in the prefs editors.

The **Edit** menu offers at least three functions: *Reset to Defaults* resets all settings in the Prefs editor to the system's default settings. *Last saved* restores the settings in the Prefs editor to the settings last saved with *Save As*. Finally, *Restore* resets the settings in the Prefs editor to the state they were in when the editor was opened.

The **Options** menu includes at least the item *Create Icons?*. When enabled, this option ensures that saved settings are given their own icon and can be launched by double-clicking.

INFO **Further menu items in Prefs**
Some Prefs editors such as Palette, Pointer or WBPattern offer additional menu items in the *Edit* and *Settings* menus. These special cases are discussed in each of the Prefs sections.

Self-explanatory controls in all Prefs editor windows: Save, Use and Cancel

Save, Use, Cancel

All Prefs editors have the same three control buttons at the bottom of the window: *Save*, *Use* and *Cancel*.

If you are satisfied with the result of the settings, you can save the settings as the current system default for further use by clicking the **Save** button.

If you only intend to use the settings for a short time or to test, select **Use**. Once you reboot the system, the settings you have made will then be lost. This is because the Workbench loads the default settings from the *Sys:Prefs/Env-Archive* directory, which can also be accessed as *ENVARC:*, every time the system is booted.

If you are not satisfied with the settings you have changed, or if you do not want to change them any further, close the Prefs editor by clicking on the **Cancel** button.

ASL (requester prefs)

You can control the ASL file requester, as well as the screen and font requesters, using the ASL prefs editor.

Function

The ASL editor has been an integral part of the operating system since AmigaOS 3.9. In this window you can configure the look and feel of the ASL-based file requesters. The size and position of the window and the sorting of the contents in the requester window can be adjusted according to your personal needs.

In order for changes made by the ASL editor to take effect, you must exit the editor by clicking *Use* or *Save*, and you must also exit the corresponding program from which the requester is to be opened. Try it out: make changes in the ASL prefs and then close the ASL editor by clicking on *Use*, quit *MultiView* if it is active, restart MultiView and click on *Project > Open* in the menu to see the changes made to the position, size or sorting in the ASL file requester.

The ASL editor is divided into two areas: *General* and *File Requester*, as you can see below:

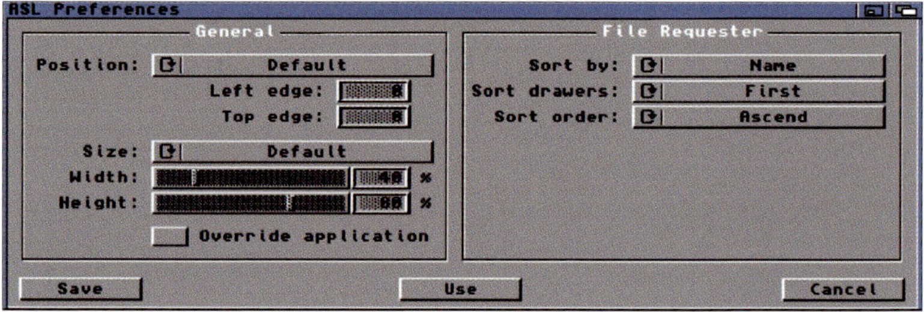

Neat ASL prefs editor for individual changes to file, screen and font requester

Position and size

The **General** section affects the file, screen and font requesters. Specify the *position* of the requesters using the cycle gadget. The *default* value aligns all requesters according to the operating system's specifications.

Center in window opens the file requester in the center of the window of the associated program, *Center on screen* opens it centered on the screen in use. *Top left of window* opens the file requester at the top left of the window, *Top left on screen* opens it at the top left of the screen. The *Mouse pointer* options opens the file requester directly at the mouse pointer.

The *Left edge* and *Top edge* text gadgets are only available for editing the positioning options *Top left on window* and *Top left on screen*. With these you can define the margin width for the left and top window margins.

You can set the window size of the requester using the *Size* cycle gadget. *Default* refers to the operating system's specifications. If you select *Relative*, you can adjust the width and height of the requester windows as a percentage of the entire screen by typing the percentage into the string gadget or by dragging the sliders.

If checked, the *Override application* option overrides the specifications for the size and position of the requester window specified by the initial program.

TIP **Recommended settings**
We recommend the position option *Mouse pointer*, which shortens long onscreen mouse paths and increases everyday efficiency.

Sorting in requesters

The **File Requester** section has three options that directly affect only the operating system's file requesters.

The *Sort by* option determines the order in which the contents are sorted by *name*, *date* or *size* (i.e. file size).

The *Sort drawers* option determines the listing of directories in combination with files: drawers can be displayed *first* (all directories before files, i.e. default setting), *last* (all directories after files) or *mixed* (directories and files mixed).

Finally, the *Sort order* option changes the sorting order between *ascending (A-Z)* or *descending (Z-A)*.

For example: when size sorting combined with mixed drawer display and descending order, the largest files and directories would be displayed at the top of the file requester list, while the smallest items would be displayed at the bottom.

DefaultIcons (icon prefs)

The DefaultIcons prefs editor, formerly known as DefIcons, links filetypes with icons.

Function

To set default icons for filetypes that do not have their own icons, use the DefaultIcons editor. When a new file of an unknown format is created or copied from another system, it usually does not have its own icon. This is the point at which the DefaultIcons system comes into play.

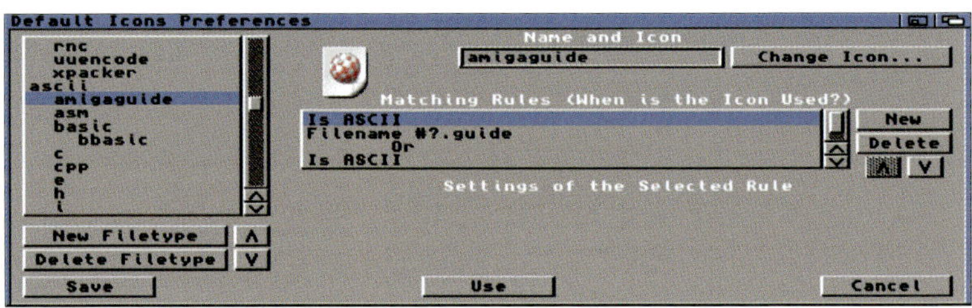

The long list of file types contained in the DefaultIcons editor can be extended to suit your needs.

In addition, DefaultIcons can be used to set the default application to open each known filetype. Image formats such as jpeg, png and iff are supported by AmigaOS 3.2, as well as sound formats (wav, aiff etc.) or text formats (txt, guide etc.). When double-clicking on such icons, the all-rounder *MultiView* is often used, as it can display images and texts or play sounds with the appropriate datatype.

The DefaultIcons editor can be used to change the icons and the default program that are connected with a group of filetypes or with a single filetype.

Launching DefaultIcons by double-clicking its icon will open a dedicated window.

Structure of DefaultIcons

The DefaultIcons editor shows a list of all currently available filetypes on the left-hand side. Below the list are two buttons, *New Filetype* and *Delete Filetype*, that allow you to either create a new filetype or *delete* a filetype. The position of the filetype in a group can be adjusted using the up and down arrows next to those buttons.

If a filetype or a group of filetypes is selected from the list, information about it is displayed on the right-hand side. By default, the name and the two buttons *Change icon* and *Advanced settings* are displayed next to the icon of the filetype or group of filetypes.

Changing a default tool

To change the default tool for a filetype, click the icon itself to open the icon information. Under the Icon tab you will see the path and name of the *default tool* that is connected to the icon. You can use the file requester or the string gadget to select a suitable tool to display the filetype (enter the full path and name of the tool in this text box). At present, *MultiView* is frequently specified as the standard for many icons. Don't forget to save any changes you make in this requester.

Changing an icon

The *Change Icon* button opens a new requester with three options to change the icon properties. In addition to deleting the icon (*Delete it*), an alternative icon can be set (*Import another...*), or the current icon can be handed over to *IconEdit* (see section 4.5) for further editing (*Open it in IconEdit*).

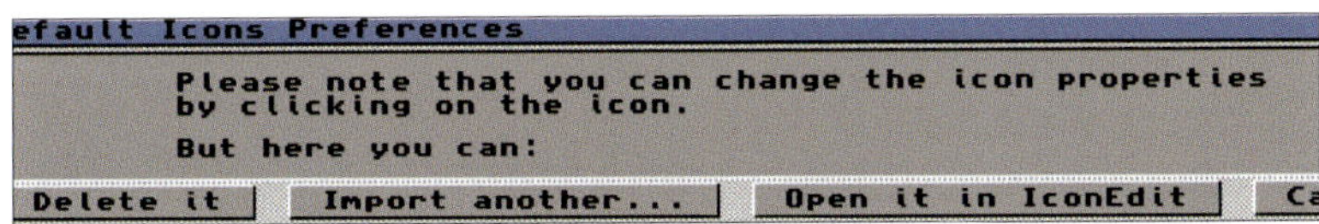

Requester for changing the icon properties alongside the DefaultIcon editor: delete, import or edit the icon.

Defining matching rules for filetypes

Clicking the central long *Advanced Settings* button displays the matching rules for the selected filetype. These operators define in which cases the icon is used. Although filetype groups can also have matching rules, their core task is to act as a container for similar filetypes. Various rules for matching the filetype can be created for the filetypes. For example, there are several rules for AmigaGuide to identify the filetype. This filetype can be matched by the ending *#?.guide* and by the text content *@DATABASE* at the beginning of the ASCII text. Clicking on an existing operator will show the options for the selected rule.

There are four buttons next to the matching rules field: you can add additional rules with *New*, remove existing rules with *Delete* and change the order of the rules easily with the up and down arrows.

Similar filetypes are grouped in containers such as image or text. This makes it easy to keep track of default icons.

Matching rules

The following matching rules, called *comparison operators* in earlier versions of the operating system, can be used:

Contains: In the text gadget of the same name, enter the character string that should be found in the file at the position specified via the cycle gadget. Options are *At Offset*, *anywhere* and *after spaces*. Note the checkbox next to the *case sensitive or Binary* option, which takes the upper and lower case of characters into account. If a character in the specified character strings cannot be displayed, you can define the ASCII value of the character in hexadecimal notation, e.g. \xff for decimal 255 or \x0a for decimal 10. If you want to identify HTML files, for example, you could enter the value *<head>* in the *contains* text gadget.

File size: This checks for a specific file size. If, for example, certain files always have the same size, this can be used to easily assign a default icon to these files. The file size can be input into the file size string gadget using digits.

Filename: Here you can enter a complete name, an extension or a partial pattern of a file. Wildcards such as #? are permitted. For example, all files with the extension *.iff* are assigned to the matching tool if you enter the value *#?.iff* as the pattern in the *Filename* text gadget. Although this procedure is very fast, it does not work for IFF images without an extension, for example.

File attributes: Here you will find a large list of attributes that determine the files and that can be selected using cycle gadgets. For example, attributes can be set for the readability, writability, executability or deletability of files, as well as the exclusion of states such as *Script* or *Not archived*.

or: This rule will link different operators with each other, e.g. for the guide format: *#?.guide* or *@database*. This means that the name of the file to be checked must either end in *.guide* or its contents must contain the character string *@database* for it to be matched positive as an AmigaGuide file.

Is Ascii: This operator lets the system check whether the file is a text file or not. The use of this operator is only intended for ASCII formatted filetypes.

Container with sub-filetypes: If this operator is set, any other defined operator can lead to the selected filetype being matched, but its icon is only used if a subclass of the filetype also matches and does not itself have a icon.

Font (font prefs)

The Font editor allows you to set the fonts used for various areas in the Workbench, as well as their size and attributes.

Function

Once AmigaOS 3.2 is installed, the *Topaz* font is used by default for all elements on the Workbench, for the menu as well as for icon names and other elements. You can use the Font editor to specify the fonts used, both the font type and the size, as well as attributes such as font color, background color or shadow. Double-click on the *Font* icon in the *Prefs* drawer to open its window, which is clearly laid out.

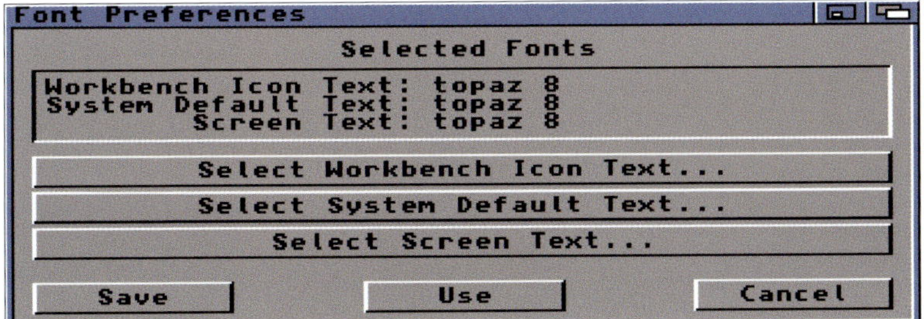

A simple overview of the Font prefs editor: three buttons affect changes to the fonts for Workbench icon text, standard default text and screen text.

TIP **Fonts in applications**
In certain tools that can be launched from the Workbench, such as ProTracker or DeluxePaint, predefined fonts are set. In such cases, the settings in the Font preferences have no effect on these specific defaults.

Font text types

The overview shows the font names for three different text displays. You can change these individually using the three buttons at the bottom. Clicking one of the buttons will open a requester for choosing the font.

Use **Select Workbench Icon Text** to change the font for labeling icons in all Workbench windows. You can also specify the text and background color for this text type.

Specify the font set for displaying data via **Select System Default Text**. Among other things, this affects the display of window contents in *View by name* mode (instead of *View by icon*).

Finally, you can even change the font used for menus, the Workbench title bar and requester windows. This is done via **Select Screen Text**.

If you want to change the font for more than one of the three text types, you must make the adjustments one after the other. However, you do not need to leave the Font preferences to do so. Once you have made all the settings as explained in the following sections, exit the Font preferences by clicking *Use* to test the display before finally saving the settings. The Workbench will then be reset (i.e. not rebooted!). You will be asked to close all open program, project and Shell windows on the pub screen. The Workbench will then rebuild itself with the new font settings.

If you are happy with the settings, switch back to the Font preferences and click *Save* – if not, make further changes or click *Cancel*. If you have not saved, the fonts displayed during the next boot process will be as they were before the changes were made.

Text requesters

In the three requester windows for the text types (icon text, default text and screen text), the fonts available on the system are listed on the left and their font sizes in points are listed on the right.

Use the scroll bar or arrows to scroll through the list of available fonts. The active or chosen font and font size for the selected text type will be highlighted and displayed with their current status in the preview area at the bottom of the window.

Use the left mouse button to select a suitable font from the list on the left and an available font size from the list on the right.

Each and any font can be used for the Workbench icon text and for Screen text. For System default text, however, the use of a so-called monospaced font is required, which displays all characters with the same width. *Topaz* or *Courier* are such fonts, for example, but *Times* or *Helvetica* are not.

Once you agree with the changes, close the requester using the *OK* button – if not, click *Cancel*.

TIP **Force update**
If you change the font used for the text of the Workbench icons, you will need to refresh the icons in all the open windows. To do this, choose *Workbench > Update all* from the Workbench menu.

Color selection for icon texts

The Workbench icon text requester offers a special feature: icons fonts can be set with additional text and background color attributes. You can make these changes using the color selector and the *Mode* cycle gadget. For example, if you are using a dark background for the Workbench and windows, the icon text could be set with white text on a black background to achieve better readability and a more stylish look.

If you have selected the *Text* option from the *Mode* cycle gadget and then chosen a color from the *Text color palette*, the icon text will be displayed in that color on a transparent background. If you change the mode to *Text+Field*, you can also

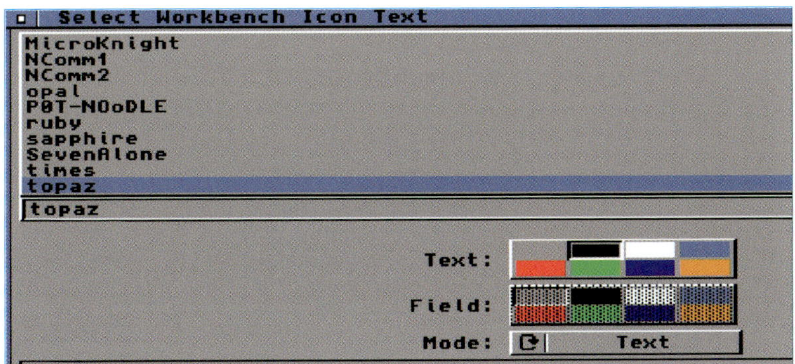

For Workbench icon text, you can specify the font, text color and background color.

specify a background color in the *Field color palette*. Make sure you choose two colors that are clearly different from each other. Failing to do so will make the text difficult to read and the system more difficult to navigate.

The number of available colors is determined by the active *ScreenMode* editor for screen preferences. The exact color values used for this display are specified by the *Palette* editor for color preferences. There they can be changed in these editors if need be.

For the *mode*, two more options are available: *Text+Outline* outlines the text with the background color, and *Text+Shadow* uses the background color to display a simple shadow effect.

IControl (interaction prefs)

IControl is an essential tool for customising the interaction between the user and the operating system, its screens and windows.

Function

IControl offers a variety of options that allow you to customize the appearance and behavior of system-wide settings, such as the action buttons for dragging screens or activating a mouse wheel.

You will find *IControl* in the *Prefs* drawer of the Workbench. Once opened by double-clicking on its icon, a simple window appears with the settings divided into four sections.

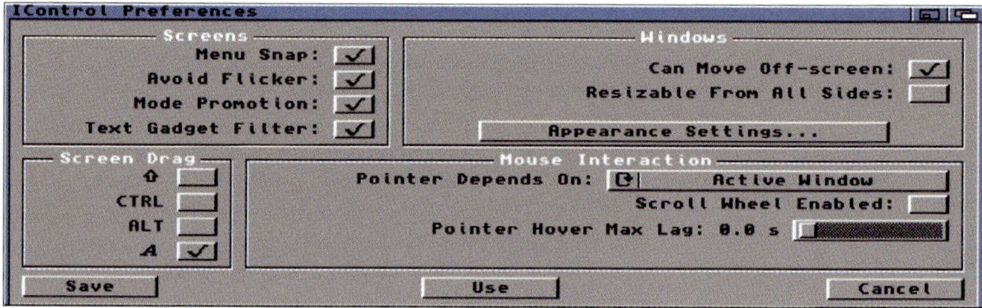

IControl lets you change the handling of Workbench screens, windows and mouse interaction.

Screens

In the *Screens* area, you can control the behavior and display of the screens on the Workbench. Four checkboxes can be used to switch the options *Menu Snap*, *Avoid Flicker*, *Mode Promotion* and *Text Gadget Filter* on and off. All of these options are activated by default.

Menu Snap: This option is intended for users who work with screens that are larger than the visible area of the monitor (virtual screen). Workbench menus are typically located in the top left-hand corner of the screen. If the left edge of the screen is outside the visible area and the *Menu Snap* option is enabled, pressing the right mouse button will shift the Workbench screen so that the menus are accessible. This shift remains for as long as you keep the right mouse button pressed down.

Avoid Flicker: This setting ensures that the *interlace display mode* is not activated for a screen in the background when a screen in the foreground is dragged down with the mouse.

Mode Promotion: This option allows you to control the software function for eliminating the *software deinterlacing feature* of AGA Amigas. By activating *Mode Promotion*, you can enable screens opened by different applications in PAL and NTSC formats to automatically use a flicker-free screen mode.

Text Gadget Filter: This option determines how control commands in text gadgets are treated: either as regular characters or as editing commands. A control command is typically created by pressing the `[Ctrl]` key and a letter key simultaneously to trigger a specific function.

The following control characters are used when entering text: `[Ctrl]+[M]` corresponds to the function of the Enter key. `[Ctrl]+[H]` deletes the character to the left of the cursor (same as the function of the backspace key). `[Ctrl]+[U]` deletes all characters to the left of the cursor. `[Ctrl]+[K]` deletes all characters from the cursor to the end of the line. `[Ctrl]+[A]` moves the cursor to the beginning of the line, `[Ctrl]+[Z]` moves the cursor to the end of the line. `[Ctrl]+[X]` deletes a complete line. *Cursor left* moves the cursor one character to the left, *Cursor right* moves the cursor one character to the right.

If the *Text Gadget Filter* option is enabled, and a control character is entered while the cursor is placed in an text gadget that does not expect numbers, the control character will be processed according to its function as described above. If the filter is deactivated, however, the control command is treated as part of the text input and appears on the screen either as an open rectangle or as a special symbol that differs from the usual characters.

Regardless of whether the option is activated or not, control commands can be inserted into an text gadget at any time. To do this, hold down the `[Ctrl]` and `[L-Amiga]` keys at the same time while pressing the desired letter key.

Screen Drag

Dragging screens means pulling the Workbench screen down while holding down the left mouse button on the title bar. In the *Screen Drag* area , you will see four keyboard keys with checkboxes: `[Shift]`, `[Ctrl]`, `[Alt]` and `[L-Amiga]`. Usually, only `[L-Amiga]` is used to drag screens. You can define alternative special key assignments for this function by activating the adjacent checkbox. This only makes sense if you frequently run applications that use the `[L-Amiga]` key and the left mouse button for other functions.

Windows

In this section, you can adjust the behavior of windows on your Workbench.

If *Can Move Off-screen* is enabled, windows can be dragged beyond the edge of the visible Workbench environment to create space. If you move a window beyond the edge of the visible area, it snaps to the edge for a brief moment and then moves beyond the edge. This allows a window to be practically clamped to an edge. This option is deactivated by default, but it is highly recommended that you switch it on after installing the OS.

Activating *Resizable From All Sides* is also recommended, as it makes everyday work noticeably easier. Once enabled, you can reduce and enlarge windows more quickly from every edge and corner. A red drag arrow will appear when you click and hold on an edge or corner. Activating this option only applies to windows that have been reopened after the change.

Appearance settings (Windows)

Clicking the *Appearance settings* button opens a window of the same name, divided into three areas. This area is a hidden gem for many users, and plays a crucial role in showcasing the screen elements in their best light. Here, you can make settings for aspect ratios that aim to make the edges of windows and screens appear more harmonious in approximately or exactly square shapes on all screens and in every resolution.

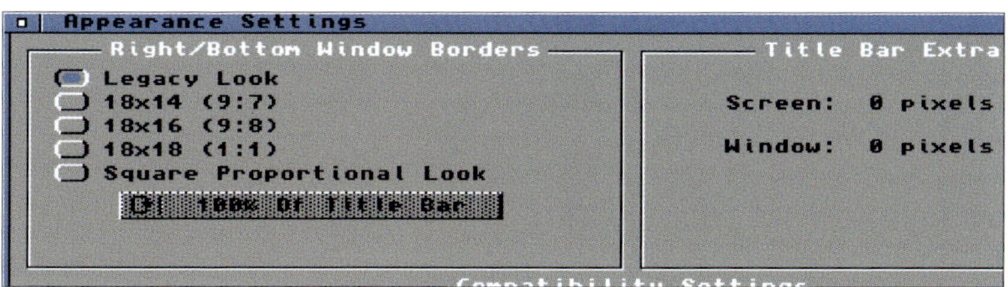

In Appearance settings, a significant part of IControl, you can adjust the size of window borders and the height of the Workbench title bar.

In the *Right/Bottom Window Borders* section, you can define the ratio between the right and bottom window borders with five simple checkboxes. *Legacy Look* sets the horizontal borders to a thickness of 2 pixels. *18×14 (9:7)* sets the horizontal borders to a thickness of 3 pixels, similar to AmigaOS 3.9 with activated aspect ratio of 1:1. *18×16* (9:8) increases the thickness of the horizontal borders to 4 pixels, as with the vertical borders. *18×18 (1:1)* increases the thickness of the horizontal borders to 4 pixels, as with the vertical borders. *Square Proportional Look* defines a square look in relation to the height of the Workbench title bar, whereby the ratio to the bar height can be determined as a percentage using the cycle gadget below. You can set the bar height to the following options: 50%, 67%, 75% and 100%.

In the section on the right, *Title Bar Extra Height*, you can easily adjust the height of the Workbench title bar and the title bars of to suit your preferences. This allows you to fully customize the look of the Workbench to your liking. The two sliders allow you to change the title bars of the *Screen* and *Window* with values from 0 to 16 pixels. The default display is 0 pixels, so the change basically results in an increase in the specified height.

Exceptions and compatibility

The *Manage exceptions* button in the *Compatibility Settings* section leads to another sub-window. Don't worry if you've made changes to the appearance settings and some special applications that run on a Workbench basis are not working correctly. You can simply exclude these from the changes you have made, and everything will be back to normal in no time! Just add the program or screen to the exception list by using the plus button and entering it into the text gadget (wildcards, also known as placeholder characters, are permitted in the text gadget).

Click to select the entry in the *Exception List* on the left. Then, activate the *Use Compatible Title Bar Height* option on the right using the checkbox. This will ensure that the third-party software displays the title bar correctly. In the *Use Compatible Window Borders* section, you can also select one of the predefined values *Never*, *Only Those Without Gadgets*, *Only Those With Gadgets* and *Always* using the radio buttons in order to react to incorrect window display in the external application as required. Leave this requester via *Save*, *Use* or *Cancel*.

The compatibility settings in IControl ensures incompatible software remains operational, despite GUI changes.

Mouse interaction

Finally, within the IControl editor, there is the *Mouse Interaction* section, which is used for configuring the mouse as an input device. There are two options to choose from in the cycle gadget called *Pointer Depends On*: with *Active window*, mouse interaction is based on the active window. Alternatively, the *Window Under Pointer* option sets the mouse behavior to the windows under the pointer, even if they are not active.

The *Scroll Wheel Enabled* option is not just useful for mice with scroll wheels and should always be checked (it is inactive by default).

The *Pointer Hover Max Lag* slider adjusts how often the Intuition system queries the pointer position and thus the speed at which the mouse pointer changes. The function has an effect on tooltips for tool icons (easy to see in *IconEdit*), on links in AmigaGuides or on websites while scrolling with the scroll wheel. If you're using a fast Amiga, leave the value unchanged at 0.0 seconds. This means that Intuition performs 50 queries per second. On slower Amigas you should reduce the value.

Input (input prefs)

The Input prefs editor lets you tweak the behavior of input devices (mouse and keyboard) and change the keyboard layout in a few simple clicks!

Function

The Input editor's window is divided into three sections: *Mouse*, *Keyboard* and *Keyboard Type*. Here, for example, you can set the movement speed of the mouse or your preferred time interval between two clicks of the left mouse button for a double-click function to be recognized by the system.

Mouse speed

Use the *Mouse Speed* slider to set the relative speed of the mouse pointer on the screen in relation to the physical movement of the mouse on a physical surface. A faster mouse pointer on screen means you need less space on your desk or mouse mat, and it's more ergonomic when you move the mouse.

There are three speed settings to choose from: 1, 2 and 3. Go wild and pick 1 if you want a slow and steady pace, or pick 3 if you're feeling extra fast and frantic! Just move the slider to set the desired value. The new mouse speed is ready for you to try out right away. Mouse speed is set to 3 by default.

Mouse acceleration

If the *Acceleration* function is active, i.e. the checkbox is ticked, the mouse pointer can be moved very quickly over longer distances on the screen. However, precision is possible over smaller distances, for example within a selection list. As the mouse speed increases, so does the speed of the mouse pointer. The mouse acceleration option is deactivated upon the system's initial installation. Test your mouse with the function switched on and off to see which setting is most comfortable for you.

Double-click delay

Set the *Double-Click Delay* slider to the desired speed for a double-click. This determines how quickly you need to double-click the left mouse button for the system to recognize the input. The duration is determined by values between 1 and 200. The default value is 75, which corresponds to a pause of approximately 1.5 seconds between the first and second double-click. The value 1 is perfect for those who double-click extremely fast, while the value 200 is perfect for slow hands, allowing an interval of just under 5 seconds.

Demonstrate and test double-click

Clicking the *Show Double-Click* button displays the duration in the adjacent field with a colored highlight that corresponds to the selected value for *Double-Click Delay*.

Use the *Test Double-Click* button below to practice double-clicking. Simply double-click on the button. If the time interval is too long, the system will not recognize the two clicks as a double-click and will display the message *too slow* as feedback. Adjust the slide as required. If the two clicks are within the time interval, feedback appears confirming: *double-clicked*.

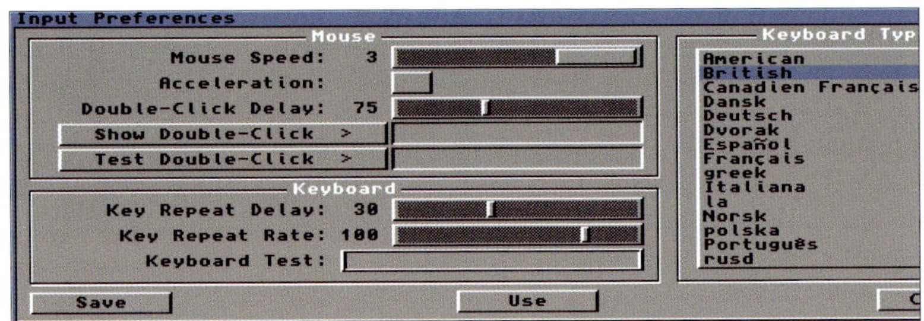

Input controls, among other things, how much time may elapse between the first and second click when double-clicking.

Key repeat delay

Most of the keys on the Amiga keyboard are assigned the function to automatically repeat keystrokes. For example, if you keep the A key held down for a long period of time, at first only one letter is entered, then after a short delay a series of letters appear until you release the key again.

The repetition only starts after an adjustable delay time. You can adjust this delay using the *Key Repeat Delay* slider. The current value of the delay is shown to the left of the slider. The default value is 35, which is equivalent to about half a second. Values between 1 and 75 are possible for the delay, which corresponds to between approximately 0.02 and 1.5 seconds.

Key repeat rate

Move the *Key Repeat Rate* slider to set the desired speed for repeated keystrokes after the initial delay. The adjustable values range from 1 to 125: the lower the value, the slower the sequence of keystrokes.

Keyboard test

In the text gadget for the *Keyboard Test*, you can try out the configured settings for the delay and speed of key repetition. Click in the input field and press and hold a key on the keyboard to immediately see the repeat settings. You can also press different keys inside the text gadget to check the layout of the keyboard.

Keyboard type

You can easily customize the mapping of your keyboard to suit your local (or any other) system. Simply mark the keyboard layout from the selection list in the *Keyboard Type* section. The appropriate assignment matches the labeling of the keys and ensures easy access to country-specific special characters. If you are not using a US keyboard, accent keys are also available. You can find more information on accent keys in section 4.7 on *KeyShow*.

Once a keymap is selected, the corresponding file in the *Devs/Keymaps* directory is activated.

The keyboard layouts shown in the table below are available in AmigaOS 3.2. You will find them displayed with the *name* in the selection list as long as they have been installed in the operating system.

Keymap file	Name in list	Language/Distribution
cdn	Canadien Français	French (Canada)
ch1	Suisse	French (Switzerland)
ch2	Switzerland	German (Switzerland)
d	German	German (Germany)
dk	Dansk	Danish
e	Español	Spanish
f	Français	French (French)
gb	British	English (Great Britain)
greek	greek	Greek
i	Italiana	Italian
la	la	Latin international
n	Norsk	Norwegian
po	Português	Portuguese
polska	polska	Polish
rusd	rusd	Russian (DE keyboard)
rusgb	rusgb	Russian (GB keyboard)
rusuae	rusuae	Russian (US keyboard)
rusus	rusus	Russian (US keyboard)
ruswin	ruswin	Russian (Windows keyb.)
s	Svenskt	Swedish
tr	tr	Turkish
usa2	Dvorak	English (Dvorak keyb.)

To check the keyboard layout, use the *Keyboard Test* text gadget in the Input prefs editor or view the modified layout using the *KeyShow* tool.

INFO **American keymap**
The *American* keyboard layout is supplied with AmigaOS without an explicit keymap file. It is used as a fallback option in case there is no other keyboard layout in the keymaps directory.

Keymap installation

If a keymap you need is missing from the selection list in the Input window, it is missing from the *Devs/Keymaps* drawer. You can install it on the system at any time by opening the *Storage* and *Devs* directories and continuing to the *Keymaps* directories. Then copy the required keymap file from *Storage/Keymaps* to *Devs/Keymaps* using drag and drop with your mouse.

If the desired keymap is missing on the system hard drive in *Storage*, it must be installed from the *Storage* disk or ADF. For example, the Shell command for the French keymap would be `copy storage3.2:keymaps/f sys:devs/keymaps/` if a storage disk is inserted in any mounted floppy drive.

Once you have copied the file, just open *Input* again and you will find the new layout in the *Keyboard Type* selection list.

Locale (country prefs)

Locale is where you set the language used by the system and country-specific settings.

Function

The *Locale* prefs editor, opened by double-clicking the *Locale* icon in the *Prefs* folder, allows you to change the system's language settings, among other things. This affects all language entries displayed in Workbench or window titles, menus, requesters and error messages. The changes do not apply to the keyboard layout – you will need to set this in the *Input* prefs editor.

As soon as a language file such as *english_british.language* (for British English) or *nederlands.language* (for Dutch) exists in the *SYS:Locale/Languages* directory, it is also displayed in the list of available languages in the *Locale window*. The language information is usually copied to the system hard drive by request during the installation of the operating system. This includes important language catalogs for individual system elements such as *prefs.catalog* or *workbench.catalog*, which are located in the *SYS:Locale/Catalogs/english_british/Sys/* directory.

INFO **Later installation of languages**
If you did not select a language for installation during the initial installation of the operating system and want to add it later, you can do this anytime using the setup routine on the *Install3.2* disk or ADF.

You can change languages, country and time zone in the handy Locale prefs editor with just a few mouse clicks.

Available and preferred languages

The *Available Languages* box displays the installed languages, for example English, French or German. By simply clicking on any of the languages listed here, it will move directly to *Preferred Languages* and become available for you to use. The language at the top of this list will be used for system displays.

If you have accidentally added the wrong language to your preferred languages, or if the order is not what you want, you can erase the entire list by clicking the *Clear Languages* button. You must then select the desired language again from the list of available languages.

The default language selection in Locale is English. Even if no other language is shown in the list of preferred languages or no other language is installed, the system switches to English.

The language change takes effect when you click *Use* or *Save*. The system reloads the settings and switches the

Workbench completely to the changed language. Applications must be closed and reopened manually for the settings to take effect on them.

Country

Country and *Time Zone* settings have an impact on country-specific conventions such as time, date and number formats. For example, a full stop is used for numbers with a decimal point in English-speaking countries, but a comma is used in German-speaking countries (for example 0.5 vs. 0,5 MB). The thousands separator in numbers can also be made country-specific with these settings, i.e. without a point, with a point or with a space.

The country selection defines the following parameters, among others: country name, units of measurement, separators, number format, combined and separate time/date information in long and short form, currency formats in credit and debit, currency symbol and international currency symbol.

To select the desired country, simply click on the entry in the *Country* list.

Time Zone

Time Zone information may be used by specific programs, but not the Workbench itself. To set the time zone, click on the desired zone on the world map. The time difference compared with GMT (Greenwich Mean Time) is displayed in white above the world map. Most central European countries, such as France, Germany, Italy or Sweden, use Central European Time (CET) and Central European Summer Time (CEST) and are therefore one hour ahead of GMT (GMT+1), whereas eastern US states such as New York, Florida or Maine are five hours behind GMT.

Overscan (margin preset)

In the Overscan settings, you can enlarge and reduce the overscan area of the screen output to suit your monitor.

Function

Depending on the screen mode used, some monitors leave a fairly wide border next to the Workbench. You can optimize this area in the *Overscan* prefs editor, which you can open by double-clicking on *Overscan* in the *Prefs* folder.

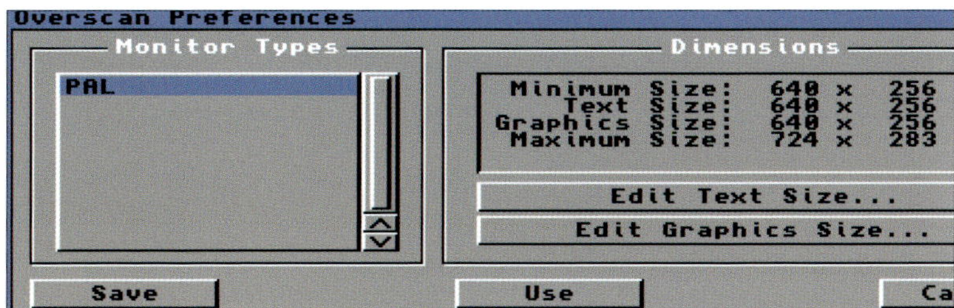

The Overscan Preferences, with a list of monitor types on the left and the Setup buttons on the right.

Monitor types and dimensions

The list of *Monitor Types* shows the currently active screen drivers. Monitor files located in the *DEVS:Monitors* directory are automatically activated when the system starts. Each monitor type controls different monitor groups.

In the *Dimensions* section, you will find size information for the different monitor types, given in pixels. The first value is the width and the second value is the height of the screen.

Changing the overscan values for a particular monitor type affects all modes of that monitor type. To change the overscan values for a specific monitor type only, select it from the list. The selected group is highlighted, and the resolution is displayed.

For PAL or NTSC modes, the dimensions for standard high-res screens (screen modes with high resolution) are listed. For multiscan modes, the sizes for productivity screens without interlaced displays are shown. For other modes within a monitor type group, sizes are adjusted according to the ratios of the listed screen modes.

The following screen dimensions are displayed: *Minimum Size* is the standard size without overscan. *Text Size* shows the current text size with overscan, *Graphic Size* shows the current graphic size with overscan. *Maximum Size* describes the maximum permissible size with overscan (for text or graphics).

Setting the overscan area

Clicking the *Edit Text Size* or *Edit Graphics Size* buttons takes you to a special screen with a black border around the edge marking the display area. Nine black rectangles serve as handles. Click and hold the individual handle points on the edges to move the dimensions. The central handle point is used to move the entire display area. The central information in the window indicates the current position and size in pixels. The display window can be any size, but all areas should remain visible as far as possible so as not to obscure the close symbol of a full-screen window, for example. If you are happy with the settings, click *OK*, otherwise click *Cancel*. As always, the changes will not take effect until you click *Save* or *Use* in the editor window.

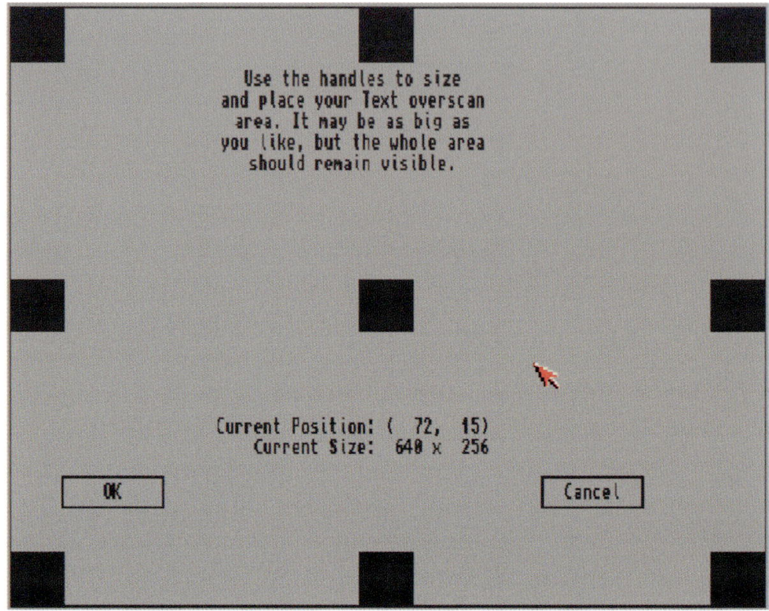

Drag the black handles to change the text or graphics over-scan area of your monitor.

Palette (color prefs)

The Palette Preferences tool lets you adjust the active colors of the Workbench and its elements.

Function

The *Palette* prefs editor, which opens in a separate window when you double-click the *Palette* icon in the *Prefs* drawer, lets you personalize the color schemes of your Workbench. This feature is particularly useful for users who wish to customize the visual appearance of their work environment to support better legibility, aesthetic preferences, or to support specific application scenarios.

The Palette window is divided into several sections: on the top left-hand side, above the color wheel, the current Workbench colors are displayed. The number of colors visible depends on whether the Workbench is being operated in color mode with four or eight or more colors. The range of the color wheel depends on the colors that can be used simultaneously in the system, for example 16 colors for OCS and ECS Amigas and 256 colors for AGA Amigas.

Each of these colors can be individually adjusted. You can choose colors either by selecting them directly from a color wheel or by making precise adjustments using the three RGB or HSB sliders. The RGB method offers direct control over the intensity of each primary color (red, green, blue), while the HSB method allows intuitive adjustment of hue, saturation and brightness.

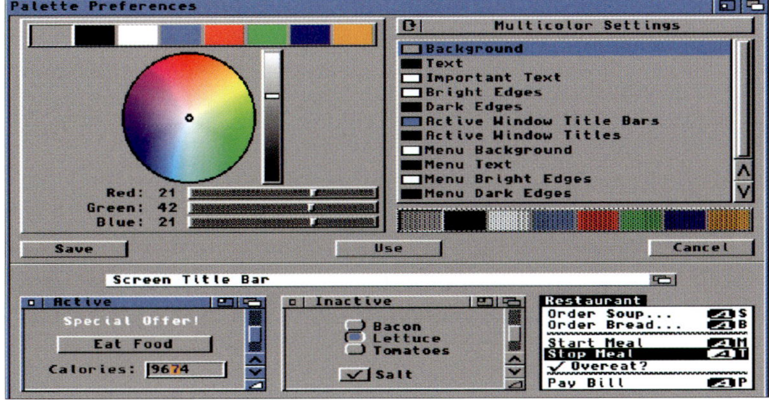

Palette is a versatile editor for coloring different Workbench elements.

Color modes

In addition to pure color adjustment, Palette also offers two options for different color modes. These are located on the right-hand side of the window and can be changed using the scroll symbol. The *Multicolor Settings* allows the use of a wider color palette, while the *4 Color Settings* limits the selection to four colors. This limitation can be useful for creating a consistent and simple color environment, or when specific applications and editors have limited color requirements.

Workbench elements

There is also an unlabeled list of specific Workbench elements on the right-hand side of the Palette window. For each of these eleven items, you can define a color from a default palette of eight (or four) colors. The list includes the following specific areas of the Workbench: Background, Text, Important Text,

Bright Edges, Dark Edges, Active Window Title Bars, Active Window Titles, Menu Background, Menu Text, Menu Bright Edges, Menu Dark Edges.

Below the list is a color selection box containing the four or eight colors from the active color palette. This area corresponds to the color selection box above the color wheel.

Preview area

If the active screen resolution is large enough (this can be changed using the *ScreenMode* preferences editor, see section 3.15), sample Workbench elements such as the screen title bar, an open drawer and an open menu are shown in a preview area in the lower part of the Palette editor window. This gives you an immediate impression of the color changes to the elements.

If the preview area is not visible as part of the Palette window because the active screen dimensions are too small, click the *Show Sample* button to see the preview in a separate window.

Selecting items and colors

By simply clicking on an item in the item list or in the preview area or preview window, you can select an item that you want to change the color of. It will then be highlighted in the item list so that you can assign a suitable color to it using the color picker at the bottom right. The top-left color selector is used to change the selected color system-wide.

TIP **Influence of white and black on symbols**

If you modify the color settings for white and black, this can affect the pseudo 3D display of the screen icons. Note that the color that replaces black should be darker than the color that replaces white.

Changing colors

The Palette editor provides you with four methods of adjusting the available colors: using the color wheel, using the hue slider next to the color wheel, using the color slider in RGB mode or using the color slider in HSB mode.

Color wheel: The color wheel displays the color spectrum in RGB mode. Click an area of the color wheel to select the color under the pointer. Alternatively, click on and hold the point highlighted in white within the color wheel and drag it to the desired position (release the mouse button to select the color).

Hue slider: The vertical slider next to the color wheel allows you to change the hue (also called shade) of a color tone. Grab and drag the bar in the slider up or down to increase or decrease the brightness of the active color.

Color slider in RGB mode: The three RGB sliders below the color wheel allow the color to be changed via the three well-known RGB channels. The color is adjusted using the red, green and blue color channels, where each channel can take a value from 0 to 255.

Color slider in HSB mode: If you switch from RGB to HSB via the *Settings > Slider Color Mode* menu, you can use the HSB color slider instead of the RGB color slider. HSB stands for hue, saturation and brightness and is a far more human-friendly way of describing color. Drag one of the sliders to see how it affects the color: *Hue* rotates the value in the color wheel, *Saturation* changes the intensity via radial shift in the color wheel, and *Brightness* sets the brightness of the active color as when adjusting via the vertical hue slider.

Color specifications

If changing colors manually is too tedious for you, why not try some of the presets? The *Edit* menu contains nine *Classic Presets* and eight *NewLook Presets*. These patterns, such as *Ocean* or *Chocolate*, *Standard AGA/RTG 3D* or *Red Light*, create beautiful color presets of various kinds and in some cases a 3D effect for the menus.

Pointer (mouse pointer editor)

The Workbench mouse pointer can take on many different shapes. It's up to you to decide what it should look like.

Function

You can use the Pointer editor to change properties such as the shape, color and size of the mouse pointer and other mouse pointer types. In the list on the left you will find all the context-sensitive mouse pointer types available on the AmigaOS 3.2 Workbench, for example the *Link* pointer (a hand), the *Busy* pointer (a clock) or the *Crosshair*. There are two options for the mouse pointer, each with two values: *Default Image* and *Custom Image* as well as *Low Res* and *High Res*.

If the *Custom Image* option is selected, the drawing area on the right-hand side is unlocked and the current pointer is shown. Here you can try your hand at creating your own mouse pointer. Select one of four colors you want from the options in the drawing area to the left of the editor. The background color is located at the top left of the color selector.

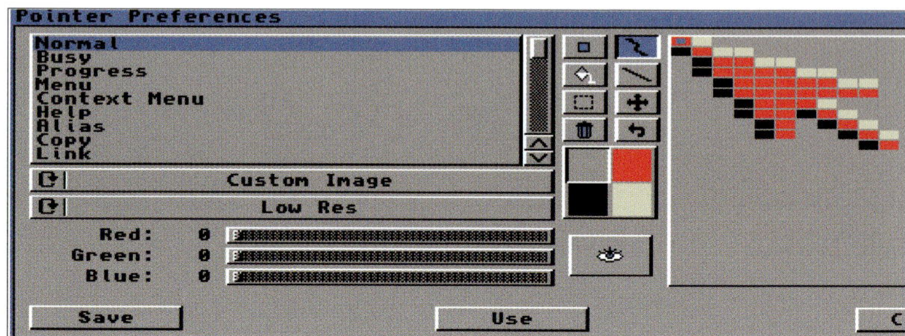

The Pointer editor contains a list of pointers (left), the editing tools (middle) and the drawing area (right).

Tools

The following tools are available for editing the mouse pointer in the area above the color selection (from left to right, top to bottom):

With the **Hot Spot** tool, you can determine the position on the mouse pointer at which an action can be triggered using the left or right mouse button. This is logically positioned directly at the tip of the standard mouse pointer. The click position in the mouse pointer can be recognized by the blue pixel with a small border. Obviously there's only one hot spot for each pointer.

You can draw a pixel-wide shape with the **Freehand** tool and fill an area with color using the **Fill** tool. Draw straight, pixel-wide lines with the **Straight Line** tool.

Use the **Select** tool – the square with a dotted border – to select areas in the image, which you can then move with the **Move** tool to the right of it. The trash can symbol represents the **Clear** tool, which can be used to delete the entire image in the editing field. The empty area is then filled with the background color. The **Undo** tool is the reversible arrow symbol at the bottom right. Use this tool to revert any mistakes that happened when drawing.

The cycle gadget for *Low Res* or *High Res* only applies to AGA or RTG Amigas. These systems can use high-resolution mouse pointers, which have twice as many pixels as low-resolution ones.

Click the **Eye** symbol to check your drawing skills. The edited mouse pointer then appears in a live preview.

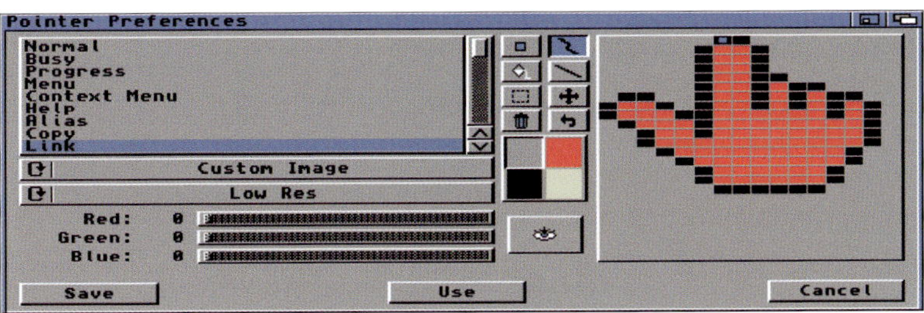

Different mouse pointer variants, such as Busy, Menu or Link, can be edited in the Pointer Preferences.

Functions in the Edit menu

In the *Edit* menu in the title bar, there are additional functions for pointers in addition to the standard menu items of the prefs. You can use *Cut*, *Copy*, *Paste* and *Erase* in combination with the selection tool to edit parts of the image. *Undo* and *Redo* let you reverse or repeat a step – it's as simple as that.

You can also import IFF images via the *Load image* item. Use the smallest possible images with four colors. *Reset Colors* set the color palette to the original colors if they have been changed. *Reset to Defaults* will set the output to its original state.

Printer (printer prefs)

The Printer Preferences control the basic settings for a printer connected to the Amiga, including the driver and any fine tuning.

Function

Even though printing on paper is becoming increasingly rare these days, inkjet, laser and even dot matrix printers are still found in many households. Since the specialized printer software *TurboPrint* has not been developed for some time, users have to rely on the default settings of the operating system.

The challenge is that the printer needs a parallel port, which only older devices have. Alternatively, a USB hardware extension must be installed in the Amiga (see section 7.5, *Hardware*) to allow newer printers to be connected via a USB port. If the printer and the Amiga have a network connection, the *lpr.device* from the Aminet can be used to send print jobs via TCP/IP (download: www.aminet.net/package/comm/tcp/lpr-dev).

Once the question of how to connect to the printer has been answered, the next question is which driver to use. In general, basic settings can be made via the *Printer Preferences* to address and control Canon, Epson or HP printers, as well as any other PostScript-capable printer.

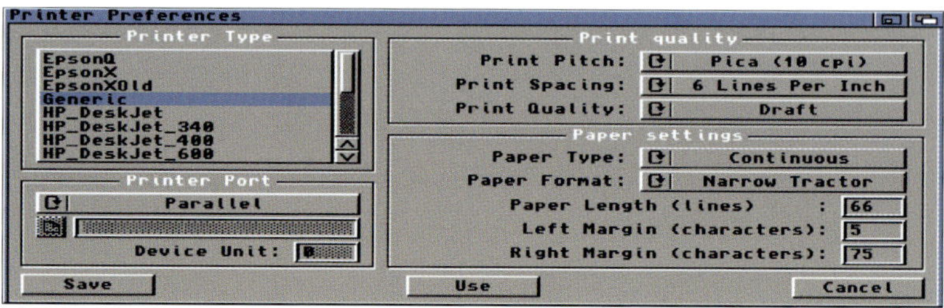

Unlike in AmigaOS 3.9, the graphics printing part is not included in the Printer prefs, but in the PrinterGfx prefs.

Clicking the *Printer* icon in *Prefs* opens a separate window. If you are familiar with AmigaOS 3.5 or 3.9, you will notice a difference in the window that appears here: previously, the *Printer* and *PrinterGfx* sections were combined in the *Printer* Preferences so that settings for text and graphics printing could be changed in one place. In AmigaOS 3.2, the two sections are once more divided into these two different preferences.

You can make settings that relate to the basic print output in the *Printer* prefs window. These include *Printer Type*, *Printer Port*, *Print quality* and *Paper settings*. Settings made here are used as default values if no other settings have been made elsewhere. Applications such as word processors usually provide their own options, which at least partially override the information of the *Printer* prefs.

TIP **PostScript as an alternative**

Printer support in AmigaOS is severely limited due to a lack of drivers from manufacturers and the lack of updates for TurboPrint. Only a few printer models are supported. We recommend using PostScript to ensure reliable printing. (see section 3.13).

INFO **Generic printer type**
If there is no printer driver for your printer (or for a printer that your printer can emulate) in either *Devs/ Printers* or *Storage/Printers*, select *Generic*, the default printer driver.

Printer type

A list of the available printer drivers currently installed in *Devs:Printers* is displayed under *Printer Type*. To select a printer (i.e. its driver), point to its name in the list and left-click on it. The selected model (or a generic printer) is highlighted.

If you want to use a PostScript printer, you need to change settings in the *PrinterPS* prefs. These settings override the specifications of the *Printer* prefs. Nevertheless, in the *Printer* prefs you must select a printer port for the PostScript printer.

Printer port

Use the cycle gadget in the *Printer Port* section to determine the connection type of your printer. You can choose between the *parallel* port, the *serial* port and a *custom* setting (i.e. a user-defined setting). If you choose *Serial*, you must check whether the transfer settings in the Serial Preferences correspond to your printer. If you choose *Custom*, you can select an output device in the file requester below – for example, a device connected via the USB port or via a network. Specify the device unit in the string gadget for a serial or user-defined printer connection. As a rule, this value is 0, unless the Amiga has several serial interfaces or USB ports, so the device units must be explicitly defined for each selected printer.

Print quality

The *Print quality* section contains specifications for print density, lines per inch and print quality. *Print Pitch* indicates the density, i.e. the number of print characters per inch (cpi) in the horizontal direction. The higher the value, the tighter the print. The following options are available: *Pica (10 cpi)*, *Elite (12 cpi)* and *Narrow (15-17 cpi)*. *Print Spacing* describes the line density and thus specifies the number of lines of text per inch (lines per inch, lpi for short) in the vertical direction. Select *6 lines per inch (lpi)* or *8 lines per inch (lpi)*: the higher the value, the smaller the space between the lines.

Print Quality sets the printout quality. If *Draft* is selected, print quality is reduced in favor of print speed. Selecting *Letter* results in slower print speed but high print quality.

Paper settings

In this area, you can make changes to the paper specifications. *Paper Type* determines the type of paper used. You can choose between *continuous* (paper fed in by tractor) and *single* sheet.

Use the *Paper Format* option to set the size of the paper used. You can choose from *U.S. Letter*, *U.S. Legal*, *DIN A4*, *Narrow Tractor*, *Wide Tractor* and *Custom*. Select the format according to the functionality of your printer.

Paper Length (lines) indicates the total number of lines that can be printed on a page between the top and bottom margins. Example: the DIN A4 paper format is common in most parts of Europe. It has a length of 29.7 cm, which corresponds to 11.67 inches. At 6 lines per inch, this results in a rounded 70 lines per DIN A4 page (US format: 11 inches and 66 lines).

The value set for *Left margin (characters)* specifies the width of the left margin, i.e. the number of blank characters from the left edge of the paper to the point at which the printer should start printing. The print density (number of characters per inch in the horizontal direction) affects the width of the margin. If *Pica (10 cpi)* is specified as the print pitch and 10 is set for the left margin, the result would be left margin of 1 inch. The value for *Right Margin (characters)*, on the other hand, determines the width of the right margin, i.e. the number of characters from the left edge of the paper to the point at which the printer should no longer print. This is not the distance from the right edge of the paper to the end of printing, but explicitly the distance from the left edge of the paper.

To change the values for paper length, left margin and right margin, select the corresponding string gadgets, delete the given value, enter a new value and confirm with the Enter key.

PrinterGfx (graphic print prefs)

The Graphics Printer Preferences, PrinterGfx for short, provides options for optimizing the printing of graphics.

Function

One of the main functions of *PrinterGfx* is the ability to influence the quality of your printouts. Here you can adjust settings such as color correction and scaling to ensure that your graphics are output on paper exactly as you want them.

You will find *PrinterGfx* in the *Prefs* drawer of the Workbench. In it, you will find a variety of settings that are tailored specifically to printing graphics.

Dithering

Dithering involves printing patterns of different colored dots (or patterns of dots of different shades) that appear as a mixed color or grey scale. This results in smoother transitions in the image making the image appear to have more colors or shades of grey. Three options are available for dithering via its cycle gadget: *Ordered*, *Halftone* and *Floyd-Steinberg*.

Ordered is the standard method for dithering. Different color intensity results from an ordered dot pattern. The dots can be different colors but have the same print density. They are printed in even rows and columns.

With *Halftone*, different color intensity is achieved by varying dot size and density.

In the *Floyd-Steinberg process*, different color intensity is the result of a complex (and therefore time-consuming) algorithm. This process results in a more even shading, as the color intensity of the respective pixel is distributed to the print dots that form this pixel and to the adjacent dots.

Printer drivers can replace these shadings with their own methods. Floyd-Steinberg dithering in particular is not suitable for all printers.

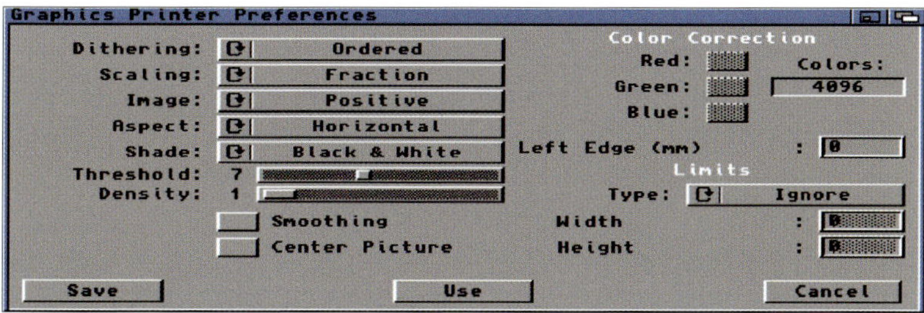

PrinterGfx bundles all settings related to the output of graphics, photos and drawings.

Scaling

Scaling refers to the true-to-scale resizing of an image. The final size of a printout is defined with the *Limits* settings at the bottom right of the PrinterGfx window. The following options are available in the cycle gadget for scaling:

By using the *Fraction* option, the size of the image corresponds approximately to the size specified under *Limits*. This may result in distortions. The pixels are reduced or enlarged as required. It is recommended to use this option for printing images with many shades, but not for text.

With the *Integer* option, the number of dots in the printout corresponds to an integer multiple of the pixels on the screen. For example, if the image displayed on the screen has a size of 320 x 200 pixels, the printed image can have a size of 320 x 200, 640 x 400, 960 x 600 pixels, etc. Use this option if the image to be printed contains thin vertical and horizontal lines (for example a grid or text).

Image

This option determines whether an image is printed as a *positive* or *negative*. Changing this option generally only make sense for black and white and grey scale printouts. If you select *Positive*, the image is printed as it is displayed on the screen. If you select *Negative*, the screen colors will be inverted in the printout. This option is comparable to the negative of a photo.

Aspect

This option is used to set the print direction for the image. If *Horizontal* is selected, the image is printed as it is displayed on the screen. If *Vertical* is selected, the image is rotated 90 degrees during printing. Note that not every program supports this setting.

Shade

Select the colors to be printed using the *Shade* option. Note, however, that this option is not supported by all printers. Four color options are available to choose from: Color, Black & White, Grey Scale 1 and Grey Scale 2.

With *Color*, colors are printed according to the screen display. If you select this option, the options in the *Color Correction* section (on the right-hand side of the PrinterGfx window) are enabled.

With *Black & White*, colors are printed either as black or as white. There is no shading. With *Grey Scale 1*, colors are reproduced in different shades of grey. With *Grey Scale 2*, a maximum of four grey levels are supported. Use the latter setting for prints of images created on an A2024 monitor.

Threshold

The *Threshold* value determines which colors displayed on the screen appear as black or white in the printout. This option only affects black and white coloring. The higher the threshold value, the more colors are printed black. When printing in grey scale or color, some printer drivers use this threshold in a different way, usually as a gamma correction threshold. In this case, the threshold value is extremely important for the quality of the printout. You can adjust the threshold value in 15 steps, whereby 7 is the preset value.

Density

The *Density* slider sets the print density for graphics. The lower the value, the faster the image will print on printers that support multiple print densities. Values between 1 and 7 are possible, with 1 being the default. If a higher density is selected, increasing the number of print dots will produce a sharper image. However, print speed will be reduced.

Smoothing

The *Smoothing* option is used to smooth diagonal lines that normally appear jagged or trapped. This option is particularly suitable for programs that create graphic printouts of text. If smoothing is enabled, it can slow down printing, but usually results in much better print quality. Please note that *Floyd-Steinberg* dithering and *Smoothing* cannot be used in conjunction with each other.

Center picture

This option is used to center the print image horizontally. If *Center Picture* is checked, the value for *Left margin* on the right side of this window will be ignored.

Left edge

You can specify the left margin of the print on the paper – in other words, how far to the right the printed image will shift – by changing the value of the *Left Edge* gadget.

Values are given in inches/10 (inches divided by 10, default for English systems) or in mm. You can change the units of measurement via the *Settings > Use Metrics System* menu (tick or untick this option). If necessary, check whether your country setting is correct. To do this, start *Locale* in *Prefs* and change the country to your location.

If *Center Picture* is enabled, the *Left Edge* value will be ignored during the printing process.

Color correction

Color correction leads to a better match between the colors on the screen and the colors on the printout. Use this function for the red, green and blue color channels as well as combinations of these colors.

Color correction limits the number of printed colors. If this option is not enabled, color printers can print all the colors available on an Amiga screen. For each color that is selected for correction, several color levels of that color are lost. The number of colors that can be printed is displayed in the info gadget of the same name to the right of the color correction checkboxes.

Color Correction can only be adjusted manually if the *Shade* setting is set to *Color*. Otherwise, the color correction fields will be greyed out.

Limits

Here you can set the limits for the *Width* and *Height* depending on the type of limit. You decide what *Type* of limit value you want by selecting it from the cycle gadget.

Use the *Width* and *Height* gadgets to set the size of the print image. The options for the *Bounded* and *Absolute* values are given in tenths of an inch or in millimeters, depending on the setting. If *Pixels* has been selected as the limit type, the values are specified in pixels. With the *Multiply* option, the width and height is given in x times. Click on the gadget to enter a value. Delete the specified value and enter the correct value. Then press the Enter key.

The *Type* cycle gadget holds these limits types to select from:

Ignore: The limits for width and height are ignored. The size of the print image corresponds to the size requested by the application. However, the width cannot exceed the following limit: (right margin - left margin) + 1 / character per inch or mm. The height is usually limited by the length of the paper.

Bounded: The size of the print image is determined by the limit values for width and height. For example, if the print image should have a size of `100` x `130` mm, enter the actual values `100` and `130` for width and height (when operating in mm mode).

Absolute: The limits for width and height are interpreted as absolute values. If the print image is to be exactly `100` x `130` mm, enter the values `100` and `130` for width and height. Then select *Absolute*. The image will be scaled according to your specifications. This can lead to distortions. When using this option, you must *select* the *Fraction* option for *Scaling*. However, if you select *Absolute,* you can also obtain a print image with a normal aspect ratio that has a specific width or height. Set the width or height to the desired value and enter `0` for the other limit value. Example: if you set the width to `100` and the height to `0`, the height is calculated so that the correct aspect ratio is displayed. If both limits are set to `0`, the image is printed with the maximum width and height required for the correct aspect ratio.

Pixels: The limits for width and height are interpreted as pixel values. If one of both limits is set to 0, the same rules apply as for the *Absolute* option. The printout has the specified width or height along with the width or height corresponding to the correct aspect ratio.

Multiply: The width and height of the original image are multiplied by the set limits for width and height. If, for example, 2 is specified as the width and 4 as the height, the printed image is twice as wide as the original picture (in pixels) and four times as high.

PrinterPS (PostScript prefs)

PrinterPS is the ultimate solution for configuring and customizing settings for printers that support PostScript.

Function

PostScript is a widespread page description language used for printing complex layouts and graphics at high quality. With *PrinterPS*, you can define aspects such as print resolution, paper size and other specific settings for PostScript printers to achieve the best possible print quality for your documents and graphics.

You can use *PrinterPS*, short for *Printer PostScript Preferences*, to configure settings for controlling the functions for PostScript printers. This prefs editor will work properly only if you have a PostScript-capable printer connected to your Amiga and have selected *PostScript* in the *Printer* prefs.

The PostScript prefs window contains a considerable number of gadgets, which are explained in detail below.

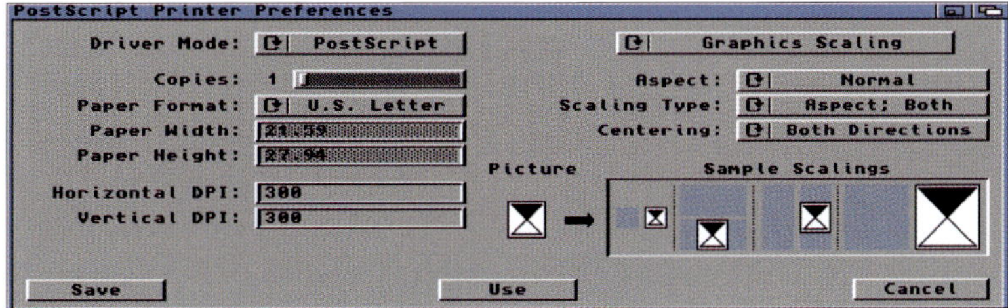

The PrinterPS prefs provides complex settings for your PostScript-capable printer.

INFO **Additional menu items**
In the *Settings* menu of PrinterPS, you will find the *Measuring System* item. Choose *centimeters*, *inches* or *points* in the submenu. The selected unit is used to display the settings for the width, height and margins. On English systems, *inches* is the default unit. On most European systems it will be *centimeters*.

Driver mode

Use the *Driver Mode* cycle gadget to choose between *PostScript* and *Pass Through*. In PostScript mode, the driver converts all text output data to the PostScript format and sends it to the printer specified in the *Printer* prefs. If *Pass Through* is selected, the data is sent directly to the port, bypassing the PostScript printer driver. The Pass Through option allows programs that already output data in PostScript format to send the PostScript data directly to the printer, in a kind of transparent way.

Copies

The number of copies of each page to be printed can be set using the *Copies* slider. The maximum is 99 copies, with 1 being the default.

Paper format, width and height

PrinterPS offers the *DIN A4* paper format, which is common in many European countries, as well as the American *U.S. Letter* and *U.S. Legal* formats, adjustable with the cycle gadget of the same name.

The information in the *Paper Width* and *Paper Height* gadgets reflects these options (e.g. 21.0 x 29.7 for A4), but is greyed out. If you set the *Paper Format* to *Custom*, you can enter the exact length and width manually and thus specify a paper format.

Horizontal and vertical DPI

You can easily define the horizontal and vertical resolution for PostScript printing: in the *Horizontal DPI* and *Vertical DPI* gadgets, enter a number for the dots per inch (dpi) for the printout. The driver uses this resolution for all dithering and processing methods. Use the exact DPI settings intended for your PostScript printer to avoid distortions in the printout.

Further options

Use the unnamed cycle gadget in the top right to choose from even more settings that are grouped into four categories: *Text Options*, *Text Dimensions*, *Graphics Options* and *Graphic Scaling*. Certain options will be displayed depending on your selection.

Text options

Font: Select the desired font for the printout. These are fonts that are integrated into the printer and are used for printing text, e.g. Courier, Helvetica, Bookman and many more.

Pitch: Select *Normal*, *Compressed* (i.e. narrow) or *Expanded* (i.e. wide) to change the text density.

Orientation: Select *Portrait* (i.e. vertical) or *Landscape* (i.e. horizontal). To print on envelopes, use *Landscape*, for example.

Tab: Here, you enter the number of characters or inches by which the printed text is to be shifted by a tabulator. There are a few options to select from: 4 characters, 8 characters, 1/4 inch, 1/2 inch and 1 inch. Use inches for proportional font sets.

Text dimensions

Margins: Define the margins for the text to be printed using four gadgets for the left, right, top and bottom margin. The margins represent the distance to the respective paper border, whereby the width and length of the paper must be specified beforehand.

Font Point Size: Specify in points the size of the font set to be used for the data sent to the printer.

Line Leading: Determine the spacing between the lines of text. This is the distance in points between the bottom edge of a line and the top edge of the following line.

Lines Per Inch: This field displays the approximate number of lines per inch (lpi). This value is calculated from the values specified for the font point size and the line leading.

Lines Per Page: This field displays the approximate number of printable lines per printed page. This value is calculated from the values for the font point size, the line spacing, the paper height and the top and bottom margins.

Graphics options

Margins: The print area for printing graphics is specified with the values for *Left Edge*, *Top Edge*, *Width* and *Height* (compare *Margins* for *Text Dimensions*). The values are given in the unit measurement system of your choice (see the related *Settings* menu).

Image: This option determines the image output as *positive* or *negative* (see also *Image* option in *PrinterGfx*).

Shading: Set the options *Black & White*, *Grey Scale* or *Color* with this cycle gadget (see also *Shade* in *PrinterGfx*).

Dithering: Select *Default*, *Dotty*, *Vertical* or *Horizontal* if you have activated *Grey Scale* as the shading scheme. *Default* corresponds to standard halftone shading. The *Dotty* option is comparable to halftone shading, but the dots are much larger, causing certain effects. If *Grey Scale* is selected, the grey shades are created using vertical or horizontal lines of different thicknesses that are arranged at close intervals.

Graphics scaling

In this settings group, you can define the size, image position and scaling factor for the print image. The effects of the options can be seen immediately in the four sample scalings at the bottom right of the window. The shaded areas represent print areas of different sizes and shapes. Changing the various settings will change the print result of the original image.

Aspect: When printing graphics, select *Normal* or *Sideways*. The desired rotation is carried out before all other processes when printing a graphic, including scaling.

Scaling Type: Select one of seven scaling types. This controls the display of the image in the print area that was defined in the margin and size settings. When selecting a proportional scaling type, the aspect ratio is retained. This is not the case with scaling types that adapt to the print area.

None: The image is printed without scaling. If the image does not fit into the specified print area, it may be cut off on the right and/or bottom.

Aspect; Width: The image width is adjusted to the width of the print area and the height is scaled according to the aspect ratio. If the image is too high for the print area, it is cut off at the bottom.

Aspect; Height: The image height is adjusted to the height of the print area and the width is scaled according to the aspect ratio. If the image is too wide for the print area, it is cut off on the right.

Aspect; Both: The image is scaled to the maximum size within the print area while retaining the aspect ratio.

Fits; Wide: The width of the image is adjusted to the width of the print area. The height is then scaled until it corresponds to the aspect ratio or the height of the print area is reached. In contrast to the scaling type *Aspect; Width,* the image always fits into the print area and is never cut off at the bottom.

Fits; Tall: The height of the image is adjusted to the height of the *print area.* The width is then scaled until it corresponds to the aspect ratio or the width of the print area is reached. In contrast to the scaling type *Aspect; Height,* the image always fits into the print area and is never cut off on the right.

Fits; Both: The image height and width are scaled to the dimensions of the print area. The aspect ratio is not taken into account.

Centering: The centering option ensures the printed content is equally distanced from each margin and is therefore centered horizontally and/or vertically on the paper. Select *Horizontal*, *Vertical*, *Both Directions* or *None*. Centering is the last process before the actual print output and takes place after scaling.

TIP **Using multiple printers**

If you want to connect more than one printer to your Amiga, copy the *Printer* prefs via `[R-Amiga]+[C]` and open the information requester of the copied prefs via `[R-Amiga]+[I]`. Change the name of the printer in the *Name* text gadget in the *File* tab and add the device type as UNIT=1 to the tool types in the *Icon* tab. This symbol then defines the settings for the new device. You can repeat this step with other printers. The new device can then be controlled and used with the Printer prefs, which are synchronized with PrinterGfx and PrinterPS for each device unit. You can also store presets for different printers in the Workbench to quickly switch between devices.

Reaction (GUI prefs)

The Reaction Preferences allow you to change the settings for the AmigaOS-native Reaction interface used by a number of programs.

Function

In AmigaOS 3.5, the *Intuition* interface was extended with new *Reaction* classes. These extensions were not available in AmigaOS 3.1.4. In AmigaOS 3.2, updated variants of Reaction classes were introduced allowing corresponding applications to work out of the box. You can significantly and visibly influence the appearance and behavior of these interfaces in the Reaction prefs editor.

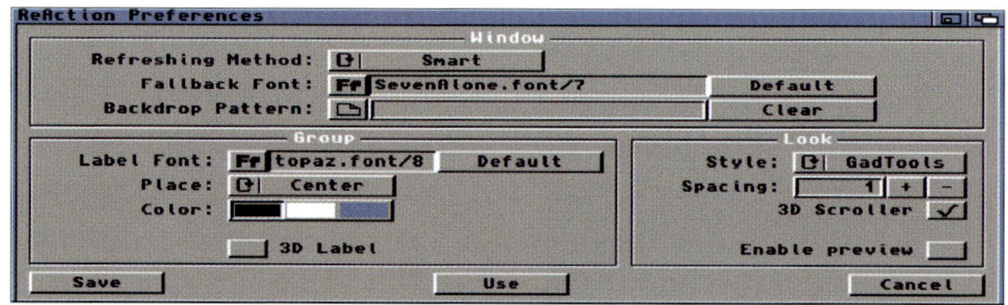

Back since AmigaOS 3.2: Reaction and the Reaction Preferences for making visual changes to the user interface.

Windows

The *Window* section lets you configure all settings for Reaction-based windows:

Refresh Method: Here you can determine the window refresh method of Reaction windows. You can choose between *Simple* and *Smart*. The *Simple* setting requires slightly less memory, but the window refresh takes longer. If you select *Smart*, more memory is used, but the window is refreshed more quickly. Select the setting depending on whether you have a lot or little memory available.

Fallback Font: Use this option to specify an alternate font for Reaction windows if the font set defined in the Font preferences is too large for Reaction windows to handle on the screen. Reaction will then attempt to switch to the fallback font. A small font size should be selected as the fallback. If you are unsure, click the *Default* button next to the font selector to use the default font.

Backdrop Pattern: This setting lets you assign an image file as a backdrop. This will be displayed in Reaction windows instead of the plain grey background.

Group

Under *Group*, you can adjust settings for groups (i.e. related items) in Reaction interfaces.

Label Font: This setting lets you select the font for group headings. You can select the font manually in a requester or click on *Default* to use the default font.

Place: Here you can define the alignment of the group headings. The cycle gadget gives you a choice of *center*, *right* and *left* alignment.

Color: Here you can change the color of the group headings. There are three basic colors to pick from.

3D Label: The *3D Label* checkbox can be used to add a pseudo 3D effect to the group headings.

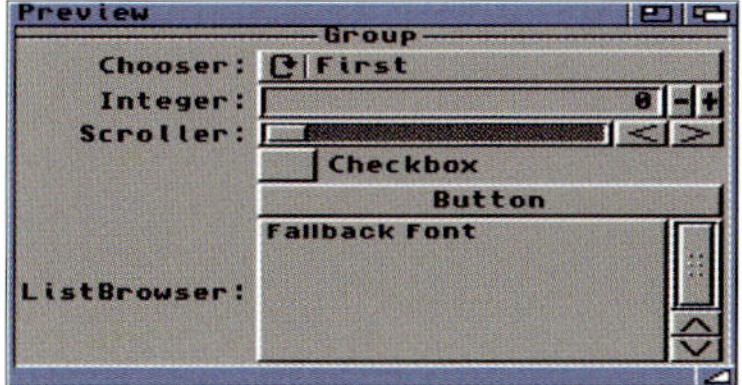

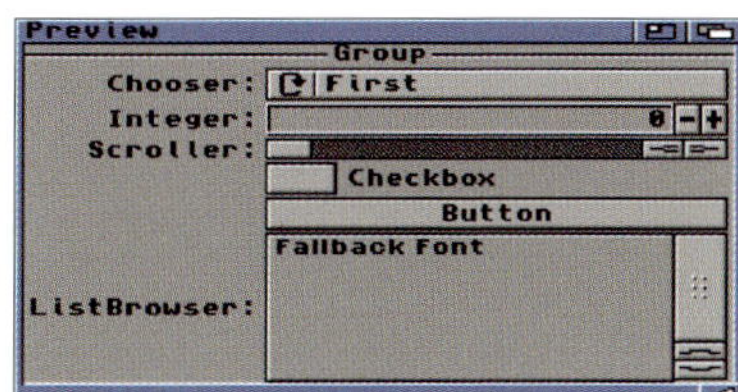

Reaction preview window comparison: GadTools style on the left, Xen style with 3D scrollbars on the right.

Look

In the *Look* group, there are three options that significantly influence the appearance of all Reaction interfaces.

Style: The most significant visual influence on the interface is probably the style option, which can be changed via a cycle gadget. This changes the appearance of scrollbars, bars and buttons on Reaction interfaces, for example. There are five styles to choose from: GadTools, Thin, Thick, Xen and Thin Xen.

GadTools is best suited for applications that make use of the GadTools style introduced in AmigaOS 2.0. Meanwhile, Xen is popular with MUI programs. The style choice is a matter of personal taste and has no influence on the system's efficiency.

Spacing: Here you can define the distances between the Reaction elements. The value is not a fixed distance, but a distance level. Larger values lead to larger distances. The default value is 1.

3D Scrollers: Enable this option via the checkbox to display the scroll bars of lists and sliders in 3D.

Enable preview: This preview function is useful for quickly testing changes. Clicking the button opens a tiny Reaction window that instantly displays the effects of changes to items of the interface.

ScreenMode (screen prefs)

You can customize the display of the Workbench to your liking via the ScreenMode settings. Here you can adjust screen resolution and color depth to suit your preferences.

Function

Undoubtedly the most important setting of the Workbench is screen resolution and color depth, which you can define in the *ScreenMode* prefs editor. You can also enable the *AutoScroll* option and find out more about screen mode capabilities.

If you have installed a graphics card with drivers, you can also select the resolutions and color depths of the graphics

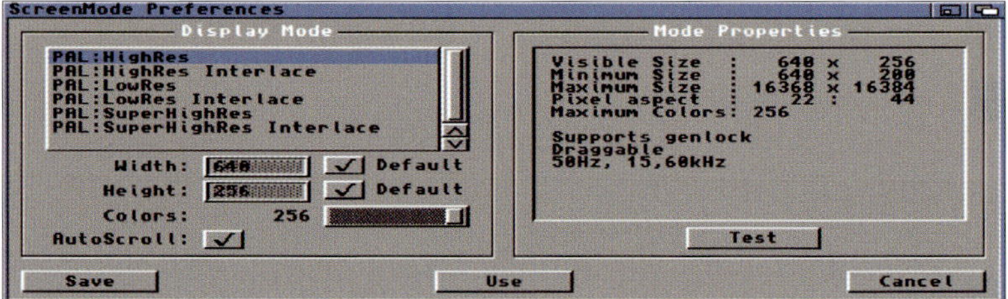

The ScreenMode Preferences, with a wide range of resolutions listed as display modes. The example shows a UAE screen with 1280×1024 pixels and 16-bit color depth (65536 colors).

card modes exactly as you want them here. The default setting is always *High Res*, regardless of the chipset available.

Display modes

In the *Display Mode* box, you will find the available screen modes currently being addressed by the drivers located in the system directory *Devs/Monitors*. Go through the list using the scroll bar and select the desired mode by marking it. The width and height provided for the selected display mode, as well as the available colors are displayed below.

Width and height

Use the *Width* and *Height* gadgets to change the size of the Workbench screen as required. Enter a value that lies between the minimum and maximum value (as specified in the information to the right). If these values are exceeded or not reached, the system automatically corrects to the minimum or maximum value.

By ticking the *Default* checkboxes, the width and height input will be locked and the and the default settings of the screen mode will be selected.

Colors

Use the *Colors* slider to set the maximum number of colors available for the screen mode. In Low Res and High Res modes, which are displayed via the chipset, more Chip RAM will be used when displaying more colors. In addition, updating the screen will be slower. If you use a graphics card in your Amiga, you can display up to 16.8 million colors. Please note there is a memory limit on graphics cards for higher resolutions and high color depths. In 16-bit and 24/32-bit modes, the maximum number of colors available is preselected, i.e. the colors slider is locked.

INFO **Recommended color depths**
16 colors – preferably 32 – should be used for GlowIcons. OCS/ECS Amigas should only be run using 8 colors for performance reasons (4 colors are sufficient for AmigaOS 3.1 icons).

Autoscrolling

The *AutoScroll* checkbox is typically ticked, meaning this option is enabled. This allows you to continue scrolling with the mouse pointer when you reach the edge of the visible screen area. This option is recommended if you have defined a width and height where only parts of the screen are visible.

Mode properties

The relevant properties of the selected display mode are shown under *Mode Properties*: visible size, minimum and maximum size, pixel aspect (i.e. aspect ratio) and maximum number of colors that can be used, plus vertical and horizontal frequency in kHz.

Depending on the screen mode, further criteria are also shown: *Requires ECS* indicates whether the mode requires a specific chipset as a minimum requirement (here: ECS). *Supports Genlock* indicates the permitted use of genlocks in conjunction with the screen mode. *Draggable* indicates that the Workbench screen can be pulled down like a window blind to reveal any other open screens behind it.

TIP **Pixel aspect ratio**
Depending on the graphics mode, the individual pixels have a different width/height ratio. In RTG modes, a ratio of 1:1 (or multiples, e.g. 17:17) should always be displayed here to ensure that the interface is displayed correctly. If this is not the case, you will need to configure your RTG system to do so. Please refer to the documentation for your Picasso96 version.

Testing the display

Once you're finished setting up the display mode, you should test the mode with your monitor to ensure it can handle the screen resolution. If you accept the changes without doing so, the Workbench will inform you that you should first carry out a test.

The *Test* button is used to check the settings. Only when the display works perfectly using the test should you use the mode permanently via *Save* or *Use*.

Serial (serial prefs)

In the Serial Preferences you can configure your system for communication via the serial port.

Function

The transfer of serial data via modems and networks requires compatibility between the communicating devices. Exact details on the required settings can be found in the documentation for your serial device. Click on the *Serial* icon in the *Prefs* drawer to open the editor, which is clearly organized and easy to use.

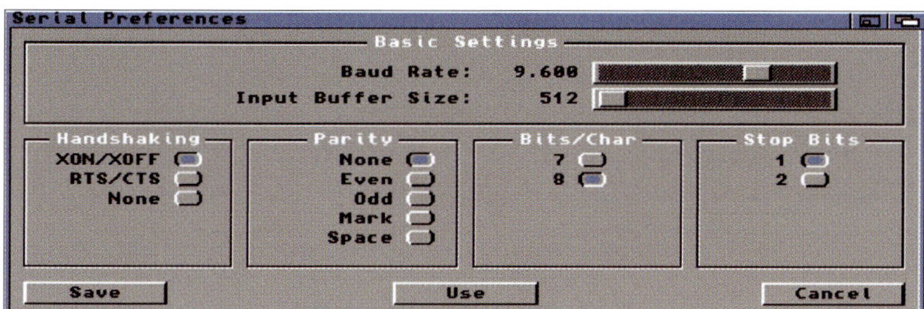

The Serial prefs with the baud rate slider. When using serial devices, you can address them with units.

Baud rate

The *Baud Rate* defines the transfer rate in bits per second (bps) of the serial port. In serial communication, bits are sent or received one after the other. As a character normally consists of 10 bits (1 start bit, 8 data bits and 1 stop bit), you can calculate the approximate number of transmitted characters per second (cps) by dividing the baud rate by 10.

Use the slider to choose one of the available baud rates: 110, 300, 1,200, 2,400, 4,800, 9,600, 19,200 or 31,250. The current setting is displayed next to the slider. The chosen baud rate must match the baud rate of the device with which the Amiga is communicating. The higher the value, the faster the data will be transferred. The default value, which is suitable for the majority of common devices, is 9,600 baud.

Input buffer size

The input buffer is a memory area that is reserved for the temporary storage of incoming serial data. You can select one of the following sizes with the *Input Buffer Size* slider: 512, 1,024, 2,048, 4,096, 8,192, 16,384, 32,768 or 65,536 bytes. The current size is displayed to the left of the slider. The higher the baud rate and the more actions the Amiga performs, the larger the input buffer should be. The value is preconfigured to 512.

Handshaking

The handshaking protocol controls the data flow between the serial port and the connected device. In order for data to be transmitted, the same protocol must be enabled for the computer and for the connected device. *XON/XOFF*, *RTS/CTS* and *None* are available protocols, to be selected with radio buttons.

XON/XOFF is the most frequently used protocol. The special characters XON and XOFF are inserted into the data transferred between the devices and are used to control the data flow.

With *RTS/CTS*, the data flow is regulated by separate control lines: RTS (Request to Send) and CTS (Clear to Send). You will need a special serial cable (available from your Amiga dealer) to connect the device to the Amiga.

If the *None* option is selected, the protocol is deactivated. The data flow will then take place without restrictions or control. A friendly heads-up: be extra careful when using this option.

Parity

Parity enables the detection of transfer errors by checking the parity bit setting. The parity bit is transmitted and set so that the number of bits set for a character always adds up to an even (or odd) number. Choose your desired *Parity* setting using the radio buttons: *None*, *Even*, *Odd*, *Mark* and *Space*.

The *None* option specifies that all bits are used for data. This is usually the one you'll want to pick when *Bits/Char* is set to 8. There is no parity check at all. *Even* specifies that the total number of 1-bits in each character, including the parity bit, must always be an even number. Conversely, with *Odd*, the total number of 1-bits in each character, including the parity bit, must always be an odd number. *Mark* limits the parity bit to 1. *Space* sets it to exactly 0.

Bits/Char

In the *Bits/Char* area, you can specify the number of bits that are transmitted through the serial port in order to send a character. This value also specifies the number of bits expected for each character received.

This value must correspond to the parity setting. If parity is set to *Even*, *Odd*, *Mark* or *Space*, set *Bits/Char* to 7, as some systems use the eighth bit for parity checking. If the option *None* is set for parity, you can set *Bits/Char* to 8. If you want to use and transfer the full 8-bit character set, you must always select 8.

Stop bits

Stop bits are additional bits that are added at the end of a character. These bits allow the computer to recognize the space between words and the end of the transmission of a character. This applies to all data sent and received via the serial port.

Two stop bits are usually required for computers with a low processing speed. For computers with a data transfer speed of 300 baud or higher, 1 stop bit is usually sufficient. If 8 data bits per char are used, you can only specify one stop bit, otherwise data will be lost during data transfer.

Multiple serial units

If your system is equipped with more than one serial interface, you can specify a default unit by adding the `UNIT` option in the Shell command line for the execution of `Serial` or by specifying the `UNIT` tool type for the program icon. This will cause an additional *default unit* gadget to be displayed in the bottom right-hand corner of the Serial prefs window. Enter the unit number of the interface to be used in this gadget if no interface is specified by another method. Here, `0` and `1` stand for the serial port of the motherboard. As a rule, the documentation for a serial device describes the unit numbers to be used for the interfaces. The settings made in the serial editor affect all interfaces.

Sound (sound prefs)

In the Sound Preferences, you can choose the method and sound signal of warning messages from the system.

Function

The Workbench provides a warning message if, for example, a program requests input or a processing error occurs. In this case, AmigaOS 3.2 produces a flashing screen. If desired, a sound can be played in addition or as an alternative to the flashing. The warning mode can be amended in the *Sound* Preferences.

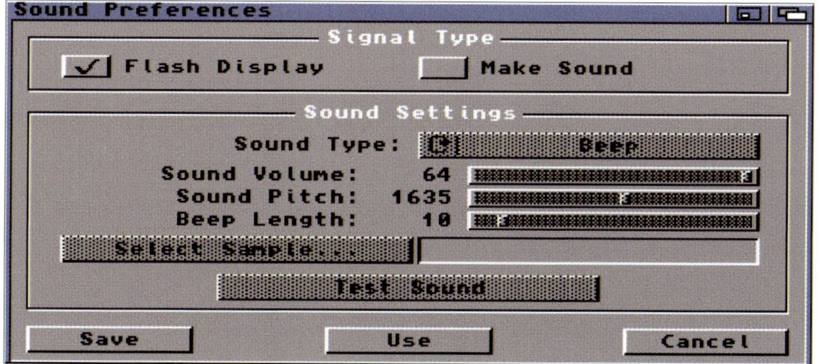

If you want a sound to be played as a warning in addition to a flashing screen, the sound's volume can be adjusted.

Signal type

In this section, you can decide whether the system should emit a flashing light and/or sound when it issues a warning. Simply tick the appropriate *Signal Type*: *Flash Display* and/or *Make Sound*.

Sound settings

If the *Make Sound* option is enabled, you can specify the *Sound Type* in the *Sound Settings* group. For a *Beep*, a manually generated tone, you can modify the *Sound Volume*, *Sound Pitch* and *Beep Length* parameters moving those three sliders. For a *Sampled Sound*, you can choose a sound file from a drive by clicking on *Select Sound* and adjusting its volume and pitch. You can use all sound formats for which a datatype is provided in the *Devs/DataTypes* drawer, e.g. IFF or WAVE.

Click on *Test Sound* to hear whether the sound or audio file meets your expectations.

Time (time prefs)

Use the Time Preferences to adjust the system time and system date.

Function

The Time prefs lets you set the date and time of the system. This affects the display and editing of files and folders for changes to be recorded chronologically. A battery-backed real-time clock (RTC) is required to be installed in the Amiga for the date and time settings to be retained even after a cold start.

Setting date and time

To change the date, enter the current year in the year gadget, and change the month using the cycle gadget until the current month is displayed. Click on the current day in the calendar overview.

Hours and minutes are adjusted with two sliders. Move the sliders to the right or left to increase or decrease the value for hours and minutes. The seconds cannot be set precisely.

TIP **Replace defective batteries**
Leaking batteries in old computers can cause major damage to the hardware. If necessary, have the battery replaced with a button cell by a specialist and have the damage repaired.

WBPattern (pattern prefs)

WBPattern lets you change the background of Workbench screens and windows, helping the user interface break free from its grey dullness and come alive with color.

Function

By default, the Workbench is not exactly bursting with color. This can be counteracted by using a pattern or a suitable image to brighten up the backgrounds of the Workbench screen and windows. You can do this via the WBPattern prefs and give your Workbench a more visual, personalized style.

After opening the Workbench pattern prefs by clicking on the *WBPattern* icon in the *Prefs* drawer, the editor appears in a smart window with two sections: adjust patterns or images on the left side, and edit patterns on the right.

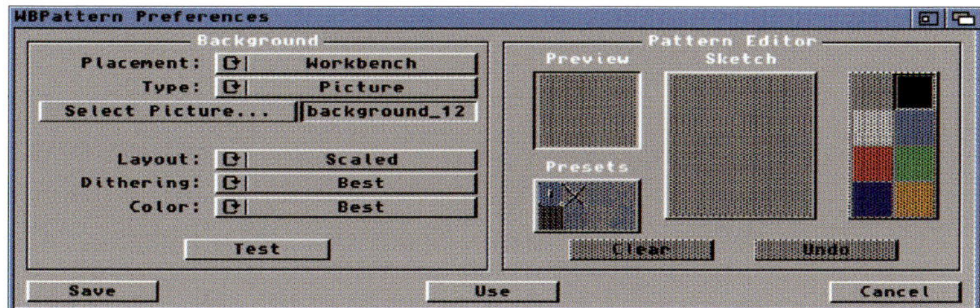

Your starting point for a more beautiful user interface: with WBPattern you can change the background of the Workbench screen and windows with images or patterns.

Background

You must first define the area you want a background to be applied to. This is done in the *Placement* cycle gadget, where you will find three options: Workbench, Windows and Screen.

Workbench defines the background of the Workbench window or the content of the visible area in *Workbench as Backdrop* mode. Activate the latter mode in the *Workbench* menu or using the keyboard shortcut `[R-Amiga]+[B]`.

The second option is *Windows*: the background of Workbench windows can be defined here. This applies to all drive and drawer windows. Shell or program windows are not affected.

Finally, the *Screen* option refers to the background of the screen if the aforementioned *Workbench as Backdrop* display mode is enabled.

Background type

The *Type* parameter allows you to set an image as the background. The resolution and number of colors of the image should match the screen settings defined in the *ScreenMode* prefs as closely as possible. You can search for and specify the image file in a file requester, which will open by clicking on the *Select Picture* button. All image formats for which a datatype is available in *Devs/DataTypes* are supported (see section 2.7, *Datatypes*).

If the image does not perfectly match the screen resolution, you can improve the display using the *Layout* parameter. This contains four options: *Scaled* changes the size of the image while maintaining its proportions, aligned to the screen resolution. *Interpolated* adds missing pixels and color gradations to the displayed image if required. *Centered* places the image in the center of the Workbench screen (not available for windows). Finally, *Tiled* arranges a small graphic into a mosaic to form a much larger overall image.

As the downsampling of image files requires processing power and memory, the display of the image can be preconfigured: the quality of *Dithering* and *Color* can be adjusted with the values *best*, *good* and *poor*. The higher the quality, the more color fields are used to display the background image and may then be missing when displaying icons on the Workbench. Test which setting best suits your system.

Pattern type

As an alternative to an image, you can use a self-created or premade pattern as a background. If you select *Pattern* as the *type*, the *Pattern Editor* on the right-hand side of the WBPattern window is enabled.

Pattern editor

In the *Pattern Editor*, you can either create your own small pieces of art as patterns or use one of the predrawn patterns. In the *Sketch* field, you can use the mouse to create any pattern using the eight colors shown on the right. A single click places a pixel in the active color at the position of the pointer; when the mouse is held down, the brush follows the movement. Switch between the colors to work out the pattern.

If you find the coloring work too tedious, simply access one of the eight predrawn patterns from the *Presets*. These presets can be recolored or modified as much as you want.

The result of the tiled pattern is displayed in the small *Preview* field for checking while painting and switching back and forth.

If you don't like the result, you can remove the pattern from the sketch by clicking the *Clear* button. The area will then be completely filled with the active color. To discard the last drawing operation, click *Undo*.

WBPattern menu

The *Settings* menu of WBPattern carries additional menu items (see section 3.1, *Preferences at a glance*) that allow you to edit patterns more efficiently.

Use the *Cut*, *Copy* and *Paste* commands to transfer images from the WBPattern editor to a program that can access the clipboard and has more extensive drawing functions, such as *IconEdit*. Use *Load image* to load IFF images into the WBPattern editor (images larger than the working area of the editor are cut off at the bottom or right-hand side when they are loaded or pasted into the WBPattern editor). Use *Erase* to delete the data in the entire workspace, *Undo* to undo the last action performed and *Restore* to restore the last undone state.

Test

A firm click on the *Test* button will display the changed image or pattern background in the Workbench backdrop or screen and in all open windows. The change is done live, without windows having to be closed beforehand. This is the best way to get a good idea of any changes before making them final.

Workbench (Workbench prefs)

The Workbench Preferences are a real jack-of-all-trades in terms of the visual and functional customization of the graphical user interface.

Function

Since AmigaOS 3.5, the Workbench Preferences have been integrated into the Prefs as the central area for controlling the system. It should be one of the first points of contact after setting up the system. It can be used to hide physical drives (and make them visible again), change the look of icons or the content of the Workbench title bar, and much more.

Hidden devices

Physical drives, i.e. floppy drives, hard disks and HD partitions, the RAM Disk or CD-ROM drives, are listed in the *Hidden*

Devices list. By default, these are visible, i.e. they are displayed on the Workbench screen. If you want to make individual drives invisible, simply click the drive's name in the list. The drive will then be hidden on the Workbench screen itself, but can still be accessed as usual by the Workbench or any program.

The invisible option is useful, for example, for drive partitions that do not require direct access from the Workbench, e.g. Gotek drives or the installation partition on an AmigaOS 3.2 CompactFlash card.

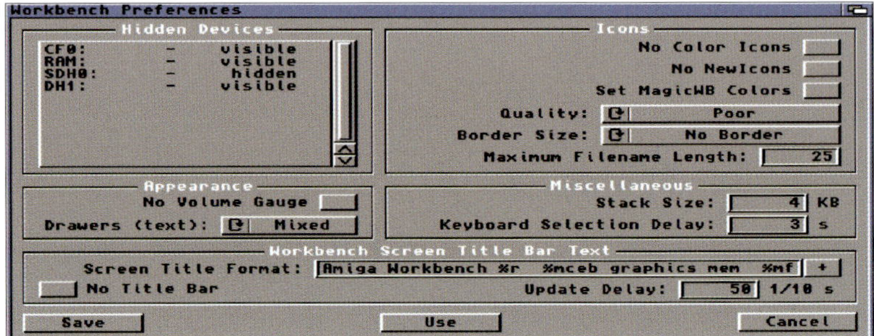

Plenty of functions in a single window: hide devices, edit the title bar, set stack size and much more.

Look of icons

In the *Icons* group, you can set the appearance of the icons on the Workbench screen. If you tick *No Color Icons*, the eight-color icons that were standard in AmigaOS 3.1 or earlier will be displayed, if available, instead of NewIcons or GlowIcons. This setting is recommended for newly installed systems (without GlowIcons installed), but not for installations based on 3.1 with NewIcons or 3.5 or 3.9.

If you activate the *No NewIcons* option, the respective standard icon of a file, if available, is displayed and not any existing NewIcons variant. The option *Set MagicWB Colors*, available since AmigaOS 3.9, is useful if you use lots of older MagicWB icons: this option changes the color coding and ensures MagicWB icons are displayed in the correct colors.

The *Quality* cycle gadget lets you choose the exact color range you want for your icons. You can choose between four quality levels: *Best*, *Good, Poor* and *Bad*. If you choose a higher quality level, the icons tend to look better. However, there are fewer colors available that can be used by programs on the Workbench. You can tell that there is an excessive amount of color if *IconEdit* opens its own screen on startup or the background image loses quality. If you change the quality to a lower level, there is a chance that IconEdit will be displayed on the Workbench again. Our recommendation for the quality level is *Good*.

The border appearance of the icons can also be changed globally: the self-explanatory options *No Border*, *Small*, *Medium* and *Large* can be found in the *Border Size* cycle gadget. As an exception, individual icons can still be used that do not have a border even if the global border is switched on.

The *Maximum Filename Length* in the *Icons* group is quite interesting. File names with up to 25 characters are usually displayed on the Workbench screen. By changing the value in the input field, you increase or decrease the displayed part of the filename, but not its actual length.

Note that the permitted filename length depends on the file system of the drive used and its settings (see section 2.12).

Appearance

Since AmigaOS 3.5, the windows for volumes such as hard disks or RAM Disks have had a bar on the left-hand side where the occupied and free storage is shown visually. This so-called *fill level* display can be hidden for all affected windows by activating the *No Volume Gauge* checkbox in the *Appearance* section.

The *Drawers (text)* cycle gadget determines how directories are to be handled globally in file requester lists: *Mixed* (directories mixed with files), *Top* (first directories, then files) or *Bottom* (first files, then directories).

Memory stack

Under *Stack Size* in the *Miscellaneous* section, you can set the memory stack for programs launched from the Workbench without an icon. For all other program, the stack size is defined in the related icon. The default stack size is 4 kilobytes. You can increase this value to 16 kilobytes or more depending on the memory configuration of your system.

Keyboard selection delay

The cumbersome *Keyboard Selection Delay* option defines the time interval in seconds after which the buffer for the keyboard-controlled icon selection is completely emptied. This ensures that an input from the keyboard is regarded as an independent input and not as a continuation of an icon name.

In other words, if you press a letter key in an active window, the system automatically jumps to the first icon with this initial letter. If you press another letter key within the time interval, the input is recognized as the second letter of the name. If the delay time expires, i.e. you need longer than the specified time value to enter another letter, this is interpreted as entering a new name. By default, the keyboard selection delay is set to 3 seconds.

Changing the Workbench title bar

A tool for real power users is the option contained in the *Workbench Screen Title Bar Text* section. By default, the Workbench displays its name and the system's available memory in its white top title bar. However, the entries in this title bar can be highly customized using the text gadget for the *Screen Title Format*. Free text and predefined values are permitted. For example, `%maem` indicates the available, free total memory in megabytes, `%ir` means the number of active programs and `%is` is the number of open screens. If you click the + button next to the text gadget, the *Title format item wizard* opens in a new window. You will be able to choose from predefined values from different topics: *memory* (e.g. various RAM specifications in bytes, kilobytes, megabytes or per cent), *version number* (Kickstart or Workbench), *processor* (CPU and FPU), *env variable* (environment variable), *release string* and *system info* (e.g. running programs, active disks). If you select a value and click *Insert*, the given value is entered at the position of the cursor in the title format text gadget as soon as you click *Use* or *Save*.

No title bar and status updates

With the option *No Title Bar*, available since OS 3.9, the Workbench title bar is hidden and the background image extends over the entire height of the WB screen. If you right-click into the screen and hold down the button, the title bar will be displayed.

Finally, the inconspicuous *Update Delay* option is shown at the bottom right of the Workbench Preferences. The value, given in 1/10 seconds units, determines the interval at which the details in the Workbench title bar will be refreshed. A value of 50 would indicate 50 tenths of a second, i.e. an interval of 5 seconds. If you want to increase or decrease the interval, make a suitable change, e.g. 10 for 1 second or 100 for 10 seconds.

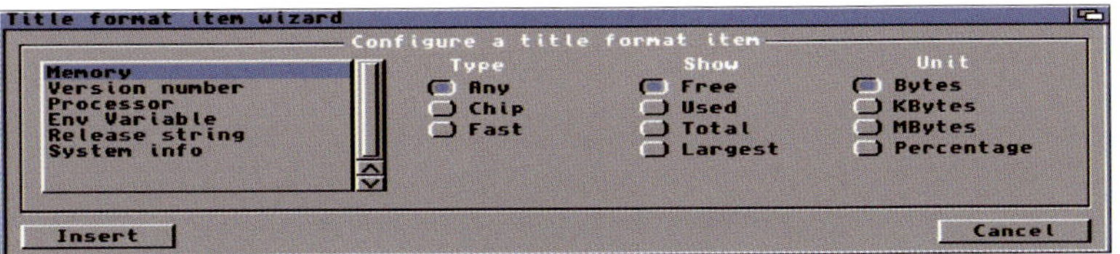

The Title format item wizard helps users customize the Workbench title bar with predefined values.

EnvArc (settings directory)

All system settings changed in the various Preferences editors are stored in the EnvArc directory.

Function

The *Prefs* directory contains a drawer that is not visible at first glance (due to the lack of an .info file). All system settings that you change via the different preferences editors are saved in this drawer. Each time the system is launched, these settings, which are necessary for the Workbench, are loaded into Fast RAM (*RAM:ENV*, to be precise) in order to be active while the Workbench is being used. For example, if you select a system language in *Locale*, this setting is saved in the *locale.prefs* file in *EnvArc*. These settings are then loaded and activated the next time the system is started. Please note that `ENV:` is actually a soft link to `ENVARC:` – it is no longer copied when `ENVARC` is started.

Contents

To display the *EnvArc* drawer, use the `[R-Amiga]+[+]` keyboard shortcut. You can now view the contents of the directory. The *Versions* subdirectory, for example, contains the version number of the AmigaOS.

System settings are stored in the *Sys* drawer. In addition to settings that have been made and saved in the individual prefs, the so-called default icons are also stored there (see section 3.3). If you have a look in this drawer, you will see a wealth of default icons and some *.prefs* files that contain settings information.

If you install third-party software on the Amiga with presets, this information is usually also stored in a subdirectory of EnvArc.

TIP **Beware of damage**

Please be very careful when using EnvArc. Do not change or delete any files without good reason, as the consequence could be that the system cannot start properly. In the worst case, you may need to reinstall AmigaOS.

Programs

4

The Tools and Utilities drawers are packed with handy little programs to make your life easier and your work more efficient. You've got the Calculator, for example, and TextEdit, which is great for creating and editing text files, along with MultiView, the excellent all-purpose tool for viewing and playing files of different types. Not forgetting the Shell – so powerful, it has its own chapter in this book. And that's not all! You'll find lots of other small but useful system programs in the System, Commodities, and WBStartup folders.

Calculator (pocket calculator)

A program that forms part of the basic equipment of all modern operating systems is a calculator. An electronic calculator is also supplied with AmigaOS 3.2.

Start up the calculator by double-clicking on the *Calculator* icon. Use the mouse to operate it by clicking the buttons displayed on the screen. Alternatively, enter data directly via the keyboard using the standard keys or the numeric keypad.

Functions

The function of each button is as follows:

`CA`	deletes all entries and resets the calculator to 0 (for clear all)
`CE`	deletes the current entry
`*`	multiply
`/`	divide
`+`	add
`-`	subtract
`.`	decimal point
`<<`	deletes the last character entered
`±`	changes the sign of the current input (positive numbers become negative and vice versa)
`=`	displays the calculation result

Menus

When making entries with the keyboard, the `[Return]` and, on the numeric keypad, `[Enter]` keys are equivalent to the equals sign `[=]`. Use the `[Backspace]` key to delete entries.

Three menu items are available in the Calculator program: *Project*, *Edit* and *Window*.

The *Project* menu contains the following items: *Clear Entry* deletes the current input. *Clear All* deletes all entries and resets the calculator to zero. *Quit* exits the program.

The following items are available in the *Edit* menu: *Cut* copies the current entry to the clipboard and deletes the current entry or result. *Copy* copies the current entry to the clipboard, but keeps the data for further calculations. *Paste* inserts the current content of the clipboard into the input field of the calculator.

The *Window* menu only contains the menu item *Show tape*. If you select this function, the entries and calculation results are displayed in a separate window, as with a physical calculator that has a printer, i.e. you receive an additional overview of all entries and calculation steps. You can copy the data displayed in the window to the clipboard for further use in another program.

Shell command

Like most other utility programs, you can execute the calculator via the Shell:

```
CALCULATOR [PUBSCREEN <public screen name>]
[TAPE <window>]
```

The `TAPE` parameter corresponds to the *Show tape* menu item and creates an output window of a specific size with a display of all inputs and outputs. The exact dimensions of the window are defined in this way:

```
TAPE=RAW:x/y/width/height/title/options
```

The `PUBSCREEN` parameter defines a specific screen on which the graphical user interface is displayed. If the name of the screen is not found, it is displayed on the default screen (the Workbench screen).

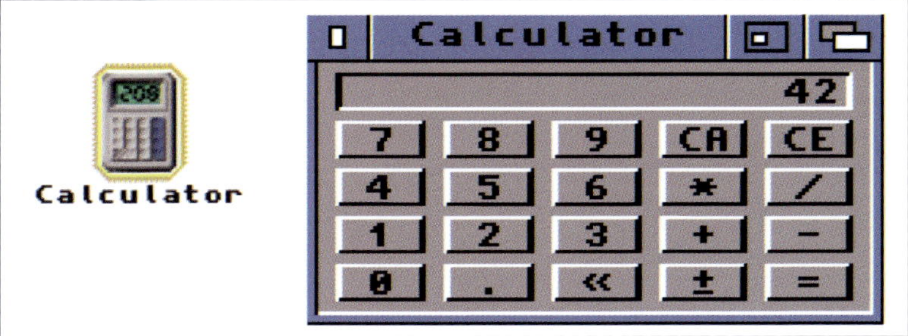

Simple but effective: the calculator has always been part of the standard repertoire of AmigaOS and offers the most important mathematical functions.

CMD (output redirection)

The CMD tool redirects the output of a device, such as a printer, to a file.

Function

The output from devices such as a printers or faxes, or an analysis tool, can be redirected to a file by CMD. The tool itself does not come with a graphical user interface for this, so it needs to be controlled in detail via the Shell.

Shell command

CMD understands the following command format:

```
CMD <devicename> <filename> [arguments]
```

Either `SERIAL` or `PARALLEL` are permitted as the *device name*. For example, if you want to save the output of a printer to a file, the device name must be the same as in the Printer preferences. To put it simply: if the printer is connected to the parallel port on the Amiga, use `PARALLEL`; for the serial port, use `SERIAL`. *Filename* corresponds to the name of the file created.

If you execute CMD by double-clicking its icon rather than via the Shell, the output via the parallel port (e.g. output to a printer) is stored in a file called *CMD_file* in the RAM Disk by default.

Arguments

CMD supports various arguments, which can also be concatenated. `SKIP` skips any type of initial expression (typically used when redirecting a screen expression). `MULTIPLE` redirects the output to several files until the command `Break` is issued or you enter `[Ctrl]+[C]` on the keyboard. `NOTIFY` informs you about the progress of the output. Corresponding messages are displayed directly on the screen. `DEVICE` redirects from another user-specific device.

Example

Use the following command sequence to save each output via the serial port to a file called *cmd_file*, which is located on the RAM Disk:

```
CMD SERIAL RAM:cmd_file
```

GraphicDump (screen printout)

You can use GraphicDump to print out the content of the current screen.

Function

If you have multiple active screens, as is common on the Amiga, the screen in the foreground will be printed. The program waits 10 seconds after the icon has been double-clicked before printing to give you time to bring the desired screen content to the foreground.

Shell command

`GRAPHICDUMP [TINY|SMALL|MEDIUM|LARGE|<xdots>:<ydots>]`

The size options correspond to the *ToolTypes* accepted by the program and determine the width of the printout: `TINY` corresponds to a quarter of the total width that the printer allows, `SMALL` to half, `MEDIUM` to three quarters and `LARGE` to the full width that the printer interprets as permissible. The height of the printout retains the proportions of the screen.

To define exact dimensions, you can also give absolute values in pixels: `XDOTS` corresponds to the absolute width in pixels, `YDOTS` to the absolute height in pixels.

Examples

To create a printout of the foreground screen that is half the size of the full width of the printer, just run the command sequence `GraphicDump SMALL`.

With `GraphicDump 600:300` you can create a printout that is exactly 600 pixels wide and 300 pixels high.

HDToolBox (drive preparation)

HDToolBox is a tool designed for hard disks and other block-oriented drives. It is primarily used to divide such drives into a number of areas, which is also referred to as partitioning.

Functions of the HDToolBox

In addition to its main function of partitioning drives, HDToolBox can perform other functions such as initializing a hard drive through *Change Drive Type*. The procedure for partitioning and initializing drives is explained in detail in this section.

Other functions are now obsolete, such as changing the list of bad blocks with *Modify Bad Block List*, low-level formatting with *Low-level Format Drive* and checking the data on the disk with *Verify Data on Drive*. Clicking the *Help* button displays a help guide. Please note that HDToolBox is available in English only, regardless of your language settings.

Advantages of partitioning

Partitioning under *Partition Drive* offers several significant advantages for daily work with the Amiga:

1. The operating system, applications, and data – such as images or documents – can be structurally separated.

2. You can run multiple AmigaOS versions simultaneously. Use one for emergencies if your regular system fails after tinkering. Or run different versions, like OS3.2 and OS3.9, side-by-side. You will need to ensure that a compatible Kickstart ROM is used in each case.

3. You can use different file systems, such as FFS, SFS and PFS, at the same time.

4. It is a simple fact that the more files a file system contains, the longer it takes to check its structure. Other maintenance tasks such as backups will also take longer.

Not all drives need to be partitioned. Floppy disks are not partitioned, nor are USB sticks or SD cards.

Historical and new formats

The original Amiga computers (Amiga 500, Amiga 2000, Amiga 600, Amiga 1200, Amiga 3000, Amiga 4000, etc.) initially used SCSI hard disks, and later more cost-effective IDE hard disks (see information on SCSI and IDE on page 180).

These two data interfaces are now outdated, and serial successors have replaced them: IDE or PATA has been surpassed by the standard *Serial ATA* (*SATA*), and SCSI has been superseded by *Serial Attached SCSI* (*SAS*), more commonly found in server environments. This has had an impact on the availability of hard drives with those legacy connection types. New IDE and SCSI hard drives are no longer typically available from computer hardware resellers. Given these considerations, exploring alternative options for your hard drives is essential. Read more in the information section on *alternatives to hard drives* on the next page. We have also summarized the most important hardware extensions for you in the *Next Steps* chapter.

Hard Disk Files in the emulation

In an Amiga emulator environment, such as WinUAE for Windows or the portable FS-UAE for Linux, Mac OS X and Windows, it is possible to set up *hard disk files*, also called *hardfiles* (*HDF*). In the FS-UAE Launcher, you can find this function by clicking with the left mouse button on the colorful Amiga tick in the top left-hand corner; in WinUAE, it can be found in the side menu under *CD & Hard drives*. Use *HDF Creator* or *Add hardfile* to create new HDF files.

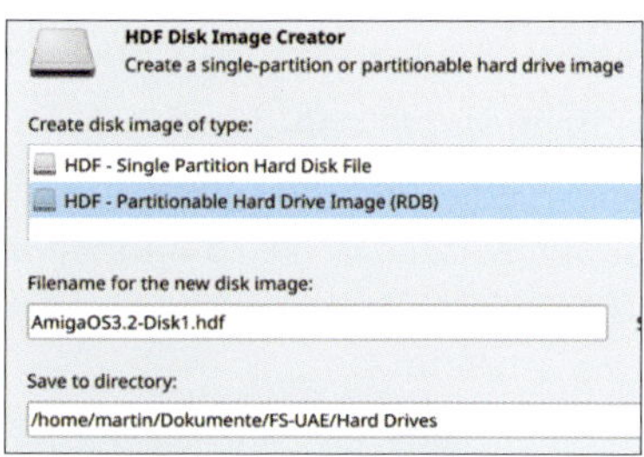

How to create a 2 GB "hard disk" in FS-UAE

There are two types of HDF file: an *HDF (Single Partition Hard Disk File)*, which contains only a single partition (this device appears immediately in AmigaOS on boot); and an *HDF (Partionable Hard Drive Image (RDB))*, which comprises a complete hard disk, including the Amiga RDB partition table.

INFO: SCSI, IDE and alternatives to hard drives

SCSI

SCSI, pronounced “skasi”, means *Small Computer System Interface*. Originally, and as in the Amiga, data transfer took place in parallel. *Units* address the devices connected to the bus. For SCSI with a bus width of 8 bits, this is a maximum of eight devices, including the controller. This is the number supported by the SCSI controllers in the Amiga 3000 and 4000T. For *Ultra Wide SCSI*, *UW-SCSI* or *SCSI 3* for short, the maximum number of devices that can be supported is theoretically 16, including the controller. In practice, the maximum number is likely to be lower due to the length and quality of the cables used. This standard is supported for the Amiga by the *CyberStorm Mk3 / PPC UWSCSI controller* from phase5. The controller is usually preassigned unit 7, but the units of other devices can be freely assigned using jumpers. With SCSI, drives are usually accessed using *Direct Memory Access* (*DMA*), which places less strain on the CPU than the access method used by IDE controllers in the Amiga sector. The speed is also at least higher than that of the IDE controllers installed in the Amiga 1200 and 4000.

IDE

IDE stands for *Integrated Drive Electronics*. This name comes from a time before standardization, just as *AT Attachment* (*ATA*) or more precisely *Parallel ATA* (*PATA*). A maximum of two drives can be attached without a 4-way adapter. The Amiga 1200 and Amiga 4000 had a PATA controller. There are PATA controllers with higher speed such as the *Elbox FastATA controller* and PATA controllers on newer expansion cards for the Amiga. One device is the *master*, the other device is the *slave*. Set the jumper on the boot hard drive to *master* and on the other hard drive or CD/DVD drive to *slave*. It's as easy as that.

Alternatives to hard drives

For SCSI-based Amigas, a *ZuluSCSI to SD adapter* is a good alternative to outdated SCSI hard drives. *Compact Flash to IDE adapters* are available for IDE. Such adapters must make the CF card available to the AmigaOS as a device with *random access*. This function is called *True IDE*. Ask for advice from an Amiga retailer who has these adapters in stock. Make sure you buy high-quality SecureDigital or CompactFlash cards! See also sections 8.1 (FAQ) and 7.5 (Hardware recommendations).

Alternatively, you can integrate a directory from the host system. This will use the host file system. This completely eliminates the partitioning steps. One approach is to install the operating system in a hard disk file and store your data in a directory on the host computer. For programs, a host directory makes it easier to share with several emulated Amigas.

You can read about WinUAE's capabilities in more detail in section 1.3 about *Preparing WinUAE*.

Vampire V4 with CF card

The Apollo Vampire V4 Standalone FGPA computer boots from a CF card. However, a CF card with AmigaOS 3.2 installed on it will not boot the computer without further adjustments. The *ApolloBoot* bootloader and its instructions simplify the installation and booting of AmigaOS 3.2 on the Vampire V4 Standalone (www.apollo-computer.com/apolloboot.php). The software also takes care to load a Kickstart ROM suitable for AmigaOS 3.2. If you intend to only install AmigaOS 3.2, the *SOLO* version is for you. *OMNI* and *TRIO* are for users who also want to install other operating systems and AmigaOS versions. If you want to install AmigaOS 3.2 manually, use *ApolloBoot ZERO*.

ApolloBoot must be registered for free with the developer Willem Drijver. The website specified above lists suitable links to a web form.

RDB (Amiga Rigid Disk Block)

The Amiga's *Rigid Disk Block* (RDB) standard was vastly superior to the *Master Boot Record* (MBR) standard, which was common in the PC sector at the time. The standard, which was not so rigid in terms of possibilities, made it easy to set up ten or more partitions on a disk. For a long time, MBR was limited to four partitions. More than four partitions could be achieved by marking a primary partition as extended and adding logical partitions within it.

However, the RDB standard, which is based on a series of linked blocks, also has certain legacy issues. For example, dividing the addressing of individual blocks on the drive into cylinders, heads and sectors is outdated. Fortunately, *HDToolBox* provides a suitable function under *Change Drive Type* to automatically determine suitable values for this addressing on a new device.

RDB, in a broader sense, comprises the actual rigid disk block, which only contains general information about the drive. This block refers to the individual partition blocks for the partitions, in which the start, size, bootability and number of buffers are stored, among other things. If required, RDB also refers to blocks that contain file system drivers. This means you can boot from a partition with a file system that is not contained in the Kickstart ROM. This can be an alternative file system such as Smart File System or a newer version of Fast File System.

As of version 4 of AmigaOS, the version for PowerPC-based computers, AmigaOS no longer loads file system drivers from the file system area of the RDB. This makes little sense as they are compiled for 68k processors. AmigaOS 4 and higher already contains the necessary file system drivers.

AmigaOS 3.2, however, loads drivers from the file system area of the RDB. All of this information is located in an area at the beginning of the disk, which has a maximum size defined when the device is set up, which is usually sufficient for all typical use cases.

TIP

Using HDToolBox from AmigaOS 3.9 (or not)

The AmigaOS 3.2 HDToolBox does not offer all the functions of the AmigaOS 3.9 HDToolBox. For example, device driver selection via the ASKDEVICE argument or icon option, functions for saving and restoring an RDB, and translation into languages other than English are missing. After copying the *hdwrench.library* and *resource.library* from OS3.9 into an OS3.2 installation, HDToolBox from OS3.9 does run in principle. Among other things, it is possible to create or delete partitions and install a drive. However, the function for restoring the RDB did not work properly in our tests within FS-UAE. The only HDToolBox that is officially supported is the one in AmigaOS 3.2. If in doubt, we recommend you use this version! The following instructions refer to this version 47.10 of HDToolBox.

INFO **Upcoming HDToolBox replacement in AmigaOS 3.3**
For AmigaOS 3.3, a replacement for HDToolBox is in the works with *PartitionEdit*, which automatically lists all drives and takes a big step forward in usability. AmigaOS 3.2/3.3 developer Camilla Boemann revealed this in her presentation at Amiga38. A release date for AmigaOS 3.3 has not yet been officially set.

Steps to set up a new device

In order to make a new device available to AmigaOS, a number of steps are required:

1. If you have not already done so, **connect** or plug in the device. Ensure the Amiga is switched off first. Be sure to follow the information provided in this book and in the manufacturer's instructions.
2. If the device does not yet have an **RDB** (Rigid Disk Block), installed one using *Change Drive Type*.
3. The device must be **partitioned** into one or more parts using *Partition Drive*.
4. Optionally, set up a new **file system**. This step is required only if you are using a file system that is different from the default file system that comes with AmigaOS 3.2.
5. **Format** the partitions to be used with a file system such as *Fast File System* or *Smart File System*.

Once these steps have been completed, you will be able to install AmigaOS and its applications, and otherwise copy data to the file systems on the partitions.

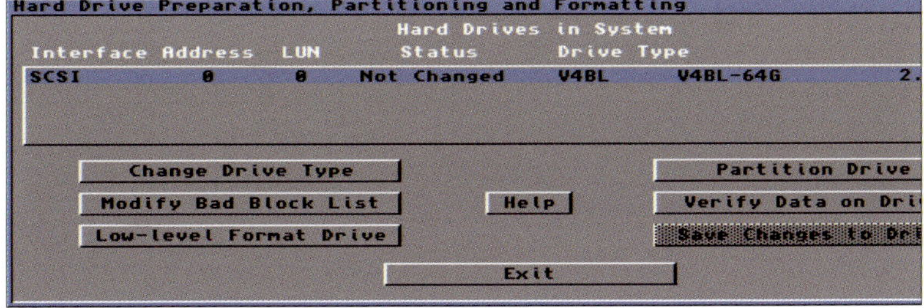

HDToolBox on the Apollo Standalone V4+ FGPA computer

The following sections provide a detailed description of each of these steps. Depending on what you are planning to do, you can skip certain steps. For example, to add a new partition in a free area on an already connected device with RDB, only steps 3 and possibly 4 and 5 are required. However, please read all sections. This will help you get the full picture.

It is recommended that you use only the HDToolBox included with AmigaOS 3.2 for partitioning. You won't have to worry about how the RDB is structured internally, but you can be sure the result is fully compatible with AmigaOS 3.2. While *HDToolBox* versions from other AmigaOS versions up to 3.9, as well as *Media Toolbox* from AmigaOS 4 and higher, should still be compatible, this is not always the case for corresponding tools from third-party manufacturers.

There is one exception to this recommendation: the UW SCSI controller on the *CyberStorm Mk3* and *CyberStorm PPC* from phase5 feature an *NCR 53C770* chip with firmware that uses its own API for managing the Ultra Wide SCSI capabilities. In this case, use the manufacturer's *SCSIConfig* tool (download: www.aminet.net/package/driver/media/CS-SCSI-Tools-31).

TIP **Back up important data!**
In extreme cases, all of the data on an existing device can be rendered inaccessible by errors in setting up a rigid disk block and partitioning a device. As such, it is strongly recommended that to double-check each step taken, and it is a good idea to back up any important data to an external drive that can be disconnected while HDToolBox is running.

Connecting or plugging in a new device

To connect a new device, first read the instructions for your Amiga or for the third-party controller installed in your Amiga.

Otherwise, pay attention to the correct polarity for IDE or PATA hard drives. Pin 1 is marked with a red line on good cables. This must be correctly aligned with pin 1 on the controller connection and the hard drive or CF adapter. Set the jumper on the boot or system hard disk to *master* and the second device to *slave*.

For a 4-way adapter, follow the instructions in its manual. However, please note the following information: the *IDEfix* software commonly used for 4-port adapters does not work properly with many versions of AmigaOS, including AmigaOS 3.2. A good alternative is the *AtapiMagic* software available on Aminet (download: www.aminet.net/package/driver/media/AtapiMagic).

With SCSI 2, you must also pay attention to the correct polarity! Good SCSI cables are protected against polarity reversal, but there is no guarantee for this. However, UW SCSI or SCSI 3 cables can only be connected in one way. **Caution:** Damage to the hardware is possible if the polarity is incorrect!

For SCSI, be sure to set the jumper on each device to the appropriate unit number. Be sure to omit unit number 7, as this is usually used by the controller. A good approach is to jumper the system drive to unit 0, and then all other disks and CD/DVD drives consecutively thereafter.

With SCSI, and especially UW-SCSI, pay attention to the termination at both ends of the SCSI bus. It is recommended that you use active terminators, as these send the data back.

The widely used SCSI controllers A2091 and A590 are limited by default to a maximum volume size of 4 gigabytes. We recommend either activating *SCSI Direct* for the file system or using the *GuruROM* update for these controllers to be able to use partitions larger than 4 GB. Information on direct SCSI access and drives and partitions larger than 4 GB can be found in the *Partition settings* section.

Starting HDToolBox

New devices, such as a hard disk, SSD, CF card or partitionable HDF file in an emulation environment, do not have an RDB partition table by default. Use HDToolBox to create one.

On a running system, you will find HDToolBox inside the *Tools* drawer on your system drive. To run it during the installation process instead, however, open the *AmigaOS3.2CD*, and open the *Install* drawer. Click *CopyToRAMandRun_HDToolBox* to copy the program to the RAM Disk and run it directly from there.

After starting HDToolBox, a new window with the cumbersome name *Hard Drive Preparation, Partitioning and Formatting* will open. The interface will be in English even if AmigaOS 3.2 has been fully installed with support for another language. The upper part of the window contains a list of detected and accessible drives in a section called *Hard Disk Drives in System*.

If this list is empty, the connected drive is connected to a controller with a different driver than the *scsi.device*. On an Amiga 3000 or Amiga 4000T, this is responsible for the built-in SCSI controller, and on an Amiga 4000 (D) it is responsible for the built-in IDE controller. Other controllers use different drivers. The driver software of some controllers, such as the FastATA controllers from Elbox, also include their driver under the name *scsi.device*. Other manufacturers might use different names. Consult the instructions for your controller to find out what the driver is called.

A small selection of controllers is shown in the following table, *A variety of device drivers*. A good starting point for your own research is the *Amiga Hardware Database* website (https://amiga.resource.cx). In some cases, there are even hardware drivers available for download.

A variety of device drivers

Controller	Drivers
Apollo V4 standalone CF card	2nd.scsi.device
Blizzard SCSI Kit	1230scsi.device, 2060scsi.device
CyberStorm Mk 2SCSI	cybscsi.device
CyberStorm PPC UWSCSI	cybppc.device
Elbox FastATA 4000 / ZIV	scsi.device
Fastlane Z3	z3scsi.device
GVP turbo cards with SCSI controller	gvpscsi.device
GVP turbo cards with IDE controller	gvpat.device
Terrible Fire 534, 1230, 1260	ide.device or ehide.device
WarpEngine 040	warpscsi.device
WinUAE, FS-UAE, ...	uaehf.device

INFO **Unique to CyberStorm PPC UWSCSI**

For the CyberStorm PPC UWSCSI controller, use the partitioning tool supplied with the controller. You can find more information on this in the section *Steps to set up a new device* on page 183. Please also read the manufacturer's instructions.

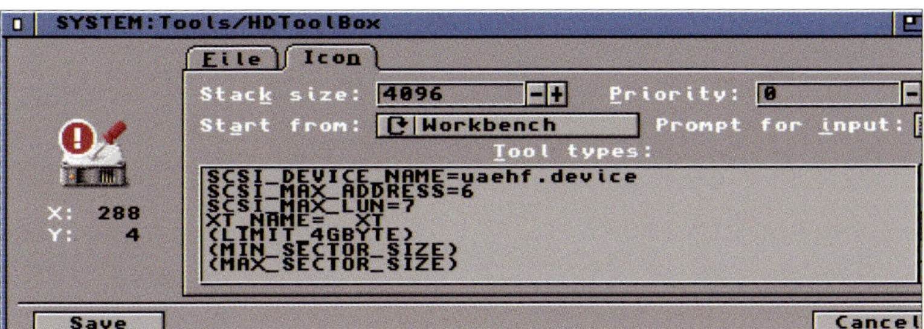

A suitable setting for emulators such as FS-UAE and WinUAE

Enter the name you have determined for the driver in the icon properties for the *HDToolBox* icon under SCSI_DEVICE_NAME. The default setting here is *scsi.device*. Alternatively, start HDToolBox from the command line directly with the driver name, e.g. `HDToolBox uaehf.device`. Remember that HDToolBox is located in the RAM Disk during installation after clicking on *CopyToRAMandRun_HDToolBox*. For SCSI controllers, use the icon properties SCSI_MAX_ADDRESS to set the SCSI *unit* up to which the program will scan. This way, you can exclude optical drives with higher unit numbers or reach the higher unit numbers for *Ultra Wide SCSI* – or simply reduce the search time for drives by limiting it to the highest unit number used.

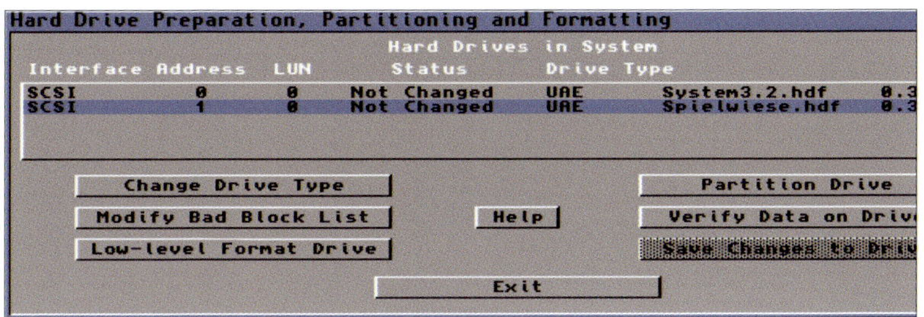

HDToolBox with two FS-UAE drives

If the driver name is correct, the devices connected to the controller should appear in the hard drives list when HDToolBox is launched. Under *Interface* it should say SCSI, unless you have an ancient XT drive. This is followed by the *Address* and *LUN* number, the *Status* and the *Drive Type*. The address will be the *unit* number for SCSI, and usually either `0` for master or `1` for slave in the case of IDE. The *LUN* or *Logical Unit Number* specifies the logical unit for drives with several *logical units*. This can apply to CD changers, for example, but is not usually relevant for hard drives. The *Device Type* provides information about the manufacturer, model name and version number of the firmware. For UAE-based emulators such as FS-UAE or WinUAE, the name of the HDF file can be found there.

Devices that already contain an RDB that you have not modified in the current HDToolBox session will be displayed in the *Status* column as *Not Changed*. Changes to the RDB remain in the main memory of your Amiga until you click on *Save Changes to Drive*. The new device should appear under *Status* as *Unknown*. However, it may also be an optical or tape drive.

Setting up an RDB

Launch HDToolBox as described in the previous section *Starting HDToolBox*. Select a device that HDToolBox does not yet recognize properly. The new device should appear in the device table under *Status* as *Unknown*. Not every drive shown as *Unknown* has to be a hard drive – it can also be an optical drive or tape drive. If in doubt, try all drives marked as *Unknown*. However, only save changes if you are sure you have selected the correct drive.

When HDToolBox is started after a new drive has been connected, the following message may be displayed: *Drives have been added or removed from the system*. The tool wants to write the change to an existing drive. For example, if a drive with unit number 2 is added, HDToolBox wants to write the information to the drive with unit number 1. For such a drive, the *Status* column will then show *Changed*. Select such a drive and click the button *Save Changes to Drive*. The same can happen when removing a drive.

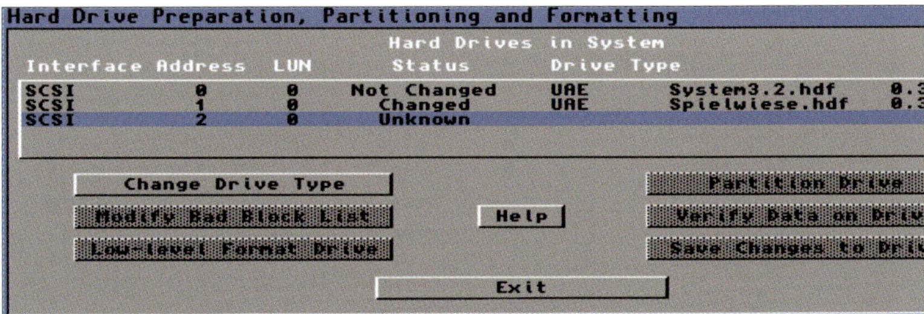

A new drive in FS-UAE will initially be displayed with the "Unknown" status.

Select the new drive with the *Unknown* status. For devices that HDToolBox does not "recognize", the tool will only let you click on *Change Drive Type*. In this case, a list of device types will appear under the heading *Select a Drive Type* that is typically empty. There may be a suitable definition for your device here. However, it usually makes sense to create a new device type with *Define New...* and read out the configuration. To do this, first click on *Define New...* and then on *Read Configuration* in the new *Define a New Drive Type* window. The program should fill in the entry fields with suitable values. If desired, adjust the manufacturer name in *Manufacturers Name* and the device name in *Drive Name*. They will appear later in the drive list. As a rule, the default values will already be correct.

You do not need to worry about how the *cylinders*, *heads* and *blocks per track* or *per cylinder* behave. The only important thing is that the recognized capacity shown under *Size* matches the capacity of the drive.

Nowadays, the values given for cylinders, heads and blocks per track usually have nothing to do with reality. HDToolBox calculates a geometry that fits the capacity of the drive and leaves enough flexibility for partitioning, because a partition must always start at the beginning of a cylinder.

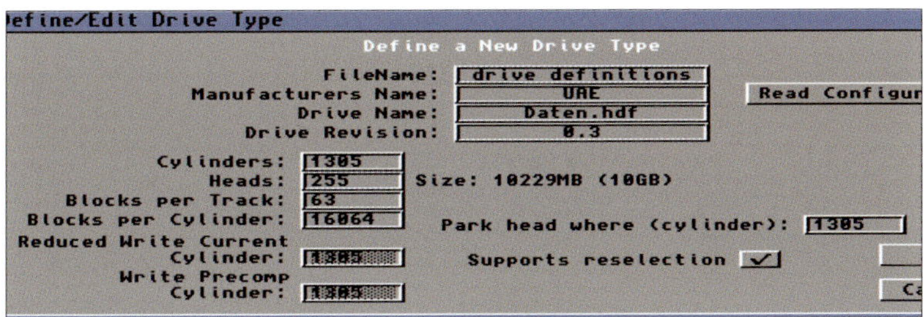

A suitable drive type for a new drive in FS-UAE, here seen in the "Define/Edit Drive Type" subwindow.

If the results are correct, click *Ok* and *Ok* again in the previous window. The program will now display the drive as *Changed* under *Status* in the HDToolBox window. Click *Save Changes to Drive* to save the changes. You can now partition the device.

If the results are not correct, check that you have selected the right device. If not, exit the program as a precaution to avoid inadvertently saving the changes for the wrong device.

Partitioning a drive

To partition a device, select it in the device list and then click on *Partition Drive*. If HDToolBox does not display the drive you want, it may be connected to a different controller that uses a different driver. In this case, read the section *Starting HDToolBox*. If *Unknown* appears in the *Status* column, it means that no RDB has been set up for the device. Read the previous section *Setting up an RDB*.

Typically, after you have set up a new drive, you now simply need to click on *Save Changes to Drive* and then *Save Changes to Drive* in the *Hard Drives in System* display. After a restart, you will receive two or more partitions of the same size with Fast File System in international mode as the DOS type by default, which you can format directly. Their device names will be *DH0:*, *DH1:* etc. with the first letter of the manufacturer's name of the device in front. In the emulation environment, this will be, for example, a *U* for *UAE*. However, even in this case, it makes sense to enter a higher number of file system buffers in *Partitioning Drive* mode by clicking *Advanced Options* under *Buffers* and then pressing the Enter key.

The block size of 4 KB used in a typical HDToolBox setup is not useful in all cases, especially with a file system that accommodates smaller files, such as those of AmigaOS 3.2. You will find specific recommendations on this below and in section 2.12 on *File systems*.

You may therefore want to make further adjustments. To do so, select the desired drive and click on *Partition Drive*. The program will display the new *Partitioning Drive* window with an overview of the defined partitions.

Standard partitioning of the HDToolBox for a 10 GB drive

For some controllers, you may even need to adjust specific values! Potential modifications may include changing the size of a partition, creating a partition, deleting a partition, changing the settings for a partition, changing the file systems for a partition via DOS type, changing the file system settings and loading a file system from a third-party manufacturer into the RDB.

The following is a basic guide to the partitioning interface in HDToolBox, followed by a section for each of these customizations. HDToolBox initially only carries out all changes in the main memory. Only when you click on *Save Changes to Drive* in the parent window will the changes be saved to the drive. So make sure that you do not simply quit the program with *Exit* if there are still changes to a drive that you want to save.

The *Partitioning Drive* window shows the SCSI address and the LUN, followed by a graphical view of the drive's memory and its partitions. The area for the current partition is filled in black, while the area for all other partitions is shaded in black and white. The program marks any free area with the standard grey background color of the window. On the left it says *Cyl 0*, while on the right it shows the number of cylinders on the drive. These days, this value usually has nothing to do with reality. HDToolBox calculates a geometry that fits the capacity of the drive and leaves enough flexibility for partitioning. Partitions on AmigaOS must always start at the beginning of a cylinder. At the end of the area for the selected partition you will see a blue triangle by default, which is used to change the size of a partition. Left-click and hold to drag the partition to the desired size.

Below this section are four buttons: deleting a partition *(Delete Partition)*, creating a new partition *(New Partition)*, reverting to the default partitioning *(Default Setup)* and showing a short guide *(Help)*.

Underneath this setting, by default, HDToolBox shows a text gadget for the *Partition Device Name*. The information under *Bootable* also indicates whether the partition is bootable. To the right of this is the file system that is set with the DOS type – in standard partitioning this will be *International (FFS)*, i.e. *Fast File System* with support for umlauts. Press *Ok* to apply changes to the partitioning and *Cancel* to discard them. You must also save any changes you have made in the parent window with *Save Changes to Drive*. Once you have saved the changes, a restart is required for AmigaOS to apply the changes.

All other functions, such as advanced options for the partition and the option to set the DOS type and load additional file systems into the RDB, can be accessed by clicking on the field next to *Advanced Options*. This includes the important setting for the number of file system buffers under *Buffers*.

Important: Always press the Enter key after making a change in a input gadget within HDToolBox. Otherwise, in some cases, the program will not adopt the change. For example, the program will register a change to the partition's device name without pressing Enter, but not an adjustment to the number of buffers!

The Advanced Options offer a much wider range of settings.

INFO **Beware of data loss!**
Any data that already exists on a partition will become inaccessible if you change its position or size! This can also be caused by deleting a partition. If you change the partitioning of a drive that is already partitioned, be careful not to make any data inaccessible that you still want to access!

Recommendations for partitioning

It is almost impossible to give a specific recommendation for all application scenarios. However, we would like to give you a few pointers. Think about which types of data you want to separate. It is common to set up one partition for the system and a separate partition for everything else. AmigaOS 3.2 occupies less than 20 MB after installation on a Fast File System with a block size of 2 KB. Of course, the programs you install will occupy space too. Accordingly, a simple partitioning for a small hard drive with 4 GB could look like this, for example:

1. partition *DH0*, file system name *System*,
   FFS with 2048 byte block size, 1 GB
2. partition *DH1*, file system name *Work*,
   FFS with 2048 byte block size, long file names, 3 GB

If you have a larger disk, just make the second partition a bit larger. If you want to store large files, choose a block size of 4096 bytes.

Alternative the drive could be partitioned according to system, programs and data, with an optional partition for large files and a small partition for a copy of the AmigaOS 3.2 CD, update archives and possibly important drivers like Picasso96 as an emergency system. Even if the system and programs are separated, additional files will end up on the system drive when applications are installed, including libraries, device drivers or fonts. For a 40 GB device, the partitioning might look like this:

1. partition *OS*, file system name *System*,
   FFS with 2048 byte block size, 500 MB
2. partition *INSTALL*, file system name *AmigaOS3.2CD*,
   FFS with 1024 byte block size, 200 MB
3. partition *PRG*, file system name *Programs*,
   FFS with 2048 byte block size, 2 GB
4. partition *DAT*, file system name *Data*,
   FFS with 4096 byte block size, 5 GB
5. partition *DAT2*, file system name *Data2*,
   SFS, possibly with DOS type *SFS\02*, remaining GB

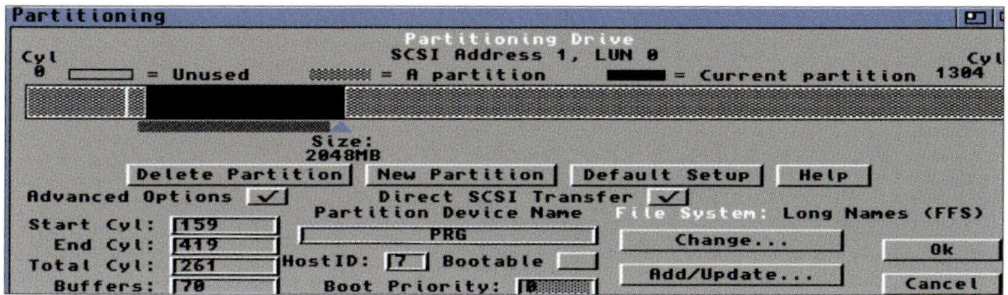

An example of a 10 GB drive in FS-UAE with system, emergency system, programs in FFS and data in SFS

As a general rule, you should only create a partition as large as you actually need it to be. As such, you could even have areas on your hard drive that are unpartitioned and unformatted!

If you have an extra hard drive with 80 GB just for data, for example, a single partition with *SFS 2* may be enough. Or you could create one partition for documents, one for music and one for large files. As long as you observe the restrictions of the file system, there are few limits to your creativity.

In an emulation environment like FS-UAE or WinUAE, you have the added benefit of being able to store data directly on the disk of the host system in a dedicated directory structure, bypassing the Amiga file system.

We highly recommend reading the following sections and the section *File Systems* (from page 101) to gain a comprehensive understanding of the available options and recommended settings.

TIP **Storing data on the host system**
In an emulation environment, host system directories are suitable for storing larger amounts of data. Read more about this in the introduction to the section *Partitioning with HDToolBox*. This allows you to circumvent the limitations of Amiga file systems previously available for AmigaOS 3.2. It also makes it easier to exchange files. The directories shared in the emulated Amiga from the host file system are accessible on the host system, for example via the file manager. Files for an AmigaOS 3.2 installation can even be stored directly in a directory on the host system. AmigaOS file system attributes that cannot be written directly to the host file system by an emulator such as FS-UAE or WinUAE due to incompatibility are stored in files with the **.uaem* name extension. Do not delete these files on the host system if you want to keep the AmigaOS file system attributes! Data stored in a hard disk file will only appear on the host system as a hardfile, which is useful for keeping an overview. Up to version 3.1.66, you can only define four drives via the FS-UAE interface. You can add more drives by editing the configuration file.

Creating a new partition

To create a new partition, you need free space on a drive. By default, HDToolBox will fill the free space on a new drive with two or more partitions of the same size. Therefore, you will need to delete or reduce the size of a partition before creating a new one.

Attention: First, click on *New Partition* and *only then* on an area with free space. Otherwise, HDToolBox may move an existing partition within the free space and, if you apply and save the changes, make the data on it inaccessible! If you clicked on an empty area without initiating *New Partition* first, don't worry! Just move the partition back to its original location. If you want to be absolutely sure, click *Cancel* to discard the changes.

By default, HDToolBox will use the entire free area for the new partition. If necessary, make the partition smaller by dragging the blue triangle. For more information, see *Changing the size of a partition*. Finally, under *Partition Device Name*, change the device name for the new partition, which HDToolBox has named *CHANGE_ME*. If necessary, adjust other settings, in particular the file system to be used, the number of buffers, and the block size for Fast File System. Enable direct SCSI access if required, too. See sections *Changing partition settings* (page 196) and *Changing file system settings* (page 198).

In a standard setup, HDToolBox uses *DH0:*, *DH1:* etc. with the first letter of the manufacturer's name of the device as a prefix. In an emulation environment, this will be e.g. a *U* for *UAE*. It is also common to simply use *DH0:*, *DH1:* etc. without a prefix. You can use any individual name with up to 30 characters. HDToolBox allows you to enter 31 characters, but not all parts of AmigaOS seem to support this. At least, when booting, a window will appear asking you to insert the corresponding drive.

In any case, long names tend to be rather unwieldy. Descriptive names such as *OS:* for the operating system, *PRG:* for programs, *DAT:* for data, *WRK:* for work files or *PLY:* for entertainment software are certainly a more interesting alternative to the standard names. At least with AmigaOS you have this luxury, whereas with Windows you have to make do with C:, D:, etc. Lame!

Positioning a partition

Left-click in the area for a partition, hold down the button and drag the partition to the desired position. Alternatively, click in the free area to the left or right of the partition to adjust the position more precisely.

If you want to determine the exact position of a partition, open the advanced options under *Advanced Options* and change the value in *Start Cyl*. Be sure to confirm with Enter so that HDToolBox accepts the change!

Attention: Changing the position of a partition makes any data on it inaccessible!

Changing the partition size

Once you have selected your partition, you will see the standard blue triangle at the end of the area. This is your gateway to changing the size of your partition. Click and hold the left mouse button on it to drag the partition to the desired size.

Alternatively, open the extended options under *Advanced Options* and change the value for the number of cylinders under *Total Cyl*. Or change the value for the last cylinder of the partition under *End Cyl*. In both cases, press Enter afterwards so that the program accepts the changes. HDToolBox will automatically adjust the other value.

INFO **Beware of data loss!**
Changing the partition size can make any the on it inaccessible! This also applies to enlarging a partition! If you want to enlarge a partition that contains data, you must first back up the data, reformat the partition and then copy the data back again. Be smart!

Deleting a partition

Select the desired partition and then click *Delete Partition* to remove it. Make sure you select the correct partition. The same applies here as before: deleting a partition makes any data on it inaccessible! (We can't stress this enough!)

Once you have made the changes, save them and restart your Amiga.

Changing the settings of a partition

Select the desired partition and edit the partition name under *Partition Device Name*. Read the section on *Creating a new partition* for tips on choosing useful names. Then click on *Advanced Options*, if you have not already done so, to display them.

For controllers from 1990 onwards, tick the box for *Direct SCSI Transfer* to enable direct SCSI access, unless your controller is a *Commodore A2090* or the controller on the *CyberStorm Mk3* or *PPC* turbo cards from phase5. For a long time, the only hard drives available for the Amiga were smaller than 4 gigabytes. Amiga drivers from this period did not support larger hard drives because they were limited to 32-bit addressing. With direct SCSI access, AmigaOS bypasses the 64-bit standards NSD and TD64 for *TD_READ/TD_WRITE* for access beyond the 4-gigabyte limit after checking the capabilities of the drive. For controllers that cope well with this,

AmigaOS bypasses weaknesses in the implementation of these standards. For the controllers on the CyberStorm Mk3 or PPC accelerator cards, it is recommended to use the manufacturer's own tools. See the section *Steps to set up a new device* (from page 183).

To make a partition bootable, make sure you tick the *Bootable* box. If necessary, change the *Boot Priority:* by default, the first floppy drive has a priority of 5, all others have priority the `-10`. The default value for partitions is `0`. A higher value means a higher priority. If you select a value above 5, AmigaOS will no longer boot from floppy disk by default. You can of course still select a floppy drive in the boot menu. See the section about the *Amiga boot menu* in the *Power User* chapter. The default value is suitable for systems with only one bootable partition. If you have more than one bootable partition, simply give the preferred partition priority 1, for example.

Press the Enter key after changing the value. Otherwise, HDToolBox will not apply the change.

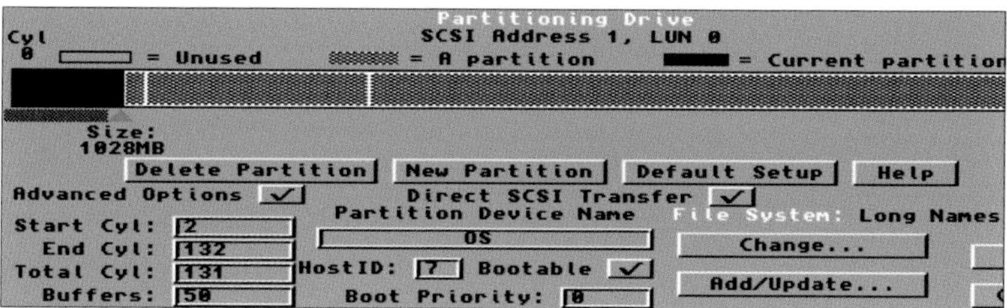

Partition settings for a bootable Fast File System under AmigaOS 3.2

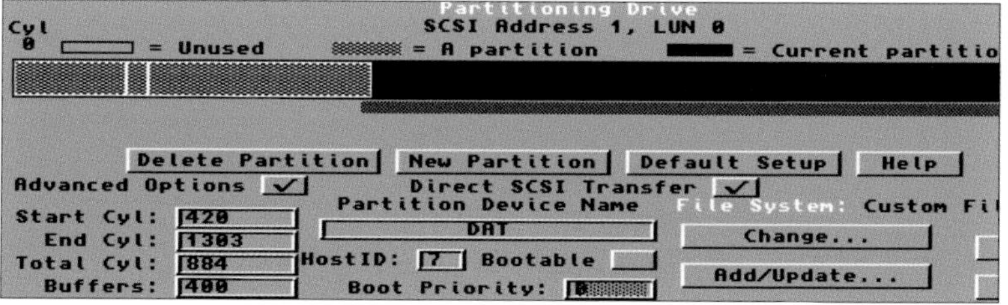

Partition settings for a Smart File System for data files storage

Recommended number of file system buffers

Under *Buffers*, set the number of file system buffers. The default value of 30 is usually too low, especially for the Smart File System and the Professional File System. For the Fast File System, the value may be appropriate depending on the block size. The memory used is calculated by multiplying the number of buffers by the block size of the file system. The following table provides a guide. The upper limit can be exceeded for Amigas with a lot of memory. Please note that the value only applies to this partition – other partitions are added to the main memory consumption! With the Fast File System, this does not bring any major performance gains, as this file system does not necessarily use the buffers to buffer metadata. See also the section *File systems* (page 101) in the *Basics* chapter. Information on the block size can be found in the following section *Changing file system settings*.

File system	Block size	Recommended number of buffers
FFS	512 bytes	50-100
FFS	1024 bytes	30-100
FFS	2048 bytes	30-70
FFS	4096 bytes	30-50
SFS	512 bytes	100-1000
PFS	512 bytes	70-500

Changing file system settings

Select the desired partition and open the extended options by clicking next to *Advanced Options*, if you have not already done so. Click on *Change...* to see the settings for the file system. Select the desired file system under *File System*. In addition to the *Fast File System*, which is the default file system, you will find only *Custom Filesystem* and *UNI\01*. The latter is a partition for use with a Unix-like operating system such as Amiga Unix. If you would prefer to use the Professional File System, for example, read the following section, *Managing file systems*.

INFO **Changing file systems**

If you change the file system at this point from Fast File System to Smart File System or Professional File System or vice versa, the data stored on the partition will become inaccessible. You must reformat the partition to be able to use it with the new file system.

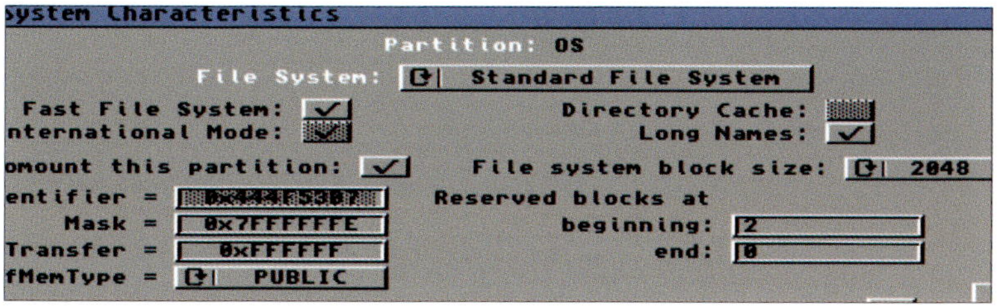

File system settings for a bootable Fast File System under AmigaOS 3.2

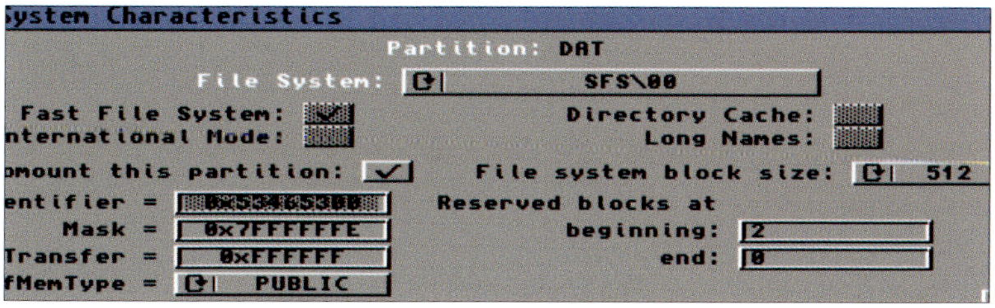

File system settings for a Smart File System for data file storage

To use the Fast File System, make sure the *Fast File System* option is enabled. Otherwise you will get the old Amiga standard file system with checksums, which is no longer recommended for hard disks in particular and is now known as the *Old File System (OFS)*.

To support umlauts, the *International Mode* is useful. With these two options, it is compatible with older AmigaOS versions down to AmigaOS 1.3. The *Directory Cache* introduced with AmigaOS 3.1 is not very useful as it slows down other accesses.

If you want to use file and directory names longer than 31 characters, enable *Long Names*. Names can then be up to 107 characters long. Note that this does not work with AmigaOS versions lower than 3.1.4. AmigaOS 4 also supports long file names. The Linux driver for the Amiga Fast File System, *affs*, does not yet support long names. HDToolBox automatically updates the corresponding DOS type for *Identifier*. The Smart File System, Professional File System and, from AmigaOS version 3.1.4 upwards, CrossDOS support long file names with up to 107 characters.

For DOS types and filename lengths, see also the section *File systems* in the chapter *Basics*.

TIP **Character length in AmigaOS**

The Amiga Workbench limits the length of file names to 25 characters by default. Together with *.info* as the file extension for the icon, this results in 30 characters. If you want to use longer names, launch the *Workbench Preferences* and enter the desired maximum length in the *Icons* group under *Maximum Filename Length*, e.g. 101 characters if you want to use up to 106 characters. If you enter 102 characters for up to 107 characters, the prefs editor will automatically fix this to 101 characters.

Select a suitable block size for the file system used under *File system block size*. For a Fast File System on hard disks, CF/SD cards or USB sticks, i.e. everything else than floppy disks, a block size of 1 to 4 KB makes sense. HDToolBox 47.10 in AmigaOS 3.2 already uses 4096 bytes for standard partitioning. This value is too high for file systems that tend to store smaller files. This includes the file system on which you install AmigaOS 3.2. A block size of 1 or 2 KB is also sufficient here. For Smart File System (SFS) and Professional File System (PFS) use 512 bytes instead. Larger block sizes do not improve performance, they just waste space. More details on this can be found in the *File systems* section (2.12) in the *Basics* chapter.

Caution: Changing the block size for an existing file system makes the data on it inaccessible (yes, we said that already – sorry for repeating it). You must reformat the partition in order to be able to use the new block size.

The values in *Mask* and *MaxTransfer* are patches for controllers and mass storage devices from the late 1980s. The first SCSI and XT controllers to support the RDB standard came out in 1988. The A2091 could be installed in the Amiga 2000, while the A590 could be connected to the A500. They could access memory directly, but only for the address space of the 68000 processor in the Amiga 500 and 2000, i.e. 24 instead of 32 bits. The value in *MaxTransfer* defines the amount of data that the driver can transfer in one DMA access. The value in *Mask* is a bit mask that defines which memory is accessible for the DMA transfers. *BufMemType* also serves this purpose. Use *24BITDMA* for the A2091 and A590.

For controllers from Commodore and Great Valley Products (GVP), no adjustments to *MaxTransfer* and *Mask* are required for AmigaOS 3.2. Other controllers from 1990 onwards should also be able to cope with the standard values. For older controllers in particular, please read the controller's original manual. A safe value for *MaxTransfer* is 0×1FE00.

Caution: If the MaxTransfer value is too high for the controller, errors may occur during data transfer. Your saved data may contain errors without being notified by an error message.

Managing file systems

Select any partition and click next to the *Advanced Options* to open its window, if you have not already done so. Click on *Add/ Update...* to switch to the *File System Maintenance* window, the file system administration center.

You will be presented with a list of file systems. The DOS type is in the *Identifier* column, the version is in the *Version* column, the size of the file system driver is in the *Size* column, and its name is in the *File System Name* column.

International (FFS) version 47.4 is usually shown there. The DOS type is specified as *DOS\03* or 0x444F5303. However, the file system is also used for DOS types *DOS\01* to *DOS\07*, for example for DOS types that support long file names.

If you want to use SFS or PFS, install the files for the file system according to the instructions in the section *File systems* in the chapter *Basics*, and referring to the manual of the file system.

To add a file system, click *Add New File System*. Select the *Smart File System* file for SFS or the *pfs3aio* file for PFS. Once installation is complete, you will find the file systems in the *L* directory of the system drive. You can also access this directory via the *L:* assignment.

In the next step, check the version number. For the Smart File System, this will be at least version 1 revision 277, i.e. 1.277. For the Professional File System, this will be at least version 19 revision 2, i.e. 19.2. For CrossDOS, this will be version 45 revision 39, i.e. 45.39. Do not change the version numbers! If the version numbers do not match, check whether the correct version of the file system is actually installed.

Under *Enter DosType for File System*, enter 0×53465300 or *SFS\0* as the DOS type for the Smart File System. Click *OK* to add the file system. If you would like to use files larger than 4 gigabytes minus 2 bytes and partitions larger than 128 gigabytes, add the file system again with the DOS type 0x53465302. However, be sure to read the notes in section 2.12 on *File systems* in the *Basics* chapter. There is currently no data recovery tool for this DOS type so proceed with caution!

For the Professional File System (PFS) with direct SCSI access, enter 0x50445303 or *PDS\03* as the DOS type instead.

Use *Update File System* to update an existing file system. The procedure is the same. The DOS type remains the same, though, which makes sense. This option is useful for the Fast File System if the version in the Kickstart ROM is out of date. In this case, select the file *Fast File System*.

Click *Delete File System* to get rid of a file system.

Caution: Do not remove a file system that you are still using. Otherwise you may make the data on it inaccessible.

ystem Maintenance

File Systems on SCSI Address 1, LUN 0

Identifier	Version	Size	File System Name
0x50445303	19.2	59120	Custom File System
0x53465302	1.277	98252	Custom File System
0x53465300	1.277	98252	Custom File System
0x444F5303	47.4	30532	International (FFS)

d New File System... | Delete File System | Update File

An RDB with FFS, SFS and PFS

Formatting

Formatting is the process that creates the file system set via the DOS type on the drive and uses the *Format* tool. Restart your Amiga after partitioning. Select the icon representing the partition you want to format on the Workbench. Select *Format disk* from the *Icons* menu. Alternatively, open the *System* drawer and double-click on the *Format* program. In the latter case, a list will appears showing all detected drives. These are either partitions or, in the case of floppy disks and non-partitioned SD cards or USB sticks, entire drives. To use *Format* as a Shell command, see chapter 5 on the *Shell*.

Enter the name for the file system. AmigaOS will show this name on the Workbench and in requester windows. For example, *DF0* is the name of the floppy drive, and *Pictures* is the name of the inserted floppy disk. In the case of a partition, *DAT* is the name of the partition and *Data* is the name of the file system.

For the *Fast File System*, the *Format* tool already sets the options according to the DOS type set for the partition, e.g. *Fast File System* and *International Mode* for *DOS\3*, and *Long*

File Names for *DOS\7*. If you do not want to create a *recycle* bin, remove the tick next to *Put Trashcan*. The *Directory Cache* is generally not useful. See section 2.12 on *File systems*. Click on *Quick Format* to format the drive. Performing a slow format by clicking on *Format* is not necessary with reasonably modern hard drives, as these automatically sort out faulty blocks. This method also takes considerably longer depending on the drive's size.

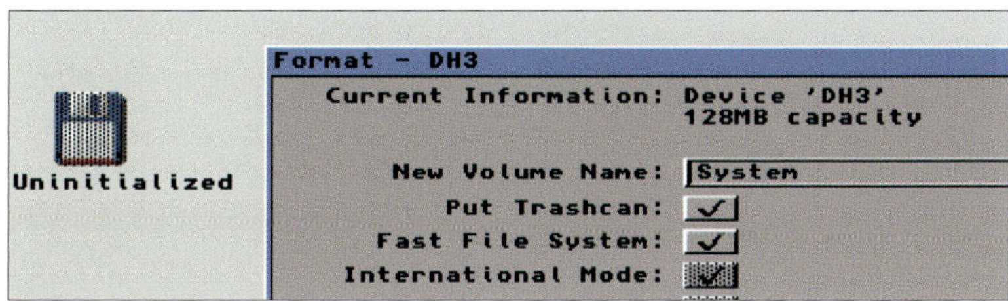

Formatting a Fast File System prior to installing OS 3.2

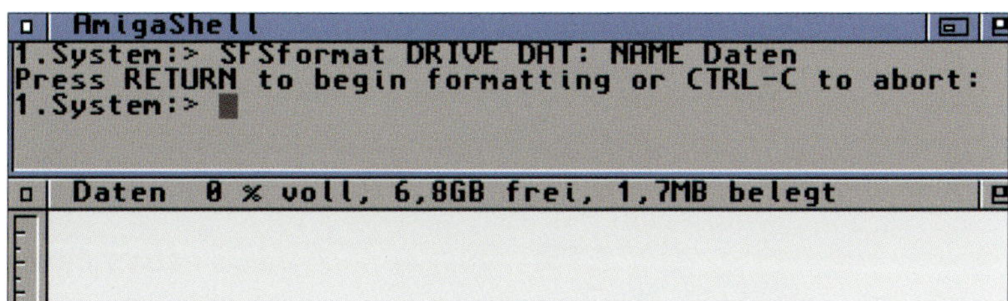

Formatting a Smart File System for data storage

The procedure for using the *Professional File System* is quite similar. However, being a different file system, all options apart from *Put Trashcan* are missing here. If required, you can enable support for *Long File Names* after formatting by using the `SetFnSize` command. Alternatively, you can use the `PFSFormat` command to specify the maximum filename length and the maximum number of entries in the directory for recently deleted files. The program also supports large partitions. See also the previously mentioned section *File systems* (from page 101).

Drives that use the *Smart File System* can only be formatted with the `SFSformat` command, e.g. with `SFSformat DRIVE DAT: NAME Data`. Optionally, this works with the argument `CASESENSITIVE` to enable case sensitivity and with `NORECYCLED` to disable the directory for recently deleted files. You can find information on this in the *File systems* section. It is advisable not to use the `CASESENSITIVE` option for file systems containing the operating system or programs, as a discrepancy in upper and lower case can result in a multitude of errors.

Once you have finished formatting, you can change the icon for the new drive as you wish. By default, the icon will be the symbol for a floppy disk, which is not really suitable for partitions. Select the icon and choose *Information* from the *Icons* menu. Then drag the icon that you like from the Workbench into the area with the icon in the information window and save the change. In this window you can also find out which device driver – *Device* – and which DOS type – *Handler* – is being used.

Installing AmigaOS or copying data

Once the partitions have been set up and formatted, the device is ready for the installation of AmigaOS and programs, and/or the copying of data. For the installation of AmigaOS, read the chapter *Installation*.

To copy your data, use the Workbench or the `Copy` command, if necessary with the arguments `ALL` and `CLONE`. You can learn how to use the command in the *Basics* and *Shell* chapters. For example:

```
Copy Old-Files: Files: ALL CLONE BUF=500
```

A file manager such as *Directory Opus*, or a tool that mirrors directory trees such as *BackUp* (download: www.aminet.net/package/disk/bakup/BackUp), is also well suited for this.

Saving and restoring the RDB

Unlike the HDToolBox from AmigaOS 3.9, the HDToolBox for AmigaOS 3.2 does not offer the function for saving and restoring the RDB. Don't worry, you can use the *ReadRDB* command (download: www.aminet.net/package/disk/misc/ReadRDB). The command `ReadRDB device=scsi.device UNIT=1 FILE SYS:RDB_scsi.device_0` will read the RDB from the first IDE drive of an Amiga 4000, for example. With the command `ReadRDB DEVICE=SCSI.device UNIT=1 FILE SYS:RDB_scsi.device_0 WRITE` you can write it back.

Recommendation: It is a good idea to backup the RDB file to a different drive than the drive from which the RDB originates!

We recommend you first try backing up and restoring with a test drive to get a feel for how the process works, e.g. in FS-UAE or WinUAE using a test HDF file.

TIP **Beware of data loss!**
Restoring an RDB is a potentially dangerous operation. Make sure you restore the correct RDB for the drive in question! This applies if you have connected the drive to another controller in the meantime. The backed up RDB must also be up-to-date. For example, if you have added a partition since making the backup and want to import the RDB from a file that does not yet contain the information for this partition, the data on the partition will no longer be accessible! Make sure you use a name that best describes the relation of the drive and RDB.

```
AmigaShell
1.System:> ReadRDB DEVICE=uaehf.device UNIT=1 FILE SYS:RDB_uaehf.device_1.bak
   Device to access: uaehf.device, unit: 1
   Disk vendor, product & revision : UAE      System3.2-Neu.h  0.3
   Cylinders................1305   Blocks per cylinder.......16064
   Sectors per track..........63   Bytes per block.............512
   Heads.....................255   Interleave....................1
   Low cylinder................2   High cylinder..............1304
   Size in megabytes.......10236
   Reselection is ENABLED.
   No disks exist to be configured after this one on this controller.
   No LUNs exist to be configured greater than this one at this SCSI Target ID.
   No Target IDs exist to be configured greater than this one on this SCSI bus.
   Drive does NOT support SCSI synchronous mode.
   Saved RDB to file SYS:RDB_uaehf.device_1.bak.
1.System:>
```

```
AmigaShell
1.System:> ReadRDB DEVICE=uaehf.device UNIT=1 FILE SYS:RDB_uaehf.device_1.bak WRITE
   Device to access: uaehf.device, unit: 1
   File SYS:RDB_uaehf.device_1.bak contains the following information :
   Disk vendor, product & revision : UAE      System3.2-Neu.h  0.3
   Cylinders................1305   Blocks per cylinder.......16064
   Sectors per track..........63   Bytes per block.............512
   Heads.....................255   Interleave....................1
   Low cylinder................2   High cylinder..............1304
   Size in megabytes.......10236
   Reselection is ENABLED.
   No disks exist to be configured after this one on this controller.
   No LUNs exist to be configured greater than this one at this SCSI Target ID.
   No Target IDs exist to be configured greater than this one on this SCSI bus.
   Drive does NOT support SCSI synchronous mode.

   WARNING: Going to overwrite the RDB of device uaehf.device,
   unit 1, with file SYS:RDB_uaehf.device_1.bak that contains the above information.
   IS IT WHAT YOU REALLY WANT TO DO (y/n) ? y
   Written file SYS:RDB_uaehf.device_1.bak to RDB.

1.System:>
```

Saving an RDB with ReadRDB (top) and restoring it (bottom)

IconEdit (icon editor)

IconEdit is a dream come true for those who like to customize the appearance of their Workbench, allowing you to create new icons and modify existing ones.

Function

The tiny *IconEdit* program, located in the *Tools* drawer, allows you to create your own icons from scratch or edit existing icons according to your own wishes. In this way, you can customize the Workbench to suit your personal preferences.

After starting *IconEdit*, the program window opens and displays the standard Workbench icon for programs, known as the *default icon*, in a drawing area.

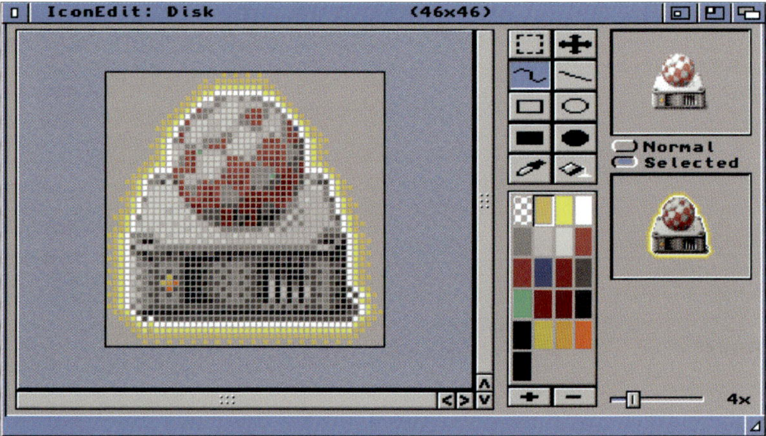

IconEdit showing an icon in the drawingboard (left), editing tools (center) and how the icon looks in Normal and Selected mode (right).

Interface

The IconEdit window is divided into three sections: on the left-hand side you will see the *drawing area* in which the icon to be edited can also be enlarged to make pixel work easier. This is the where you can create new icons and edit existing icons.

On the right is a preview of the icon in its two states: normal and selected. The version to be edited can be switched between using the *Normal/Selected* radio buttons. At the bottom right, the zoom factor inside the drawing area can be adjusted using the slider. You can change it continuously from 1x to 16x.

The color selection area and various drawing tools and aids such as freehand drawing, circles or rectangles, lines and a fill function are located in the middle section of the window. The functions of each of these eight tools will be explained below.

Drawing area

The *drawing area* on the left-hand side is the actual workspace. You can modify the icon displayed here using tools such as freehand drawing with the available colors, or create a completely new icon and then save it. You can also zoom in and out.

Color selector

The colors that are available to use when drawing an icon are displayed in the *color selector* in the center. The number of colors availablc depends on the active screen mode. Eight colors are visible by default, and even more in colorful mode. Try switching the editing mode back and forth between *classic* and *colorful* using `[R-Amiga]+[1]` and `[R-Amiga]+[3]` (more on this later).

Active colors are highlighted when selected. The top left field in the color selection box with the checkerboard pattern is for applying transparency. To test this, place a pixel on the drawing area by pressing the left mouse button with the active color.

Under the color selection box you will discover two new functions in AmigaOS 3.2: with + you can add a new color using a color circle or three color sliders (RGB/HSB); with – you can remove the active color.

Tools

Use the **Marquee** `[M]` tool to select a portion of the drawing area. Press, hold and drag the mouse to the desired position. The selection will be marked with a blue frame and can be cut, copied, pasted and deleted using the common editing functions in the *Edit* menu or via shortcuts (see the *Edit menu* section for details).

The **Move** `[V]` tool can be used to move the entire contents of the drawing area or just a selection. Drag the board or the selected area to the desired position (press, hold, move, release).

The **Pen Freehand** `[P]` tool can be used to quickly edit the icon. Select the tool using the mouse or the `[P]` key and click with the left mouse button in the drawing area to make a pixel in the selected color appear at the position of the mouse pointer. Hold down the mouse button and move the pointer in the drawing area to make pixels appear along the course of the pointer. This will not intended for straight lines – rather, for quick edits.

You can easily draw a straight line using the **Line** [L] tool. Click and hold the mouse button in the drawing area to define the length of the line from the starting position. The line will be created when you release the button. Hold [Shift] while dragging the line to force the line to be drawn vertically or horizontally.

You can create rectangles using two tools: **Rectangle** [R] and **Solid rectangular block** [B]. The former draws an outlined rectangle, the latter a filled rectangle. To draw a rectangle, position the mouse pointer in the drawing area and press and drag the object with the left mouse button. The shape will be created square if you hold the [Shift] key while drawing.

The two ellipse tools work in a similar way to the rectangle tools: **Ellipse** [E] and **Solid Elliptical Disk** [D] draw ovals and circles an outline or as a filled object, respectively. The position of the mouse pointer forms the center of the object when you press, hold and drag the left mouse button on the drawing field, to give the object the desired shape and size. The ellipse is created when you release the mouse button. If you hold down the [Shift] key at the same time, the two ellipse tools will form a circle.

The pipette symbol represents the **Color Picker** [I] tool. Click anywhere in the drawing area to identify the color at that position and activate it in the color selection box.

The last tool, in the bottom right, is the **Flood Fill Paint Bucket** [F] and is used to fill enclosed areas with the selected color. This can be a circular or rectangular outline, as well as a hand drawn, closed area. You can create a circle with a yellow outline and red fill in just a few simple steps. This tool makes it possible! Select the desired color and click on the area to be filled. Colored areas can be recolored.

TIP **Zoom function**
Drawing can be made more precise if you zoom in with the mouse wheel while holding down the [Ctrl] key in the drawing area (and then zoom out again). Zooming in takes place at the position of the mouse pointer. When zooming out, the icon is centered.

Classic vs. Colorful

An important aspect of IconEdit is the *editing mode*. In the *Images* menu, under *Currently editing*, you can switch between *Classic* and *Colorful* modes with the two normal and selected states. The icons and color schemes displayed in the IconEdit window will change accordingly. For multi-colored, multi-variant icons, you should select *colorful* mode, which features GlowIcon effects.

Normal vs. Selected look (Highlight menu)

AmigaOS distinguishes between normal and selected icons on the Workbench to make it easier to work with files. The operating system uses icons with two variants for this, in which an icon can only change slightly when switching from *normal* to *selected*, or look completely different. You can change between the current editing variants using the radio button.

The first step in defining the appearance is the *Highlight* menu, which has the *Classic* and *Colorful* submenus for those two editing modes. Use this to define the look of the icon in its selected (highlighted) status, i.e. after a single mouse click.

There are three options to choose from under *Classic* in the *Highlight* menu: *Invert* inverts the colors so that light areas appear dark and dark areas appear light (for example, white to black and black to white). *Backfill* highlights the background when selected. And *Image* shows a modified or completely different icon variant when selecting the icon.

There are two options under *Colorful* in the *Highlight* menu: with *Image*, a glowing outline can be applied to the icon to indicate if it has been selected thanks to the GlowIcon system, or you can apply a completely different image. *Dimmed* is a simple display technique in which the brightness of the icon's colors is automatically reduced from the normal display. Glowing and dimming can also be combined in GlowIcons mode.

Menu functions in IconEdit

IconEdit can be easily operated via its graphical user interface. But under the hood, i.e. in the menu bar, there are many other functions to be discovered in addition to the highlight menu mentioned above.

Project menu

In the *Project* menu, you can create a new icon with *New*, load an existing icon with *Open* or save the file with *Save* or *Save as* under an existing or new name. Close IconEdit with *Quit*.
All system-wide keyboard shortcuts work in IconEdit. When creating and opening a new icon, a requester will ask if you want to save the open icon. Note that *New* does not create an empty icon, but uses a template based on the selected *type*, as follows:

Type menu

You can define the type of the icon to be edited in the *Type* menu. AmigaOS 3.2 distinguishes between five different types of icons. *Disk* includes drive icons and is originally derived from floppy disk, but is used for all drive types such as hard disks or CF cards. *Drawer* includes directory icons. Programs of all kinds, whether tools or games, are stored with the *Tool* icon type. This identifies them as directly executable software on the Workbench. *Project* icons are used for files that have been created with an application. The *Garbage* icon type identifies the AmigaOS *trashcan*, a place where unwanted data finds a temporary home until it is finally deleted.

Edit menu

The *Edit* menu contains standard functions that use the clipboard of AmigaOS. This makes it possible to import content within IconEdit, as well as from a drawing tool.

The command list includes *Cut* (deleting the entire icon or a selection in the drawing area while copying its content to the clipboard), *Copy* (copying the entire icon or a selection to the clipboard), *Paste* (pasting the content in the clipboard into the drawing area) and *Erase* (deleting the selection in the drawing area and filling it with transparency). You can also *select* the entire drawing area with *Select All* and use the *Undo* and *Redo* functions to undo work steps or redo undone ones. Sounds complicated, but it's really simple (and practical)!

Two clip commands are exclusive here. An existing image file can be opened with *Insert Image*. Select the file you want to open with the requester that appears. Place the image in the drawing area and move it using the *Move* tool. With *Save Selection*, the content of the clipboard, which was previously filled with the *Cut* or *Copy* function, can be saved as an image file. The storage location is specified within a requester.

Images menu

The *Images* menu introduces some interesting features. The *Currently editing* sub-item changes the editing mode, as described in detail in the section *Classic vs. Colorful* (page 208). Add a color variant with *Extend with Colorful Images* if none is available and delete the color variant using *Remove the Colorful images* if required.

The *Exchange* function switches the image content back and forth between *normal* and *selected* mode. If an image is available in normal mode, the image can be copied to the *Selected* area using *Duplicate*. This is also possible in the opposite direction, depending on the active function, i.e. it is always copied from selected to unselected status. With *Use Template*, the icon automatically receives a pattern background, while *Exchange Black/White* inverts a classic icon, i.e. performs a color inversion.

A new feature is the *Add Glow Effect* function, which automatically creates the familiar glow style for the respective icon status. You no longer need to paint the glow yourself. This function is of course intended for the selected state. This also applies to the creation of a darkened style (see above) with the *Add Dimmed Effect* option.

Settings menu

The *Settings* menu contains two useful functions. *Use grid?* is a drawing aid in which a transparent grid is placed over the contents in the drawing area. This makes the individual pixels more visible when working with the tools. The grid will not be visible in the finished symbol. You can permanently save a setting customized to your personal needs with *Save Settings.*

Changing icon sizes

Oversized icons are permitted on the Workbench and can even fill the entire screen. You can determine the dimensions of the icon using the *Resize Canvas* function in the *Images* menu. In the requester that appears, the width and height of the icon can be defined using the input field or the + and – buttons. The default dimensions are 46 x 46 pixels. If necessary, you can reset any changes you have made using *Resize Canvas To Standard Size.*

Saving default icons

Say you want to change the default icon for a newly created project. To do this, change the icon type to *Project* in the Type menu and create a new icon in the menu via *Project > New.* After you have changed the look, save it via *Project > Save as* under the name *def_project.info* in the *Sys:Prefs/Env-Archive/Sys* folder, as this is where all the standard icons, the *DefaultIcons*, are located.

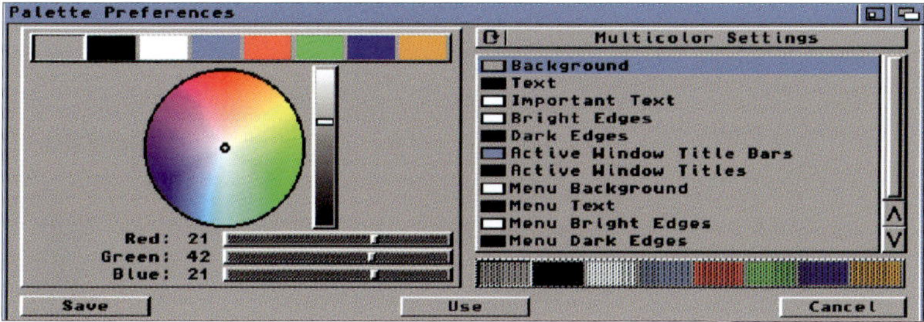

Essential to IconEdit: the available color palette is defined in the Palette Preferences.

InitPrinter (printer initialization)

InitPrinter initializes a printer according to the definitions set in the Preferences.

Function

A printer connected to the Amiga is automatically initialized the first time it is accessed, but if the printer has been switched off since then, it is recommended that you initialize the printer again with *InitPrinter*.

InitPrinter can be run by double-clicking on its icon in the *Tools* folder or from within the Shell using the `InitPrinter` command without arguments. In the latter case, the Shell prompt will disappear and only reappear after the printer is reset. If no printer is found, a system message will indicate a printer problem. Close the message by clicking the *Cancel* button.

Shell command

`INITPRINTER`

KeyShow (keyboard layout display)

KeyShow displays the current keyboard layout set for the system. This corresponds to the settings in the input preferences.

Function

After double-clicking on the *KeyShow* icon in the *Tools* drawer, the keys that appear on the keyboard when a single key is pressed are displayed. For example, the *Q* key displays a small *q*.

If you press one of the so-called qualifier keys, such as *Alt*, *Shift* or *Ctrl*, that key will be shaded grey and the rest of the keys will be shown as if you had pressed the key along with

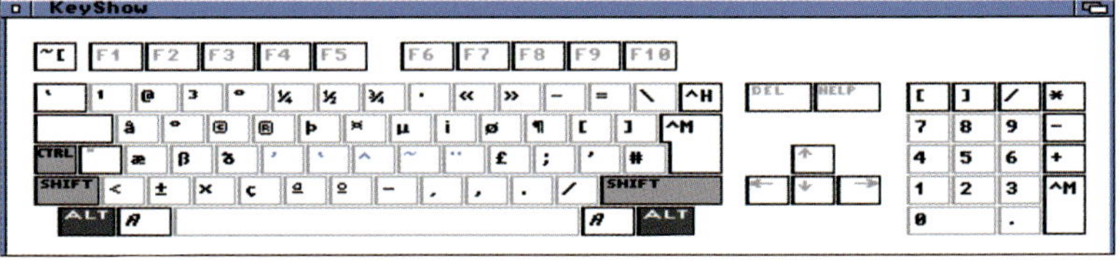

A helpful solution to keep track of your keys: with KeyShow, you can find your way with ease.

the qualifier key. This also works with two or more qualifiers. Selecting the qualifier key again will disable it, and the rest of the keyboard will appear as if the qualifier key had not been pressed.

Shell command

Use the Shell to run the tool with the `Keyshow` command. No further arguments are available.

PrepCard (PCMCIA integration)

With the help of this handy little tool, adding PCMCIA expansions to a compatible Amiga is a breeze.

Function

The Amiga 600 and 1200 both feature a PCMCIA slot on the left side of their case. This slot can be used to connect hardware for system expansions. *PrepCard* makes it possible to use a PCMCIA memory card in these Amigas as a storage medium or a memory extension. PrepCard can be started by double-clicking its icon or executing a command in the Shell.

Shell command

```
PREPCARD [DISK | RAM]
```

The `DISK` option prepares a PCMCIA card for use as a *CC0:* drive. Writing and reading to and from a card prepared in this way will then work the same as any other drive such as a hard disk or floppy disk. A battery-buffered PCMCIA card is recommended for permanently storing data.

The `RAM` option prepares a PCMCIA card for use as a memory expansion. When you boot the machine with a card prepared in this way, the memory on the card is added to the RAM memory of your Amiga. With the exception of ROM (read-only memory) cards, you can do this with any compatible PCMCIA card.

The `DISK` and `RAM` options are mutually exclusive, i.e. if you specify both options, the first option will be used and the second option will be ignored. If you use PrepCard on an Amiga without a PCMCIA slot, an error message will be displayed.

You can read more about useful peripherals in the *Hardware Extensions* (7.5) section in the *Next Steps* chapter.

PrintFiles (data print output)

PrintFiles is the fastest way to print out your digital data. It goes from monitor to printer in a flash.

Function

The PrintFiles utility has the simple task of outputting the content of text files to your printer. It is located in the *Tools* drawer and is launched from the Shell or by double-clicking on its icon.

Shell command

`PRINTFILES [-f] <filename> [<other filenames>]`

The command `PrintFiles Work:Book/Chapter2.txt` sends the contents of the text file *Chapter2.txt* in the folder *Book* on the *Work:* drive to the connected printer. If you do not have a printer connected to your Amiga, you will see an error message in the Shell window (or the Workbench). Simply click *Cancel* to resolve this issue.

You can print several files at once using the `FILE` argument. If PrintFiles cannot find or open one of the files listed, it simply skips that file and continues with the next one. Printouts are made according to the printer settings defined in the Preferences.

Add a page break when printing several files using the `-f` option to print single files on a new page. Without this, the printout of the next file will always start on the page where the printout of the previous file ended.

A simple example: `PrintFiles Text1.txt -f Text2.txt -f Text3.txt` prints the three text files (Text1, Text2, Text3), each with a page break in between.

Using on the Workbench

Using *PrintFiles* via an icon on the Workbench will feel a little odd: select the first file you want to print with a single mouse click and then select all the other files you want to print while holding down the `[Shift]` key. You can also select the files you want to print by drawing a frame around the corresponding icons with the mouse. Once you have selected all the desired files, continue to hold down the `[Shift]` key and double-click on the *PrintFiles* icon.

To add a page break between each printed file by default, simply add the tooltype `formfeed=true` to the PrintFiles icon settings.

ShowConfig (configuration display)

Want to know which expansions or which ROM is in the Amiga? ShowConfig will give you this information and more.

Function

ShowConfig, which can be found in the *Tools* drawer, is a useful helper that summarizes all the relevant information about the running Amiga system in a central window. Here you can find out, for example, which processor or which custom chips are built into the Amiga, or how much memory it has. Furthermore, ShowConfig can provide a comprehensive list of available expansion cards.

ShowConfig uses the so-called *boards.library* by Marcus Gerards to display the ever-growing list of expansion boards. The library is located in *SYS:Libs* as part of AmigaOS 3.2, but can be updated manually when new versions are released (download: www.aminet.net/package/util/libs/BoardsLib).

If there is a CPU or a CPU card with a *Memory Management Unit* (MMU) or mathematical co-processor (FPU) in the Amiga, ShowConfig refers to the *MMULib* package, which is added during the installation process of AmigaOS 3.2.

Shell command

ShowConfig can be run by double-clicking on its icon or running the Shell command `SHOWCONFIG [function]`. When started inside the Shell without arguments, `ShowConfig` displays a summary of the system information directly in the Shell window. While `ShowConfig GUI` opens the user interface of the program, `ShowConfig DEBUG` shows details of the built-in expansion cards.

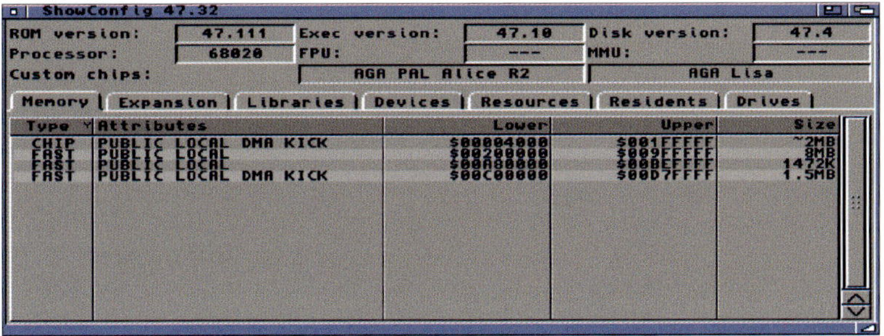

ShowConfig displays all system information at a glance.

TextEdit (text editor)

This simple yet super-effective editor is here to make your life easier! Use it to write text, scripts or listings without worrying about formatting.

Function

Another standard utility in AmigaOS 3.2 is *TextEdit* from the *Tools* drawer. This text editor is simple to use but has all the power you could possibly need to work efficiently on text documents. Several documents can be open at the same time, making it easy to compare and copy content back and forth. Open text documents are arranged in individual tabs above the input area. Modified text documents that have not yet been saved are marked with an asterisk (*). The editor also has a useful search and replace function.

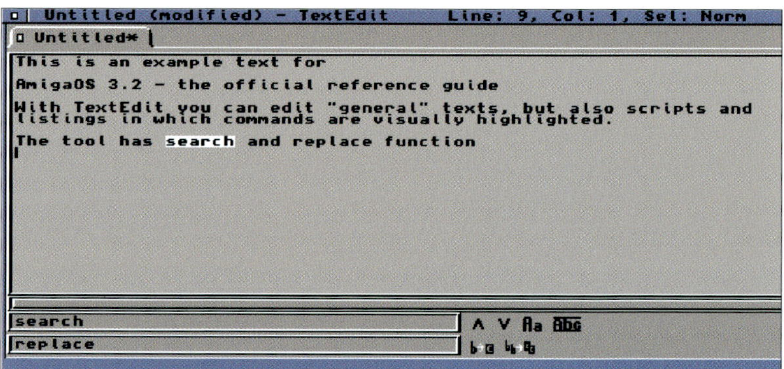

A simple text document in TextEdit without formatting. The search and replace function is at the bottom of the window. Files are arranged in tabs above the input area.

Using TextEdit

As in any text editor, you can navigate and place the cursor, i.e. the current editing position, using the mouse or the four arrow keys. You add text at the cursor. The location of the cursor is shown in the status bar by line and column, corresponding to line and character. To switch between open text documents, click on the file's corresponding tab at the top.

File types

TextEdit processes the content as plain text in ASCII format without formatting. It therefore does not provide the ability to style text in bold or italics, integrate tables or make font size changes, as is known from specialized word processing software such as WordWorth or Final Writer. However, TextEdit is able to highlight content on the screen to make editing easier. For example, coding instructions are displayed in bold if you change the *file type* in the menu from the default setting *Generic text* to *Assembler 68k*, for example. Other file types are *ARexx*, *Shell script* and *C*, each of which is displayed slightly differently.

Go to *Settings > Filetype Options* to change the behavior of the different text types. In the window that appears you can edit things like line breaks and line number display. Click the arrow next to the entries to change other settings such as *indentation* and *highlighting*.

Menu commands

TextEdit supports a range of keyboard shortcuts to streamline your work. All of the commands can also be executed from the menus. Use the *Project* menu to create *new* text documents, *open* existing ones or *save* a file that has been edited (including with a *save as* function). The standard shortcuts are [R-Amiga] combined with [N], [O] and [S], and for *Save as*, [Shift]+[S]. If several text files are open at the same time, you can jump to the previous tab with *Reveal previous* or `[R-Amiga]+[,]`, and to the next tab with *Reveal next* or `[R-Amiga]+[.]` You can stop editing a file with *Close* or [R-Amiga]+`[W]`. However, if the document has not yet been saved (denoted by a * symbol in the tab name), a requester will appear informing you that any changes made when closing without saving will be lost. *Project > Quit* closes the entire tool. You will be prompted to save any unsaved text before quitting.

The *Edit menu* also contains familiar functions. Mark text with the mouse or the cursor keys while holding down the Shift key. *Cut* or `[R-Amiga]+[X]` copies any selected text to the clipboard and removes the content from the document. *Copy* or `[R-Amiga]+[C]` copies any selected text to the clipboard but leaves it in the document. *Paste* or `[R-Amiga]+[V]` inserts the copied or cut content from the clipboard at the cursor position in the text field. The entire text of a document can be selected using *Select all* or `[R-Amiga]+[A]`, including any text that is outside the visible area.

The *Undo* or `[R-Amiga]+[Z]` function, which can be used to undo previous work steps, is essential for text editing of all kinds. This can be the entry of single characters, as well as the insertion of content from the clipboard. If you have inadvertently undone one step too many, you can *restore* the changes you have made with the [R-Amiga]+[Y] shortcut.

Search, replace, jump and convert

TextEdit comes with a reliable function for searching and replacing content. To initiate a search, head to *Edit > Search* or use the keyboard shortcut [R-Amiga]+[F]. This will open a text gadget at the bottom of the window, wherein the text to be searched for can be entered. Elements matching specific criteria in the currently displayed text are highlighted with a designated color within the edit area. In addition to the search field, the up and down arrows can be used to jump to the previous or next location. The first option next to it makes the search case-sensitive (e.g. a search for the character string *Amiga* would only find the text *Amiga*, but not *amiga)* while the *Match whole word* option only searches entire text segments (e.g. searching *write* will find the character string *write*, but not *rewrite*).

The search function is supplemented by the extended *Search & Replace* tool, which can be found in the *Edit* menu or with [R-Amiga]+[H]. For example, if you want to replace *Atari* with *Amiga* in the current document, enter *Atari* in the upper search field and *Amiga* in the lower replace field. After pressing [Enter], the words are swapped. The adjacent *Replace and search for next* option replaces the current finding and jumps to the next location; the *Replace all* option does as described in one quick step. If it is not currently required, you can *hide* the search and replace gadgets tool via the menu or with [Esc].

The *Go To* or [R-Amiga]+[T] function is particularly useful for navigating long documents and listings. Enter a line number in the text field followed by Enter to jump directly to that line.

The *Transform Selection* menu contains four functions for making frequent quick changes. You can change spaces to tabs, tabs to spaces, lowercase letters to uppercase letters and uppercase letters to lowercase letters in selected text elements.

Bookmarks

Bookmarks (found in the *Edit > Bookmarks* submenu) are a trusty friend when editing long texts, especially over a longer period of time. Just as you might mark a reading position in a book with a bookmark, you can use digital bookmarks in TextEdit to find important text sections or paragraphs. Use the somewhat ambiguous *Toggle bookmark* command or [R-Amiga]+[M] to set a bookmark in the current line, which will then be marked with a symbol to the left of the text. You can also jump to the previous and next bookmark or delete (clear) all bookmarks in the open document from the same submenu.

Settings

The *Settings* menu contains options that affect how you work in TextEdit. *Save settings* to reuse them later. Enabling Monospaced Font affects the spacing between characters, i.e. the font used in the text area is switched between proportional or non-proportional. Furthermore, you can save the selected window size with *Remember Window Geometry*, and show information on the file type options in case you need more detail.

Clock (system clock)

Whether displayed digitally or in analog, with the clock you can always keep an eye on the time. This utility has been part of AmigaOS since the earliest days.

Function

The well-known *Clock* from the *Utilities* drawer can be used to display the time on the Workbench at any time on request, either as a digital display with numbers consisting of hours, minutes and seconds, or as an analog display. Clock may not be pretty, but it does its job technically flawlessly – provided the correct time has been set in the *Time Preferences*, and the battery in the real-time clock or the RTC module in the Amiga is working.

Using Clock

When the clock is started, it appears on the Workbench by default as an analog clock with a white face. The width and height of the clock can be changed as required using the size symbol in the bottom right-hand window. If you prefer the digital version with purely numerical information, which fits neatly into the Workbench status bar, you can change the display format via the *Project menu* or the keyboard shortcuts `[R-Amiga]+[D]` for the digital clock or `[R-Amiga]+[A]` for the analog clock.

Analog clock settings

The appearance of the analog clock can be modified slightly in the *Settings* menu: if you tick the *Date* option, the date will be displayed digitally below the clock in the format *DD/MM/YY* (date/month/year, each with two digits). The *Seconds* option switches the analog second hand on and off.

Digital clock settings

The appearance of the digital clock is simple and clear, as are its corresponding options in the *Settings* menu. With the *Date* option enabled, the clock switches back and forth between the time and date every few seconds. Under *Settings > Digital format*, there are five options for showing the time that only differ if you look closely: assuming the system time is set to 9 o'clock, 13 minutes, 32 seconds, the settings from top to bottom would correspond to a display of 9:13, 9:13 am, 9:13:32, 9:13:32 am and 09:13:32 respectively.

Use *Settings > Save Settings* to permanently set the look and position of the clock, whether for the digital or analog format.

Alarm clock

Use the alarm clock function to be notified at the specified time: set the time for a reminder message to be sent using the hour and minute sliders in *Settings > Set Alarm*. Confirm the alarm clock setting with *Use* and switch on the alarm clock via Settings > *Alarm* or `[R-Amiga]+[M]` – the Amiga will then ring you awake at the desired time.

INFO **Setting the time**
The clock is set using the Time Preferences, which is explained in the Prefs section.

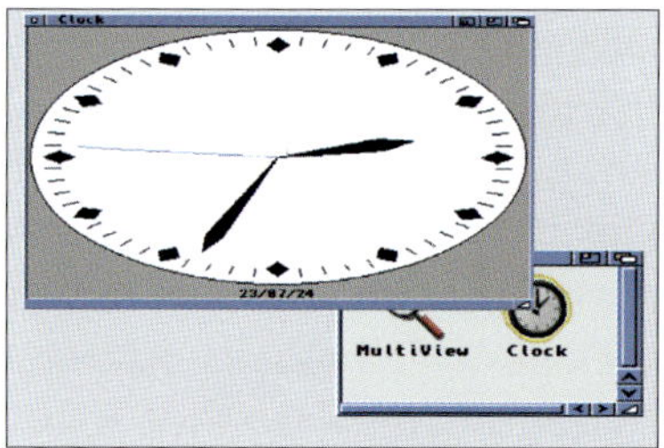

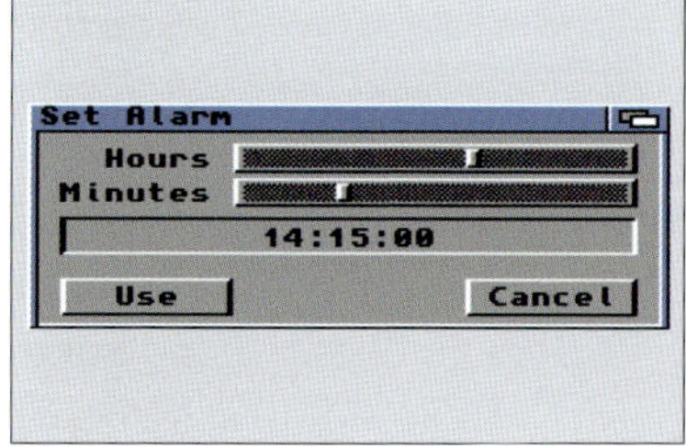

The analog clock face and alarm clock feature of the Amiga clock

MultiView (file viewer & player)

MultiView is the Swiss army knife of AmigaOS. Its versatility means it can display a wide range of files, and its modular expansion capabilities make it an invaluable asset.

Function

Images, text, sound, animations, AmigaGuides – the universal *MultiView* is almost a complete all-rounder: provided a datatype is available for a file, Multiview can show or play it. Alongside the *DataType* system, MultiView has been an elementary part of AmigaOS since version 3.0 and continues to be maintained.

DataType system

A suitable datatype must exist for a file format to be displayed or played in MultiView. These definition files must be located in the system directories *Devs/DataTypes* and *Classes/DataTypes*. Preinstalled datatypes include JPG, PNG and AmigaGuide. Aminet and other sources provide datatypes for a wide variety of standard and exotic formats, e.g. WebP, SVG, MPEG, FLI and Windows icons

TIP **Managing DataTypes**
Try to keep the operating system lean: if you no longer need a file format, simply move its datatype from *Devs/DataTypes* to *Storage/DataTypes*. After a reboot, the datatype will no longer occupy any RAM.

Using MultiView

To launch *MultiView*, double-click its icon in the *Utilities* drawer. A requester will appear on the screen in which you can navigate through the directory structure to the file to be opened. If you select a file and click *Open*, it will be loaded, regardless of whether it is an image or an icon, an animation, text (scripts are also recognized), audio or an AmigaGuide. Close a file simply by clicking the close gadget.

Showing an image

When you open an image file, e.g. IFF, JPG or PNG, the image will be displayed in a window. The speed of the display and the number of colors displayed are determined by the active screen resolution and the number of colors on the screen, as well by as the performance of the Amiga.

Showing an animation

When you open an animation, such as a GIF, a window will appear with a panel that you can use to control the animation. Press the *Play* button to start the animation. Use the buttons to the left and right of *Play* to rewind and fast-forward the animation. The timeline next to it indicates the current position of the animation by means of the black square icon.

Playing audio

When you open a sound or music file, e.g. WAV, AIFF or MOD (ProTracker), a window with a loudspeaker symbol will appear. Click on the icon to play the audio file.

Showing text

When you open a text file (TXT, ReadMe or script), it is displayed in a separate window. You cannot edit the text. Use an external editor such as Text Editor, Vim or CygnusEd to edit the file.

Showing AmigaGuides

When you open an AmigaGuide file (with the extension *.guide*), it is displayed in its own special window. As with a web page, you can click on links to other text sections or completely new documents and thus jump within the document or to external documents. This is done using the rectangular boxes, which are usually, but not always, labeled with text. This allows for complex structures in documents of all kinds, such as extensive instructions, lists of information on events, or a list of Amigas used in famous and significant places, such as shown below.

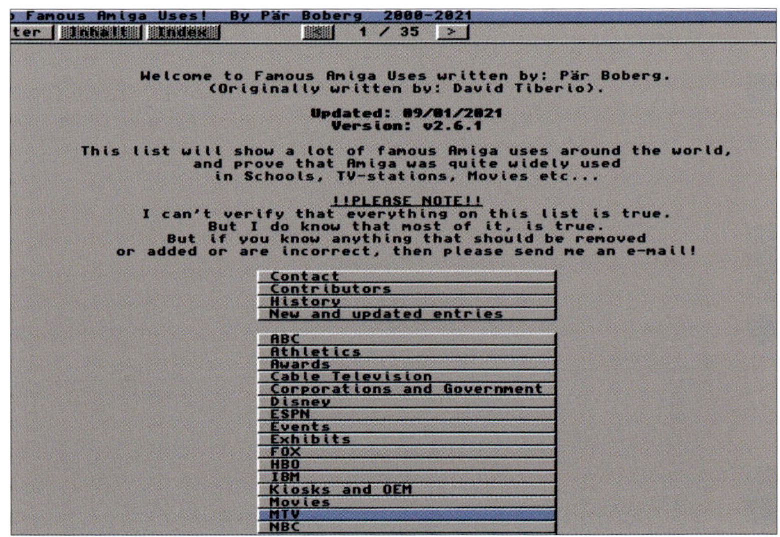

MultiView showing the open AmigaGuide "Famous Amiga Uses"

Above the display area, a control bar features various buttons for navigation and help. The help button leads you to the individual help area of the respective AmigaGuide or to a general help page, which explains how buttons, menus, keyboard commands, the mouse and cursor keys work in AmigaGuides.

Navigation in AmigaGuides

The MultiView navigation bar is invaluable for navigating an AmigaGuide document. It contains several useful functions for moving through the document with ease, similar to a modern web browser. If a function is unavailable, it will appear greyed out and unclickable.

The *Index* button shows the AmigaGuide's keyword list if it has one. *Contents* displays its table of contents – content overviews of subsections are also shown here. Use *Back* to return to the previous page and *Next* to move through any pages you have called up prior to the *Back* button. The section number is in the center of the bar, with two control buttons to the side, < and >, to move backwards and forwards through the AmigaGuide.

MultiView menu

The MultiView menu is divided into five submenus: *Project*, *Edit*, *Navigation*, *Window* and *Settings*.

Under *Project* you will find the sub-items *Open*, *Save as...*, *Print*, *About* and *Quit*. *Open* lets you display or play any file supported by DataTypes. *Save as...* saves the active file under a new name anywhere on a volume. Click *Print* to output an image or document to the connected printer. Click on *About to* display information about the open file in a window. In the case of images, for example, resolution and color depth are listed. *Quit* closes the MultiView instance.

The commands in the *Edit* menu are also familiar. *Mark* lets you to select a specific part of an image or text. *Copy* transfers the content of the entire file or the selected area to the clipboard, *Paste* inserts the copied content from the clipboard, *Select All* selects all areas of a text or image file, while *Clear Selected* removes this selection.

The *Navigation* menu is only enabled when displaying text. In a text document, use *Find* to search for specific text sequences: enter the text in the input requester and start searching by pressing Enter or clicking *OK*. Any found text sections are highlighted in color. Use *Find Next* and *Find Previous* to jump to the next or previous location.

You can open a separate MultiView screen via the *Window* menu. This detaches the display from the rest of the Workbench. To do this, the *Use Separate Screen* option must be ticked, i.e. enabled. Regardless of whether it is in a shared Workbench screen or a separate screen, the size of the display window can be changed with *Minimize*, *Normal* (proportional) or *Maximize*.

Any changes you make can be saved for future use – simply go to *Settings > Save As Defaults*. If you do not save them, they will expire when MultiView is closed.

MultiView and DefaultIcons

MultiView is also used in conjunction with the DefaultIcons system. File types for images, text documents, sounds or animations are assigned a preset icon on the Workbench so that the user can recognize them without any confusion. As such, MultiView is automatically defined as the standard display tool. If you double-click one of these files on the Workbench, the file will be displayed or played directly with MultiView.

Find (file/directory search)

Find is a fantastic tool that lets you search for files and directories on your drives with ease.

Function

The *Find* tool is located in the *System* folder, though you can also access it from the menu via *Window > Find* or with the shortcut `[R-Amiga]+[F]`. By default, Find will search all drives for files with the exact name you specify. For example, next to the cycle gadget *With the exact name,* enter the string *Assign.* Click the *Start* button in the bottom right to initiate the search process.

Searched, found: Find detects files and drawers

Using Find

If you uncheck the *All* box in the top right of the window, you can select a drawer to search in using the *Search from* selector in the top left. Click *Volumes* in the requester to list and choose an entire drive for the search. Confirm with *OK*.

The cycle gadget contains four search options: *With the exact name*, *Whose name contains*, *Matching the pattern*, *Containing the string*. The program will search the contents of files with the latter option, which naturally takes considerably longer. For example, select the system drive to search in and tell the program to search for all files containing the string *Assign* using the *Matching the pattern* option. Compare the outcome with those that result from the options *With the exact name* and *Whose name contains* to get a better understanding of the differences.

The program does not differentiate between upper and lower case when searching. You can change the default search settings via the icon tool types. Using the following instructions, the program will search for all files containing the string *Assign* in the system drive by default after clicking on *Start*.

```
FROM=SYS:
MODE=STRING
FIND=Assign
```

You can edit the icon tool types in the information window. Access it from the Workbench menu *Icons* > *Information*.

FixFonts (font updating)

FixFonts is the tool you need to take control of your fonts. It updates the .font files in the Fonts directory.

Function

The *FixFonts* program updates the *.font* files in the *Fonts:* directory. By default, the assignment points to the *Fonts* drawer in your system drive. Depending on your installed programs or customizations, the assignment can also point to other directories containing fonts.

Using FixFonts

Use the FixFonts program if you have installed new font files or deleted existing font files. There is a separate *.font* file and a directory of the same name for each installed font. For example, the *Topaz* font has the file *topaz.font* and the directory *topaz* with the file 11, which can display the corresponding font size 11. The AmigaOS Kickstart ROM also includes Topaz in font sizes 8 and 9. Other bitmap fonts included as standard in AmigaOS 3.2 are Courier, Diamond, Emerald, Garnet, Helvetica, Opal, Ruby, Sapphire and Times.

The *Intellifont* system utility is the best way to manage so-called vector fonts (see section 4.18).

Format (drive formatting)

The Format system tool is used to format all types of drives, including hard disks, floppy disks or CF cards.

Function

Use *Format* to prepare drives or drive partitions for use with your Amiga. By default, it uses the *Old File System*, which is compatible down to AmigaOS 1. For PC disks, the *CrossDOS file system* is used. For partitions on hard disks, SSDs, USB sticks or other drives, the partition's DOS type determines the file system used. Details on the advantages and disadvantages of the file systems included in AmigaOS, as well as file systems available from third-party sources, can be found in section 2.12. Under *CrossDOS*, you can also find out how to use the driver for PC floppy disks. The tool can also be used as a Shell command. You can read more about this in chapter 5 on the *Shell*.

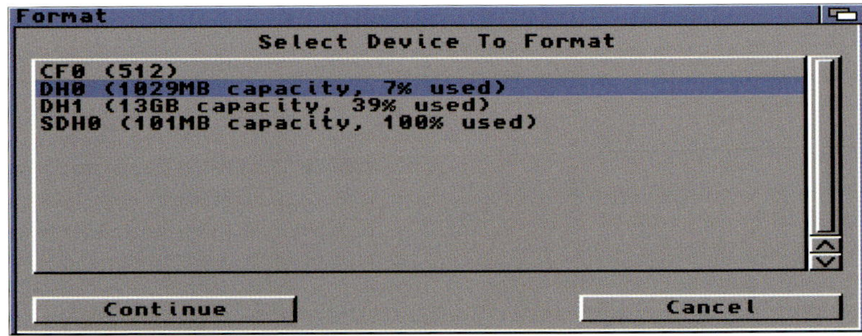

Format identifies the drives available for formatting

Using Format

After starting *Format* by double-clicking its icon, a list of formatable drives will appear. AmigaOS understands this to mean all inserted writable removable media, as well as all partitions on hard disks or SSDs. The list also includes all drives that already contain a file system. For drives without a file system, the program will only show the capacity and the device name; for drives with a file system, it will also show the current capacity. For double-density disks, *Format* displays 880 KB for the Amiga format and 720 KB for the PC format, and twice as much for high-density disks, at 1760 KB and 1440 KB respectively.

How the Workbench displays unformatted drives

Another way to start the tool is to click on the icon of the drive to format on the Workbench screen and select the *Format disk* menu item in the *Icons* menu, or double-click on the *Format tool* icon while holding down the `[Shift]` key. For a newly created partition or a removable disk without a file system, the Workbench will display the disk as *Uninitialized*. For an unformatted PC disk, the Workbench will display it as *Unreadable*. The `Info` command shows the available drives. It displays *Not a DOS Disk* or *Unreadable Disk* for unformatted drives.

After formatting a drive that already contains a file system with files and directories, AmigaOS will display it as empty. The existing data can then only be restored, and with great effort, using a rescue tool – and only if the drive was formatted quickly. Always ensure you select the correct drive when formatting!

After selecting the drive, enter your desired drive name. You can also select whether you want to set up a trashcan. The *Format* requester only shows further options for the *Old File System* and the *Fast File System*. It is typically recommended that you choose the Fast *File System*. Activate *International Mode* to support umlauts, or select *Long File Names* to support file names of up to 107 characters. Enabling *Directory Cache* is generally not recommended. You can read more on this in the section 2.12 on *File systems*.

The formatting tools provided for third-party file systems offer additional options. For example, *SFSformat* offers additional options for the *Smart File System*. In testing, only formatting was available with this tool. For the *Professional File System*, on the other hand, the manual recommends using *PFSFormat*, which also offers additional options. You can find out more about these commands in section 2.12 on *file systems*.

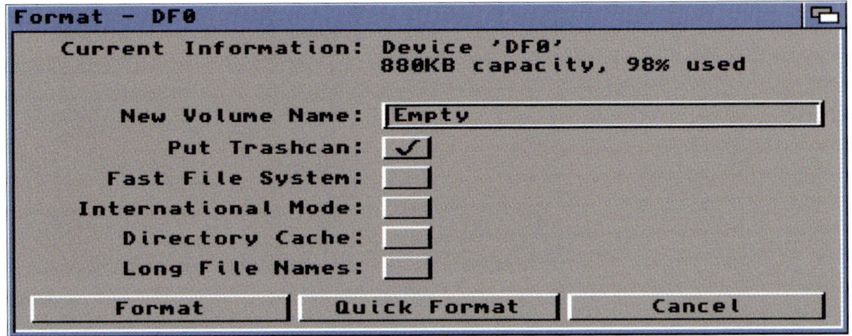

Options in the Format requester for the Old File System and the Fast File System

Finally, click either the *Format* or *Quick Format* button to format the drive. For floppy disks, it is recommended that you perform a slow format via the *Format* button. The tool will overwrite all the sectors of the drive, which ensures that the disk can be completely written to without errors. For partitions on hard disks and SSDs, as well as USB sticks, fast formatting via *Quick Format* is more useful, as the firmware of such drives handles faulty sectors independently. Flash storage devices such as SSDs or USB sticks will also age faster under a slow format due to the additional write accesses performed. In addition, slow formatting takes a very long time, especially with large hard drives.

Once formatting has been successfully completed, the Workbench will display an icon with the drive name you have selected. You can now make full use of the drive, i.e. copy files and directories to the drive or install software.

Help (help system)

AmigaOS 3.2 provides comprehensive documentation that clearly outlines system functions.

Function

Click the *Help* icon in the *System* drawer to open the AmigaOS reference manual, which is only available in English. Alternatively, press the `[Help]` key on an Amiga keyboard to call up the docs, or type `Help` in a Shell window. The AmigaOS documentation contains the following chapters – the underlined text points to the chapters in this AmigaOS 3.2 Reference Manual, currently in your hands, containing detailed descriptions.

Contents

1) *Foreword:* introduction and acknowledgments.
2) *AmigaOS 3.2 Features:* a summary of the new features of AmigaOS 3.2.
3) *Workbench Basics:* basic instructions for operating the Workbench, including instructions on using the mouse, menus, icons, and DOS drivers including *RAM:* and *RAD:*. → Chap. 2 / p. 76
4) *The Shell:* everything about the AmigaOS Shell, with an introduction, an overview of its newer functions and internal commands, as well as notes on Shell programming. Includes basic information for each command. → Chap. 5 / p. 256
5) *Workbench Programs:* a description of all the programs that you can start from the Workbench. → Chap. 4 / p. 172
6) *The DataType Subsystem:* an overview of the DataType system that can be extended by third-party-providers and allows programs to open files of different types without having to implement the reading and display of the files themselves. → Section 2.6 / p. 94
7) *Device & File System Quirks:* information on device names, DOS-types and file system rights. → Section 2.12 / p. 101
8) *AmigaOS Command Reference:* a list of AmigaOS commands with descriptions. → Chap. 5 / p. 278
9) *ARexx:* an overview of Shell commands for ARexx and the ARexx ports of MultiView, TextEdit and Workbench. ARexx is a programming language included in AmigaOS with which you can remotely control Amiga programs that support it. → Chap. 6.5 / p. 356

10) *Frequently Asked Questions:* a compilation of frequently asked questions and answers sorted by section. Version 47.2 of the FAQ is also available on the Aminet (www.aminet.net/package/docs/help/AmigaOS_3.2-FAQ). AmigaOS 3.2.2 contains version 47.3, dated December 26th, 2022. → Section 8.1 / p. 448
11) *Amiga Error Code Identification:* notes on the various types of error messages in AmigaOS, including color codes when booting, Guru Meditations and Amiga DOS error codes. → Section 8.2 / p. 453
12) *The Amiga Early Startup Control*: a description of AmigaOS boot menu options with instructions on how to choose the boot drive, configure the display options and view a list of expansion cards. → Section 6.2 / p. 337
13) *HDToolBox:* details on the partitioning tool. Two small guides explain how to partition and format a drive and how to add or update file system drivers. → Section 4.4 / p. 178
14) *AmigaGuide hypertext documents:* instructions on how to write your own AmigaGuide documents. The OS3.2 manual is also written largely in AmigaGuide. → Section 6.4 / p. 351
15) *MountList and Mount Files:* a description of all the options for mounting lists and files, the so-called DOS drivers. This makes devices accessible to AmigaOS. In many cases, simply copying existing DOS driver files and making the necessary adjustments is all that is required. → Section 4.19 / p. 233
16) *Keyboard and Mouse Shortcuts:* a list of global keyboard shortcuts and mouse commands, as well as keyboard shortcuts in Shell windows. → Section 6.3 / p. 344
17) *Scripts in S:* a description of the Shell and ARexx scripts located in *S:*, including the general, the user and the shell start sequence, as well as an ARexx script called *Win* for opening a directory. → Section 6.1 / p. 326
18) *Environment Variables:* an explanation of how local and environment variables work and where AmigaOS stores them. → Section 3.21 / p. 171
19) *Macintosh file systems summary:* a summary of the Mac file systems supported by AmigaOS. → Section 2.12 / p. 101
20) *Help and Support:* information on where you can get support and help as an AmigaOS user. Plus links to the FAQ and the manufacturer's support forum (https://forum.hyperion-entertainment.com). → Section 1.1 / p. 16

Intellifont (vector font management)

Intellifont is your one-stop shop for all things vector fonts! Install, delete and change fonts with a simple click.

Function

AmigaOS has got you covered with native support for vector fonts in *CompuGraphic* format (CG), in addition to the far more common raster fonts. Raster fonts are perfect for defining individual characters via a rectangular matrix of dots, also known as a bitmap. There are separate bitmaps for each font size. A vector font is a cutting-edge way to define a single character. It does this by using a polyline defined by points with specific coordinates, which allows you to scale it to any size without losing any quality.

The Intellifont tool lets you manage these CompuGraphic fonts. You can install new CG fonts and remove old ones with this little helper, as well as set which sizes the AmigaOS font requester should offer for a CG font.

AmigaOS already contains three vector fonts: *CGTimes*, *CGTriumvirate* and *LetterGhotic*. They are located inside the *Fonts* drawer in the *_bullet_outlines* diretory. Some files for vector fonts are located in *_bullet*. For each CompuGraphic vector font there is a related *.font file*, as with bitmap fonts.

Use Intellifont to make CompuGraphic fonts available on your AmigaOS.

Using IntelliFonts

Once you start Intellifont from inside the *System* drawer, you will see a window with two lists. The list on the left, called *Source Typefaces*, shows available CG fonts in a defined folder. The list on the right, called *Existing Fonts & Typefaces*, shows all the fonts that are already installed. This includes pure bitmap fonts. Intellifont marks CG fonts with a black dot after the font name.

For example, download the *AlexAntiqua.lha* archive from Aminet (download: www.aminet.net/package/text/bfont/AlexAntiqua) and extract it to the RAM Disk. Then select *RAM:* with the file requester above *Source Typefaces*. As soon as you click on the *Alex-Antiqua-Book* font in the *Source Typefaces* list, the program displays a plus sign in front of the font name. Click again to remove the plus sign. This allows you to select the desired fonts from a directory with several fonts in one go. Finally, click on *Install Marked Typefaces* while the font is marked with a plus. Intellifont will install the font and define the sizes 15, 30, 45, 60 and 75 for the font requester. By default, the tool uses the *Fonts* directory on the system drive as the target. Other destinations to which *FONTS:* refers are also available for selection.

The *Alex Antiqua* font does not display properly at size 15. To create a new size for an already installed font, click on *Modify Existing Typefaces*. Select the *Alex-Antiqua-Book* font and size 15 and click on *Delete Size*. Enter *size* 20 in the input gadget, followed by the Enter key, and click on *Add Size*. Optionally, click on *Create Bitmap* to create a real raster font for the size. This makes the font accessible to programs that are compatible with bitmap fonts only. It also saves your Amiga from having to calculate the bitmap font used for the screen display from the vector font for frequently used sizes. Finally, click on *Perform Changes*. Only then will Intellifont create size 20 for the *Alex Antiqua* font as a raster font. You will find the new raster font

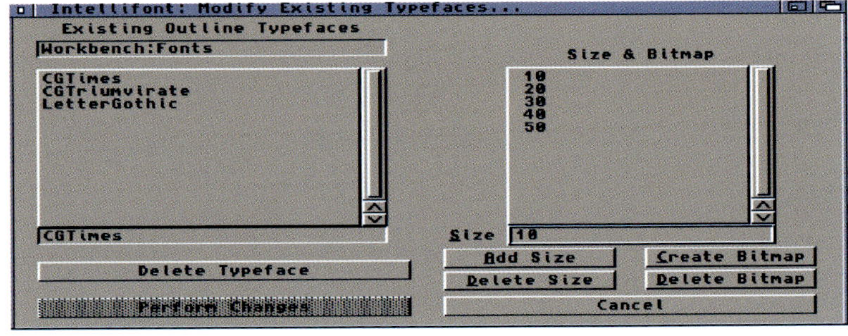

The requester for changing existing vector fonts

in *FONTS:AlexAntiquaBook*. Clicking *Cancel* in the modification requester makes the program forget the requested changes. If necessary, you can remove the raster fonts again using *Delete Bitmap*. Use *Delete Typeface* to remove an entire font.

You can choose any size for your font using the font requester. Simply enter the desired size into the input gadget below the sizes list. AmigaOS will remember the sizes you enter until the next time you restart, after which the requester will only offer the predefined sizes. The *bullet.library* automatically calculates the requested size for CG vector fonts. You can also specify a different size for raster fonts, but you will notice a considerable loss of quality. It is recommended that you only use the predefined sizes for raster fonts.

Font engines

Aminet has additional engines for fonts in other formats. For example, *ttf.library* (download: www.aminet.net/search?query=ttflib) let you integrate TrueType fonts into AmigaOS, meaning TrueType fonts installed under Linux and Windows can be used. Unlike *TTEngine* (download: www.aminet.net/package/util/libs/ttengine-68k), it uses the *bullet.library* contained in AmigaOS and cannot achieve maximum display quality due to limitations in this library. However, it is compatible with all programs that use AmigaOS features. *TTFManager* is a utility for installing TrueType fonts.

Features of third-party software

Some programs do not use the operating system's libraries to manage vector fonts, such as word processors and DTP software. These programs sometimes also support vector fonts in other formats such as TrueType and often achieve higher quality.

Mounter (device registration)

Mounter simply helps you manually mount file systems.

Function

The *Mounter* tool lets you manually mount file systems that have not yet been mounted. It has a graphical user interface and can run as a commodity in the background. The standard shortcut for displaying it is `[Alt]+[Shift]+[F10]`. Alternatively, it can be used as a Shell command (see chapter 5 on the *Shell*).

Mounter is used where AmigaDOS does not automatically mount file systems. This may be a partition for which *automatic mounting* is not active. You will find this option in *HDToolBox* when partitioning a drive with *Partition Drive* after switching on the Advanced *Options* by clicking the *Change* button. The option is called *Automount this partition*. AmigaDOS also sometimes does not automatically mount file systems on certain (e.g. partitioned) removable media. This can be a USB hard drive or a USB stick, for example. Amiga file systems on standard floppy disks are mounted automatically by AmigaDOS.

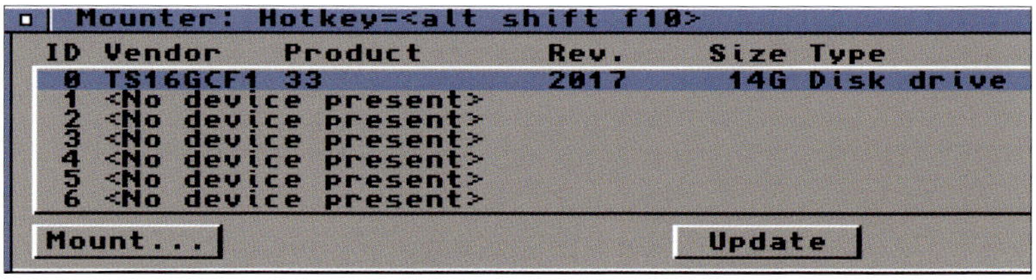

```
Mounter: Hotkey=<alt shift f10>
ID Vendor    Product          Rev.      Size Type
 0 TS16GCF1  33               2017      14G Disk drive
 1 <No device present>
 2 <No device present>
 3 <No device present>
 4 <No device present>
 5 <No device present>
 6 <No device present>
Mount...                                 Update
```

Mounter lists all detected devices

Using Mounter

By default, *Mounter* searches for devices using the *scsi.device* driver (for *device driver names*, see *Starting HDToolBox* from page 178). Use the `DEVICE` tool type to specify a different driver. Once started, *Mounter* displays a list of detected devices. If you click on one of the devices and on *Mount*, you will see a list of partitions with mountable file systems. After selecting one of these, you can mount it by clicking on *Mount*.

If the file system is already mounted, the program will unmount and remount it. Using *Mounter* on the file system on which the booted AmigaOS system is located makes no sense as assignments such as *C:* will still point to the previously mounted but now no longer available file system. As such, be sure to only mount file systems that are not yet mounted. Alternatively, prevent this behavior with the tool type `NOREMOUNT`. With `NOUNMOUNT`, you can prohibit the unmounting of a file system on a partition with the same name.

All other Shell parameters can also be specified in the list of tool types of the icon. For example, you can create a project icon with *SYS:System/Mounter* as the default program to mount a specific file system in a specific partition on a specific device. However, be careful with the `PARTITIONS` parameter. The notation for multiple partitions when used as a icon characteristics is `DH2:|DH3:`, where instead of the space character used in the Shell, the vertical bar | is used.

NoFastMem (disabling Fast RAM)

NoFastMem forces the system to disable the Fast RAM memory, allowing games and other software that does not comply with the system to start.

Function

With *NoFastMem* you can temporarily switch off the Fast RAM. AmigaOS distinguishes between Chip and Fast RAM. Chip RAM is the main memory that is accessible by the Amiga custom chips such as Denise or Lisa, Agnus or Alice, as well as Paula. The custom chips use it primarily for graphics and sound data. The processor and the custom chips share bandwidth for accessing Chip RAM. This reduces the maximum memory bandwidth for the processor, especially with higher resolutions and copper or blitter operations. Therefore, depending on the Amiga model and add-on cards, there is additional Fast RAM that can only be accessed by the processor.

The first Amiga models did not contain any Fast RAM as standard. As a result, some older games and programs are unable to cope with Fast RAM and will not run at all.

Using NoFastMem

Click on *NoFastMem* in the *System* drawer or enter `NoFastMem` in a Shell window to temporarily disable the Fast RAM. It will remain switched off as long as the tool is running. You can stop it either by clicking on it again or by ending the already running program. To do this, press `[Ctrl]+[C]` in the Shell window in which it is running, or use the command `Break` with the process number for *NoFastMem*. Discover this with the `Status` command.

Alternative

An alternative to NoFastMem, which supports more tricks for getting older, bulkier games running, is *WHDLoad* (download: www.whdload.de). The main purpose of this software is to install demos and games that were intended for floppy disks onto hard disks or SSDs. However, it supports many additional options, such as temporarily disabling certain Amiga functions so as to run non-system compliant games and demos.

RexxMast (ARexx initialization)

The ARexx interpreter implemented in AmigaOS is launched with RexxMast from the System directory.

Function

The *RexxMast* command starts the ARexx interpreter built into AmigaOS. When booting into the Workbench, the startup sequence located in *S:Startup-Sequence* checks whether RexxMast is present. If it is, RexxMast is automatically launched.

You can find a lot of information on system-relevant programming with *ARexx* in the comprehensive section 6.5 on *ARexx* on page 356.

Commodities

Commodities are small utilities that run in the background and make daily work easier. Typical examples are Exchange and FKey.

Commodities are extremely useful in everyday life. Users will hardly notice their presence as they work silently in the background. *ClickToFront*, for example, automatically brings the window under the mouse pointer to the foreground.

Directories

Commodities are located in two directories: *Tools > Commodities* and *WBStartup*. If you want to launch a commodity automatically when the Amiga boots up, move it to the *WBStartup* drawer assigned to *SYS:WBStartup*.

The *Exchange* commodity provides an overview of all the active commodities that can be controlled there.

Priority tool type

The priority of a commodity as it relates to other programs can be set by using the `CX_PRIORITY` tool type when launched via the Shell. The default priority value for all programs is `0`. This value can be altered to give a program a higher priority so that the program is executed before all other commodity programs with a lower priority value. For example: `cx_priority=10` assigns priority `10` to the related commodity.

All nine commodities at a glance, from AutoPoint to NoCapsLock

Window tool type

CX_POPUP and CX_POPKEY are standard tool types that apply to all commodity programs that can be controlled in their own windows. If CX_Popup=no is specified, the window of a program will not be opened when its icon is launched. The default setting is CX_Popup=yes.

Shortcut tool type

Use CX_POPKEY to define a keyboard shortcut for opening the hidden window of a commodity program. The keyboard shortcut will have no effect if the commodity has not already been started. With CX_Popkey=F9, for example, [F9] is defined as the keyboard shortcut for the commodity. Combinations of two keys must be separated by spaces and framed by double quotes. For example, CX_Popkey="Shift F4" defines the double key assignment [Shift]+[F4].

AutoPoint (focus window)

Function

With the *AutoPoint* commodity, the window located under the mouse pointer will be automatically activated with a short delay. Launch AutoPoint from the Workbench by double-clicking on its icon. AutoPoint will activate immediately – no separate window will open.

To disable the commodity, double-click the icon again. You can also quit *AutoPoint* from within the *Exchange* commodity.

Shell command

`AUTOPOINT [CX_PRIORITY <priority>] [KEEPSTRINGS]`

The `KEEPSTRINGS` option prevents AutoPoint from automatically setting the focus of a window with an active string gadget as long as the mouse is not moved.

If you started the commodity via the Shell, it can be quit with the shortcut `[Ctrl]+[C]`.

Blanker (screensaver)

Background knowledge

Screen burn-in occurs when static images or image elements such as menus or logos are displayed on a screen over a long period of time. This mainly affects older screen technologies such as CRT monitors, and especially plasma screens, which are rarely used today. Modern OLED screens are also affected by this effect but usually only temporarily, while modern LCD screens are less susceptible to burn-in.

To minimize the risk of burn-in on CRTs and plasmas, it is advisable to use dynamic images and activate a screensaver. Though the risk of burn-in is significantly reduced on a modern LCD or OLED screen, it does not hurt to take precautions, especially when static images are displayed over a long period of time.

Function

AmigaOS has a somewhat outdated yet functional screensaver in the form of *Blanker*. If *Blanker* is active, the screen is automatically blanked if no keyboard or mouse input is detected within a defined period of time.

Using Blanker

Double-clicking the *Blanker* commodity opens it in a separate window. You can change the period of time after which the screen is hidden when the mouse and keyboard are inactive in the text gadget. The entry is made in seconds, with 60 seconds being the default setting. For example, if you only want to hide the screen after 5 minutes of inactivity, enter the value 300 in the text field.

Enable *Cycle Colors* and *Animation* to influence the look of the screensaver. If *Animation* is ticked, a white vector line animation is displayed as a screensaver. If you enable the *Color*

Cycle option, the line animation will be made up of continuous RGB colors. As soon as the animation option is deactivated, a purely black screen is displayed as the screensaver.

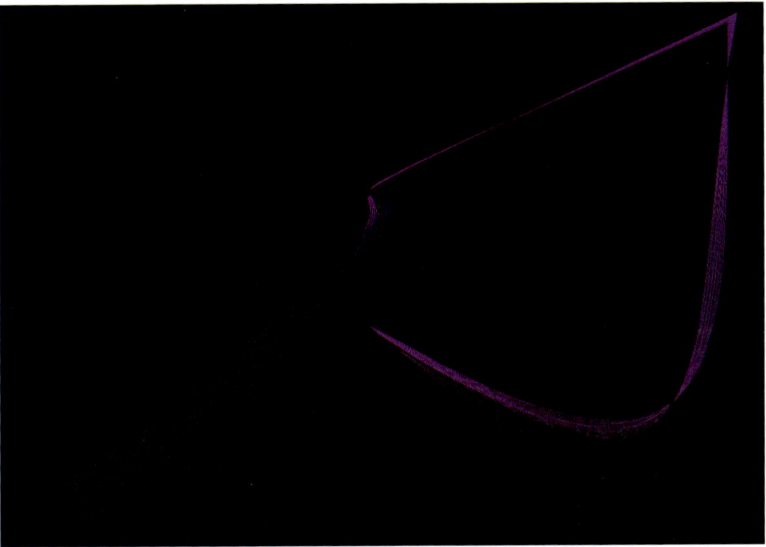

Blanker with animation and color cycle options activated

To ensure the Blanker window does not interfere, hide it using the shortcut `[R-Amiga]+[H]`. If you want to switch off the Blanker completely, use the keyboard shortcut `[R-Amiga]+[Q]`. Alternatively, open the *Exchange* Commodity, select the *Blanker* entry there and click *Remove*.

Shell command

```
BLANKER [CX_PRIORITY <priority>] [CX_POPKEY
<key>] [CX_POPUP=<yes|no>] [SECONDS <timeout>]
[CYCLECOLORS <yes|no>] [ANIMATION <yes|no>]
```

Entering `Blanker` in the Shell will start the screensaver with a black screen. The commodity supports a number of arguments, some of which correspond to the options in the Blanker

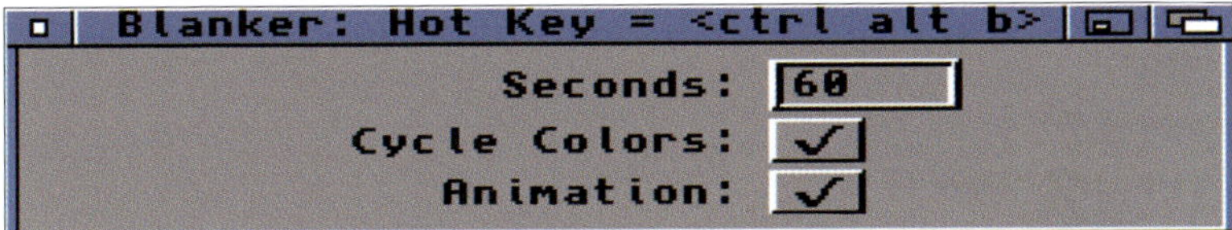

A Blanker setup showing seconds value and display style

window: `SECONDS` (for seconds), `ANIMATION` (for animation) and `CYCLECOLORS` (for color cycle). The other arguments follow the patterns described *(tool types for Commodities)*.

```
Blanker SECONDS 120 ANIMATION YES CX_POPUP=NO
```

runs Blanker without a window and calls up the screensaver with a white animation 120 seconds after user inactivity. The keyboard shortcut `[Ctrl]+[C]` can be used to close Blanker if it is run from the Shell.

ClickToFront (window to front)

Function

The practical *ClickToFront* commodity makes it possible to bring a window to the foreground without having to move windows around and click the foreground/background icon. You can bring a window to the foreground using ClickToFront by simply double-clicking on the window you intend to bring to the front.

TIP **ClickToFront and qualifiers**
ClickToFront supports the *qualifier* feature, meaning you have to press a special key while double-clicking to bring the window to the foreground. The special keys `[L-ALT]`, `[R-ALT]` and `[CTRL]` are supported by the characteristics `Lalt`, `Left_Alt`, `Ralt`, `Right_Alt`, `CTRL` and `CONTROL`. `NONE` describes the status of *no special button*. If desired, you can specify these characteristics separately by selecting the ClickToFront icon and accessing its icon settings via the *Icons > Information* menu. Switch to the *Icon* tab to see information on the qualifiers that are active for this commodity in the *tool types* list. The qualifiers `Left_Alt`, `Right_Alt`, `Ctrl` and `None` are active by default.

Using ClickToFront

To activate ClickToFront, navigate to *Tools > Commodities* and double-click the *ClickToFront* icon. No window will open for this commodity.

We recommend moving the ClickToFront commodity to the *WBStartup* drawer so it's started automatically when you boot into the Workbench.

To disable the commodity, double-click the *ClickToFront* icon once more. Alternatively, use the *Exchange* commodity to exit or deactivate the program, as described under Exchange.

CrossDOS (convert DOS texts)

Function

The *CrossDOS* commodity offers precise controls for text conversion on active CrossDOS drives *(PC0:* and *PC1:*, provided their DOS drivers are located and mounted in the *Devs/ DosDrivers* directory). The CrossDOS window provides a quick overview of all available drives and allows you to customize *text filters* and *text translation* settings for each drive.

Open the commodity with a double-click on its icon or the keyboard shortcut `[Ctrl]+[Alt]+[C]`. It will appear in its own tiny window.

Using CrossDOS

The list on the left side of the CrossDOS window contains the device names of all the CrossDOS drives currently enabled in AmigaOS. Select the drive to access its corresponding settings.

The *Text Filtering* option allows you to remove control characters from DOS text files that are not required on the Amiga: DOS text files usually contain control characters for *carriage* return (*CR*) and *line* feed (*LF*) at the end of each line; in addition, one or more *end-of-file* control characters (*EOF*) can be set at the end of DOS files. Amiga text files, however, only require line feed control characters (*LF*). As a result, these characters must be adapted accordingly when transferring DOS text files to the Amiga and vice versa. This can be achieved by making sure that the *Text Filtering* box is checked during any copying processes from the floppy disk.

The *Text Translation* option controls the conversion of the Amiga character set into the DOS character set. In some DOS files, an eighth bit (high bit) is set for certain ASCII characters to give the character a new meaning, for example in the case of umlauts. Such mutated vowels must be converted to other code numbers on the Amiga.

If you select *ASCII-7* as the translation type (see below), the text in the file will be converted to standard ASCII text. This type of text conversion only takes place when the file is read from the DOS disk. Although the eighth bit is filtered out (i.e. deleted) when the file is read, it is not reset when the file is written to the DOS disk.

Four options for text filtering and translation are hidden in the *Translation Types* cycle gadget. The *ASCII-7* option converts to standard ASCII text, while *INTL* preserves international characters such as é, ð or ö. *DANSK* is used to filter Danish text data, while *MAC* filters ASCII files from a Macintosh that have been transferred to a DOS floppy disk.

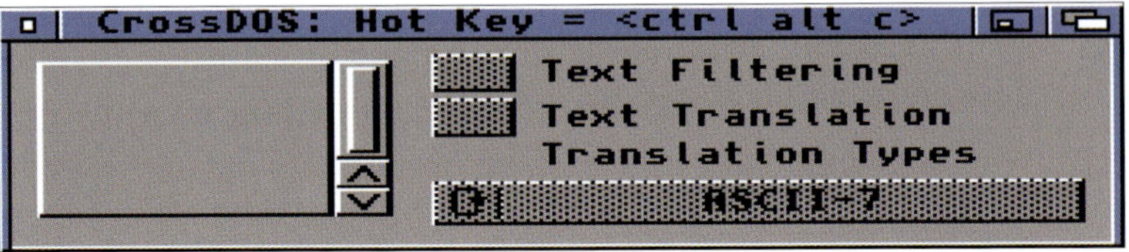

The compact CrossDOS window: mounted DOS drives such as PC0, PC1 etc. are listed on the left, while on the right you will find three quick settings for text conversion.

You can hide the CrossDOS window by clicking on the close gadget or using the `[R-Amiga]+[H]` shortcut. To switch the commodity off completely, use the shortcut `[R-Amiga]+[Q]` or go to the menu via *Project > Quit*. Alternatively, open the *Exchange* Commodity, select the *CrossDOS* entry from the list and click on *Remove*.

Exchange (manage commodities)

Function

Exchange is the central hub for managing and terminating commodities and programs with ease. It's like having your own personal task manager right there in the operating system.

Using Exchange

Exchange can be launched by double-clicking on *Tools > Commodities > Exchange* or using the keyboard shortcut `[Ctrl]+[Alt]+[Help]`. It will open in a separate window.

In the *Available Commodities* section, Exchange lists the active programs and states the name and task of the selected program inside the information field. If you select an entry, you can switch it from *active* to *inactive* (and back to active again if required) using the adjacent cycle gadget to put the corresponding commodity into pause mode. Clicking on *Remove* quits the selected commodity completely.

If a tool or commodity has its own window, it can be opened and closed by clicking the *Show Interface* and *Hide Interface* buttons. In the latter case, the corresponding commodity is hidden but it remains active.

To hide the Exchange window, click on the close gadget or use the shortcut `[R-Amiga]+[H]`. If you want to close it completely, use the keyboard shortcut `[R-Amiga]+[Q]` or go to the menu via *Project > Quit*.

We recommend copying Exchange to the WBStartup directory and leaving it there permanently. This is the best way to ensure it is active at all times.

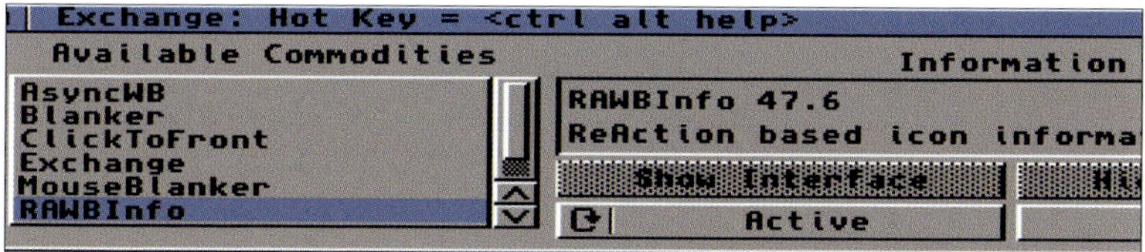

The commodity center of AmigaOS 3.2: Exchange lists all active commodities and tools. You can hide and show them, activate and deactivate them, or close them completely.

FKey (assign function keys)

Function

The ten function keys on the Amiga keyboard – F1 to F10 – are unassigned by default on the Workbench. With the *FKey* commodity you can assign different functions to these keys and turn them into to your own super shortcuts (see section 6.3 on *shortcuts*). This can save you the hassle of navigating to applications or entering recurring text strings.

The function can be used on the F keys alone or in combination with other keys, for example F3 or F4+ALT.

Using FKey

When you start the commodity via *Tools > Commodities > FKey*, a new window will open. The *Defined Keys* selection list will show assigned key combinations as soon as you specify them (it is empty by default). Simply use the *New Key* button to add a new shortcut, while *Delete Key* will remove any existing marked shortcuts.

The *Command* cycle gadget offers eight basic commands that you can assign to a shortcut (see below). Three of these commands require an additional individual entry in the *Command Parameters* string gadget.

If an existing shortcut is to be assigned to another command, select the shortcut under *Defined Keys* and change the assignment using the cycle gadget.

To save your FKey settings permanently, go to the menu *Project > Save Defined Keys*.

The close gadget hides FKey, retaining the function of the assigned shortcuts. To close FKey completely, go to *Project > Quit* or select the *FKey* entry in the Exchange commodity window and click on *Remove*.

Shortcut functions

The following eight commands can be assigned to function keys using the Command cycle gadget:

- *Cycle Windows* moves the rearmost window to the center foreground of the Workbench screen and marks it.
- *Cycle Screens* moves the rearmost screen to the foreground.
- *Enlarge Window* enlarges the active window to the maximum height and width, i.e. up to the right-hand side and the bottom of the screen.
- *Shrink Window* reduces the active window to the smallest possible size.
- *Toggle Window Size* switches the size of the active window between minimum and normal, fulfilling the same purpose as the zoom gadget. The command is also applied to windows that only have a zoom gadget, but no size gadget.
- *Insert text* inserts a defined character string into an active text gadget or console window (such as the Shell) at the position of the text cursor. The character string must be input in the *Command Parameters* string gadget and can have a maximum length of 255 characters. If the function button for the *Insert Text* function is pressed while the text cursor is not in an element suitable for text input, the execution of the function will be ignored.
- *Run Program* opens a program without having to click through a long directory structure. In the *Command Parameters* string gadget, enter the program's name, full path and any optional arguments.

- *Start ARexx Script* executes an ARexx script. The script's name, full path and any optional arguments must be defined in the *Command Parameters* string gadget. If you enclose the script name in double quotes, the script will be converted into an ARexx string file (see *ARexx* section 6.5).

Define individual F keys and F key combinations with FKey to start programs or change the size of windows, for example.

TIP **Key combination with multiple keys**

The key sequence does not have to consist of just one key – it can include several keys that must be pressed simultaneously (not one after the other) to execute a defined command. Instead of *F1*, enter *F1 Alt*, for example, to define the shortcut `[F1]+[Alt]`.
Note: The key entries must be separated by a space, not by a comma or plus sign.

Example for setting up FKey

If you use a program such as *Directory Opus* or *TSgui* as part of your everyday work, simply place a shortcut on an F key to start the program quickly: in FKey, click on *New Key* and enter *F1* in the input field for the shortcut, for example. In the *Command* area, use the cycle gadget to select the option *Run program*. Define the path and name of the program in the *Command Parameters* string gadget. Depending on your system and the location where the software was installed, this may be something like *Work:Tools/DirectoryOpus/DirectoryOpus*, for example.

This applies to all programs, whether native to the Workbench or installed separately. Additional arguments may also be specified. For example, you can display the time on the Workbench quickly by entering the command sequence *DH0:Utilities/Clock digital 200 0* into the *Command Parameters* string gadget. This will open the Clock on the Workbench as a digital version slightly indented at the top edge.

MouseBlanker (hide pointer)

Function

The *MouseBlanker* commodity hides the mouse pointer when an input is made on the keyboard. Then as soon as you move the mouse, the pointer becomes visible again.

You can start the commodity by double-clicking on it; another double-click on the icon stops it. You can also end it by opening the *Exchange* commodity, selecting *MouseBlanker* from the list and clicking *Remove*.

Shell command

```
MOUSEBLANKER [CX_PRIORITY <priority>]
```

MouseBlanker can be run from the Shell with the command `MouseBlanker` and supports the `CX_PRIORITY` argument for setting the priority, as described in the Commodities features (see page 236). When executed from within the Shell, the commodity can be stopped with the `[Ctrl]+[C]` shortcut.

NoCapsLock (switch off Caps Lock)

Function

The Caps Lock key on the keyboard is used to permanently enable capitalization. When pressed, all letters entered on the keyboard will automatically output as uppercase letters, regardless of whether the Shift key is pressed or not. Caps Lock only affects the input of letters, not numbers or special characters.

On the Amiga, a luminous diode is integrated into the Caps Lock key which indicates whether the Caps Lock function is switched on or off. To disable the Caps Lock function, the Caps Lock button must be pressed again.

Using NoCapsLock

The Caps Lock key can be disabled by using the *NoCapsLock* commodity. This means that if you unintentionally press the key it will have no effect on the casing of letters when writing text.

To activate NoCapsLock, double-click its icon in the *Tools > Commodities* drawer. No window will open. To deactivate the commodity, double-click its icon again, or open the *Exchange* commodity, select the *NoCapsLock* entry and click *Remove*.

If you generally find the Caps Lock button annoying and want NoCapsLock to remain permanently activated even after a reset, simply move *NoCapsLock* to the *WBStartup* drawer.

NumericPad (redirect numeric keypad)

Function

The *NumericPad* commodity redirects entries that should be made on the numeric keypad to corresponding keys on the conventional part of the keyboard. This is an invaluable feature for Amiga 600 users, as it lacks a numeric keypad.

Using NumericPad

After starting NumericPad from inside the Commodities drawer by double-clicking its icon, press the Caps Lock key to activate redirection to the Amiga keyboard. You will find the "virtual" numeric keypad positioned around the *L* key. To deactivate redirection of the numeric keypad, press the Caps Lock key again.

Shell command

```
NUMERICPAD [CX_PRIORITY <priority>]
```

WBStartup

The *WBStartup* drawer (located in SYS:) contains programs that are automatically loaded into the system when AmigaOS 3.2 is booted. Six programs are included by default. You can store additional executable commodities in the drawer so that they are automatically activated at the next start.

The standard content of the WBStartup drawer: AssignWedge, AsyncWB, AutoArrangeIcons, DefIcons, MenuTools and RAWBInfo.

AssignWedge (requester extension)

Function and usage

AssignWedge is a useful function that expands the system's volume requester (*"Please insert volume X in any drive."*). In addition to the two default options *Retry* and *Cancel*, the user can use two additional functions:

Assign can be used to manually create an assignment, for example to designate a drawer as a volume; and *Deny* can be used to permanently reject a requested drive until the next restart in order to prevent new requester windows constantly popping up.

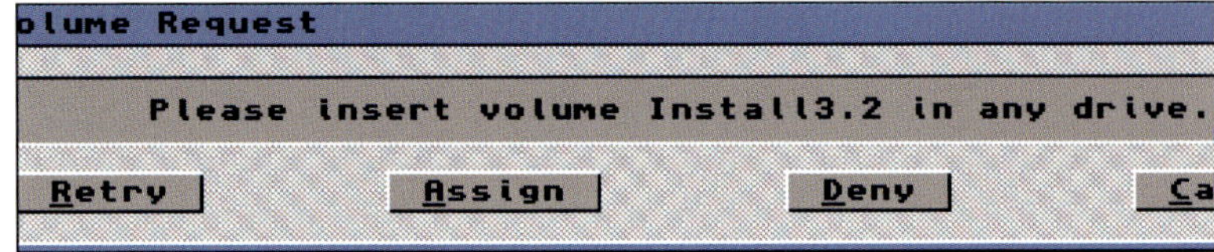

AsyncWB (function extensions)

Function and usage

The AsyncWB commodity extends the operating system with small functions that are very useful in everyday life:

1) The copy and delete processes within the Workbench are executed asynchronously with AsyncWB, which means that the user does not have to wait until a process has ended to run other Workbench tasks.
2) The *Copy* and *Delete* commands in the *Icons* menu of the Workbench are extended by AsyncWB with a separate, Reaction-based graphic progress bar and a *Cancel* button.
3) The *Execute command* function in the *Workbench* menu is extended by AsyncWB with a history functionality, so that the user can search for previously entered commands using the cursor keys (up and down) to quickly run them again. The history information is saved in the log file *ENVARC:Sys/AsyncWB.history*. Furthermore, the *Execute command* window now includes a file requester gadget, making it easier to locate files.
4) The *New drawer* command in the Workbench's *Window* menu now offers the additional option *Icon*, which, if enabled, creates a suitable info file for the new drawer. The drawer will then be automatically visible in every window display mode.

Shell command

The AsyncWB commodity can also be enabled (and disabled) from within the Shell by entering `AsyncWB`. It has several options such as `NOHISTORY` (to switch off history logging) or `BUFSIZE` (to set the buffer size). See chapter 5 on *Shell* for more information.

AutoArrangeIcons (icon sorting)

Function and usage

AutoArrangeIcons rearranges or tidies up the icons in the active window. The keyboard shortcut `[R-Amiga]+[Y]` will run two ARexx scripts that will do the following: reset the active window to its default size and sort the icons it contains by name. A *snapshot* of the active window is then taken.

You can run this commodity from the Shell by entering `AutoArrangeIcons` or via the *Tools* menu in the title bar menu.

DefIcons (icon link)

Function and usage

DefIcons is an extremely useful commodity that attempts to determine the type of a file on the basis of a configuration file and to link that file with a standard icon – a so-called pseudo-icon – if it does not already have one.

DefIcons is already preconfigured, but can be fine-tuned with the *DefaultIcons* preferences (see page 120). DefIcons can be activated or deactivated by double-clicking its icon. Entering the `help DefIcons` command in the Shell lists the DefIcons schemes with all arguments.

MenuTools (help menu item)

Function

If the MenuTools program is located in the *WBStartup* drawer, the *Help* menu item will appear in the *Tools* menu of the Workbench title bar. MenuTools is an ARexx script that can be opened and modified with any Amiga text editor. This way you can create your own menu items and open your favorite applications or games with them.

RAWBInfo (information requester)

Function

RAWBInfo is an extended information requester. If you select an icon and call up the *Information* function from the *Icons* menu, a separate window will open with information and changeable attributes relating to this icon.

RAWBInfo uses Reaction for its GUI and can be opened from the Workbench menu or with the keyboard shortcut `[R-Amiga]+[I]`.

The details shown in the info requester include, for example, the size of a directory, the option to create and replace icons for a selected object, the conversion of icons and the setting of a large selection of arguments for handling the respective icon type.

Using RAWBInfo

The structure and contents of the information window vary slightly depending on the icon type, i.e. on whether the information is to be provided for a drive, a drawer, a program, a project (e.g. an AmigaGuide file) or a trashcan. Common to all views is the title bar, which always shows the path of the icon, and the icon image on the left-hand side of the window. Below the icon, the position of the icon is shown with X and Y coordinates in pixels. X corresponds to the horizontal axis, Y to the vertical axis, in each case starting with the values `0`, `0` for a position at the top left of the window.

You can drag any other icon from Workbench and drop it onto the icon in the info window to replace it. You can undo this change by clicking *Cancel*. Use the *Save* button to save the changes you have made.

Apart from the icon types *drive* and *trashcan*, the information in the main area of the info window is bundled in two tabs, which are explained below: *File* (for programs and projects) or *Drawer*, and *Icon*.

File/Drawer tab

For programs, projects and directories, the *Name* field displays the name of the icon in a text gadget where you can make changes. The icon type is listed in round brackets after the text gadget. For programs and projects, *Version* information is displayed below. Click the gadget or press the `[?]` key to call up the information. Not every icon has a version number – if this is the case, *not available* is displayed.

This is followed by the *Last change* information, which indicates the date of creation or the last change to the object in the format day and time, as well as the *Size* of the object in bytes and blocks. For directories, you can click on the *Size* button to determine the number of files and subdirectories contained in the drawer.

The info window for the *drive* icon type is slightly different. This applies to hard drives and CF and SD card hard drive replacements, as well as floppy drives, CD-ROMs and other drives. In addition to a name text gadget and the size as listed above (in bytes and blocks as well as the number of files and directories on this drive), the drive capacity is also listed as *used* and *free* space. The drives info window also contains the device name and driver (device and handler), the file system used, the creation date and the status of the drive (e.g. readable/ writable for hard disks).

Protection bits (see next paragraph) and comments can also be defined for drawers, programs, projects and trashcans. The *Comment* string gadget can contain 79 characters and be used freely. Some programs automatically insert information here, e.g. the URL of downloaded files, while other icons contain the author copyrights or additional version numbers.

Protections bits

Protection bits can be set for drawers, programs, projects and trashcans inside the info window using the six checkboxes *Read*, *Write*, *Delete*, *Execute*, *Archive* and *Script*.

If *Read* is enabled, the file can be read. If it is disabled, the project cannot be opened. *Write* determines the write protection of a file. If it is not set, i.e. inactive, a file cannot be overwritten. If the *Delete* protection bit is set, i.e. active, a file can be deleted from the drive. If it is not set, the file cannot be removed.

To make a program or script executable, you must set the protection bit to *Execute* (or remove the bit to prevent execution). The *Archive* protection bit is set by backup or archiving software and indicates if a file or drawer has already been archived.

Marking the *Script* bit indicates if a script file can be executed from the Shell only (read more about scripts in chapters 5 and 7).

Icon tab

The *Icon* tab defines important details for opening a program or project. You can use a file requester to specify the default tool used to open a project, for example. Or if you want to open IFF

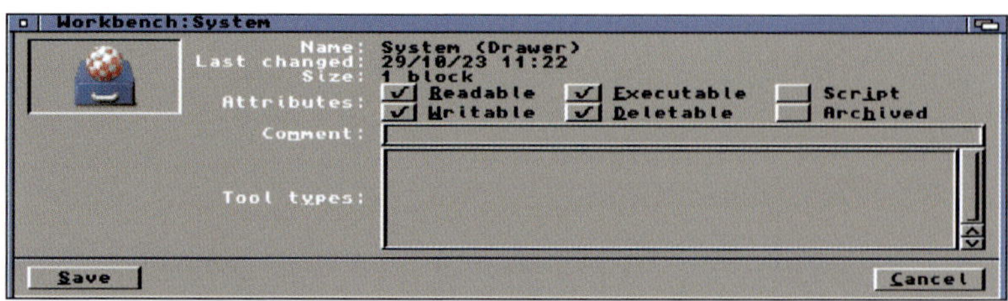

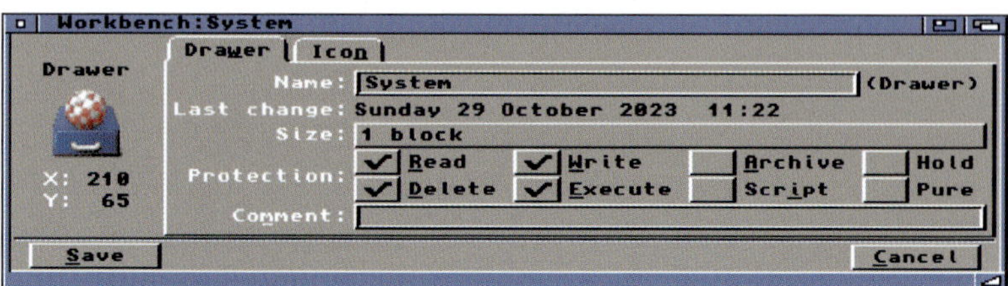

The icon requester in the old design (above) and the modern design created by Reaction (below). RAWBInfo must be active to enable the modern look.

images with a different viewer, rather than the system default MultiView, for example, you can make the corresponding change here too.

Further settings can be adjusted here for projects and programs. *Stack size* specifies the memory capacity to be reserved in RAM for a program or project. Make changes via the text gadget or with the +/- buttons. You can also set the *Priority* value here, which indicates the priority of the program task in relation to the usable processing time compared to other actively executed programs in *multitasking*. The default priority value is 0. To grant a program less processing time, lower the value in the gadget; to prioritize it higher, increase the value. It is recommended to keep the priorities between a minimum of -5 and a maximum of +5 to avoid system instability.

The drop-down list under *Start from* defines the launch options. If you change the value to Shell or ARexx instead of the default start from the Workbench, you can make the system wait for an input when starting.

RAWBInfo offers different settings for the *drawer* icon type in the *Icon* tab. You can use three cycle gadgets to determine the display of icons in the drawer. If you select the *Show* option *As parent*, the display will be based on the parent drawer. In *Show*, you can choose between *Only icons* (i.e. display only files with an associated *.info file*) and *All files*. In *View*, you can sort the display of the drawer contents by icon, name, date, size or type. And in

Sort, you can change the alphabetical sorting of the icons in the drawer to *forward* or *reverse*, meaning ascending or descending.

Tool types

The *Tool types* section lets you adjust the start behavior of a program or project. Instructions for the screen name (example: `Pubscreen=MyScreen`), file type (example: `Filetype=Text`), logging (example: `nolog`) and other settings can be entered into this text gadget.

Definitions in inside parentheses are ignored during execution. To quickly include or exclude features, simply hold down the Shift key and click on the line that is holding the tool type instructions.

RAWBInfo menu

RAWBInfo bundles four items with advanced functions into its own Workbench menu: *Project*, *Type*, *Icon Image* and *Tool types*.

Project menu: If several info requesters are open at the same time, you can quickly switch between these windows with *Next* or *Previous*. If available, the *Version* item shows additional details about the author and date and, if applicable, the CPU, unlike the version information in the info window. *Save* saves the icon, *Load default icon* replaces the current icon with the default icon, *Save as default icon* replaces the default icon with the current version, and *Delete icon* removes the icon. *About* contains the version number of RAWBInfo and more details. Click *Quit* to exit the tool.

Type menu: Five types are available here for the icon that is currently shown: Drive, Drawer, Tool, Project and Trashcan.

Icon image menu: This menu offers a variety of functions related to the processing of icons. *Default* loads the icon that has been predefined in *DefIcons* to create a standard icon for a file that does not yet own an .info file. *Copy* places the current icon into the clipboard, *Paste* replaces the current icon with the icon copied to the clipboard, and *Restore* restores a state prior to a change. The *Convert to palette mapped* menu item changes the icon to the *MagicWB*, *Default* or *Screen* (*GlowIcon* if set) palette.

Under *Extras*, there is an additional submenu with three functions. *Remap 1.3/2.0* changes the color display of icons from the style of AmigaOS 1.3, with four colors, to the extended style of AmigaOS 2.0 and upwards. *Image to icon* converts a

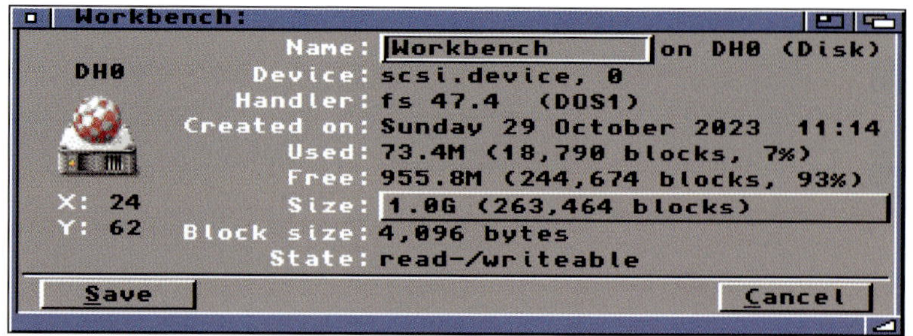

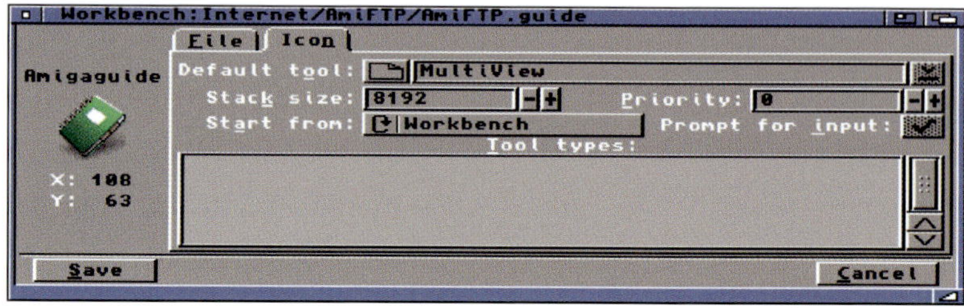

The RAWBInfo information requester for drives (top) and projects (bottom, with active icon tab). Note the extended customization options for projects, tools and drawers.

selected image into an icon. *Delete alternate image* only deletes the image that is displayed when the icon is selected (e.g. the glow effect of the GlowIcons) – if an icon does not have an alternative image, it will appear dimmed when selected.

In the *Icon image* menu, you can display content from the clipboard with *Show clip*, transfer the current icon to the icon editor for visual editing via *IconEdit*, or *load* and *save* an icon image.

The *Frameless* option removes an unwanted frame around the icon, *Drop NewIcons data* skips the NewIcons format. *Drop planar data* speeds up the loading time of a GlowIcon by not additionally saving the icon in the outdated style of AmigaOS 2.0. This means that no additional icon layer is created, which would increase the file size.

Tool types menu: Here you will find functions that relate to the tool types of the icon. You can *clear* (delete), *sort* in alphabetical order, *restore*, *disable all* or *enable all* features, and *toggle* attributes between active and inactive.

The Shell

5

The Shell is the command line interface of AmigaOS. This "CLI" has been included since the first versions of AmigaOS. However, AmigaOS 3.2 brings a whole range of new functions to the Shell: alternative script interpreters, an improved command history and, for the first time, Tab completion. The ability to use Pipe to link commands is a feature already implemented in AmigaOS 3.1.4. It is integrated directly into the Shell. Executing multiple commands in a subshell is also included.

A typical Shell session

To illustrate how it works, here is a brief look at how a typical Shell session might run. If you don't understand all the concepts yet, don't worry. More detailed explanations will follow in later sections.

First, start the Shell by double-clicking on *Shell* in the *System* drawer. A Shell window will open under the title bar of the Workbench screen.

TIP **Standard Shell window**
The window opens by default with a height of 130 pixels and the width of the screen. The desired size and position can be set in the tool types in the icon settings. With `WINDOW=CON://700/300/AmigaShell/CLOSE/ICONIFY`, the default program *SYS:System/Shell* defined in the icon settings positions the window with a size of 700 by 300 pixels where the mouse pointer is located.

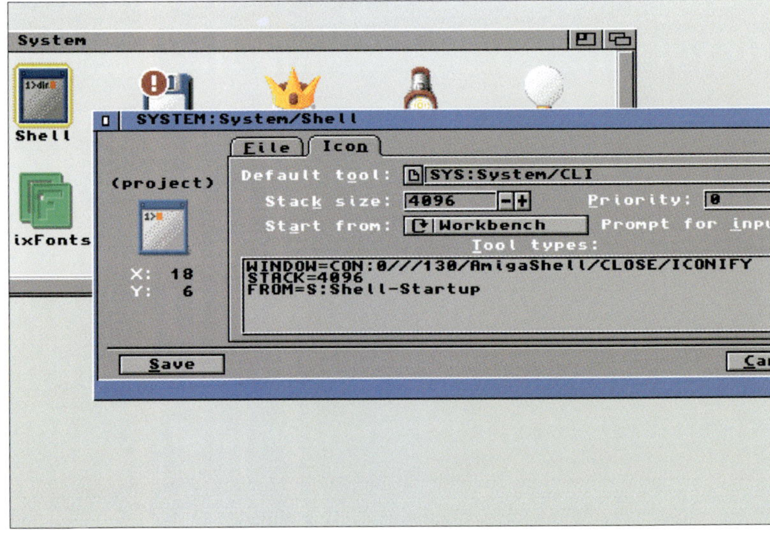

Use the Shell icon settings to define a perfect position and size of the Shell window.

To get started, the `Info` command shows an overview of the available drives and their assigned names. To do this, type in `Info` and press the `[Enter]` key.

TIP **Upper and lower case**
In contrast to typical Unix shells, the Amiga shell is not case sensitive: `Info`, `info`, `INFO` and `InFo` all indicate the same command.

```
AmigaShell
1.System:> info

Mounted disks:
Unit          Size        Used          Free Full Errs
CD0           No disk present
DF0           No disk present
DF1           No disk present
DH3          4095M     4194304       4194303  50%    0  Re
INSTALL       200M       78378        127252  38%    0  Re
OS           1838M        7077        934393   1%    0  Re
RAM           130M          76        133977   0%    0  Re

Volumes available:
Amiga [Mounted]
AmigaOS3.2CD [Mounted]
Ram Disk [Mounted]
System [Mounted]
1.System:>
```

Info shows all disks and their assigns, e.g. DH0: & System.

Next, the `Clear` command clears the Shell window. Use `Dir` to get an overview of the files and directories in the top directory of your system drive.

One disadvantage of the `Dir` command is the unsorted display of directory names. The `List` command with the appropriate option provides a remedy. With `List SORT name` you get a list of the directory sorted by name. However, if you also prefer to see the folders before the files, as in the `Dir` output, use `List SORT REVERSETYPE,NAME`.

The `List` and `Dir` commands also show the contents of subdirectories if the `ALL` option is added. Try it out with `Dir ALL` or `List ALL`. It may take a while for the command to show the contents of all subdirectories. You can interrupt the command before it finishes by pressing `[CTRL]+[C]`.

Adapting the *S:User-Startup* script can be a typical task. Use `List S:` or `Dir S:` to display the contents of the directory to

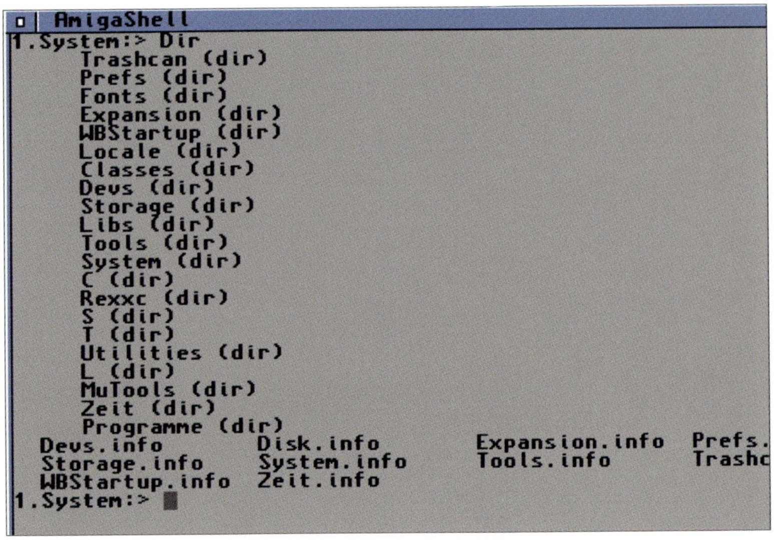

```
AmigaShell
1.System:> Dir
     Trashcan (dir)
     Prefs (dir)
     Fonts (dir)
     Expansion (dir)
     WBStartup (dir)
     Locale (dir)
     Classes (dir)
     Devs (dir)
     Storage (dir)
     Libs (dir)
     Tools (dir)
     System (dir)
     C (dir)
     Rexxc (dir)
     S (dir)
     T (dir)
     Utilities (dir)
     L (dir)
     MuTools (dir)
     Zeit (dir)
     Programme (dir)
  Devs.info          Disk.info          Expansion.info   Prefs.
  Storage.info       System.info        Tools.info       Trashc
  WBStartup.info     Zeit.info
1.System:>
```

The Dir command showing the contents of the parent directory of a system drive.

which the `S:` assignment refers. Use the `CD` command built into the Shell to change to the corresponding directory. To do this, type `CD S:`.

It is a good idea to create a copy of the file before making any changes. You can do this by typing the command `Copy User-Startup User-Startup.bak CLONE`. The `clone` option is useful for backups. It sets the time, file comment and permissions to the same values as the source file. Edit the file with `TextEdit S:Startup-Sequence`. For example, add the line `NewShell CON:424/568/600/200/BOOT-SHELL/CLOSE/ICONIFY` to the end of the file to automatically obtain a Shell window with 600 x 200 pixels at the bottom right after booting with a screen resolution of 1024 x 768 pixels. You will see this after booting as soon as you move the Workbench window to the background.

TIP **Tab completion**

With Tab completion, you do not need to type the name *User-Startup* in full. Type in U, followed by `[TAB]`, and see what happens.

```
AmigaShell
1.System:> List SORT NAME
C                                   Dir ----rwed Heute      10:45:14
Classes                             Dir ----rwed 19-Sep-21  15:55:41
Devs                                Dir ----rwed 13-Apr-21  02:43:34
Devs.info                          1862 ----rw-d 13-Apr-21  02:43:34
Disk.info                          2372 ----rw-d Heute      10:27:08
Expansion                           Dir ----rwed 19-Sep-21  15:54:34
Expansion.info                     1788 ----rw-d 13-Apr-21  02:43:34
Fonts                               Dir ----rwed 19-Sep-21  15:55:45
L                                   Dir ----rwed 19-Sep-21  15:55:37
Libs                                Dir ----rwed 19-Sep-21  16:15:23
Locale                              Dir ----rwed 19-Sep-21  15:54:34
MuTools                             Dir ----rwed 19-Sep-21  15:59:05
Prefs                               Dir ----rwed 19-Sep-21  16:15:30
Prefs.info                         1656 ----rw-d 13-Apr-21  02:43:33
Programme                           Dir ----rwed Heute      11:00:26
Programme.info                     1484 ----rw-d Heute      11:00:16
Rexxc                               Dir ----rwed 19-Sep-21  15:54:39
S                                   Dir ----rwed 19-Sep-21  16:15:30
Storage                             Dir ----rwed 13-Apr-21  02:43:34
Storage.info                       1898 ----rw-d 13-Apr-21  02:43:33
System                              Dir ----rwed Heute      10:34:11
System.info                        2034 ----rw-d 13-Apr-21  02:43:34
T                                   Dir ----rwed 19-Sep-21  15:54:40
Tools                               Dir ----rwed 19-Sep-21  16:26:34
Tools.info                         1926 ----rw-d 13-Apr-21  02:43:33
Trashcan                            Dir ----rwed 19-Sep-21  15:53:30
Trashcan.info                      2916 ----rw-d 13-Apr-21  02:43:34
Utilities                           Dir ----rwed 13-Apr-21  02:43:33
Utilities.info                     1952 ----rw-d 13-Apr-21  02:43:33
WBStartup                           Dir ----rwed 13-Apr-21  02:43:33
WBStartup.info                     1990 ----rw-d 13-Apr-21  02:43:33
Zeit                                Dir ----rwed 19-Sep-21  16:15:19
Zeit.info                          1484 ----rwed 19-Sep-21  16:15:02
12 files - 22K bytes - 21 directories - 68 blocks used
1.System:>
```

The list command with its output sorted alphabetically by name.

If you just want an emergency Shell with a window that is always in the background, try `NewShell CON:424/568/600/200/Boot-Shell/BACKDROP`. You will only see this if you move all other windows, including the Workbench window, to another location.

TIP **CD command integrated directly into the Shell**
It is not necessary to enter the `CD command`. The Shell usually recognizes automatically when you enter a path to a directory and switches to it.

Did you notice how the `List S:` command displayed the output unsorted by default? This is the default behavior. With `alias List "List SORT NAME"` you get a sorted output by default in the current Shell. If required, add this alias to the Shell startup sequence in the file *S:Shell-Startup*. You can find more information on this in the section *The Shell start sequence* in this chapter on page 273.

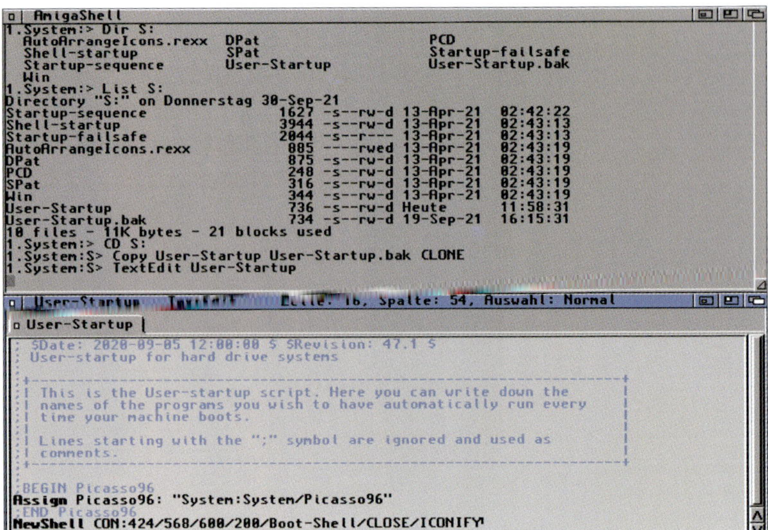

This image shows how to create a backup copy and then edit the user-startup file.

Basics of the Shell

In this section, you will learn all about the basic functions of the Shell. You will also be introduced to a number of exciting new Shell functions.

In addition to numerous basic functions, the Shell offers many new options, such as nesting and combining commands with the && and ( ) operators, extended redirection options, recursive alias expansion, nesting of backticks, the evaluation of control characters in character strings (*binary expansion*) and much more.

A complete overview of new functions can be found in the *AmigaOS 3.2 documentation* under *The Shell / New Features: Changes in the Shell*. There is a link to *Shell Syntax for Experts*, for all those who want to delve even deeper into the treasure chest of the Shell.

Finding help

In the previous section on a typical Shell session, you will have learned some commands and options. Would you like to know more? Then the `Help` command will be of use to you. Without any parameters, this command opens the table of contents of the *AmigaOS 3.2 Reference Manual*. However, you can also enter the name of a program, command or other topic. For example, try `Help Dir`, `Help NewShell`, `Help Shell`, `Help AssignWedge`, `Help Input` and `Help Help`. Among other things, `Help NewShell` shows you how the window specification for `CON:` is structured. Alternatively, click on the *Help* icon in the *System* drawer or press the [HELP] key on your Amiga keyboard. In programs that support this, you will receive help for the program by pressing this key. The AmigaGuide files with the name extension *.help* are located in *HELP:*, which points to *SYS:Locale/Help*.

TIP **Help function deluxe**

With the `DS` option you can also search for other help files beyond *HELP:*, and with the `CS` option you can even search the contents of the files.

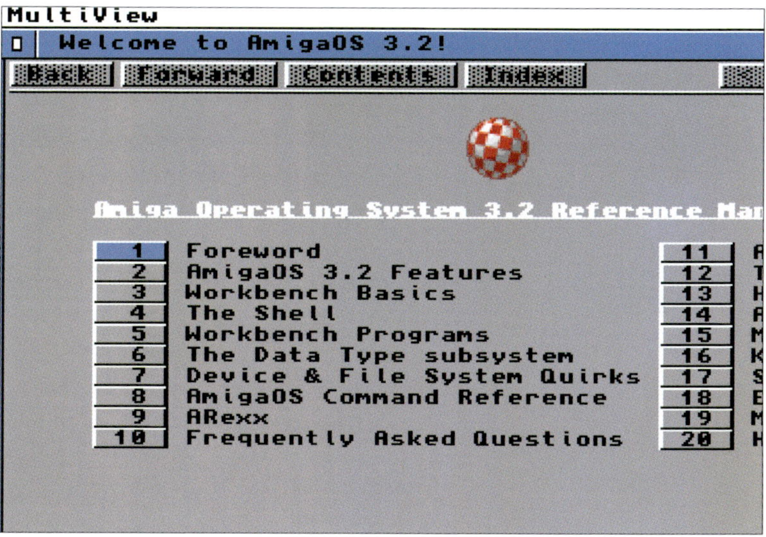

Contents of the AmigaOS 3.2 Reference Manual

Keyboard shortcuts

The AmigaOS 3.2 Shell supports the typical keyboard shortcuts known to date. For example, `[Shift]+[Left arrow]` jumps to the beginning of the line, and `[Shift]+[Right arrow]` jumps to the end of the line. Being able to pause a long command output is also quite convenient, for example for the command

`Dir SYS: ALL`. You can do this simply by typing a Space or another displayable character or by pressing `[Ctrl]+[S]`. You can then continue either by removing the character or by pressing `[Ctrl]+[Q]`.

Further shortcuts are explained in the table below. Section 6.3 about *keyboard shortcuts* lists the most important keyboard shortcuts inside the *Shell* subsection.

Key combination	**Function**
[Shift]+[Left arrow]	at the beginning of the line
[Shift]+[Right arrow]	at the end of the line
Space bar or any other character	stop output (continue by removing the character)
[Ctrl]+[S]	stop output
[Ctrl]+[Q]	continue output
[Ctrl]+[W]	delete word to the left of cursor
[Ctrl]+[X]	delete current line
[Ctrl]+[K]	delete everything from the cursor to the end of the line
[Ctrl]+[U]	delete everything backwards from the cursor to the beginning of the line
[Ctrl]+[J]	start new line

Tab completion

Since version 47, i.e. in AmigaOS 3.2, the Shell supports the automatic completion of commands, path specifications and variables using the tabulator key `[TAB]`. This function can save you a lot of typing.

Open a new Shell, type `D` and press the `[TAB]` key twice. The Shell shows a selection of commands and paths. Tab completion is useless for accessing the *Devs* directory, as you must enter at least *Dev* followed by the `[TAB]` key for a unique assignment. So either type *Dev* and then press the `[TAB]` key or *Devs* and then press the `[Enter]` key. Use the `Dir` command to get an overview of the directory. Then type do and press `[TAB]`. The Shell in OS3.2 completes to *DOSDrivers*.

Yet another mode toggles through multiple completion options after they are displayed by pressing `[TAB]` again. You activate this with `Set SHELLCOMPLETION CYCLE`. However, if you want to see all the possibilities the first time if there are several options, use `Set SHELLCOMPLETION EARLYLISTING`. You can reach both features together using `SHELLCOMPLETION CYCLE, EARLYLISTING`.

Try the options out to find your favorite. You can enter them in the *S:Shell-Startup* file.

Command history

Before AmigaOS 3.2, the CON handler implemented the so-called *command history*. This list of previously entered commands makes it possible to execute or modify a command again without having to re-enter it completely. As of AmigaOS 3.2, the Shell, in version 47, takes over this task. As a result, only entries from the Shell are stored in the history. Entries that are programs started in the Shell are now ignored.

The keys `[Arrow up]` and `[Arrow down]` scroll through previous commands. The [Shift] key can also be used to search in the history. The position of the cursor plays a decisive role here. If it is at the end of `Dir C:`, for example, the Shell will find all lines beginning with `Dir C:`. If the cursor is located in a line `Dir all` between `Dir` and `all`, the Shell will find all lines that begin with `Dir` and end with `all` – unless you use `[Ctrl]+[R]` instead, as the Shell then only uses the beginning of the line as a search pattern and ignores all characters after the cursor.

The variable `histsize` defines the maximum length of the Shell's command history. If this is undefined, the Shell will remember a maximum of 256 lines. With `Set histsize 1000`, however, the Shell will remember a maximum of 1,000 lines. Set this variable in the Shell start sequence in *S:Shell-Startup* to permanently adjust the maximum length for all newly started Shells. Use the `History` command to display the history of the current Shell, save it to a file or reload a history.

Paths, devices, drive names and assignments

Path specifications in AmigaOS follow the pattern *drive:path/to/directory*. As before, upper and lower case is not important. Such a path specification should be complete or absolute. An example is: `CD System:S/Startup-Sequence`, where in this example *System:* is the name of the drive on which the system is installed. Device names and assignments can also be specified as an alternative to the drive.

A device name is the name of the partition, as it can be viewed or changed in the partitioning program *HDToolBox*, for example, or the name of the device. An example of a typical device name is *DH0:*. However, other names up to 30 characters long are also possible! For example, a drive with data could be called *Data:* and its corresponding partition with the file system called *DAT:*.

Not every device has a file system for storing files and directories. For example, *PRT:* stands for the printer. Some devices work with removable media, such as *CD0:* for the first CD, DVD or Blu-ray drive, or *DF0:* for the traditional first floppy drive.

A selection of device names:

Device name	Function
CD0	first CD/DVD/Blu-ray drive
DA0	first drive for a disk saved as an ADF file
DF1	second floppy disk drive
DH0	typical name for a partition on a hard drive or SSD
RAM	the RAM Disk, whose data is only stored in the system's main memory
PRT	printer
SER	serial port, e.g. for a modem
PAR	parallel port, e.g. for parallel networking of two Amigas

Assignments are shortcuts that can be used to call up any path. Some of them are standard in AmigaOS. For example, `SYS:` refers to the drive from which AmigaOS has booted. The absolute path above could therefore also be *SYS:S/Startup-Sequence*. However, it can be even shorter, as *S:* points to the standard script directory: *S:Startup-Sequence*.

The *C:* assignment, which points to *System:C*, is particularly important. This is where the Shell commands are located.

The `Assign` command provides an overview of all assignments. It can also be used to create new assignments. For example, `Assign R: RAM:` would make the RAM Disk accessible under the abbreviation `R:`. An assignment can also refer to several destinations.

A selection of standard assignments with *System:* as the name for the system drive as an example:

Assign	**Target directory**	**Function**
SYS:	System drive	system drive from which AmigaOS has booted
C:	System:C	Shell commands
DEVS:	System:Devs	device drivers, including monitor and printer drivers (PRINTERS:), mount files (DOSDrivers), keyboard mappings (KEYMAPS:)
ENV:	Ram Disk:Env	settings at runtime - click on "Use" within a preset (preferences)
ENVARC:	System:Prefs/Env-Archive	permanently saved settings, standard icons - click on "Save" within a preset (Preferences)
HELP:	System:Locale/Help	documentation and help files
L:	System:L	handlers and file systems such as CDFileSystem
LOCAL:	System:Locale	localization files, language and country definitions
LIBS:	System:Libs and System:Classes	libraries and classes that programs can access
REXX:	System:S	ARexx scripts
S:	System:S	system scripts such as startup-sequence and user-startup
T:	Ram Disk:T	for temporary files

The assigns *S:*, *System:S*, *Sys:S* and *DH0:S* (if the system is located on volume *DH0)* therefore all refer to one and the same directory.

There are also relative path specifications. For example, if *System:S* is the current directory, then the specification of *Startup-Sequence* is sufficient. However, if the Shell is located in *System:C*, it will not find the *Startup-Sequence* file there if, for whatever reason, there is a file there with that name. In this case, the absolute path continues to work. It is also possible to jump up one level with /. This is how the relative path */S* would work. Alternatively, : (colon) always jumps to the top directory of a drive. Accordingly, the relative path *:S* also works.

File pattern

AmigaDOS offers the option of capturing several files or directories at once using file patterns. As the `dos.library` implements this functionality, it can also be used by any application.

AmigaDOS file patterns differ from file patterns under Linux, Windows or Mac OS X. What they have in common is the `?` (question mark), which stands for exactly one character. The `#` (hash) stands for no character or any number of characters, followed by the character that may occur more than once. Thus, `#A` stands for none or any number of characters followed by the letter A. #? stands for any number of characters, `C:A#?` shows you all commands that begin with *A*, while `C:#?A#?` shows you all commands that contain at least one *A*. As AmigaDOS does not differentiate between lower and upper case, a lower case *a* will also fit.

This procedure offers more flexibility than the common `*` (asterisk) for any number of arbitrary characters. If you still want to use `*`, you can activate it under AmigaOS 3.2 with one of many commands from Aminet. `Wildstar ON` from the Aminet archive *ksc_Wildstar* works perfectly under AmigaOS 3.2 (download: www.aminet.net/package/util/cli/ksc_Wildstar). Unlike #?, however, * must not be used alone, as a single asterisk also stands for the current console window (see section *Input and output redirection*). So `C:*` will work for you, but not `*`.

There are even more ways to work: the `|` character (vertical bar) enables an either/or. For example, `A|B` stands for *A* or *B*. All commands that begin with *A* or *B* are shown by `Dir C:(A|B)#?`. The brackets start a subordinate pattern and thus define the sequence. The % character does not represent a character. Therefore `A(B|C|%)` stands for *AB*, *A* and *AC*.

File patterns can be negated with the tilde ~ and the familiar brackets. For example, `~(#?.info)` stands for all files that are not icons. Last but not least, square brackets can be used to specify a selection of characters. For example, `[ACF]#?` stands for everything that starts with *A*, *C* or *F*, while `[B-E]` applies to everything that starts with *B*, *C*, *D* or *E*. Negation is also possible: `[~A-Z]` must not contain a letter in the corresponding position.

The reference documentation for AmigaOS 3.2 does not currently contain a section for file patterns, as was the case in manuals for all versions prior to 3.2. In the documentation wiki for AmigaOS 4, however, there is a description of many options in English (see https://wiki.amigaos.net/wiki/Pattern_Matching).

Input and output redirection

Each command executed by the Shell receives three input/output streams: an input stream for user input, an output stream for the output of commands and a special output stream for error messages. Each command also inherits the *console handler* of the Shell, accessible via the special filename `*` or the special device name *Console:*. By default, the current Shell window is the standard input, the standard output and the standard error output.

These data streams can be easily redirected. With `Dir C: >RAM:commands.txt`, the list of commands in *C:* ends up in the *RAM:commands.txt* file. With the command sequence `Dir does-not-exist >RAM:error.log` (in case that *does-not-exist* can't be found), the output also ends up in the file by default. Use `*>` to separately redirect the error output: for example, with `List RAM: RAM:does-not-exist >RAM:list.txt *>RAM:list-error.log` (with non-existent *RAM:does-not-exist*) the error output ends up in *RAM:list-error.log* and the list of files and directories in *RAM* has its output in *RAM:list.txt*.

The default input can be redirected too: `Date >RAM:date` writes the current time and date to the *RAM:date* file. With `Date ? <RAM:date`, the date can be set again. The question mark is required, otherwise the command will not accept any input from the standard input.

By default, the Shell overwrites the specified file when redirecting the standard output or the standard error output. With `>>` or `*>>`, however, the Shell appends the new output. With `<>`, standard input and standard output end up in the same file. With `*><` the standard error output is written to the standard output. However, this is the default anyway.

Prior to the DOS library of AmigaOS 3.2, version 47, it was unusual to consistently use the error output for error messages. As of AmigaOS 3.2, Shell and AmigaDOS commands route error messages to the standard error channel, as do other programs that use the *PrintFault()* function of the DOS library. In addition, existing Shell scripts completely decouple commands with `Run <>NIL:` from the Shell, which means that the error output would no longer be redirected. As a result, existing scripts would no longer function correctly. For these reasons, the Shell without `*>` redirects the standard error output to the standard output. Further compatibility rules are explained in the *AmigaOS 3.2 Reference documentation* under *Shell / Shell Syntax / Redirection of Input/Output/Error Streams*.

You can also use * and CONSOLE:. The command sequence Type CONSOLE: >RAM:console.txt writes everything you enter to the *RAM:console* file until you press [Ctrl]+\\. Make sure you only press this shortcut once. It will end the input. If you press this shortcut in a Shell window while the Shell is waiting for a command input, the Shell assumes that you do not want to enter any further commands – and exits.

Pipes

Pipes are a mechanism for providing the output of a program to another program as input. This was already possible in older AmigaOS versions via the queue handler. For example, List >PIPE:text or List to PIPE:text writes the output to a pipe channel called *text*. This can be output again unsorted with Type <PIPE:text or sorted with Sort <PIPE:text. The output of more than one command can also be redirected to the same pipe channel. The output can then be processed by another command.

New with the pipe handler version 45 in AmigaOS 3.2 is the possibility to forward the output of a command directly with the pipe character | to another command as input. The above example can thus be shortened to List | Sort. This option activates the standard startup sequence *S:Startup-Sequence* by loading the module *L:System-Startup*. More than two commands are also possible: with List | Sort | More, the sorted output of List ends up in the *More* text viewer, which displays it page by page. The next line is displayed when pressing [Enter], and the next page is shown by pressing the Space bar. If you cancel the output prematurely with [Q] or [Ctrl]+[C], the Shell also terminates the previous command. For this to work, it makes sense to use the queue handler from AmigaOS 3.2. Other third-party implementations or older versions may not be suitable for the piping described here.

Another option is to append the output of two commands to each other with ||. For example, with List C: || List S: the lists with the content of *C:* and *S:* appear one after the other. They can be collectively redirected to another program. For example, List C: || List C: | More forwards both outputs one after the other to the text viewer.

The Shell starts everything to the left of a | or || character in a sub-Shell. Therefore, `Set A=1 | Echo $A` returns the output *$A* instead of *1*. The Shell sets the variable `A` in the sub-Shell, but the `echo` command no longer notices that.

The Shell start sequence

Every time you open a Shell window or a program starts a Shell, the Shell executes the commands in the *S:Shell-Startup* file – at least as long as you do not specify a different startup file with the `FROM` argument.

In this Shell start sequence you can use `aliases` to define your own command shortcuts, change the Shell prompt or increase the standard stack size, for example. The file supplied with AmigaOS 3.2 already contains some activated example aliases from line 17 onwards. This includes an alias that redirects the `ls` command, which will be familiar to Linux users, to `List`, or an alias that calls the AmigaDOS command `Clear` instead of the DOS command `CLS`.

The Shell start sequence sets the standard prompt in line 63 and the standard display program for the Shell's new DataTypes support in line 55. In the comments from line 64 onwards you will find a guide to the options for an alternative Shell prompt with an example in line 100. Remove the comment character before the `prompt command` and open a new Shell window to test the effect.

Examples of adjustments to the completion of commands can be found in lines 28 and 33. The first command switches off completion completely. The second activates switching through the options with the `[Tab]` and `[Shift]+[Tab]` keys. If you want to test the effect of one of these commands without immediately changing the Shell start sequence and starting a new Shell, simply copy the corresponding command into a Shell window with `[R-Amiga]+[C]` and `[R-Amiga]+[V]` and execute it. This is also a good way to explore the possibilities of a Shell prompt.

The command `Stack 8192` in line 42 ensures fewer crashes with programs that require a larger stack than the standard 4096 bytes, although the question remains as to whether the allusion to the book The *Hitchhiker's Guide to the Galaxy* is purely coincidental. Anyone using software ported from Unix or similar stack-hungry programs should set a higher value, such as `stack 32768`, if sufficient memory is available.

If you only want to use the higher stack value or other customizations such as additional or different assignments with the `Assign` command for certain Shells, copy the *S:Shell-Startup* file to *S:Programming-Startup*, for example, adapt it accordingly and call the `NewShell` command with the argument `FROM S:Programming-Startup`. Alternatively, copy the *Shell* icon from the *System* directory, launch its icon information via `[R-Amiga]+[I]` and change the `from=` icon attribute according to your requirements.

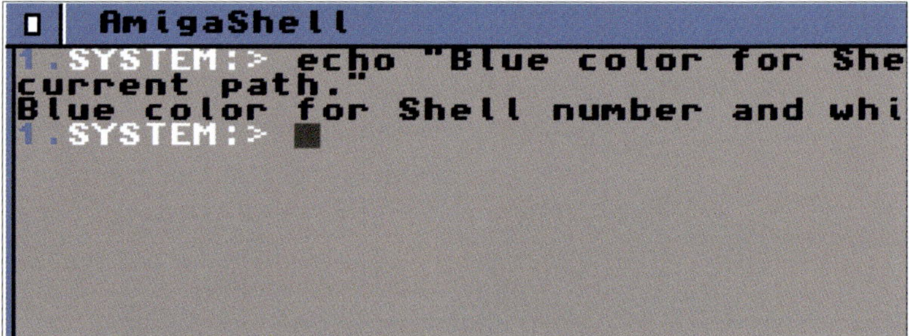

An alternative prompt, taken from the original shell-startup file. It changes the color of the Shell instance to white and the color of the current path to blue.

Listing: The Shell start sequence S:SHELL-STARTUP

```
; $VER: Shell-Startup 47.4 (14.11.2020)
;
;+----------------------------------------------------------------+
;| The following are Shell configuration options that you can enable  |
;| by just removing the ";" symbol in the line you want to activate, |
;| or by adding it, in case you want to disable it.                  |
;+----------------------------------------------------------------+
;
; Aliases
; =======
;
; Creates alternative names for AmigaOS commands. It is useful to
; reduce the amount of key strokes required to run a command, and also
; serves as an aid when you are more familiar with other naming for
; the same functionality on other Operating Systems.
;
ALIAS CLEAR "ECHO NOLINE *"*E[0;0H*E[J*" "
ALIAS CLS CLEAR
ALIAS XCOPY "COPY CLONE "
ALIAS LS LIST
;
;-----------------------------------------------------------------
; TAB Expansions
; ==============
;
; Disables TAB expansions.
;
;SET SIMPLESHELL ON
;
; Will enable cycle mode with early listing and exclude .info files
; from being selected unless explicitly suggested.
;
;SET SHELLCOMPLETION CYCLE, EARLYLISTING
;
;-----------------------------------------------------------------
; Stack Size
; ==========
;
; Increases the amount of memory allocated for a program for its stack
; usage. Default is 4096 bytes.
;
;STACK 8192
;
;-----------------------------------------------------------------
; DataTypes Support
; =================
;
; The Shell is aware of the Amiga DataTypes system and can be setup
; to display datatypes automatically, just by typing the filename on a
```

```
; CLI/Shell. For that, the file to be displayed must have its "e "
; (executable) bit cleared and must be supported by a datatype that
; is known to the system. Furthermore, the variable "$VIEWER" must be
; set to the path of a command that is able to display datatypes.
;
SET VIEWER MULTIVIEW
;
;---------------------------------------------------------------------
; Prompt
; ======
;
; Default prompt that displays the Shell number and current path
;
PROMPT "%N.%S> "
;
; With the use of Escape Sequences, the prompt can be further tweaked.
; The following is a complete list of Escape Sequences:
;
;          *Ec           Clears the window and resets all modes to defaults.
;          *E[0m        Resets graphics modes to defaults.
;          *E[1m        Turns on text boldface.
;          *E[3m        Turns on text italic.
;          *E[4m        Turns on text underlining.
;          *E[7m        Turns on reverse video text.
;          *E[8m        Makes text match background color.
;          *E[22m       Turns off boldface.
;          *E[23m       Turns off italics.
;          *E[24m       Turns off underlining.
;          *E[27m       Turns off reverse video.
;          *E[28m       Returns the text color to normal.
;          *E[30m       Turns on text color0 (background, default grey).
;          *E[31m       Turns on text color1 (shadow, default black).
;          *E[32m       Turns on text color2 (shine, default white).
;          *E[33m       Turns on text color3 (accent, default blue).
;          *E[3#m       Turns on text color# (4-7).
;          *E[39m       Turns on text default color (color1).
;          *E[40m       Turns on text background color0 (default grey).
;          *E[41m       Turns on text background color1 (default black).
;          *E[42m       Turns on text background color2 (default white).
;          *E[43m       Turns on text background color3 (default blue).
;          *E[4#m       Turns on text background color# (4-7).
;          *E[49m       Turns on default text background color (color0).
;          *E[#u        Sets maximum length of lines in window to #.
;          *E[#t        Sets maximum number of lines in window to #.
;          *E[#x        Starts text # pixels from left edge of window.
;          *E[#y        Starts text # pixels from top edge of window.
;
; And now lets go to an example:
; Set blue color for Shell number and white color for current path.
;
;PROMPT "*E[0m*E[33m%N.*E[32m%S>*E[0m "
;
;
;------------------ End of Shell-startup file ----------------------
```

DataTypes support

Since version 45, the Shell starts the preset display tool under certain conditions for files that can be displayed by active datatypes from *DEVS:Datatypes*. To do this, the file must not be executable. If necessary, remove the executable permission with `Protect file -e`. Furthermore, use `SetENV Viewer Multiview SAVE` to set *MultiView* as the display program, for example. The program should support DataTypes in order to be able to display or play all formats supported by DataTypes. The Shell will now automatically start *MultiView* for the specified file in order to display it.

Try out the function after setting the environment variable, for example, by entering `SYS:Prefs/Presets/Backdrops/background_640_512.png`. Tab completion in AmigaOS 3.2.1 does not yet take this function into account, which is why you have to enter the filename yourself.

Alternative script interpreter

With `Protect RAM:backup +s` you can inform the Shell that the *RAM:backup* file is a Shell script file. From now on, this can be called up without preceding with the `Execute` command. As of version 40 of the Shell, this also works with ARexx scripts.

As of AmigaOS 3.2, this is also possible with any other interpreter with a small modification at the beginning of the file: with `#!` – or the more Amiga-like `;!` – at the start of a script file you will specify the desired interpreter. For example, with `#! C:Perl` the Shell automatically loads the Perl interpreter *C:Perl* for a script with script permissions. The default behavior of the Amiga Shell can be explicitly specified with `;! Execute`.

A creative use is described in the *AmigaOS 3.2 reference documentation* under *The Shell / New Features: Changes in the Shell / Alternative script interpreters*. Write

```
;! Type HEX
Hello World!
```

into a file that is not called *HEX*, e.g. *RAM:Hello*. Set the script permission with `Protect RAM:Hello ADD s` and execute the new script by entering the name to see what happens. The Shell places the filename between the `Type` command and the `HEX` option.

Where is the scroll bar?

Have you noticed that even the greatly expanded Shell and the greatly expanded *CON handler* of AmigaOS 3.2 are lacking something? Exactly – we are missing the vertical scroll bar. This would make it possible for us to see the text that has scrolled out of the window.

INFO **Scrollbars in the next AmigaOS version**
In AmigaOS 3.3, the Shell window will contain a scroll bar as well as optional tabs for several Shell sessions in one window. The AmigaOS 3.2/3.3 development team has already revealed this.

Scrollbars are currently only available using external tools. One of the recommendations is *ViNCEd* by Thomas Richter (download: www.aminet.net/package/util/Shell/ViNCEd). The current version 3.106 on Aminet is from July 2022, so it is relatively up-to-date. The readme text mentions that ViNCEd works best with AmigaOS 3.1.4 or better. Thomas Richter is one of the developers of AmigaOS 3.1.4, so compatibility should be ensured. The width of the scrollbar is also correct.

The popular *KingCON-Handler* will also continue to work for the time being (download: www.aminet.net/package/util/Shell/KingCON_1.3). Still, the latest version 1.3 dates back to 1994, and the scrollbar with KingCON is narrower than the standard setting for AmigaOS 3.2.

If you want to use ViNCEd, check exactly which options you want to use during installation. For the purest possible AmigaOS 3.2 experience, it is recommended not to have the Shell icon replaced, not to have the CON:-handler replaced by

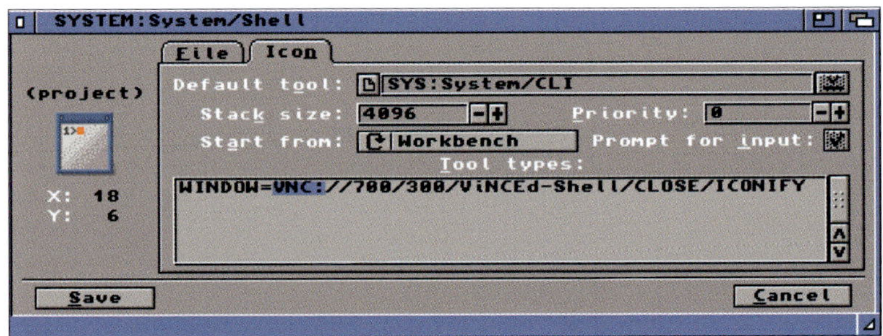

Icon properties for a minimal ViNCEd Shell window

```
ViNCEd-Shell
  68020.library              68030.library                68040.library
  68060.library              680x0.library                amigaguide.library
  asl.library                boards.library               bullet.library
  commodities.library        datatypes.library            disassembler.library
  diskfont.library           gtlayout.library             icon.library
  iffparse.library           locale.library               lowlevel.library
  mathieeedoubbas.library    mathieeedoubtrans.library    mathieeesingtrans.library
  mathtrans.library          memory.library               mmu.library
  nonvolatile.library        old-intuition.library        Picasso96API.library
  realtime.library           reqtools.library             rexxreqtools.library
  rexxsupport.library        rexxsyslib.library           rexxtricks.library
  triton.library             tritonrexx.library           ttf.library
  type1.library              version.library              vnc.library
  workbench.library
1.System:> Dir DEVS:
     Monitors (dir)
     DataTypes (dir)
     DOSDrivers (dir)
     Printers (dir)
     Keymaps (dir)
  clipboard.device       DataTypes.info          DOSDrivers.info
  Keymaps.info           mfm.device              Monitors.info
  parallel.device        postscript_init.ps      printer.device
  Printers.info          serial.device           system-configuration
  trackfile.device
```

Almost only the scroll bar: a minimal ViNCEd Shell window

ViNCEd and not to include ViNCEd automatically when booting. In addition, you should not allow the `StringSnip` and `UnixDirs` commands to start automatically at boot time nor should you allow the `TrueMultiAssigns` patch to be applied automatically. This is the only way to ensure your regular Shell will behave like the original AmigaOS 3.2 Shell.

For a Shell with scrollbars, copy the regular *Shell* icon from the *System* drawer. Open the settings on the new icon with *Icon > Information* and switch to the *Icon* tab. For the `Window` icon feature, replace the device name `CON:` with `VNC:` and add `/SHELL` after `ICONIFY`. With a size of 700 by 300 pixels for the new window, the command looks like this (without spaces!): `Window=VNC:///700/300/VINCED-SHELL/CLOSE/ICONIFY/SHELL`.

If you want it to be even more minimal, just omit the `/SHELL` at the end so that ViNCEd does not automatically run in Shell mode, provided it is not set as the default setting with `SetVNC` under `Shell`. In this case, you will get the standard Tab completion of the AmigaOS 3.2 Shell instead of the extended options of ViNCEd.

Alternatively, you can go "all in" and replace the boot Shell with ViNCEd if necessary (download: www.aminet.net/package/util/Shell/ViNCEd_Boot_Shin). Read ViNCEd's excellent instructions. The program is much more than just a terminal emulator with Shell functionality.

This will certainly make it easy to bridge the time until the release of AmigaOS 3.3 is released with its integrated scrollbar.

Shell commands

Several new commands have been added in AmigaOS 3.1.4 and 3.2. They are useful additions to the existing command repertoire. Each command is explained in detail in the following sections. You will also find useful examples from everyday life.

New commands

The commands that have been added in AmigaOS 3.1.4 and 3.2 include `AmigaModel`, `DAControl`, `GuessBootDev`, `MD5Sum`, `MountInfo`, `Owner`, `Reboot`, `WBLoad` and `Win`.

By default, the `AmigaModel` and `GuessBootDev` commands are only stored on the installation medium. If required, copy them to your system drive with the AmigaOS 3.2 CD inserted using `Copy AmigaOS3.2CD:C/AmigaModel AmigaOS3.2CD:C/GuessBootDev C: CLONE`.

`DAControl` integrates, creates or ejects Amiga disk file images. This enables quick access to a disk stored in an ADF file. If the AmigaOS 3.2 CD is inserted, `DAControl LOAD AmigaOS3.2CD:ADF/Install3.2.adf` will mount the install disk, for example. You can also copy both commands mentioned above from the install disk to your system drive. To do this, replace *AmigaOS3.2CD* with *Install3.2*.

The `AmigaModel` command shows which Amiga model you are using. The `GuessBootDev` command guesses the boot drive. With `MD5Sum`, you can calculate or check *MD5*, *SHA-1* and *SHA-256* checksums of files.

The `MountInfo` command shows the mount list for a device. For example, try `MountInfo CD0:` for the first CD-ROM drive.

With `Owner`, you can set the owner of files or directories – this does not currently have any special meaning in AmigaOS itself, but does make sense in combination with network software such as *Envoy*.

The `WBLoad` command starts a program as if it had been started directly from the Workbench. Try it out with `WBLoad SYS:Prefs/Workbench`.

The `Win` Shell script opens a Workbench window for the specified directory. Good to know: `Win` is a Shell script that is located in the *S:* directory:

You can find out more about the individual commands in the *All commands* section, which begins on the next page.

Internal commands

An entire set of commands are Shell-internal only. These include `Alias`, `Ask`, `CD`, `Echo`, `Else`, `EndCLI`, `EndIf`, `EndShell`, `EndSkip`, `Execute`, `FailAt`, `Get`, `GetENV`, `History`, `If`, `Lab`, `NewCLI`, `NewShell`, `Path`, `PopCD`, `Prompt`, `PushCD`, `Quit`, `Resident`, `Run`, `Set`, `SetENV`, `Skip`, `Stack`, `SwapCD`, `UnAlias`, `UnSet`, `UnSetENV` and `Why`. These are commands that can either only be implemented in the Shell itself or for which this makes sense for performance reasons.

A number of these commands, such as `Ask`, `If`, `Else`, `EndIf`, `Skip`, `EndSkip`, `Lab` and `Quit`, are suitable for programming Shell scripts. You can read more about this in the section *Shell programming* from page 318. The other typical commands are usually located as files in *C:*. The internal commands are of course not located there.

All commands

On the following pages you will find descriptions of each command. Information is limited to the most important options and typical use of each command. Further information in English can also be found in the *Help* chapter of the *AmigaOS Command Reference*. The `Help` command allows you to access help from within a Shell.

AddBuffers

This command adds buffers to a drive. AmigaOS stores these in main memory (RAM) and uses them to speed up access to the drive. Default values are 5 for a floppy drive and 30 for a hard drive or SSD. However, the default *startup sequence* in *S:Startup-Sequence* increases the number of buffers for the first floppy drive *DF0:* to 15, if available. For floppy drives, 30 buffers are recommended in an Amiga with 512 KB RAM. The optimum value for a partition on a hard disk or SSD depends on its file system and size. It makes sense to increase the default value used by HDToolBox if there is sufficient main memory. See the sections on *file systems* (2.12) and *HDToolBox* (4.4).

The `AddBuffers DF0:` command shows the current number of buffers for the first floppy drive. With AddBuffers DF0: `10` you add another 10 buffers, with `AddBuffers DF0: -10` you remove them again. Add the command in the user startup sequence *S:User-Startup* if you want to make this change permanently. For partitions on hard disks and SSDs, it makes sense to set the value within *HDToolBox*. The number of buffers can also be specified for additional drives mounted from a file via the mount list. For example, take a look at the

SYS:Storage/DOSDrivers/RAD mount list for a resettable RAM Disk with a fixed size. `Buffers = 5` is set there by default to five buffers, which is sufficient for a disk in main memory.

AddDatatypes

The `AddDatatypes` command makes new datatypes known to the system. The *DataTypes* system of AmigaOS allows programs that make use of it, such as the *MultiView* program, to display files of all supported types. This is not limited to different image formats. There is also a datatype for help files in AmigaGuide format, for text files and for IFF animations.

The start sequence *S:Startup-Sequence* executes the command to make all installed datatypes known to the system. An installer script for a new datatype also typically runs this command. With the `REFRESH` option, the command adds all newly installed datatypes in *SYS:Classes/Datatypes*. The `Quiet` option prevents the output of any error messages. Otherwise, individual datatypes can be specified, such as with `AddDatatypes png jpeg`. The `LIST` option provides a list of all datatypes. The location for currently inactive datatypes is *SYS:Storage/Datatypes*.

Alias

The Amiga Shell supports abbreviations for commands, so-called aliases. The built-in `Alias` command defines those. Following `Alias D Dir`, the character `D` is sufficient to list the current directory. With `Alias S SYS:`, you change to the top directory of the system drive by simply typing `S`. `Alias M MultiView` shortens access to the *MultiView* display program.

The Shell will append the arguments at the end. You specify a different position with `[]`. `Alias Hex Type [] HEX` creates the new alias `Hex`, which uses the `Type` command to display a file in hexadecimal format with printable ASCII characters. This is useful for analyzing binary files. Users of Unix-like operating systems implement the typical `nl` command for outputting text files with line numbers using `Alias NL Type [] NUMBER`. You can get rid of the alias again with `UnAlias NL`.

Aliases are only ever valid in the current Shell and its child processes. A Shell started from within the current Shell with `NewShell` therefore inherits the defined aliases. A Shell started elsewhere, for example by clicking on the *Shell* icon in the *system drawer* of the system drive, is not affected by newly defined aliases. If you want to make an alias permanently available, enter the alias in the Shell start sequence in *S:Shell-Startup*.

The following aliases are already defined there, which should be familiar to users of MS-DOS or Unix-like systems:

Alias	Function
Clear	delete contents of the Shell window
CLS	delete contents of the Shell window
Ls	Unix notation for the List command
XCopy	copy with timestamp and rights (copy clone)

AmigaModel

The new `AmigaModel` command attempts to find out which Amiga model is in use by estimating its specifications and reports this to you. If you are using an emulator, the command shows the Amiga model configured there. It may happen that the wrong model is displayed. The command can be found on the AmigaOS3.2-CD or Install3.2 disk. If necessary, copy it to *Sys:C/* to be able to use the command like any other command without specifying a path.

Ask

The `Ask` command is suitable for keyboard input in Shell scripts. It displays a prompt and then waits for an entry. Without `TO`, `NUMERIC` or `STRING`, the command expects a yes-no statement with `Y` or `YES` for `yes` and `N` or `NO` or no input at all for `no`. It then sets the return value to 5 for yes and 0 for no. With `NUMERIC`, the command queries a number instead; with `STRING`, it queries any character string. With `TO`, the result ends up in the specified local variable. Otherwise, the command outputs it to the standard output.

For example, `Ask Continue?` can be used to query whether a script should continue to run. The query is made with `If WARN`. With `Ask STRING "Name?" TO NAME`, the command writes the specified character string to the variable `NAME`, which can be output with `ECHO $NAME`. See also *Shell programming* starting on page 318.

Assign

Assignments are abbreviations that can be used to call up any path. An overview of this function can be found in the section *Paths, devices, drive names and assignments* (page 265). There you will also find a list of all standard assignments. You can obtain a list of all assignments with `Assign` or `Assign LIST`. The options `VOLS`, `DIRS` and `DEVICES` restrict the output to drives, directories or devices.

TIP **Add default assignments**
Changing the default assignments can impair the functionality of your system. However, it can be useful to add another path to a default assignment such as *Libs:* for function libraries with the ADD option.

A new assignment can be created using the `Assign` command. For example, `Assign B: Work:Pictures` makes the *Work:B* directory available via the abbreviation `B:`. To remove an assignment again, use `Assign B:`. While an alias like `Alias Scripts: S:` is generally possible, assignments are much more suitable for paths. Assignments apply not only to the running Shell and all Shells started by it, but also globally in the system, both within the Shell and in software with an user interface.

An assignment can be extended by a further path. For example, `Assign Libs: Work:Libs ADD` makes the libraries in *Work:Libs* accessible to the system. Use the command sequence `Assign Libs: Work:Libs remove` to remove the additional path. You can also specify several paths at once, for example: `Assign Music: Data:Music RAM:Music`.

Usually, AmigaDOS immediately looks for the target directory for the assignment and opens a requester if this is not available. With the `DEFER` or `PATH` option, AmigaDOS waits until the first access to the assignment. The `DEFER` option is also suitable for rarely used assignments. In this case, AmigaDOS does not look for the target directory until the first access. Thus, `Assign Floppy: DF0: DEFER` resolves the assignment to the name of the floppy inserted in the *DF0:* drive at that time. Alternatively, the `Assign Floppy: DF0: PATH` assignment remains generic and works for any inserted floppy disk. Such path-based assignments are only possible with one destination.

With `EXISTS`, the command tests for the existence of an assignment and sets the return value to 5 for `WARN` if it does not exist. With the `DENIED` option, the command shows a list of all denied accesses to a drive if `AssignWedge` is active. Option `DISMOUNT` removes a device or drive from the list without freeing up the resources. This can only be canceled with a restart. In AmigaOS 3.2, however, `DISMOUNT` in conjunction with the `shutdown` option of the `mount` command also enables a device to be cleanly logged off. The command with the `FROM` option reads a whole list of assignments from a file.

AssignWedge

`AssignWedge` is a clean new implementation of the popular AssignWedge patch. If `AssignWedge` is started, the requester asking for a volume contains the additional options *Assign* and *Reject*. By default, the *WBStartup* drawer contains an icon that starts `AssignWedge`. You can test the difference with `CD DoesNotExist:`, followed by `AssignWedge quit` and `CD DoesNotExist:`.

Start AssignWedge again by clicking on the icon or via the Shell with `AssignWedge <>NIL: &` in the background.

Avail

The `Avail` command displays how much main memory your Amiga is using according to Chip RAM, Fast RAM and total RAM. In the *Available* section, the command displays the available memory in bytes. This may not be the amount that a program can request in one go – that is what the *Largest* column is for. In *Maximum*, the command shows the total amount of memory used. With `CHIP`, `FAST` or `TOTAL`, it only shows the number of free bytes for Chip, Fast or total RAM. With `FLUSH`, the command attempts to unload unused character sets, translation catalogues, libraries or device drivers.

```
AmigaShell
1.System:> Avail
Type   Available     In-Use   Maximum    Largest
chip     2039184      41584   2080768    2032208
fast   138075088   12919856 150994944  127144952
total  140114272   12961440 153075712  127144952
1.System:> Avail CHIP
2039184
1.System:> Avail FAST
138075088
1.System:> Avail TOTAL
140114272
1.System:>
```

Example output of the Avail command

Break

Use `Break` to send signals to processes. By default, this command sends the signal `C`, which you can also trigger for the currently running process in a Shell with `[Ctrl]+[C]`. Use `D` to end a script instead, and `E` to end a commodity program. The `F` signal is currently not used.

Select the target process either via its process number or with `NAME` via the name, or with a pattern. For example, `Break NAME "AmigaGuide#?"` would stop the processes for all AmigaGuide documents displayed in *MultiView* or other programs. This means that navigation in such documents will no longer work. You can end *MultiView* itself with `Break NAME Multiview`. The `Status` command provides an overview of the running processes including their process numbers.

CD

Using the `CD` command without any parameters shows the directory in which the Shell is currently located. In combination with a parameter, the command changes to the corresponding directory. CD supports absolute paths, relative paths and file patterns. This is how `CD SYS:Prefs/Env-Archive/Sys` changes to the directory with permanent system settings and standard icons. If the Shell is already in *SYS:Prefs,* then `CD Env-Archive/Sys` is sufficient. With `CD /` you can change directory, with `CD //` you will move up two directories. With `CD SYS:Li#?` you might change to the directory *SYS:Libs* if the name of no other directory matches this pattern.

In cases where the Shell can clearly distinguish between a suitable path and another input, such as a command name, you can alternatively omit the command. For example, `SYS:` is sufficient to change to the top directory of the system drive.

Refer also to the internal commands `PopCD`, `PushCD` and `SwapCD`.

Copy

The `Copy` command copies files or entire directories with their contents. `Copy S:User-Startup S:User-Startup.bak` will create a backup copy of the user startup sequence. The new file is given the same permissions, but adopts the current date. Using the `DATES` argument, the command adopts the date of the source file, and with `NOPRO`, the new file receives the standard permissions *rwed* for read, write, execute and delete, instead of the permissions of the source file. The command takes over any comments of the source file with the `COM` option. The `CLONE` command takes over the date, permissions and comment. This is particularly useful for backup copies of entire directories.

The `Copy` command overwrites a file that already exists if it is not delete-or write-protected. If it is delete- or write-protected, `Copy` issues an error message unless you use the `FORCE` argument. In this case, the command removes the protection and overwrites the file.

TIP **Beware of data overwriting**
When copying entire directories in particular, make sure the target of the copy action is correct! Otherwise the command will overwrite files with the same name, provided they are not delete- or write-protected – and with FORCE, even protected files are overwritten!

You can copy the files in a directory using, for example, `Copy SYS:Devs RAM:` or `Copy DEVS: RAM:`. However, the files in the *Devs* directory would end up directly in the root directory of the RAM Disk. `Copy SYS:Devs RAM:Devs` would create a directory called *Devs* in the target instead and copy the files there. However, the command ignores files located in the subdirectories of the source directory. In this example therefore, any files from *Monitors*, *DataTypes*, DOSDrivers, *Printers* and *Keymaps* will be skipped. The `ALL` argument is required to copy them. As such, the `Copy SYS:Devs RAM:Devs ALL CLONE` command sequence will create a 1:1 copy of the *Devs* directory in the RAM Disk. For each copied file, the command displays a line with the name of the file and the note *...copied.* With `QUIET` you will only see error messages, which are of course easy to find in the output.

By default, the `Copy` command uses 200 buffers of 512 bytes each, i.e. around 100 KiB. When copying large amounts of data, especially larger files, a higher number such as `BUF 500` can increase the speed. `BUF 0` lets `Copy` adapt the number of buffers to the size of each file to be copied. When copying very large files, this can lead to a lack of memory for other applications! For copying to the RAM Disk, even 200 buffers are a waste of memory. If you wish, you can reduce this to something like 20 buffers, for example.

A possible call for backing up the system drive would therefore be `Copy SYS: Backup:System ALL CLONE`. With `Copy SYS: Backup:System ALL CLONE >Backup:System-Backup.log *>Backup:System-Backup-Errors.log` the regular messages of the command end up in the log file *Backup:System-Backup.log*, and error messages are stored in the log file *Backup:System-Backup-Errors.log*.

TIP **Alternatives to Copy**
The Copy command is not suitable for updating backup copies. It will copy all files again each time it is used, including files that have not changed at all. In addition, it will not delete files from the target that have been deleted from the source. A tool for mirroring directory trees such as *BackUp* by Daniel Westerberg is better suited for such purposes (download: www.aminet.net/package/disk/bakup/BackUp).

The `NOREQ` switch can be used with the command in a script. In this case, `Copy` prevents any AmigaOS requester windows during copying and returns an error instead. Compare `Copy S: DoesNotExist:` with `Copy S: DoesNotExist: NOREQ` and see the difference. Of course, this only works as long as no drive or file system called *DoesNotExist* actually exists.

CPU

The `CPU` command indicates which processor and coprocessor is installed in the system, checks for the presence of a specific CPU, checks for the presence of the appropriate library for the installed processor and allows individual CPU functions to be switched on or off. For an Amiga with a 68040 processor, the output looks like this:

```
System: 68040 68882  no FastROM (INST: Cache Burst)
(DATA: Cache CopyBack)
```

In most cases, it's not necessary to switch individual processor functions on or off. The corresponding caches for instructions and data are already activated. However, it may be necessary for some older games or other programs to switch off caches used in the various CPUs in order to make the software executable. The simplest solution, for example, is to try to start the relevant program after executing the `CPU NOCACHE` command. There is a whole range of other options such as `NODATACACHE`, `NOINSTCACHE`, `NOBURST`, `NODATABURST`, `NOINSTBURST`, `NOCOPYBACK` and as well as options specifically for the 68060. So if `CPU NOCACHE` does not produce the desired result, it is a good idea to try all the options that apply to the processor. By omitting the `NO` prefix on the option (e.g. `BURST` instead of `NOBURST`), the command switches the corresponding function back on. WHDLoad is a good alternative for games, as this special software often offers a customized configuration for the game in question (more on this in section 7.6).

The `CPU` command is no longer responsible for FastROM functionality, which copies the content of the slow Kickstart ROM chip into faster RAM. Manufacturers of processor expansion cards usually supply a suitable tool for this.

With `CPU CHECKINSTALL`, you can check for the presence of the processor library best suited to the processor installed or configured in the emulator. AmigaOS 3.2 already contains suitable libraries for the 68020 to 68060 processors, so that the return value for the check that can be queried with `Echo $RC` is `0`. Depending on the processor board used, it may make sense to use the libraries supplied by the manufacturer instead.

It is also possible to test for the presence of a specific CPU. If a 68040 processor is installed, `CPU CHECK 68040` returns the value `0` and `CPU CHECK 68060` returns the value 5.

Date

The `Date` command outputs the system time or resets it. Without arguments, the command outputs the current system time. For example, `Date 1-Jan-22` sets the date, `Date 19:00`, sets the time, and both are set with `Date 01-01-22 19:00:00`. The command understands the English name of a weekday as well as `YESTERDAY` or `TOMORROW`. Alternatively, the command combined with `TO` writes the system time to a specified file.

The system time is lost the next time the system is switched on and off. To save it in a battery-buffered hardware clock, see the `SetClock` command.

DAControl

In earlier AmigaOS versions, access to ADF files was only possible using additional software. AmigaOS 3.2 now contains the driver *trackfile.device* for this purpose. It supports *double density images* with 880 KB and *high density images* with 1760 KB in the *Amiga Disk File* format (further information on ADF can be found in sections 2.11 and 2.12). The maximum number of disks that can be used and stored as files depends on the amount of main memory available. The device names are *DA0:*, *DA1:*, *DA2:* etc.

The command `DAControl LOAD AmigaOS3.2CD:ADF/Workbench3.2.adf` integrates the *Workbench3.2* disk that is stored on the AmigaOS 3.2 CD as an ADF file. The command either uses an existing device without a disk or creates a new device. File patterns are also possible. For example, DAControl LOAD AmigaOS3.2CD:ADF/#?.adf integrates all ADF files from the CD right away – and consumes the corresponding amount of main memory. With DEVICE DA4:, you can enter your own device name when attaching an individual ADF file. If a device with a specific unit number already exists, the notation UNIT 4 also works. By default, the command includes an ADF file as write-protected . You can allow write access with WRITEPROTECTED=NO. Alternatively, create an icon for an ADF file and enter C:DAControl as the default program. You can then use WRITEPROTECTED=NO as an icon attribute.

Use DAControl EJECT device DA4: or DAControl EJECT UNIT 4 to eject the floppy disk from the corresponding drive. Alternatively, use DAControl CHANGE AmigaOS3.2CD:ADF/diskname.adf UNIT 4 to change the inserted disk. You can also insert the same disk again to remove or activate write protection with WRITEPROTECTED=NO or WRITEPROTECTED=YES.

Depending on the file system used, mounting the same disk more than once can lead to a crash. With USECHECKSUMS=YES, the command should create checksums to avoid this case. However, the command will refuse to mount the same image file even without this option. It will recognize the copying of the file to another device or under a different name. In addition, the command will not display checksums when used with info SHOWCHECKSUMS. It is therefore usually sufficient to leave this option unchecked.

Use DAControl CREATE RAM:disk.adf to create a new image file, which the command will conveniently mount straight away. This DD disk is formatted with the *Old File System*. With FILESYSTEMTYPE ffs you can use the Fast File System, and with FILESYSTEMTYPE ffs+longnames you will get additional support for long filenames. If you want to create a high density disk, use DISKTYPE HD. Both can be combined with each other. With FILESYSTEM you can load a completely different file system if required, and with LABEL you can assign a name for the new disk. So DAControl CREATE RAM:Data.adf LABEL Data FILESYSTEMTYPE ffs+longnames DISKTYPE HD would create a high density disk called *Data*, featuring the *Fast File System* and support for long file names.

You can create a bootable disk with BOOTABLE. This is particularly suitable if you want to create a customized Workbench disk for a real floppy drive, because write access to an ADF file on a hard disk, SSD or even a RAM Disk is much faster. Once you have copied all the required files, you can copy the disk to a real floppy disk using `DiskCopy`.

You can obtain an overview of the mounted disks with `DAControl INFO`. Optionally `SHOWVOLUMES` also makes visible the disk name and date of creation, while `SHOWBOOTBLOCKS` provides information on the boot block.

For more information about what the command is doing, use `VERBOSE`. When ejecting or changing a disk, the driver waits a minimum of up to five seconds if write or read accesses are still running. You can specify a longer time limit with `TIMEOUT`. Or you can use `SAFEEJECT` to ask the file system to end all disk accesses instead. It is also possible to temporarily store the contents of mounted disks in main memory. See the options `ENABLECACHE`, `PREFILLCACHE` and `CACHESIZE` in the *AmigaOS 3.2 reference manual*. For ADF files on fast volumes or the RAM Disk, cache is likely to play less of a role.

Dir

The `Dir` command shows a sorted list of files in a directory. It can also show a list of subdirectories within a directory, but unsorted. With the `FILES` option, the command only shows files, and with the `DIRS` option it focuses on directories only. The `ALL` option also shows the contents of the subdirectories. Thus, `Dir SYS: ALL` shows you the complete contents of the system drive.

Of course, this command also works with file patterns. `Dir Devs:#?.device` shows you all device driver files. In addition, combining the command with `INTER` provides an interactive mode in which the command asks what to do after each entry. Press the `[Enter]` key to get the next entry. Press the `[E]` key followed by `[Enter]` to look into a directory . Press the `[B]` key followed by `[Enter]` to move up a directory . Execute a Shell command with the `[C]` key. `Dir` combined with `C TYPE`, for example, uses the `Type` command to show the content of the current file.

The `Type` command with the `HEX` option is suitable for binary files. However, the complete filename must be specified, for example `C Type "Dir" HEX` (if `Dir` is currently located in *C:*). Furthermore, `DEL` followed by the `[Enter]` key deletes the current entry if it is a file or an *empty* directory. Finally, press `[Q]` to exit the interactive mode and return to the Shell.

DiskChange

Use the `DiskChange` command to notify the system when a disk, cartridge or other drive media has been swapped. This is only necessary if the drive does not recognize the change automatically. The command's only argument is the drive name.

DiskCopy

The `DiskCopy` command copies the contents of one storage medium, such as a floppy disk, block-by-block to another storage medium. For example, `DiskCopy DF0: TO DF1:` copies the contents of the floppy disk in the first floppy drive to the floppy disk in the second floppy drive. Use `NOVERIFY` to skip checking the written data. By default, the target media is given the name of the source media. Use `NEWNAME` to specify a different name. If you want to create several copies, use `MULTI`. In this case, the command loads the contents of the disk into main memory and allows you to make several copies.

It is not recommended to copy all types of media in this way. A file-based copy usually makes more sense, especially for flash-based media such as USB sticks or SD cards. The command copies disks in standard formats. Some Amiga games use a special format that cannot be copied with this command.

DiskDoctor

The `DiskDoctor` command has been almost completely rewritten for AmigaOS 3.1.4. True to the motto *primum non nocere, secundum cavere, tertium sanara – first do no harm, second be careful, third heal* – version 2 of DiskDoctor now only supports checking a drive or rescuing data from a drive to a target directory. It no longer supports the notorious repair of a drive on the spot known from previous versions of `DiskDoctor`. And for good reason: in the past, this often led to a complete loss of data.

The program has two modes. With `EXAMINE`, `CHECK`, or without specifying a mode, it checks the structure of a drive. With `COPY`, it saves data. In both cases, DiskDoctor only supports the proprietary Amiga file systems. This includes the *Old File System* from 1986 up to the different variants of the *Fast File System* from 1987, such as *International* (1991), *Dircache*, aka *DCFS/FastDir* (1992), and the mode for long file names, *Long Name File System*, aka *LNFS* (2006). DiskDoctor is not suitable for recovering data from file systems such as PFS or SFS. The command runs from Kickstart 2.04 onwards and requires nothing else. It can therefore be started from an otherwise empty but bootable floppy disk.

For example, the command `DiskDoctor EXAMINE DF0:` checks the disk inserted in the first floppy drive. The `VERBOSE` option shows more detail. With the QUIET option, the program will not display any messages about what it is currently doing. Optionally, a log will end up in the specified file with LOGFILE, where DiskDoctor logs as if VERBOSE was specified.

If you want to use the result of a check process to subsequently recovery files, you can write it in binary format in a so-called DABI file, which DiskDoctor can reuse. That may look like this: `DiskDoctor EXAMINE DH4: TODABIFILE=DH1:DiskDoctor-DH4.dabi VERBOSE`.

Rescuing files works, for example, with `DiskDoctor COPY DF0: to Data:Saved-DF0`. By default, DiskDoctor will only copy files that are known to the program not to be corrupted or deleted. The command also ignores files for which it is not clear from which directory they originated. With ALL, DiskDoctor copies all files. With DELETED, ORPHANED and/or DAMAGED, DiskDoctor only copies deleted files, files from unknown directories and/or damaged files. In this way, the different types of recovered files can be separated from each other in several passes. To speed up the rescue process, you can use a DABI file from the corresponding check process with FROMDABIFILE. Time-based filtering is also possible with SINCE and UPTO. Both options accept either a date such as `Yesterday` and `12-Dec-21` or a time such as `11:31:30`. If a time is specified, the command starts from the current day. If a date is specified, it uses `00:00:00` of the respective day as the time. By using MINIMUMSIZE and/or MAXIMUMSIZE, the command will filter by size. It is recommended to save the files in a newly created directory. However, if the directory already contains data, for example from previous recovery attempts, DiskDoctor overwrites an existing file with the same name with OVERWRITE=REPLACE or uses a different filename for the newly recovered file with OVERWRITE=KEEP.

If you want to check which files DiskDoctor will copy when run, use the PRETEND option. This option is also useful for estimating how much storage space the recovered files will require. With EXPLAIN, the program explains why it is copying or not copying a particular file.

If you use a block size other than 512 bytes for a file system, as is highly recommended for partitions with a Fast File System on a hard drive or SSDs, specify this with BYTESPERBLOCK. As a rule, DiskDoctor tries to read entire tracks, as this is faster. With SLOW, however, the program reads block by block and thus will sometimes save more data, as it does not discard the entire track in the event of a read error on one block. Conversely, using the command with `BLOCKSPERTRACK` will optionally copy larger areas, which can increase performance. A larger buffer size than the standard 8192 bytes also ensures higher performance. You can specify this using the `FILEBUFFERSIZE` option. As the AmigaOS floppy driver usually rejects read accesses to corrupt blocks, DiskDoctor accesses floppy disks directly by default without going through the floppy driver. If in special cases the program does not automatically recognize a floppy drive, the option `RAWFLOPPYACCESS ALWAYS` switches to direct access. For direct access, the maximum number of read attempts can be specified with `maxreadretries=10`, for example.

The `DiskDoctor` command supports a range of other settings and options. You can specify the file system type and details of how you want to access the drive, such as by NSD, TD64 or SCSI, as well as the MaxTransfer value. A detailed English manual, which can be accessed via `HELP DiskDoctor`, explains those additional options.

DPAT

Similar to `SPAT` (see page 314), the tiny `DPAT` script allows commands with two arguments that do not support file patterns to be used with file patterns. The script uses the `list` command to build a list of files, then uses it to create a script with multiple command calls, which it then executes.

A practical example is to move all LhA archives to a specific directory by typing `DPAT RENAME #?.lha Data:Archives`.

Echo

The `Echo` command outputs the specified character string on the standard output. For example, `Echo "Hello world"` outputs the character string *Hello world*, followed by a line feed, which the command with `noline` optionally omits. If the character string contains spaces, it must be enclosed in double quotes. Optionally, the command only outputs part of the character string. For example, `Echo "Hello World" FIRST 0 LEN 5` only displays the character string *Hello*. If `FIRST` is missing, the command starts counting from the right end of the string. So `Echo "Hello world" LEN 4` displays the string *orld* .

Ed

`Ed`, a full-screen text editor, allows you to edit text files. You will need to provide a filename. With `WINDOW "CON:0/0/640/480/Edit text"`, Ed opens a separate window with the specified position and size and the specified title. If Ed does not recognize the number of characters per line and the number of lines per page for foreign terminals, these can be specified with `WIDTH` and `HEIGHT`. With `TABS 8` you can set the number of spaces per Tab to 8. The default is 3. The text editor supports direct commands and indirect commands. You can access the direct commands by pressing `[Ctrl]` followed by the command key. For example, `[Ctrl]+[A]` inserts a line after the current line, while `[Ctrl]+[B]` removes a line.

A selection of direct commands:

Command	Function
[Ctrl]+[A]	insert line
[Ctrl]+[B]	delete line
[Ctrl]+[D]	scroll text down
[Ctrl]+[E]	move the cursor to the beginning or end of the current display
[Ctrl]+[F]	swap upper/lower case
[Ctrl]+[G]	execute the last extended command (see below)
[Ctrl]+[H]	delete character to the left of the cursor
[Ctrl]+[O]	remove word or space
[Ctrl]+[R]	move the cursor to the end of the previous word
[Ctrl]+[T]	move the cursor to the beginning of the next word
[Ctrl]+[U]	scroll text upwards
[Ctrl]+[V]	redraw display
[Ctrl]+[Y]	delete from the cursor to the end of line
[Ctrl]+[]]	move cursor to the start or the end of the line

You can perform advanced commands by pressing the `[Escape]` key. A prompt with * will appear at the bottom of the window, prompting you to make a further entry. Press `[Q]` and then `[Enter]` to exit the editor. If any changes have not been saved, the tool will prompt you again. Use the `sa` command to save the file instead, or optionally save it with `sa /RAM:Test.txt/` to a file with the specified name. Use `e /old/new/` to replace one character string with another throughout the document. By default, Ed distinguishes between upper and lower case when searching. The extended command `uc` switches the distinction off, and the extended command `lc` switches it on again. Of course, the newer *TextEdit* is a convenient alternative to `Ed`, but `Ed` is also able to automatically apply a collection of advanced commands to a file. Save the commands in a file and call up the tool, e.g. with `Ed RAM:Test.txt with RAM:Ed-commands`. The quoted text file *Ed-commands* could contain the following:

```
e /apple/pear/
sa
```

A good alternative for automatically editing files is the line-based editor `Edit` (see page 295).

A selection of the advanced commands:

Command	Function
A /text/	insert a line with the specified text after the current line
B	moves the cursor to the end of the text
BE	marks the end of a block at the cursor position
BF /text/	searches backwards for the specified text
BS	marks the start of a block at at the cursor position
CE	moves the cursor to the end of the line
CL	moves the cursor one position to the left
CR	moves the cursor one position to the right
CS	moves the cursor to the start of the line
D	deletes the current line
DB	deletes the selected block
DC	deletes the character at the cursor position
E /text/replace/	replaces all occurrences of the text
EQ /text/replace/	replaces all occurrences of the text, but prompts first
EX	extends the right margin
F /text/	searches for the specified text
IB	inserts a copy of the selected block
IF /file/	inserts the specified file
J	merges the current and subsequent lines
LC	distinguishes between upper and lower case (default)
M line number	moves the cursor to the specified line
N	moves the cursor to the beginning of the next line
P	moves the cursor to the beginning of the previous line
Q	exits the program without saving
RP	repeats the last command until an error occurs
S	splits the line at the cursor position
SA /file/	saves the file
SB	displays the selected block on screen

SH	shows file information
SL position	sets the left edge to the specified position
SR position	sets the right edge to the specified position
ST number	set the number of spaces moved per Tab
T	moves the cursor to the beginning of the document
U	undoes changes to the current line
UC	does not distinguish between upper and lower case letters
WB /file	saves the selected block
X	saves the file and exits the program

Edit

Edit is another programmable text editor. The command requires the path location of the file to be edited, which must already exist.

Edit is a line-based text editor that is rarely used these days. However, the program offers powerful options for automatically changing a file. You can find out more information with Help Edit.

EndShell

The EndShell command terminates the current Shell process. Only execute this command if the Workbench or another Shell process is still running, otherwise you will no longer be able to control your Amiga without restarting. If no other process is running within the terminated Shell, AmigaOS closes the corresponding Shell window. A synonym for EndShell is EndCLI.

Eval

The Eval command calculates integer mathematical expressions. For example, Eval 2*3+5 outputs the number 11. Incidentally, the program has only observed the mathematically correct evaluation order AmigaOS 3.2! In addition to basic arithmetic operations with +, -, * and /, the command also supports modulo (mod), negation (-), and (&), or (or or |), exclusive or (^), not (not), shift left (lsh), shift right(rsh) and bitwise match (eqv).

With TO, the result ends up in a file instead. As environment variables are also stored in files, this is useful for programming loops in Shell scripts. Read more on this in the section on Shell programming (see page 318).

The LFORMAT option selects the output format. The default is the decimal output %N. Alternatively, the command displays the result with %X8 as an eight-digit hexadecimal number, with %C as a character and with %O8 as an eight-digit octal number. Please note that it is essential that you specify the length for hexadecimal or octal output, otherwise the command will run indefinitely!

Line feeds can be added to the output format with `*N`. As of AmigaOS 3.2.1, the command alternatively supports the `HEX` option for hexadecimal output.

This command also supports octal and hexadecimal numbers as input. For example, `Eval 0x1E / 010 lformat "The result is %N.*N"` outputs the string *The result is 3*, as 30 (hexadecimal 0x1E) divided by 8 (octal 010) equals 3.75 and the command simply omits the fractional part after the decimal point. As of AmigaOS 3.2.1, the command also understands `$1E` as input for the hexadecimal number.

Execute

The `Execute` command runs AmigaDOS Shell scripts and optionally replaces certain placeholders in the script with the parameters specified in the command execution. As of AmigaOS 3.2, this command is included in the Kickstart ROM. The installer for version 3.2.1 also installs the command to *C:*, as many programs and installation routines expect it there.

The `Execute` command expects a script name as a parameter. For example, `Execute S:Shell-Startup` would execute the Shell startup script again. An example of replacing placeholders can be found in the section on Shell programming from page 318 onwards.

Fault

`Fault` is an internal Shell command for which there is no entry in the *AmigaOS Command Reference* chapter or the list of *Internal Shell Commands* in the *AmigaOS 3.2 Reference Manual*. The command outputs the matching error message for an AmigaDOS error number. For example, `Fault 205` returns the message *Object not found*.

More information on this can be found in chapter 8.2 on *Error Codes* in the *DOS errors* section of this book.

Filenote

You can set, change or delete comments for files or directories using the `Filenote` command. For example, `Filenote RAM:Fruit.jpg "A bowl of apples, pears and bananas."` sets the corresponding comment for the image file *Fruit.jpg*. You can see the comment with `List RAM:Obst.jpg` or in the information window of the Workbench. Deleting the comment works with `Filenote RAM:Fruit.jpg ""` or simply with `Filenote RAM:Fruit.jpg`.

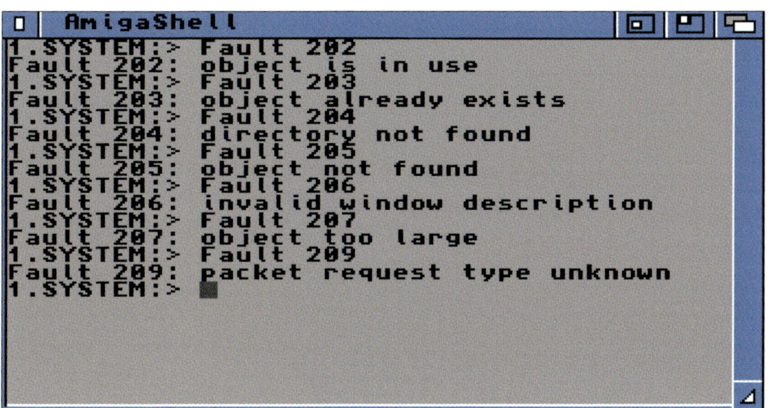

A selection of typical AmigaDOS errors

The command supports various file patterns. With the `ALL` option, the command sets the comment for all files and directories within and below the specified directory. With `QUIET`, the program does not display its progress.

Incidentally, the `Copy` command only copies a comment if you specify the `COM` or `CLONE` option.

Find

The `Find` command is indispensable for Amiga users. You can use the program via a graphical user interface, which is explained in more detail in the Programs/*System* section 4.14 on page 224. Executed from the Shell, `Find` sets the search parameters as specified, but does not execute the search itself.

`Find FROM S: CONTAINS "Start"` initiates a search for all files under *S:* that contain *Start* in the filename. Clicking the *Start* button begins the search that has been preset by the command execution. This can be customized in the user interface. The `PATTERN` option button activates the search for files whose names correspond to an AmigaDOS search pattern. Specifying a filename sets a search for exactly that filename. A search for a character string in a file can be specified with `STRING`.

Alternatively, the `Search` command also displays search results directly in the console window.

FindResident

The `FindResident` command checks for the presence of a specific Kickstart ROM module. It can then provide information about the hardware used. For example, `FindResident cdui.library` checks for an Amiga CD32. The `FindResident` command can only be found on the HDSetup disk. Copy it from the disk to your system drive with `Copy HDSetup3.2:C/FindResident C: CLONE`, if necessary.

FixROMLibs

The start sequence of the install disk or CD of AmigaOS 3.2 uses the `FixROMLibs` command with 47 as the argument. If the command finds the *icon.library* and the *workbench.library* in a lower version, for example due to an outdated Kickstart ROM, it removes them from the *ROMTag list*. This causes AmigaOS to load the newer versions from the disk. This is particularly important for an Amiga 4000T, as its Kickstart ROM contains the *icon.library* in version 40, while the *workbench.library* from the install disk requires a newer version. The Workbench would therefore not be able to start without `FixROMLibs`.

Format

The `Format` command formats a drive for the Amiga. This program has its own graphical user interface. It can also be executed inside the Shell. Details on how the program works can be found in the *System* section on page 226.

Use `Format DRIVE DF0: NAME pictures` to format a floppy disk in drive *DF0:*. Without `NOICONS`, the tool creates an icon and a *Trashcan* directory. It formats the drive track by track. With `QUICK`, the program runs faster, which is particularly recommended for partitions on hard disks or SSDs, as well as USB sticks and memory cards, as described in the *System* section.

By default, the program uses the *Old File System (OFS)* format, which is compatible down to AmigaOS 1. As of AmigaOS 2.04 it is possible to use the newer, faster and recommendable *Fast File System*, which offers a little more storage space. Umlauts in file names work better with `INTL`. With `DIRCACHE`, the disk will have a directory cache, but in many cases this makes little sense. Drives formatted in this way will only work from AmigaOS 3 onwards. `LONGNAMES` supports file names longer than 30 characters. Find out more about the options in section 2.12 on *file systems*.

Get

The `Get` command displays the value of a specified local variable. For example, `Get amount` shows the content of the `amount` variable, which may previous have been set by `Set`, e.g. with `Set amount 10`. Local variables are only valid in the current Shell and its child processes. A local variable can also be displayed with the `Echo` command, e.g. with `Echo $amount`.

AmigaOS does not differentiate between upper and lower case for variable names. `Set` shows a list of all local variables.

GetENV

The `GetENV` command displays the value of the specified environment variable. These variables, stored in *ENV:*, apply to any Shell. For example, `GetENV Language` reveals the current language setting, while `GetENV Versions/Release` shows the active AmigaOS version.

An environment variable can also be shown with the `Echo` command, e.g. with `Echo $Language` (in this case, though, it can only show a variable in *ENV:* directly, not a subdirectory). AmigaOS does not differentiate between upper and lower case for variable names. `SetENV` without parameters returns a list of all environment variables. `Dir ENV: ALL` will show the variables in subdirectories. *ENV:* also contains configuration files with binary content, which are not useful to view with `GetENV`.

To set environment variables, use the related `SetENV` command, which is described on page 313.

Group

The `Group` command sets the group for a file or a directory. It can also work with file patterns or recursively with `ALL`. For example, `Group Admin.txt admin` sets the group for the *Admin.txt* file to the *admin* group. The group can be specified as a number from 0 to 65535. With `GROUPS` as an option, the `List` command displays the groups of directory entries, if set.

Currently, however, users and groups are only relevant in AmigaOS in conjunction with network file systems such as *Envoy*. AmigaOS itself does not feature user and group management.

GuessBootDev

The `GuessBootDev` command does exactly what its name implies: it estimates which drive the system has booted from and outputs the result of this estimation. This information can be useful for installation scripts, but in many cases the *SYS:* assignment should be sufficient. By default, the command is only located on the AmigaOS3.2 CD or the Install3.2 disk. If necessary, copy it to *C:* to be able to use it like other commands without specifying a path.

History

The new `History` command displays the last 256 commands executed in the active Shell. In addition, a call such as `History SAVE RAM:commandhistory.txt` saves this command history as text. It can also be loaded again with the `LOAD` argument. You can find out more about this command in the *Command history* section of this chapter on page 265.

Info

The `Info` command shows information about the existing disks or partitions. This includes the drive name, the used and free space, the memory allocation in per cent, the number of soft disk errors, the status and the name of the disk. A block is usually 512 bytes in size. In terms of status, the command distinguishes between *read-only* and *read/write*. If no device is specified, `Info` will show details for all disks and partitions built into the system.

```
AmigaShell
1.System:> info

Mounted disks:
Unit      Size      Used       Free Full Errs   Status   Name
CD0       No disk present
DA0       879K      1717         41  98%    0  Read Only  Extras3.2
DF0       No disk present
DF1       No disk present
DH3      4095M   4194304    4194303  50%    0  Read/Write Amiga
INSTALL   200M     78378     127252  38%    0  Read/Write AmigaOS3.2CD
OS       1838M      7298     934172   1%    0  Read/Write System
RAM      6859K        94       6765   1%    0  Read/Write Ram Disk

Volumes available:
Amiga [Mounted]
AmigaOS3.2CD [Mounted]
Extras3.2 [Mounted]
Ram Disk [Mounted]
System [Mounted]
```

Example output of the info command with a mounted ADF file

Install

If you want to make a floppy disk or memory card bootable, use the `Install` command. `Install DF0: CHECK`, for example, checks whether a boot block already exists. `Install CC0:` writes a boot block to a card disk. The command is based on the existing file system. It uses an FFS boot block for the *Fast File System* and an OFS boot block for the *Old File System*. With `FFS` as an option, it will always be a FFS boot block.

With `NOBOOT`, the command writes a non-bootable boot block to the drive. **Caution:** A game disk that uses its own disk format and which AmigaOS displays as a non-AmigaDOS disk might be made permanently unbootable by the `Install` command.

Installer

The `Installer` tool is often used to set up a program on a hard drive or similar. It reads a special script file with instructions for installing software. You will not typically notice this step, as the installer is usually already registered as the default program for an icon of such an installer script.

The installer will need to know the path to a script that it is supposed to process. It distinguishes between different user modes. For a novice (value `0`), the installation runs completely automatically. For a beginner (value 1), the program will ask a few questions during setup, while an expert (value 2) will need to confirm each and any action. You can specify the minimum mode with `MINUSER` and the default mode with `DEFUSER`. `APPNAME` sets the name of the program, while `LANGUAGE` defines the default language for the installation.

Logging is also supported: use `LOGFILE` to specify the path to the log file for the installation and `NOLOG` to switch off logging. The tool supports do-as-if, which you can turn off with the `NOPRETEND` option.

IPrefs

In everyday Amiga use, there is no need to manually invoke the `IPrefs` command. When run by the startup script *S:Startup-Sequence*, it loads and activates the settings from the **.prefs* files stored in *ENV:Sys*. The program will continue to run in the background and react automatically to changes to the settings.

It only makes sense to start the command manually if you have booted into safe mode with the safe start sequence in *S:Startup-Failsafe*. For detailed instructions, see sections 6.2 on *early startup* and 6.11 on the *start sequence*.

As of AmigaOS 3.2, `IPrefs` always applies all changes at once instead of redrawing the screen several times. The program also tells you the names of the windows that still need to be closed.

Join

The `Join` command joins two or more files into a single file. Example: `Join part1 part2 part3 AS Text`.

List

The `List` command shows the contents of directories in the same way as the `Dir` command. Without an argument, the command shows the contents of the current directory. It accepts directory or file names and file patterns as arguments. If a directory is specified, the command will show its content. With the `FLAT` option, the command show just the directory, for example to see its permissions. `List` works *recursively* with the `ALL` option, i.e. to show the contents of the subdirectories and their substructures. With `PAT`, the command filters according to the specified file pattern, and with `SUB`, it filters according to the extent to which the specified character string is contained. With `DIRS`, it will show only directories, with `FILES`, it will show only files. With `UPTO` and `SINCE`, it will show entries up to or from a certain date. For example, `List SINCE 1-Dec-2021` shows all entries from 1 December 2021 and later.

By default, the List command shows the name of each file or directory, its size in bytes, its access rights and the date and the time of the creation or last modification of the file in one line. If there is a comment, the command displays this in a separate line, preceded by a colon. The size in blocks is shown with BLOCKS. Time information can be omitted with NODATES. The KEYS option also shows the block number of each file header and each directory. The command omits the header and footer with NOHEAD. With QUICK, the command only shows file or directory names. For example, List SYS: QUICK NOHEAD only shows the names of all files and directories in the system drive.

Output is unsorted by default. With SORT NAME, the command sorts by name; with SORT DATE, by date; with SORT SIZE, by size; and with SORT TYPE, by type. You can reverse the sort direction with REVERSE in front, and sorting criteria can be combined. For example, List with SORT REVERSETYPE,NAME displays directories in front of files, and in alphabetical order. With SORT RESERVESIZE,NAME, you will receive a list sorted first by size, then by name.

You can also use LFORMAT to format a list completely according to your own wishes. In this case, the List command combined with LFORMATQUOTE SHELL, LFORMATQUOTE WILDCARD or LFORMATQUOTE SHELL,WILDCARD will format names with spaces or other special characters, as well as names with file patterns for further use in Shell scripts. For file patterns, this only works with capitalized placeholders such as %S instead of %s?. Placeholders define what List displays. Here, %S stands for the filename and %S%S for the path and the filename. There are also other placeholders (see table). For example, List LFORMAT "%L %S%S" FILES shows the size first and then the path and the name of each file.

Placeholder	**Contents**
%A	file attributes (rights)
%B	size in blocks
%C	comment
%D	date
%E	file extension (e.g. .info)
%F	complete path without name
%G	group
%K	key block
%L	size in bytes

%M	`name without file extension`
%N	`name`
%O	`path from argument with name`
%P	`path from argument without name`
%R	`link destination`
%S	`name`
%T	`time`
%U	`users`
%V	`permissions for the group and others`

LoadModule

The `LoadModule` command installs resident modules in a reset-proof manner, similar to what `SetPatch` does for ROM updates. A list of installed modules is shown if used with the `LIST` option.

A typical use case is making libraries reside on the drive if the Kickstart ROM contains outdated versions. An example of this is: `LoadModule libs:icon.library libs:workbench.library REVERSE`. However, as the `SetPatch` command already does this in a different way, the command would have to be inserted into the *startup sequence* before the `SetPatch` command. This is particularly relevant for the Amiga 4000T, which is the only Amiga that lacks the *workbench.library* in the Kickstart ROM for AmigaOS 3.0/3.1.

AmigaOS 3.2.1 contains some changes to the Kickstart ROM regarding boot animation, *graphics.library*, *dos.library*, *ram-handler* and the Shell. The start sequence runs the `LoadModule` command with the `ROMUPDATE` option, which updates obsolete modules of an existing Kickstart ROM according to the softkick method and then restarts the Amiga. If your Amiga has an accelerator card with MapROM functionality, it is recommended that you replace the entire Kickstart ROM right away. With emulators such as FS-UAE or WinUAE, you can use the new Kickstart ROM straight away. Kickstart ROM files with the *.rom* extension are used for all these purposes. The files with the extension *.bin* are used to burn the ROM yourself.

LoadMonDrvs

The `LoadMonDrvs` command loads monitor drivers stored in *Devs:Monitors*. The standard *startup* sequence in *S:Startup-Sequence* runs this command. Otherwise, `LoadMonDrvs` fixes some incompatibilities with certain RTG software. The command is also used as a default program in the icons of monitor drivers, so that double-clicking on the driver loads it.

LoadResource `LoadResource` loads parts of the operating system or libraries and other components from third-party manufacturers into main memory in a non-resettable manner to reduce access times later on. This can be useful for disk-based systems.

For example, `LoadResource Libs:asl.library` loads the ASL library into main memory, and `LoadResource Fonts:topaz/11` loads the Topaz font in size 11. Of course, this only makes sense for resources that AmigaOS does not already load into main memory when booting, that are likely to be accessed later. If you want to ensure that AmigaOS does not release the resource at a later time, use the `LOCK` option. A locked resource can be unlocked with `UNLOCK`.

Caution: Locking too many resources with too little main memory can cause problems for memory management. In addition, locking for device drivers, i.e. resources with the extension *.device*, does not work.

LoadWB The `LoadWB` command loads the Workbench at the end of the standard startup sequence in *S:Startup-Sequence*. If you have closed the Workbench by mistake, but you still have a Shell window open, you can use the command to reload it.

Lock Use the `Lock` command to lock or unlock write access to devices. For example, `Lock DF0: ON` locks write access to the floppy disk in the first floppy drive. A password can also be specified. `Lock DF0: OFF` switches write access on again. Write protection is realized at the software level and is only effective until the file is unlocked or the computer is restarted.

MakeDir Directories can be created with `MakeDir`. For example, `MakeDir RAM:Photos` creates a directory called *Photos* on the RAM Disk. The command creates an entire directory hierarchy with the `ALL` option. Example: `MakeDir "RAM:Photos/Holidays/Scotland" ALL`.

MakeLink The new `MakeLink` command creates *links*. Its execution is similar to that of the `Copy` command. The name of the link is therefore the first argument (`FROM` option), and the target of the link is the second argument (`TO` option). There are hard links and soft links. The `MakeLink` command creates hard links by default. A hard link points directly to another file, i.e. without a diversion via a path name. It therefore only works within a file system and not across partitions. The command only creates hard links to directories with the FORCE option, as this can lead to confusion as to what the parent directory is. A created soft link (SOFT option) refers to the target via a path name. It is therefore possible to refer to any target on a different file system. The target must exist unless you specify FORCE as an option. If a relative path is specified as the destination, the command uses the source directory as the starting directory. The `List` command displays soft link destinations and, with `unresolved softlink` in the last line, also shows the number of soft links for which the destination does not exist. The `Dir` command shows whether a directory entry is a hard (`<hl>`) or soft (`<sl>`) link. Not all file systems fully support links.

More

Although the `More` text viewer is located in *SYS:Utilities* rather than the standard directory for commands, *C:* or *SYS:C*, it can be used as an excellent Shell command. `More S:Startup-Sequence` displays the startup sequence of AmigaOS. The command displays a page of text and then waits for keyboard input. The Enter key takes you to the next line, and the Space bar lets you go to the next page. To scroll back one page, press [B] or the Backspace key. It is also possible to scroll using the arrow keys. The command reveals all other key combinations after pressing the [H] key. Press [Q] to end the command.

Key shortcut in MORE	**Function**
space bar, down or right arrow	next page
backspace, [b], arrow up or left	previous page
Enter key	next line
[<]	first page
[>]	last page
[q] or [Ctrl]+[c]	exit
[h]	display key assignment
[%] followed by percentage	skip to the specified position
[/] followed by search word	search (case-sensitive)
[.] followed by search word	search (case-insensitive)
[E]	editing with editor from ENV:Editor

The `More` tool allows you to search for specific text. With */Assign*, you can search for *Assign* exactly according to upper/ lower case. With *.Assign*, `More` is case-insensitive. In both cases, `[N]` shows the next occurrence.

Mount

Use the `Mount` command to make new devices known to AmigaDOS. The command scans the *Devs:MountList* and the *Devs:DOSDrivers* and *SYS:Storage/DOSDriver* directories for the appropriate mount file. For example, `Mount PC0:` uses the file *SYS:Storage/DOSDriver/PC0* to make PC floppy disks with a FAT file system accessible via the first floppy drive. Use the `FROM` option to specify your own mount file. The command also accepts file patterns. The *S:Startup-Sequence* contains the operation `Mount Devs:DOSDrivers/~(#?.info)` to mount all DOSDriver files from this directory.

New in AmigaOS 3.2 is the option to cleanly unload a handler or file system with `SHUTDOWN`. The device remains intact. For example, `Mount PC0: SHUTDOWN` will release the *CrossDOS* file system. However, AmigaDOS will load it again as soon as you insert a new PC disk. Alternatively, `Assign PC0: DISMOUNT` removes the device again. Note that the `Assign` command itself does not release the resources, i.e. the handler or the file system. It therefore makes sense to always execute `Mount SHUTDOWN` first.

Mounter

Another tool for mounting file systems is the `Mounter` command. The program can also run as a commodity with a graphical user interface (see page 233). It supports drives set up according to the *Rigid Disk Block (RDB) standard*. The command parameters can also be replaced as icon attributes in conjunction with a project icon, for example.

The command `Mounter DEVICE uaehf.device UNIT 0 PARTITIONS "Install:"` mounts the file system on the *Install* partition. This file system could suitably contain a copy of the files and directories on the AmigaOS 3.2 CD. If no specific partitions are specified, the program will attempt to mount mountable file systems from all partitions on the drive. Several specific partitions can also be specified, e.g.: `PARTITIONS DH2: DH3:`. When used as a icon attribute, though, the notation would be `PARTITIONS=DH2:|DH3:`.

The `Mounter` program usually attempts to remount file systems that have already been mounted. To do this, it first unmounts such a file system and then remounts it again. This makes little sense for the file system on which the booted AmigaOS resides, since allocations such as C: will still point to the file system that was previously mounted, yet is now no longer available. You can prevent this behavior with the `NOREMOUNT` option. With `NOUNMOUNT`, you generally prohibit the unmounting of a file system on a partition with the same name.

`Mounter` uses the parameters from RDB to mount the file system of a partition. This avoids the need to first create a mount file for a file system that has not yet been mounted and then mount it with `mount`. Use `MASK` and `BUFMEMTYPE` to overwrite the corresponding information on the buffer memory with your own values.

Owner

The `Owner` command sets the owner for a file or directory. It also works with file patterns or with `ALL`, recursively. For example, `Owner Admin.txt admin` sets the owner for the *Admin.txt* file to the user *admin*. With `USERS` as an option, the `List` command displays the groups of directory entries, if set. The user can also be specified as a number from 0 to 65535.

Users and groups are currently only relevant in AmigaOS in connection with network file systems such as *Envoy*. AmigaOS itself does not contain any user or group management.

Path

This internal command shows where AmigaDOS searches for executable programs. These can be AmigaDOS commands or programs with a graphical user interface.

The default search path first contains the current directory, then typical system directories such as *System*, *Utilities* and *Tools*, and finally *C:*. In turn, the *C:* assignment can refer to several directories. See the section on *Assign* (page 281).

The `Path` command can also change the search path. For example, `Path Extras3.2:Tools ADD` adds the *Tools* directory from the specified AmigaOS 3.2 disk to the search path. If one is not present, `Path` will ask for a floppy disk to be inserted to display its paths. With `QUIET`, there is no prompt. The command always adds new paths at the end of the path list before *C:*. This is impractical if you want to use your own version of a command. With `HEAD` in addition to `ADD`, the path ends up at the beginning of the list. With `REMOVE` you can get rid of a path again, e.g. `Path Extra3.2:Tools REMOVE`.

PCD

Like the CD command, the PCD command changes to a specific directory. While doing this, it remembers the directory in which the Shell was previously located. A simple call without any parameters changes to the previous directory. A new call changes back to the directory to which the last execution of the command plus argument had changed. The following example illustrates how this works:

```
CD SYS:
PCD system
PCD
PCD
```

The script uses assignments in the form of FROM followed by the number of the Shell process to memorize the directory. The PushCD and SwapCD commands that are built into the Shell offer similar functionality.

PopCD

PopCD takes the top entry of the stack for working directories and changes to it. See the details about the PushCD command.

Prompt

The Shell's welcome prompt is set with Prompt. The default is %N.%S>. The placeholder %N stands for the number of the current Shell, and %S stands for the current working directory. It is also possible to display the return value of the last command, for example with Prompt $N.%S.%R>. Escape sequences can also be inserted, for example to set certain colors.

The change only applies to the current Shell. To use a different prompt permanently, change the Prompt command in the Shell start sequence in *S:Shell-Startup* accordingly. The comments in this file also contain examples of usable escape sequences.

Protect

The Protect command changes the protection bits of files and directories. The command expects the name of a file or directory or a file pattern. With ALL, it works recursively with all files and directories below the specified directory. It may make sense to set the access rights to files or directories separately. For example, the command processes files with FILES and directories with DIRS.

In addition, you can specify which permissions the command should set or delete, e.g., Protect RAM:File rwd sets *read*, *write* and *delete* flags and deletes all other flags. Alternatively, `Protect RAM:File -wd` removes the *write* and *delete* flag, and `Protect RAM:File +e` adds the right to *execute* the file. You can also use `add` and `sub` as an alternative to + and `-`. Rights can either be added or deleted in one command execution, but not both at the same time.

Reading, writing, executing and deleting should be self-explanatory. Script files with the `s` flag can be started directly without an `execute` command. Making a command *resident* means loading it into main memory to speed up subsequent access. Good backup programs optionally set the flag `a` for *archived* for each file that they back up. AmigaOS deletes this flag if a file is changed, which makes it easier to recognize which files have been changed during the next run.

By default, the `Protect` command only changes the user's rights. `GROUP` can be used to set group rights, and `OTHER` can be used to set the access for others. With `CLONE GROUP`, you can set group rights based on the rights for the user. The same applies to `CLONE OTHER` for the other users.

Flag	**Effect**
r	read
w	write
e	execute (for programs)
d	delete
s	script
p	pure (can be made resident)
a	archived
h	make resident on first access (needs p)

PushCD

Integrated into the Shell, the `PushCD` command places the current working directory of the Shell on a stack and then optionally changes to the specified directory. The `PopCD` command takes the top entry from the stack and changes to it, while `SwapCD` swaps the top entry from the stack and the current directory of the Shell. For example:

```
CD Sys:
PushCD Tools
PopCD
```

Reboot

Use the `Reboot` command to restart the Amiga. Unlike many similar programs, this command waits for write operations that are currently running to finish in order to avoid a validation process for file systems such as the Fast File System.

Relabel

The `Relabel` command is used to rename a volume. `Relabel DF0: Music` renames the disk in the first disk drive to `Music`. Instead of the drive name *DF0:*, the old name of the drive can also be specified.

RemRAD

A reset-proof RAM Drive (see page 97) is removed by `RemRAD`. The command instructs the *ramdrive.device* to delete all files on the RAM Disk and then switches the drive to *inactive*. Only a warm restart can release all the memory. If the reset-proof RAM Disk is in use, the status changes to *busy*. With `FORCE`, the command should remove a reset-proof RAM Disk that is in use. A warm restart with `reboot` will remove the RAM Disk in any case. When using more than one reset-proof RAM Disk, specify the device when removing, e.g. `RemRAD RAD:`.

The MountList file, a DOSDriver for the reset-proof RAM Disk, can be found in the *DOSDrivers* drawer in *Storage* on the system drive. Double-click on it or use `Mount RAD:` to mount the reset-proof RAM Disk on the system.

Rename

You can set new names for files and directories with `Rename`. For example, `Rename text1 text2` renames the file *text1* into *text2*. The last argument will be either a filename or a directory. For example, `Rename pic1 pic2 pic3 pictures`, or the more detailed `Rename pic1 pic2 pic3 AS pictures` moves the files *pic1* to *pic3* to the directory *pictures*. The progress indicator can be switched off with the `QUIET` option.

Resident

The `Resident` command loads commands into main memory until the next restart. The command is immediately available, reducing the need to access the disk. Several programs can access a `Resident` command at the same time without increasing main memory usage. In order to make a program resident, several programs must use it at the same time (*re-entrant*). It must also be possible to execute the program repeatedly without reloading it (*re-executable*). Most of the commands in the *C:* directory, and `More` from the *Utilities* directory, fulfill these requirements and are therefore *pure*, and have the PURE flag set by default. Compare this with the `Protect` command.

With no parameters set, the `Resident` command shows the resident list and internal commands. Executing `Resident C:List` makes the `List` command from *C: resident*. A command that has been made *resident* as *List* before will be replaced when doing so. Alternatively, a different name can be given: `Resident List2 C:List`. A path must always be specified for the command to be made resident. With ADD instead of REPLACE, the same program can be made resident under several names. For example, `Resident L C:List ADD` additionally makes the `List` command available as a resident `L`. An alternative to this would be an `Alias` (see page 280).

The sequence `Resident L C:List REMOVE` removes the command `C:List` that has been made resident as `L`. This can also be used to switch off an internal command. `Resident CD REMOVE` makes the internal command CD inaccessible. This is rather impractical for this command, so it is advisable to immediately make it accessible again with `Resident CD REPLACE`. This may make more sense for another internal command if an alternative command with the same name is installed as a file in the search path.

Run

Usually, when a command is executed, the Shell waits until it is finished and then returns to the prompt. Run is used to start a program or sequence of several programs in the background. For example, `Run TextEdit S:Shell-Startup` opens the text editor *TextEdit* for editing the *Shell start sequence*.

It is possible to combine several commands with +. To do this, write the plus sign at the end of the first command, press the Enter key, enter the second command, followed by a plus sign, followed by the Enter key and a third command if necessary, and so on.

Example of a longer copy process using the Run feature:

```
Run Copy DF0:Photos Data:Photos ALL CLONE +
Delete DF0:Photos ALL +
Echo "Copied Photos, original has been deleted"
```

The AmigaOS 3.2 Shell offers an interesting alternative to the `run` command: the & character, which is typical for Linux and Unix variants. If the & character is surrounded by spaces on the command line, the Shell executes the command in almost exactly the same way as with the Run command. Unlike with Run, however, the executed command remains linked to the standard input, so that & also works with the Ask command. In conjunction with the console handler *ViNCEd*, which must be installed separately, there is also the job control option FG, as on Linux. The console handler supplied with AmigaOS 3.2 does not support this additional function.

Commands started in the background use the same console window for the standard output as the Shell that started them. This can therefore only be closed as soon as all commands started in the background have been completed. In connection with an output redirection, processes can be completely disconnected via &. For example, after `TextEdit S:Shell-Startup >NIL: &`, the console window can be closed with the Shell, even if the text editor is still running.

Search

Use `Search` to look for files containing specific text. For example, `Search S: Load` searches for the term *Load* in all files within the directory to which the S assignment points. With `ALL`, the command also looks in the subdirectories. Alternatively, you can specify a single file or file pattern.

By default, the command displays the line number for each search location. With `NONUM`, it will omit this. The command displays the name of each file searched and each search location. With `QUIET`, only filenames with hits are displayed. If you want to see the locations where the files were found, use `QUICK` instead. With `FILE`, the command searches for filenames instead. With `PATTERN`, the command supports patterns as search terms. For example, `Search SYS: Start#? FILE PATTERN ALL` finds all files located below *SYS:* that begin with *Start*. The command is not case sensitive – but with `CASE`, the command distinguishes between both cases.

An alternative to `Search` is the `Find` program. Though it has a graphical user interface, it can only be configured via the command line. The actual search process must then be started by the user in the graphical user interface.

Set

The `Set` command sets the value of a local variable that is only visible to the current Shell and its child processes. Example: `Set amount 10`. You can delete a variable with the `Unset` command.

With no parameters set, the `Set` command returns a list of all local variables, including their content. To display the content of a single local variable, use the `Get` command.

SetClock

The `SetClock` command loads or saves the time from the battery-backed hardware clock. `SetClock LOAD` uses the time from the hardware clock as the system time, while `SetClock SAVE` saves the current system time to the hardware clock. The system time can be read and set with the `Date` command. If a badly written program switches off the hardware clock or sets its test bit, `SetClock RESET` resets the clock to a functional state.

Note: For Amiga models that do not have a battery-backed hardware clock, one can usually be retrofitted using a so-called clock or RTC (real-time clock) module.

SetDate

The `SetDate` command changes the date of a file or directory. The date set is the time of creation or the last change. For example, `SetDate RAM:Testfile 20-01-22 14:00:00` sets the date and time of *RAM:Testfile* to 20 January 2022 and exactly 2 pm. It is possible to specify only a date or only a time. The output of the `Date` command is compatible with `SetDate`. The command works recursively with `ALL`.

SetEnv

The `SetEnv` command sets the value of an environment variable that is valid for all Shells. Example: `SetEnv Editor C:Ed`. The command writes content to a file of the same name in the *ENV:* directory. The content of *ENV:* is located in the volatile working memory (RAM) and is therefore lost when the Amiga is restarted. With `SetEnv Editor C:Ed SAVE`, the command also writes the content of the variable to *ENVARC:*, which is located in *SYS:Prefs/Env-Archive*. Its content is also available in *ENV:* after a restart thanks to the *Env handler*. Variables saved with `SAVE` therefore survive a system restart. A volatile saved variable can also be saved permanently, for example with `Copy ENV:Editor ENVARC: CLONE`. To delete an environment variable, use the `UnsetEnv` command. With no parameters set, the `SetEnv` command displays a list of all environment variables. To display the content of an individual environment variable, use the `GetENV` command (see page 299).

SetFont

You can change the console with `SetFont`. For example, `SetFont courier 15` sets the scalable *Courier* font with size

15 as the font. Bitmap fonts such as *Topaz* can be scaled with limited quality using `SCALE`. By default, the command only works with fonts of a fixed character width, such as *Topaz*, *Courier* or *LetterGothic*. With `PROP`, the command allows proportional fonts, but this can lead to display errors. `ITALIC` sets an italic font, `BOLD` sets a bold font, and `UNDERLINE` sets an underlined font.

By default, the standard system text font is used for all Shells. You can define this inside the *Font* preferences.

SetKeyboard

The `SetKeyboard` command sets the keyboard layout for the console. `SetKeyboard d` sets the German keyboard layout, for example. As a rule, it should not be necessary to change the keyboard layout of the console provided the correct keyboard layout was selected in the *Input* preset. Sometimes it may make sense to temporarily switch to a different keyboard layout. Available keyboard layouts can be found in *Devs:Keymaps*. If a keymap is missing there, simply copy it from the *Storage3.2* disk.

Sort

The `Sort` command sorts the lines in a file and writes the result to another file. `Sort surnames "sorted surnames"` sorts a text file with surnames alphabetically. By default, the command uses country-specific rules for upper and lower case. The option `LEXICOGRAPHIC` forces upper case letters to be placed before lower-case letters. With `DESCENDING`, the command sorts backwards. With `NUMERIC`, it sorts numerically.

The `Sort` command compares all rows from the beginning of the file. A different start position can be specified with `COLSTART`. This is suitable, for example, for alphabetically sorting files with numbers at the beginning of each line. With the `SKIPBLANKS` option, the command skips leading spaces.

`Sort` reads the source file in blocks of 4096 bytes. A different size can be specified with `BUFSIZE`. The command works with plain text files. Documents created with a word processor such as AmigaWriter, Final Writer or WordWorth cannot be sorted with the command.

SPAT

Similar to `DPAT` (see page 292), this small script enables commands with arguments that do not support file patterns to be used with file patterns. The script uses the `List` command to generate a list of files and uses it to create a script with several command executions, which it then runs.

For example, `SPAT Ed S:S#?` runs the text editor with all files from *S:* that begin with *S*, such as the *Shell startup*, *SPat* itself and the *startup sequence*.

Stack

You can set the stack size for the active Shell with the `Stack` command. Typical stack sizes in AmigaOS are between 4,000 and 25,000 bytes. If a program run from the Shell exits with a software error, it may be due to the stack being too small. Try using a larger stack size. If sufficient main memory is available, it may be useful to initially select a stack size that is too large, such as 100,000 or even 500,000, in order to see to what extent a stack that is too small is the cause of the error. However, a large stack consumes more main memory. Using a stack that is too large by default is therefore not recommended.

The stack size for Workbench programs can be set in that program's respective icon information. If you have plenty of RAM, you can set a higher stack size as the default in the Shell start sequence in *S:Shell-Startup*, for example 10,000.

Status

The `Status` command shows a list of Shell processes that are currently running. With `FULL`, the command also shows the stack size, the priority and the *global vector size* of each process. With the `TCB` argument, the command reveals the same information without the name of the currently loaded program.

A search in the process list enables the `SORT` option, which supports the full program name, as well as the full program name with path and file patterns.

SwapCD

With `SwapCD` you can swap the top entry of the stack for working directories of the current Shell and the current working directory. By running `CD SYS:` first, followed by `PushCD Tools`, the *SYS:* directory is put onto the stack, and the directory is changed to *SYS:Tools*. The `SwapCD` command will then switch back and forth between *SYS:* and *SYS:Tools*.

TextEdit

A detailed description of the new text editor in AmigaOS 3.2 can be found in the chapter in *Programs* (see page 216). Contrary to what is described in the help guide for AmigaOS 3.2, this editor supports at least one filename as an argument. Thus, the command sequence `TextEdit S:Startup-Sequence` starts the editor, which then loads the contents of the start sequence into the editor window. This even works with multiple arguments, where the editor will open a tab for each specified file.

Type

If you only want to display the contents of a file, use the `Type` command. For example, `Type S:User-Startup` displays the contents of the user startup sequence. Line numbers are available with `NUMBER`. `TEXT-ONLY` is useful for files with binary data. In this case, the command will only show the text characters that can be displayed.

For binary files, the `HEX` option will output in hexadecimal format with the displayable characters shown opposite. With `AUTO`, the command will attempt to automatically recognize whether the file is a plain text file or a binary file based on the first 256 characters. In hexadecimal mode, `WIDTH` can be used to specify a width. By default, the program displays up to 61 characters per line.

By default, the command reads up to 2,048 characters at a time. A different buffer size is specified by `BUFSIZE`.

UnAlias

The `UnAlias` command removes an alias from the alias list of the current Shell. Other Shells running at the same time will not notice this. For more on aliases, see the `Alias` command.

Unset

The `Unset` command removes a variable from the variable list for the current Shell process. To set variables and display variable contents, use the `Set` and `Get` commands.

UnSetEnv

The `UnSetEnv` command removes an environment variable from the variable list for the current Shell process. To set and display variables, see the `SetEnv` and `Get` commands.

Any default value of an environment variable stored in *ENVARC:* or *Sys:Prefs/Env-Archive*, which is still available after a restart, can only be deleted by using the command with the `DELETE` option.

Version

The `Version` command shows the version number of a library, device or tool, or of the Workbench. With no parameters set, the command shows the Kickstart ROM version (labeled *Kickstart*) and the AmigaOS version (labeled *Workbench)*. The Workbench itself also shows which version of AmigaOS is installed in the menu under *Workbench > About...* This version differs from the version of the actual Workbench within AmigaOS. The command shows this with `workbench.library` as an argument. With no parameters set, it also sets the two environment variables *Kickstart* and *Workbench* to the corresponding version numbers. The `Version` command also understands file patterns. The versions of all libraries in *Libs:*, for example, can be shown with `Version LIBS:#?.library`. By default, the command only shows the name and version number. With `FULL`, the modification date is also shown, if available. For example, for AmigaOS 3.2.1, `Version FULL` shows 13.7.2021 as the modification date.

The `Version` command also lets you check for a specific version number using `VERSION` and `REVISION`. For example, for AmigaOS 3.2.1, `Version exec.library 48` returns the error value 5 in the variable `$RC`, as the version of the library is 47.8. For devices, a unit number can also be specified with the `UNIT` option.

Wait

In scripts, it can be useful to wait for a certain time or for a certain event. For example, `Wait 10 secs` waits 10 seconds. Minutes can also be specified with `MINS`. The command waits for a specific time with `UNTIL`. For example, `Wait UNTIL 14:30` sets a pause until 2:30 pm.

However, if a script is waiting for a task to be completed and it is not clear from the outset how long it will take, then it is recommended to wait for a file to be created. This can be achieved with `Wait FILE T:Backup/Done`, for example.

Which

With `Which`, you can find the location of a specified command or assignment. `Which Dir` shows the location of the `Dir` command on the drive, and `Which C:` shows where the *C:* assignment points to.

The command displays internal commands as `INTERNAL` and resident commands as `RES`. After running `Resident C:Dir`, *RES dir* is shown as a result of `Which Dir`. Usually `Which` only shows the first result. With `ALL`, the command searches all search paths. With an active resident `Dir` command, `Which C:Dir ALL` shows both *RES dir* and the path on the volume.

Why

You can discover why a previously executed command failed with the internal `Why` command. After typing `Dir DoesNotExist`, running `Why` displays the message *"Object not found"* if *DoesNotExist* really does not exist. The `Dir` command itself will already have returned an error message. But if a program does not do this, `Why` can sometimes provide an explanation.

Shell programming

The topic of Shell programming alone would easily fill an entire book. So here are just a few useful tips on how to get started, including explanatory examples, of course.

Introduction to Shell programming

You create or edit a Shell script the same as you would a text file, using a text editor, such as *Ed* or *TextEdit*, included in AmigaOS, or another text editor of your choice, such as *CygnusEd* or *GoldEd*. For example, use *TextEdit* to create your first script, which will consist of a single line:

```
Echo "Hello World!"
```

Save this to *RAM:Hello*, for example, and then run it with `Execute RAM:Hello`. The Shell will then display the text *Hello World!* Easy, right?

If you give the script the script access flag by using `Protect RAM:Hello +s`, then simple entering `RAM:Hello` will work. If the Shell is located in *RAM:*, then even just typing `Hello` is enough to start the script. Alternatively, you can copy the script somewhere in the search path for commands and scripts to run it from anywhere just by entering its name. For example, use `Copy RAM:Hello S: CLONE` to create a new Shell command with `Hello` implemented as a script, which you can run at any time and from any directory.

Of course, the Shell can do much more than just perform a simple output like *"Hello World!"*. A Shell script is a collection of commands built into the Shell along with external commands. AmigaOS comes with a number of external commands. There are also many other commands and programs available for download from Aminet and other sources (e.g. www.aminet.net/util/cli). The built-in commands offer a range of options for influencing the sequence of programs. For example, you can react to certain events with `If` and jump to a point in the script marked with *Lab* using `Skip`. Alongside variables and calculation functions such as those provided by the `Eval` command, loops are also possible for performing actions several times, allowing you to automate simple tasks you want to see repeated. For more complex requirements, other scripting languages like ARexx, which is built into AmigaOS, or Ruby, Python, Perl or similar, may be better.

The *AmigaOS 3.2 reference documentation* does not contain a complete reference for programming Shell scripts. If possible, please refer to the *AmigaDOS manual* for older AmigaOS versions. In the *AmigaOS 4 Wiki*, you will find an overview of the topic, which is also largely suitable for AmigaOS 3.2 (https://wiki.amigaos.net/wiki/AmigaOS_Manual:_AmigaDOS_Using_Scripts).

Existing Shell scripts are a good starting point if you want to learn about Shell programming. In AmigaOS, for example, there are some scripts that contain typical constructions such as if-then queries. The start sequence in *S:Startup-Sequence* shows the use of simple if-then queries. The `Help` command is implemented as a script as well. You can find it in *SYS:System/Help*.

Variables

Both local and environment variables can be used in Shell scripts. A local variable only applies to the current Shell and the scripts running in it. For example, you can use `Set file "RAM:examplefile"` to set the variable *file* to the content *RAM:examplefile*. However, the Shell saves an environment variable in *ENV:*. Therefore, the content of an environment variable can also be read with a script started in another Shell. You can set such a variable with the `SetEnv` command. AmigaOS loses the variable again after a restart, as *ENV:* points to a directory in the RAM Disk by default. Use the `SAVE` argument to save the content of a variable permanently. This command also saves the variable content in *ENVARC:* (see the description of the corresponding commands in this chapter for further information).

To access the content of a variable, prefix its name with a dollar sign. For example, `Echo $File` will output *RAM:examplefile* if you have set the variable content accordingly. You can also use `Get` or `GetEnv` to display the content of a variable.

If a script uses environment variables only for the purpose of the script, use a unique variable name. Note that a script can be run multiple times. One way of doing this is to compose the variable name from the name of the script, the purpose and a unique number. This provides, for example, the process number, which inserts <$$>. An example: `SetEnv CoolScriptFILE<$$> "RAM:examplefile"`.

To avoid any conflicts with the redirection of input and output via < and >, you can define other characters, for example with `.BRA {` and `.KET }`, to specify parameters. In this case, `{ARG1}` would be used instead of `<ARG1>` in the script above.

Parameter transfer

It makes sense to pass a parameter when running many scripts. This is also possible with special brackets. The following script accepts up to two arguments, both of which are optional. With `.KEY ARG1/A ARG2`, the first argument would always be required and the second argument would still be optional. There are other variants: `/N` marks numbers, `/S` marks a switch such as `FILES` in the `List` command, and with `/K` the keyword (*ARG1* in this example) must always be specified. All details can be found by typing `Help Execute`. Here is the example:

```
.KEY ARG1 ARG2
Echo "Argument 1: <ARG1>"
Echo „Argument 2: <ARG2>“
```

If-then queries

A simple example of an if-then query is:

```
Ask Continue(Y)/Cancel(N)?
If WARN
    Echo Continue
Else
    Echo Cancel
Endif
```

In this case, the `Ask` command queries a Boolean value: true or false, yes or no. The query is not localized to the language. Therefore, `Ask` always uses `[y]` for yes, and `[n]` or no for no. Depending on the answer, the script will either continue or abort.

Another variant may be more suitable for querying whether the script should continue to run:

```
Ask Continue(Y)/Cancel(N)?
If NOT WARN
    Echo Cancel
    Quit 0
Endif

Echo "Here we go again"
Echo "Memory usage:"

Avail
```

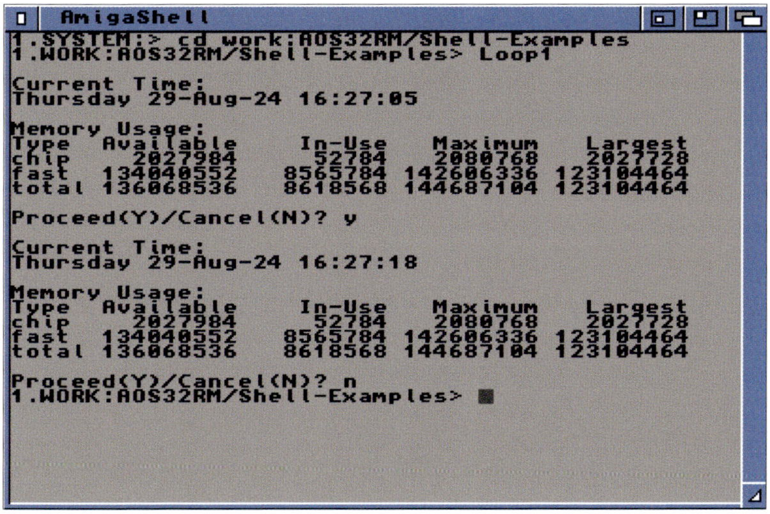

```
AmigaShell
1.SYSTEM:> cd work:AOS32RM/Shell-Examples
1.WORK:AOS32RM/Shell-Examples> Loop1

Current Time:
Thursday 29-Aug-24 16:27:05

Memory Usage:
Type   Available    In-Use   Maximum   Largest
chip     2027984     52784   2080768   2027728
fast   134040552   8565784 142606336 123104464
total  136068536   8618568 144687104 123104464

Proceed(Y)/Cancel(N)? y

Current Time:
Thursday 29-Aug-24 16:27:18

Memory Usage:
Type   Available    In-Use   Maximum   Largest
chip     2027984     52784   2080768   2027728
fast   134040552   8565784 142606336 123104464
total  136068536   8618568 144687104 123104464

Proceed(Y)/Cancel(N)? n
1.WORK:AOS32RM/Shell-Examples>
```

A simple loop

It is also possible to set a label at the end of the script and jump to it in an if-then query. For example:

```
Ask Continue(Y)/Cancel(N)?
If NOT WARN
    Echo Cancel
    Skip End
Endif

Echo "Here we go again"
Echo "Memory usage:"

Avail

Lab End
Echo "End of script."
```

Loops

Using what we've learned with an additional option for the Skip command, a simple loop can easily be built. An example:

```
Lab Loop

Echo "*Current Time:"
Date

Echo "*nMemory Usage:"
Avail

Ask "*nProceed(Y)/Cancel(N)?"
If WARN
    Skip Loop BACK
Endif
```

The BACK argument is important here in order for the Skip command to actually jump back.

A loop can have a predefined number of runs. This requires a counter, which the Eval command increments. As the command cannot write the result directly to a local variable, an environment variable is used:

```
.KEY UPPERLIMIT/A

Echo "Upper limit: <upperlimit>"

SetEnv RUN<$$> 0

Lab Start

Eval $RUN<$$> + 1 TO ENV:RUN<$$> >NIL:

Echo "Run: " NOLINE
Type ENV:RUN<$$>

If VAL $RUN<$$> NOT GE <upperlimit>
    Skip Start BACK
EndIf

UnsetEnv RUN<$$>
```

This example also shows a parameter transfer. If you save the script in a file called *Loop*, set the script flag and run the script with `Loop 5`, you will receive the following output:

```
Upper limit: 5
Run: 1
Run: 2
Run: 3
Run: 4
Run: 5
```

A simple loop

Coming up next

In the following *Power User* chapter, you will learn, among many other professional tips, how to customize your Amiga perfectly to your own requirements using various start sequences and the Shell commands you learned here.

Power user

In this chapter, we dive deep into the world of AmigaOS. Experienced users will find out how to utilize the full potential of the operating system. Learn how to optimize your Amiga with different scripted startup sequences and how best to use the Amiga boot menu. You will also get an overview of useful keyboard shortcuts that will massively speed up the way you work. And that's not all: deepen your knowledge in a detailed section on the powerful ARexx programming language and discover new ways of customizing your AmigaOS!

Startup scripts: Introduction

The default AmigaOS startup always follows an identical sequence: there is the early startup of the Kickstart ROM, then the startup sequence, followed by the user startup, then a final command to load Workbench. Each phase, and options for customizing each item, is explained in this chapter.

Startup sequence

After completing the early startup phase of the Kickstart ROM, AmigaOS loads the *Startup-Sequence* script located in *S:* on the boot drive, unless you select *Boot With No Startup-Sequence* in the boot menu or *Failsafe boot* in the boot options. The *Startup-Sequence* script does everything that is required for a proper system start.

User startup

The script then passes control to the *User-Startup* script located in *S:*, if it exists. If required, you may want to include additional commands in this script that then can be executed every time you start your Amiga.

The installer scripts of programs that you install sometimes also add additional commands there, such as assigning directories with the `Assign` command.

LoadWB and WBStartup

Finally, the *LoadWB* command included in the standard start sequence launches Workbench, which itself loads all the programs in the *WBStartup* drawer on the system drive while starting up.

Failsafe boat

Alternatively, activate the *Failsafe boot* option in the boot menu under *Boot Options*. In this case, AmigaOS executes the script from the *Startup-Failsafe* file instead. This omits, among other things, the loading of drivers, the running of the user startup and the execution of the programs in *WBStartup*.

Shell startup

The *Shell startup* script located in *S:* is not directly related to the actual boot process. The Shell executes it when it is started. This is where you enter commands that you want to execute when you open a Shell window. You can read more about this script in chapter 5 on the *Shell*.

Startup scripts: startup-sequence

This important system startup script is located in the S directory and performs all the tasks necessary for the proper startup of AmigaOS. Here you will learn about the functions and effects of the commands contained in the startup-sequence.

AmigaOS 3.2.2 contains version 47.19 of the *S:Startup-Sequence*. The section beginning in line 3 with `Version exec.library version 47 >NIL:` checks to what extent the Kickstart ROM corresponds to the current version of AmigaOS 3.2. If this is not the case, the script starts an effective update with the `LoadModule` command from line 5 until the next cold start and then triggers a warm restart. If you want to avoid this, install the latest Kickstart ROM chips in your Amiga according to the instructions (see section 1.2). If you are using a UAE-based Amiga emulator such as FS-UAE or WinUAE, there is no reason not to select the current Kickstart ROM for version 3.2.2. Make sure you use the correct ROM file for the Amiga model you are using.

The final `SetPatch` command in line 17 applies further runtime patches as required and loads support libraries for the 68030, 68040 or 68060 processors if necessary. The command execution in the *startup-sequence* redirects the list of patches to *NIL:* so that no Shell window opens when booting. You can view the output at any time using the `SetPatch` command.

If the CPU libraries required for a 68040 or 68060 are missing at startup, the *CPU CheckInstall* Section (from line 18) automatically starts the *Startup-Failsafe* script in line 25 and then ends the execution of the regular start-sequence with the `Quit` command. The installer script for AmigaOS 3.2 automatically offers to install suitable CPU libraries if a corresponding processor is available (see page 65).

The `CPU` command used for the check in line 20 returns an error value of up to 30 in the event of an error. Therefore, the command `FailAt 31` is placed before it to continue the execution of the script even in this case. After this section, `FailAt 10` in line 34 resets the error tolerance to the default value.

The `Version` command in line 35 initializes the Shell variables *Kickstart* and *Workbench* to the version numbers of the running Kickstart and Workbench. The Workbench version stands for the version of the disk part of AmigaOS, not for the version of the *workbench.library*.

For the first floppy drive, if present, the section following line 36 increases the number of buffers by 15 with the `AddBuffers` command.

The section from line 40 onwards is used to set up the system for environment variables. This consists of a disk directory, to which the assignment *ENVARC:* (for *Environment Archive*) points, as well as a directory for the variable contents valid at runtime, to which the assignment *ENV:* points. The `MakeDir` command in line 45 also creates the usual temporary directory *T* and *Clipboards* in the RAM Disk.

Starting from line 48, there are some assignments that the `Resident C:Assign PURE` command from line 47 accelerates by caching the `Assign` command in RAM. These include the assignments of *ENV:*, *T:* and *CLIPS:* to the corresponding directories in the RAM Disk.

The `FailAt 21` command at line 51 secures further assignments from line 52 as well as commands for loading drivers from line 57. The `BindDrivers` command in line 57 binds special third-party drivers from the *Expansion* directory, if available. In many cases, the directory is empty. The subsequent `mount` command binds the DOS drivers located in *DEVS:DOSDrivers*. Finally, the monitor drivers from *DEVS:Monitors* are initialized by the `LoadMonDrvs` command.

The following `SetEnv` commands in line 61 write the version numbers from the local variables *Workbench* and *Kickstart* to global environment variables of the same name without saving them permanently. The `Unset` commands then delete the two Shell variables.

In addition, the `Language` variable for the system language is initially given the value *english* for English.

Before loading and applying user settings, the `AddDatatypes` command in line 66 loads the datatypes from *DEVS:Datatypes*. These include datatypes for displaying AmigaGuide documents and various image formats such as ILBM and PNG. Finally, the `IPrefs` command loads and activates the settings in the **.prefs files* from *ENV:Sys*. This includes setting the color depth and resolution of the Workbench screen. Finally, `ConClip` activates the clipboard for console windows.

Ideally, the `LoadWB` command at the end of the *startup-sequence* opens the Workbench screen in the correct resolution. If an AmigaDOS Shell window has previously appeared due to an error output, *IPrefs* waits until it is closed. This is also why the output of some commands is redirected with *>NIL:* to nowhere – so that no Shell window opens. The `EndCLI` command at the very end of the script closes such a window.

The *IPrefs* program continues to run in the background in order to react to future adjustments to the settings, such as after using a preset from *Prefs*. As of AmigaOS 3.2, IPrefs always applies all changes at once instead of redrawing the screen several times. The program also shows the names of the windows still to be closed.

If the file *SYS:System/RexxMast* exists, the script also activates the ARexx interpreter in line 70. This is usually a good idea, as some ARexx scripts in *S:* require this and many Amiga tools need their own ARexx port and use ARexx scripts.

The `Path` command from line 72 sets up the search path for the Shell. In addition to the *C:* assignment for the directory with the external AmigaDOS commands, it also contains other standard directories such as *SYS:Utilities*, *SYS:Tools*, *SYS:Prefs* and *SYS:Rexxc*, which contain programs that can be started from the Shell. The following `MakeLink` command provides the RAM Disk with a pretty icon.

The official start process is now almost complete. If a user-startup-sequence is available in *S:User-Startup*, the `Execute` command in line 75 executes it.

Then `LoadWB` loads the Workbench, and finally `EndCLI` terminates the Shell that executed the startup-sequence.

Listing: The system start sequence
S:startup-sequence

```
; $VER: Startup-Sequence_HardDrive 47.19 (28.2.2023)
; Startup-Sequence for hard drive systems

Version exec.library version 47 >NIL:
If Warn
 LoadModule L:System-Startup ROMUPDATE
Else
 Version strap version 47 >NIL:
 If Warn
 LoadModule DOWNGRADE L:Ram-Handler L:Shell-Seg L:System-Startup
      Libs:dos.library Libs:gadtools.library Libs:graphics.library
      Libs:intuition.library >NIL:
 Else
 Version exec.library revision 9 >NIL:
 If Warn
 LoadModule DOWNGRADE L:Ram-Handler L:System-Startup
        Libs:intuition.library >NIL:
 EndIf
 EndIf
EndIf
SetPatch >NIL:

;------------------- CPU CheckInstall Section ------------------------
FailAt 31
CPU CHECKINSTALL

SET temp1 $RC

If VAL $temp1 EQ 30
 ECHO ""
 ASK "Press the RETURN key to resume booting into a restricted system."
 Execute S:Startup-failsafe
 QUIT
EndIf

If VAL $temp1 EQ 5
 ECHO ""
 ASK "Press the RETURN key to resume booting."
EndIf

UNSET temp1
;---------------- End of CPU CheckInstall Section --------------------

FailAt 10
Version >NIL:

Assign >nil: EXISTS DF0:
If not warn
 AddBuffers DF0: 15 >NIL:
EndIf
```

```
If EXISTS ENVARC:
 MakeLink RAM:ENV to ENVARC: FORCE
Else
 MakeDir RAM:ENV
Endif
MakeDir RAM:T RAM:Clipboards

Resident C:Assign PURE

Assign ENV: RAM:ENV
Assign T: RAM:T
Assign CLIPS: RAM:Clipboards
Assign REXX: S:

FailAt 21
Assign PRINTERS: DEVS:Printers
Assign KEYMAPS: DEVS:Keymaps
Assign LOCALE: SYS:Locale
Assign LIBS: SYS:Classes ADD
Assign HELP: LOCALE:Help DEFER

BindDrivers
Mount DEVS:DOSDrivers/~(#?.info)

LoadMonDrvs >NIL:

FailAt 10
SetEnv Language "english"
SetEnv Workbench $Workbench
SetEnv Kickstart $Kickstart
UnSet Workbench
UnSet Kickstart

AddDataTypes REFRESH QUIET
IPrefs
ConClip

If EXISTS SYS:System/RexxMast
 SYS:System/RexxMast >NIL:
EndIF

Path C: SYS:Utilities SYS:Rexxc SYS:System S: SYS:Prefs SYS:Tools SYS:Tools/Commodities
MakeLink RAM:Disk.info TO ENVARC:Sys/def_RAM.info SOFT

IF EXISTS S:User-Startup
 Execute S:User-Startup
EndIF

LoadWB
EndCLI >NIL:
```

Startup scripts: user-startup

The user startup sequence is located in the S:user-startup file. On a freshly installed AmigaOS 3.2 system, this will only contain a comment and a version number.

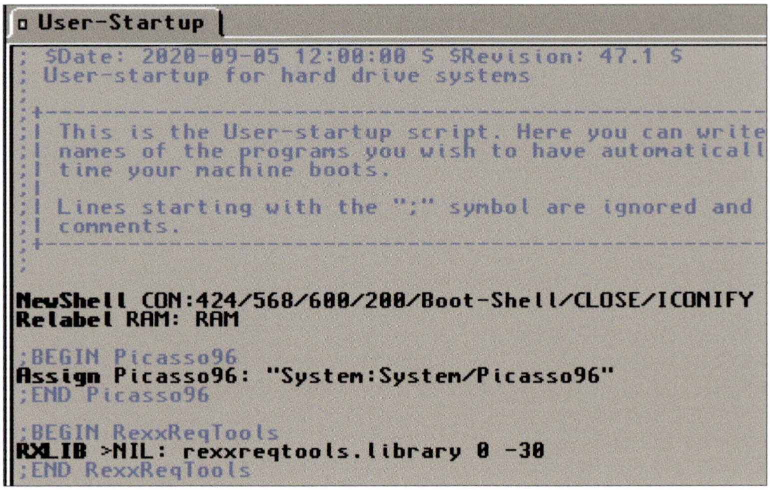

```
User-Startup
; $Date: 2020-09-05 12:00:00 $ $Revision: 47.1 $
; User-startup for hard drive systems
;
;+-----------------------------------------------------
;| This is the User-startup script. Here you can write
;| names of the programs you wish to have automaticall
;| time your machine boots.
;|
;| Lines starting with the ";" symbol are ignored and
;| comments.
;+-----------------------------------------------------
;
NewShell CON:424/568/600/200/Boot-Shell/CLOSE/ICONIFY
Relabel RAM: RAM

;BEGIN Picasso96
Assign Picasso96: "System:System/Picasso96"
;END Picasso96

;BEGIN RexxReqTools
RXLIB >NIL: rexxreqtools.library 0 -30
;END RexxReqTools
```

A relatively short user start sequence from a freshly installed system.

Function

The installer scripts of programs that you install one after the other sometimes add additional commands. The installer script for *Picasso96* does this, for example.

TIP **Using semicolons in scripts**
As in all other scripts in the AmigaDOS system, a semicolon [;] at the beginning of a line is used to exclude, i.e. ignore, the contents of a line.

Comments

Some commands are marked with comments such as `;BEGIN Picasso96` and `;END Picasso96` when added to the *user-startup*. It is recommended to leave these comments.

On the one hand, these comments make it clear where a change has been made. On the other hand, if the program is removed, an installer script can more easily detect the corresponding commands in the script and remove them, to avoid subsequent errors when the system is rebooted.

Adding commands

Use a text editor such as TextEdit or Ed to insert your own commands as required, e.g. `Relabel RAM: RAM` (if you prefer a shorter name for the RAM Disk without spaces).

Rumor has it the AmigaOS developers have used the *RAM Disk* name to motivate developers who write installer scripts and other programs that cannot handle spaces in file or directory names to fix such bugs. Because there were many such installer scripts, users who install applications were at a particular disadvantage.

You can also open a reserve Shell window with `NewShell CON:424/568/600/200/Boot-Shell/CLOSE/ICONIFY`. It is possible to do this without resetting the screen as *IPrefs* has already been started in the system start sequence.

Listing: The user start sequence
S:user-startup (modified)

```
; $Date: 2020-09-05 12:00:00 $ $Revision: 47.1 $
; User-startup for hard drive systems
;
;+---------------------------------------------------------------+
;| This is the User-startup script. Here you can write down the  |
;| names of the programs you wish to have run automatically every |
;| time your machine boots.                                       |
;|                                                                |
;| Lines starting with the";" symbol are ignored and used as      |
;| comments.                                                      |
;+---------------------------------------------------------------+
;

NewShell CON:424/568/600/200/Boot-Shell/CLOSE/ICONIFY
Relabel RAM: RAM

;BEGIN Picasso96
 Assign Picasso96: "System:System/Picasso96"
;END Picasso96

;BEGIN RexxReqTools
 RXLIB >NIL: rexxreqtools.library 0 -30
;END RexxReqTools
```

Startup scripts: startup-failsafe

A safe system startup sequence is located in the file S:startup-sailsafe that omits much of what the standard startup sequence in S:startup-sequence executes.

Function

Just a glance at the number of lines in the *startup-failsafe* script file shows that the script is limited to the essential features for bug analysis. With just under 40 lines of content, the failsafe startup sequence is just half as long as the standard sequence – especially when you consider that the file begins with an 18-line comment after listing the version number in line 1.

This comment also explains what the secure startup sequence omits: there's no checking for CPU libraries, no additional floppy buffers, no integration of DOS, graphics or expansion drivers, no clipboard for console windows, no ARexx and no application of user settings via IPrefs.

There was even room for a little humor in a comments section: anyone who edits the file runs the risk of being attacked by a horde of teenage Atari fans. (The question is, how many Atari fans are still teenagers and how many teenagers are discovering the Atari these days.)

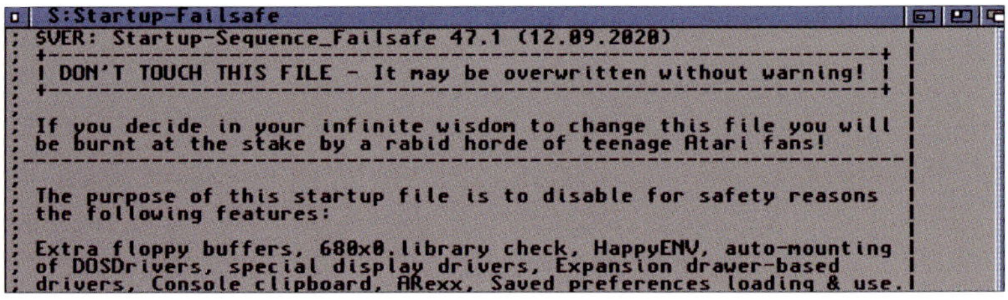

```
S:Startup-Failsafe
; $VER: Startup-Sequence_Failsafe 47.1 (12.09.2020)
; +----------------------------------------------------------------+
; | DON'T TOUCH THIS FILE - It may be overwritten without warning! |
; +----------------------------------------------------------------+
;
; If you decide in your infinite wisdom to change this file you will
; be burnt at the stake by a rabid horde of teenage Atari fans!
; ------------------------------------------------------------------
;
; The purpose of this startup file is to disable for safety reasons
; the following features:
;
; Extra floppy buffers, 680x0.library check, HappyENV, auto-mounting
; of DOSDrivers, special display drivers, Expansion drawer-based
; drivers, Console clipboard, ARexx, Saved preferences loading & use.
```

A little humor in the secure system start sequence.

Contents

The script also omits the user start sequence in *S:user-startup* and the Workbench start sequence from the *WBStartup* directory. The latter is ensured by the parameter `SKIP` when the `LoadWB` command is executed in line 42 (see next page).

The `Wait 1` command then waits for one second so that the `RequestChoice` command can open an info requester with a warning. Due to the waiting time, this usually appears above the Workbench window.

Listing: The secured system start sequence
S:Startup-Failsafe

```
; $VER: Startup-Sequence_Failsafe 47.1 (12/09/2020)                   |
; +-------------------------------------------------------------------+ |
; | DON'T TOUCH THIS FILE - It may be overwritten without warning! | |
; +-------------------------------------------------------------------+ |
;                                                                     |
; If you decide in your infinite wisdom to change this file you will  |
; be burnt at the stake by a rabid horde of teenage Atari fans!       |
;---------------------------------------------------------------------|
;                                                                     |
; The purpose of this startup file is to disable for safety reasons   |
; the following features:                                             |
;                                                                     |
; Extra floppy buffers, 680×0.library check, HappyENV, auto-mounting  |
; of DOSDrivers, special display drivers, Expansion drawer-based      |
; drivers, Console clipboard, ARexx, Saved preferences loading & use.|
;                                                                     |
; Also the WBStartup folder won't have its contents processed and the|
; user-startup won't be executed either.                              |
;---------------------------------------------------------------------|

FailAt 10
SetPatch >NIL:
Version >NIL:

MakeDir RAM:T RAM:ENV
Copy ENVARC: RAM:ENV QUIET ALL NOREQ

Assign >NIL: ENV: RAM:ENV
Assign >NIL: T: RAM:T

FailAt 21
Assign PRINTERS: DEVS:Printers
Assign KEYMAPS: DEVS:Keymaps
Assign LOCALE: SYS:Locale
Assign LIBS: SYS:Classes ADD
Assign HELP: LOCALE:Help DEFER

AddDataTypes REFRESH QUIET

Path C: SYS:Utilities SYS:Rexxc SYS:System S: SYS:Prefs
  SYS:Tools SYS:Tools/Commodities

LoadWB SKIP

Wait 1
RequestChoice " ATTENTION!                         "
 " You have booted into Failsafe mode.*nSeveral features have been
  disabled.*n*nThis is a safe environment to carry out*n*maintenance
  and troubleshooting tasks." "OK" >NIL:

EndCLI >NIL:
```

If the user settings are not applied, the output of all started programs will be in English. If you want to risk applying the settings later, you can execute the Workbench window for running commands from the title bar menu under *Workbench* with the `Execute command` or by pressing the `[R-Amiga]+[E]` keys. Enter `IPrefs` followed by the `[Enter]` key to apply the settings. If you enter the `LoadMonDrvs` command first, with a bit of luck you will also get the right resolution and color depth for the Workbench screen when using a graphics card.

This is also a way to test what is causing regular start process to fail: one by one, simply do all the things that the standard start sequence and the user start sequence execute to see where the problem lies. An alternative to this is the boot option for *tracing* the start sequence mentioned in the section on *early startup*.

Explanations for the things the secured start sequence executes can be found in the section on the standard start sequence, *Startup Sequence* from page 327.

The warning message that shows when executing the safe start procedure.

Startup scripts: shell-startup

By default, each time a Shell is started it executes the commands from the *S:Shell-Startup* file. You can find out more about the Shell startup sequence in the chapter *The Shell* in the section *Shell startup sequence* from page 271.

Boot menu: Early Startup Control

AmigaOS contains a boot menu in the Kickstart ROM. The so-called "Amiga Early Startup Control" is executed as the very first step when booting the system.

Calling up the boot menu

Early Startup Control can be called up by holding down the left and right mouse buttons simultaneously when booting the system, or by pressing the `[Help]` key on the Amiga keyboard. If your Amiga is already running, you can reboot it with `[Ctrl]+[L-Amiga]+[R-Amiga]` once there is no more read or write access to the hard disk. Make sure you save any unsaved data first.

When using a PC keyboard, such as when emulating an Amiga with software like FS-UAE or WinUAE, the Windows key is typically used for the left Amiga key and the menu key for the right Amiga key.

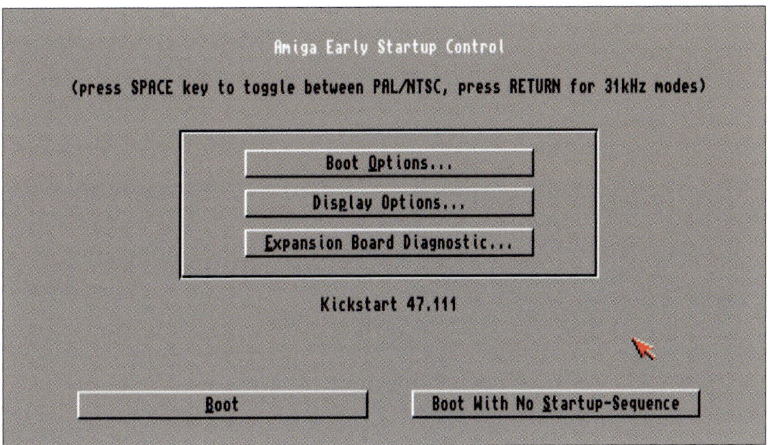

Amiga Early Startup Control.

Structure of the boot menu

The boot menu user interface offers three sub-pages:

1. *Boot Options*
2. *Display Options*
3. *Expansion Board Diagnostic*

In addition, AmigaOS 3.2 displays the Kickstart ROM version number under these three options. For AmigaOS 3.2.2, this is 47.111.

Kickstart-versions

The following table provides an overview of the current Kickstart versions:

AmigaOS version	Kickstart version
3.1.4	46.143
3.2	47.96
3.2.1	47.102
3.2.2	47.111
3.2.2.1	47.111

PAL and NTSC

You can switch between PAL and NTSC display by pressing the space bar. PAL (*Phase Alternating Line*) is the color transmission method used for analogue television primarily in Europe until it was replaced by digital television standards. NTSC is the process standardized by the *National Television Systems Committee* and is used primarily in the North American market. There are two main differences important to the Amiga:

1. The refresh rate of PAL is 50 Hz, while that of NTSC is 60 Hz. This is why images in interlace mode flicker more in PAL than in NTSC.
2. PAL resolutions have a picture height of 256 pixels – 512 pixels in interlace mode – while NTSC resolutions have 200 or 400 pixels.

PAL mode should be suitable for a Commodore 1084 monitor purchased in Europe. If there is a larger black border at the bottom, this may indicate an NTSC screen output on a PAL monitor.

For an Amiga without flickerfixer hardware, you can toggle between 15 kHz and 31 kHz modes with the Enter key (this works on Amigas with the AGA chipset, but not the OCS and ECS chipsets). This is the line frequency, i.e. how often a screen can display a line per second. The higher the value, the higher the possible refresh rate. The higher the value, the higher the resolution a CRT screen can display without flickering. However, a certain minimum value also makes sense for flat screens.

While many flat screens and CRT screens only support resolutions within a range between the minimum and maximum line frequency, a refresh rate that is too low is particularly annoying when playing games or watching videos or movies, for example.

If you're lucky, your flat-panel display will be able to show 31 kHz PAL or NTSC. However, if you see no picture or an unstable picture, try pressing the Enter key once to see if it helps.

INFO **31 kHz mode**
Only switch to 31 kHz mode if your screen is capable of 31 kHz. Prolonged operation of a screen with a line frequency that is too high can damage the screen.

This affects the display of the boot menu only. Setting options for booting AmigaOS can be found in the display options.

The 31 kHz modes were added with the optional Kickstart for AmigaOS 3.1.4. Since AmigaOS 3.2, the Kickstart version display and options for updating the ROM modules, starting in safe mode, and tracing the startup sequence and the system log have also been added.

As a general rule, all changes made in the Early Startup Control are lost on a cold start. However, the settings will survive a warm start via `[Ctrl]+[L-Amiga]+[R-Amiga]`.

Boot options

You can select which drive the Amiga should boot from in the boot options. Individual drives can also be temporarily disabled. This can be useful for deactivating *DF0:* if you want to boot from an external Gotek drive. A number of other options round off the settings.

Select the desired boot drive on the left under *Select Boot Device*. If no drive is selected, Kickstart will boot from the drive with the highest boot priority. This is listed at the top of the table under *Control Active Devices*.

The table of devices shows whether a device is *enabled*, i.e. switched on, or *disabled*, i.e. switched off. This is followed by the device name, such as *DF0:* for the internal floppy drive. The next column shows the boot priority for bootable drives or the info *not bootable* for non-bootable drives. This is followed by the DOS type and finally by the device driver. Double-click on one of the drives to deactivate or activate it temporarily.

Click on *Use* to apply the changes and return to the main page. Click on *Boot* to start the boot process. Use *Cancel* to undo the changes.

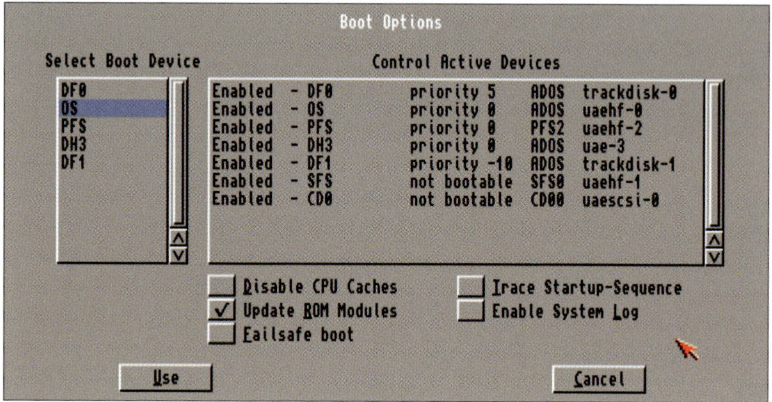

Drives can be deactivated during boot if desired.

By activating **Disable CPU Cache**, you can switch off the CPU caches. This may be necessary for some older games or other programs. Alternatively, use the CPU command or a tool such as *WHDLoad* to switch off caches. This option has no effect on a 68000 CPU as it has no caches.

Since the Kickstart for AmigaOS 3.2, some additional functions have been added: by unchecking **Update ROM Modules**, you can prevent the start sequence from updating the ROM modules.

A few more functions further simplify the debugging of the boot process. With **Failsafe boot**, AmigaOS executes the script in the file *S:startup-failsafe*. This alternative startup sequence only starts the essentials, increasing the probability of a successful start in case of problems with advanced functions, such as the integration of a graphics card via *ReTargetable Graphics (RTG)*. Alternatively, select **Boot With No Startup-Sequence** on the main page to avoid running through the start sequence at all.

Another option is to go through the regular startup-sequence command by command with **Trace Startup-Sequence**. The Shell displays each command before executing it. Confirm the command with the `[Enter]` key. The Shell skips the command with `[N]` or `[DEL]`. The `[Esc]` key cancels *tracing*, upon which the Shell will execute the rest of the start sequence without further inquiry. Alternatively, you can cancel the execution with `[Ctrl]+[D]`. If you do not cancel tracing before executing the

IPrefs command, the following system message may appear: *"Intuition wants to reset the Workbench screen. Please close the following windows: AmigaDOS."* You can ignore this message. `EndCLI`, the last command in the start sequence closes the window, and *IPrefs* will then automatically reset the Workbench screen, e.g. adjust the resolution accordingly.

AmigaOS outputs a system log to the serial interface, if available. With *Enable System Log* checked, the log will end up in the *RAM:syslog* file instead. You can read this with a program like *TextEdit*.

Diagnostics during booting

AmigaOS has various colored screen displays during the boot process that provide information about the status of the system for diagnostic purposes. For example, it can recognize whether a chip or memory element is faulty.

A complete list of diagnostic colors and their meaning can be found in section 8.2 on *error codes*.

Booting the failsafe start sequence.

Diagnostics of the extension boards

A table called **Expansion Board Diagnostics** shows a numbered list of the expansion boards built into the Amiga. Under *Type*, you can see the connection type, such as *Z2* for Zorro-II and *Z3* for Zorro-III.

This is followed by numbers for the *vendor* (manufacturer) and *product*. Next is the address and size of the memory area that AmigaOS has assigned to each expansion card. The last column, *Status*, shows the status of the card. *OK* should be shown here.

The numbers for the manufacturer and the product are not assigned to the actual name. However, this is possible for known cards during operation using the `ShowConfig` program. This program, which has been greatly expanded for AmigaOS 3.2, can be run as a command or with a graphical user interface. You will find this program in the *Tools* drawer on the system drive. If you want to open the interface from the command line, use `ShowConfig GUI`. You can even create a report about your Amiga as an AmigaGuide document with `ShowConfig REPORT RAM:MyAmiga.guide`. When needed, this document can be read with *MultiView*.

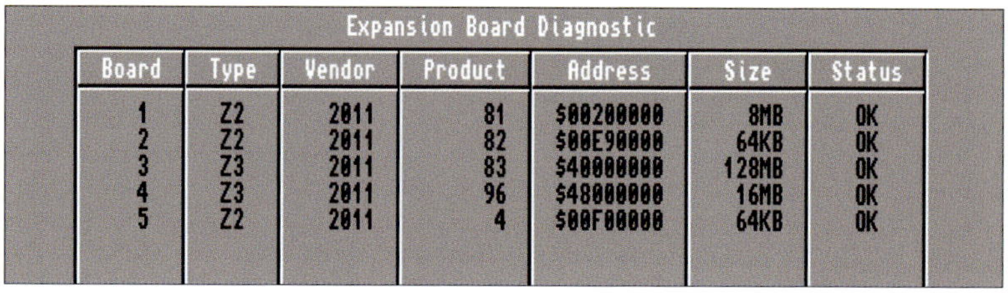

Expansion Board Diagnostic

Board	Type	Vendor	Product	Address	Size	Status
1	Z2	2011	81	$00200000	8MB	OK
2	Z2	2011	82	$00E90000	64KB	OK
3	Z3	2011	83	$40000000	128MB	OK
4	Z3	2011	96	$48000000	16MB	OK
5	Z2	2011	4	$00F00000	64KB	OK

Diagnosis of the expansion cards

Fixing errors

If an expansion board does not work, check it is properly seated. Depending on the board, certain jumpers may need to be set accordingly. The manual for the board should contain detailed information on this. You can also check the troubleshooting section of the expansion manual, if it has one. Another idea is to remove all the cards except for the one showing the error. It may be that two cards are not compatible with each other, or are only compatible if you change the order in which they are plugged in. Perhaps the card or the motherboard of the Amiga is also broken. In many cases, however, expansion board problems can be fixed. If your Amiga is equipped with a Zorro II or III daughterboard from a third-party manufacturer, that may be at fault. If your Amiga supports expansion boards out-of-the-box, such as the Amiga 2000, 3000, 4000 and 4000T, one solution might be using an original daughterboard.

A problem with an expansion board can also lead to a color error message when booting, for example the yellow color for an error before AmigaOS is ready to display a Guru Meditation. Sometimes the only thing that helps here is to rule out the causes of errors by systematic trial and error according to the Sherlock Holmes principle.

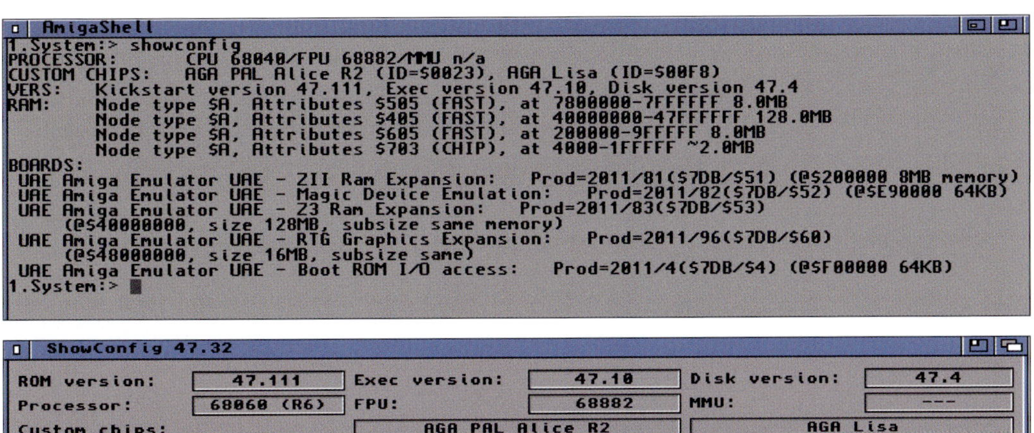

Running ShowConfig as a command in the Shell (top) and via its new graphical user interface (bottom).

TIP

Use the appropriate Kickstart version

When identifying expansion boards, make sure you use the Kickstart version that matches your Amiga model. This also applies when using a UAE-compatible emulator such as FS-UAE or WinUAE. For example, the Amiga 1200 Kickstart ROM in FS-UAE 3.1.66 sometimes does not recognize the UAEGFX graphics card when emulating an Amiga 4000.

Keyboard shortcuts

Keyboard shortcuts make AmigaOS much quicker to use – instead of navigating the screen with the mouse, these short key combinations are the way to go.

System

Shortcut	Function
[Ctrl] + [L-Amiga] + [R-Amiga]	restart the Amiga (Warm Reset)
[Esc]	end process or file requester (context-dependent)
[Help]	open help (general for Workbench or specific for prefs, tools or similar)

Workbench window

Shortcut	Function
[L-Amiga] + [N]	bring the Workbench screen to the foreground
[L-Amiga] + [M]	scroll through open screens
[Alt] + [cursor right]	show next window
[Alt] + [cursor left]	show previous window
[Shift] + click on zoom symbol of the window	maximize window
[R-Amiga] + double-click on drawer	open drawer, close higher-level drawer
[R-Amiga] + click on the close gadget	close all drawers
[R-Amiga] + [Y]	automate sorting and snapshot of icons in windows and Workbench
[R-Amiga] + [left mouse button]	copy (instead of moving) file when dragging and dropping with the mouse

TIP **Keyboard shortcuts as a menu replacement**
Many shortcuts correspond to menu commands. If a command cannot be executed in a certain context or if it is faded out in the menu, its shortcut will not work either.

Workbench menu

Shortcut	Function
[R-Amiga] + [B]	change backdrop mode ("Workbench as background")
[R-Amiga] + [E]	open "Execute command" requester
[R-Amiga] + [?]	open "About ..." info window
[R-Amiga] + [Q]	quit, i.e. close Workbench

Windows menu

Shortcut	Function
[R-Amiga] + [N]	create a new drawer in the open directory
[R-Amiga] + [K]	close drawer
[R-Amiga] + [M]	update the contents of the drawer
[R-Amiga] + [A]	select (highlight) all the contents of the active drawer
[R-Amiga] + [Z]	cancel selection
[R-Amiga] + [.]	sort and align the contents of the drawer by column
[R-Amiga] + [6]	sort and align the contents of the drawer by name
[R-Amiga] + [7]	sort and align the contents of the drawer by date
[R-Amiga] + [8]	sort and align the contents of the drawer by file size
[R-Amiga] + [9]	sort and align the contents of the drawer by file type
[R-Amiga] + [-]	only display files with icons (with linked .info file)
[R-Amiga] + [+]	show all files (including those without an associated .info file)
[R-Amiga] + [1]	show contents of the drawer according to icon (standard)
[R-Amiga] + [2]	show contents of the drawer by name (alphabetical, A-Z, 0-9)
[R-Amiga] + [3]	show contents of the drawer by date (from new to old)
[R-Amiga] + [4]	show contents of the drawer by file size (from small to large)
[R-Amiga] + [5]	show contents of the drawer by file type (alphabetically by type)
[R-Amiga] + [G]	change sorting of the contents in ascending order
[R-Amiga] + [H]	change sorting of the contents in descending order
[R-Amiga] + [F]	open the Find utility ("search files")

Icons menu

Shortcut	Function
[R-Amiga] + [O]	open file(s)
[R-Amiga] + [C]	copy file(s)
[R-Amiga] + [R]	rename file(s)
[R-Amiga] + [I]	show information on file(s)
[R-Amiga] + [S]	fix the position of the file(s) (snapshot)
[R-Amiga] + [U]	release the position of the files (unsnapshot)
[R-Amiga] + [L]	move file(s) from the drawer to the Workbench window (leave out)
[R-Amiga] + [P]	return file(s) from the Workbench to their original drawer (put away)
[R-Amiga] + [D]	delete file(s) (confirmation required via requester)

TIP **Display key assignments with KeyShow**
You can view key assignments in the preset language, as well as the effects of modifiers such as the Amiga, Shift and Alt keys, with *KeyShow* in the *Tools* folder.

Cursor navigation

Shortcut	Function
[Amiga] + [cursor keys]	move the cursor (mouse pointer) slowly
[Amiga] + [Shift] + [cursor keys]	move the cursor (mouse pointer) quickly
[Amiga] + [L-Alt]	perform left click
[Amiga] + [R-Alt]	perform right click

TIP **Reassignment of keyboard shortcuts**
Some commands that are assigned to keyboard shortcuts can be assigned to new ones using the *IControl* preferences.

Window operation

Shortcut	Function
[Alt] + [cursor up]	open higher-level drawer
[Alt] + [cursor down]	open selected drawer
[Alt] + [cursor left]	cycle through open drawers in a clockwise direction
[Alt] + [cursor right]	run through open drawers in a anticlockwise direction
[Tab]	scroll through the selection of icons in the active window
[Tab] + [Shift]	select the icons in the active window in reverse order
[Left-Amiga] + [V]	activate the button on the far left of a requester (usually the confirm button)
[Left-Amiga] + [B]	activate the button on the far right of a requester (usually the cancel button)
[Ctrl] + [cursor keys]	move all the icons in a window as a block one pixel in the respective cursor direction
[Shift] + [cursor keys]	move all the icons in a window as a block by half the screen width in the respective cursor direction
[cursor keys]	with an icon highlighted: scroll through the selected icons in the respective cursor direction
[cursor keys]	without an icon highlighted: move all the icons in a window as a block several pixels in the respective cursor direction

TIP **Underlined letters**

Some buttons and commands in AmigaOS 3.2 and the boot menu are labeled with an underscore under individual letters. These refer to keyboard shortcuts. For example, the shortcut [R-Amiga]+[E] in the *execute command* requester triggers the execution of the command. Note that AmigaOS distinguishes between upper and lower case here!

File selection (ASL requester)

These shortcuts apply to file selection requesters:

Shortcut	Function
[R-Amiga] + [P]	open parent directory
[R-Amiga] + [V]	open drives overview
[R-Amiga] + [R]	switch back to default
[R-Amiga] + [A]	refresh view
[R-Amiga] + [D]	delete file or drawer
[R-Amiga] + [M]	rename file or drawer
[R-Amiga] + [L]	select previous file or drawer
[R-Amiga] + [N]	select next file or drawer
[R-Amiga] + [#]	mark file or drawer
[R-Amiga] + [O]	confirm selection / open file
[R-Amiga] + [C]	cancel process
[R-Amiga] + [1]	list files sorted by name
[R-Amiga] + [2]	list files sorted by date
[R-Amiga] + [3]	list files sorted by size
[R-Amiga] + [+]	list files in ascending order
[R-Amiga] + [-]	list files in descending order
[R-Amiga] + [4]	put drawers at the beginning
[R-Amiga] + [5]	shuffle drawers and files
[R-Amiga] + [6]	place drawers at the end

String gadgets

String gadgets are input fields in which text can be entered, for example in requesters such as *Find*. The following shortcuts can be used here, among others:

Shortcut	Function
[R-Amiga] + [C]	copy selected text to clipboard
[R-Amiga] + [V]	insert selected text at cursor position (paste)
[R-Amiga] + [X]	place selected text in clipboard and delete (cut)
[Shift] + [cursor left] OR [Ctrl] + [cursor left]	set cursor to start of line
[Shift] + [cursor right] OR [Ctrl] + [cursor right]	place cursor at end of line
[Shift] + [Del]	delete all characters to the right of the cursor, including the cursor
[Shift] + [Backspace]	delete all characters to the left of the cursor, including the cursor

Shell

The following shortcuts, among others, are implemented in the Amiga Shell:

Shortcut	**Function**
[Ctrl] + [A]	set cursor to start of line
[Ctrl] + [Z]	place cursor at end of line
[Ctrl] + [K]	delete all characters to the right of the cursor
[Ctrl] + [U]	delete all characters to the left of the cursor
[Ctrl] + [W]	delete word to the left of the cursor
[Ctrl] + [J]	insert line break
[Ctrl] + [B]	remove line
[Ctrl] + [S]	interrupt output
[Ctrl] + [Q]	resume output after it has been interrupted
[Ctrl] + [C]	stop Shell process
[Ctrl] + [D]	cancel AmigaDOS script
[Ctrl] + [M]	Return or Enter
[Ctrl] + [H]	backspace key
[Ctrl] + [\]	close Shell window

Commodities

Individual commodities have their own shortcuts for starting, ending, saving, hiding and iconifying:

Shortcut	**Function**
[Ctrl] + [Alt] + [B]	start Blank
[Ctrl] + [Alt] + [C]	start CrossDOS
[Ctrl] + [Alt] + [F]	start FKey
[Ctrl] + [Alt] + [Help]	start Exchange
[R-Amiga] + [S]	save commodity settings (for FKey, Blanker, CrossDOS only)
[R-Amiga] + [H]	hide commodity (for Exchange, FKey, Blanker, CrossDOS only)
[R-Amiga] + [I]	iconify commodity (for Exchange, FKey, Blanker, CrossDOS only)
[R-Amiga] + [Q]	exit commodity (for Exchange, FKey, Blanker, CrossDOS only)

Boot process

Shortcut	Function
[Help] (press and hold)	open the Amiga Early Startup Menu during the boot process (corresponds to pressing and holding the left and right mouse button simultaneously; only applies in supported Amiga models)
[Space]	in the Amiga Early Startup Menu: switch screen display between PAL and NTSC (15 kHz)
[Return]	in the Amiga Early Startup Menu: change screen frequency between 15 kHz (standard) and 31 kHz (for compatible screens)
[ALT] (hold down)	activate serial debug (outputs commands executed during the boot process via the serial interface)

TIP **Find content quickly**

You can quickly locate a file in an active drawer by entering the first few letters of its filename on the keyboard. Wait three seconds to start a new search.

AmigaGuide in practice

The proprietary AmigaGuide is a powerful tool for documentation of all kinds. Here you will learn how to create your own guides.

The origin of AmigaGuide

AmigaGuide is a hypertext format developed and introduced by Commodore that is ideal for help texts, instructions and extensive documentation. It has been an integral part of AmigaOS since Workbench 2.0 and has been expanded several times since then.

AmigaGuide files have the extension *.guide* and consist of pure ASCII text. This means they can be created and edited with any text editor such as TextEdit, GoldEd or CygnusEd. On the Amiga, the *MultiView* program is in charge of displaying AmigaGuides. In order to display an AmigaGuide document correctly, the AmigaGuide file type must be present in the system directory *DEVS:DataTypes*, which is the default for the AmigaOS.

AmigaGuide documents can be viewed on other operating systems using specialized tools, for example on Windows with *AGWViewer* or *WinGuide*, on MacOS with *Grotag*, or on Linux with *AGReader*. All links can be found on the service website for this book at www.lookbehindyou.de/en/amigaos32book.

The structure of an AmigaGuide document is explained in this section along with an extended range of functions.

Structure of an AmigaGuide

Basically, AmigaGuide documents consist of a header with global commands and nodes with text and commands. Global commands and node commands must each be on a separate line. They always feature an @ character at the beginning of the line, followed directly by the command without spaces.

The `@DATABASE` command must be set at the beginning of any AmigaGuide file. This is the only way the system can identify the file type in addition to the *.guide* file extension. All other commands are optional.

The following example shows the header of an AmigaGuide-document with global commands:

```
@DATABASE "example.guide"
@AUTHOR John Doe
@$VER: example.guide 1.0 (20.6.1994)
@ONOPEN arexxscript.rexx
@ONCLOSE arexxscript2.rexx
@INDEX MAIN
@SMARTWRAP
```

Text commands, on the other hand, are placed within the text. The @ character is immediately followed by a { bracket. There must be no space between the @ and the {, otherwise the command will not be identified.

Nodes must be opened with a @NODE command and closed with a @ENDNODE command so that the viewer tool recognizes and can display the content area correctly. All content between these two commands are assigned to the node.

The following example shows two nodes with simple text commands:

```
@NODE MAIN "Title node"
This is @{B}bold text@{UB}.
This represents the first page and
thus the title node.@{PAR}
@{"Another page" LINK "NEWPAGE"}
@ENDNODE

@NODE NEWPAGE "Text commands are explained here"
New paragraph@{PAR}
Inserts a tab character into the text@{TAB}
@{"Show image" link "imagename.iff/main"}
@ENDNODE
```

Global commands

Global commands are characterized by the fact that they can be used outside of a node. They are used to define metadata, formatting and nodes.

The following overview lists the available AmigaGuide global commands in the current version, including short explanations.

Global command	Designation / Instruction
@DATABASE <filename.guide>	name of the AmigaGuide including file extension (always position at the start of the file, as this is how the format is identified)
@AUTHOR "name of the author"	name of the author
@(C) "copyright infos"	copyright information for the document
@$VER: filename.guide version.revision (day.month.year)	version of the document
@FONT <font name.font> <font size>	specifies font and font size (if not specified, the system font is used)
@MASTER <documentname. guide>	defines an AmigaGuide document as a master document
@REMARK	comments in the text
@WORDWRAP	activates automatic line breaks
@SMARTWRAP	interprets line breaks as the end of a paragraph
@AMIGAGUIDE	the term AmigaGuide(R) is labelled in bold and with a copyright symbol
@HELP <node name>	links to the node that should be displayed when the help button is clicked (if not specified, the standard help from AmigaGuide is displayed)
@TAB <number>	determines the tab spacing with a value (default: 8)
@INDEX <node name>	specifies the node to be displayed when the index button is clicked (if not specified, the index button remains deactivated)
@XREF <path/abc.guide>	references another AmigaGuide document, including relative path
@WIDTH <number of columns>	number of columns of the widest node
@HEIGHT <number of lines>	number of rows in the top node
@MACRO <macro name> <commands>	defines a macro consisting of a macro name followed by a substitution, which can contain substitutions with $1, $2 etc. The macro can then be used like a text command.

Global command	Designation / Instruction
@NODE <node name> "title of the node"	marks the start of a node. The node name must not have any spaces and its title is displayed in the title bar of the document when it is called up.
@ENDNODE	marks the end of a node. Each node must be closed. For the last node in the document, a line break is required after the command @ENDNODE.
@ONOPEN <scriptname. rexx>	executes an ARexx script when opening the document
@ONCLOSE <scriptname. rexx>	executes an ARexx script when closing the document

Node commands

Node commands can only be used within a node. They are used to determine the metadata and formatting of the node.

Node comedo	Designation / Instruction
@TITLE <window title>	specifies the title of the node if it has not already been determined with @NODE. It overwrites the title specified for @NODE.
@TOC <node name>	specifies the node that is to be displayed when the content button is clicked. The default setting is the main node.
@NEXT <node name>	specifies the node that is used for the browse function (next) when the > button is clicked. Without @NEXT, the next node in the file is selected.
@PREV <node name>	specifies the node that is used for the browse function (back) when the < button is pressed. Without @PREV, the last node in the file is selected.

In addition to the commands in this table, the global commands @FONT, @HELP, @INDEX, @MACRO, @REMARK, @ONOPEN, @ONCLOSE, @TAB, @WORDWRAP and @SMARTWRAP can also be used within a node.

Text commands

Text commands can only be used within text. This allows text formatting, hyperlinks and buttons to be realized.

Text command	**Designation / Instruction**
@{<link title> LINK <node name>}	creates a link to another node. The link is marked by a button and refers internally and to other AmigaGuides, images, sounds, mods and other formats. Example for calling up a subpage: @{"Imprint" LINK imprint page}.
@{IMG <image file with path>}	new feature for the display of images via datatypes directly in the AmigaGuide
@{B}bold@{UB}	formats as bold text
@{I}italics{UI}	formats as italic text
@{U}underlined@{UU}	formats as underlined text
@{JCENTER}, @{JLEFT}, @{JRIGHT}	sets the text alignment: centred, left-aligned, right-aligned
@{LINE}	inserts a new line
@{PAR}	inserts a new paragraph
@{TAB}	inserts a tab character
@{"beep once" BEEP}	creates a button that triggers a system beep (usually sound and flashing of the screen)
@{FG <color>}	specifies the foreground color to use as of the next character. Possible colors: background, fill, filltext, highlight, shadow, shine, text.
@{BG <color>}	specifies the background color to use as of the next character. Possible colors: see @{FG <color>}.
@{LINDENT <value>}	indents the left margin by the specified value (chars number)
@{PARI <value>}	indents the first line of the first paragraph by the specified value (chars number) (only if automatic line break is activated)
@{<button label> SYSTEM <DOS command>}	executes a DOS command via the Shell when clicking a button
@{<button label> RX <script name>}	executes an ARexx script when clicking a button
@{<button labelling> RXS <AREXX command>}	executes a single ARexx command when clicking a button

ARexx: The programming language

ARexx, the Amiga's answer to IBM's REXX, is a programming language that allows you to customize your working environment. It is particularly suited to scripts that are used to control programs.

Introduction: What is ARexx?

ARexx is an extremely powerful tool for customizing tasks. For example, you can use an ARexx script to cause an image-processing program to process an entire directory of images with a specific effect in one go, as if by magic. You can also have several ARexx-enabled applications work together to then automatically send the processed images by e-mail.

Many applications support ARexx, but what about the operating system itself? Until AmigaOS 3.1, only a few programs included with the system offered an ARexx port, such as the editor *Ed*. AmigaOS 3.5 was the first release in which the Workbench received an ARexx port.

This ARexx introduction is not a replacement for the ARexx manual that was included with AmigaOS 3.1. That can be found in HTML format on the AmigaOS 3.9 CD-ROM (in the directory *OS-Version3.9 / AmigaOS 3.9 Manual*) and read with a web browser. It describes the individual ARexx commands very well and is a good reference work. Another source is the ARexx manual in the AmigaOS documentation wiki (direct link: https://wiki.amigaos.net/wiki/AmigaOS_Manual:_ARexx).

Instead, this introduction explains how you can control the ARexx-enabled components of AmigaOS 3.2. Unlike AmigaOS 3.9, the commodities in AmigaOS 3.2 do not have an ARexx port. However, the OS 3.2 Workbench listens to ARexx commands and is compatible with the command set of the OS 3.9 Workbench. In addition, the *MultiView* and *TextEdit* programs can be controlled via ARexx in OS 3.2.

To make it easier for you to get started with ARexx, let us first show you the basics. We will also provide a number of examples to help you understand how to use the new functions.

Start ARexx

The ARexx interpreter must be active in order to use ARexx. You can start this by using the `RexxMast` command from the *System* directory of your system drive. The AmigaOS 3.2 start-sequence executes the command automatically (see section 6.1 on the *start sequence*). In addition, using the `RX` command in the Shell to execute an ARexx command or script will automatically start the interpreter. The `RexxMast` program can also be copied from the *System* drawer to the *WBStartup* drawer, but this is not necessary considering the standard start sequence of AmigaOS 3.2.

If the error message *'Host environment not found'* appears instead of the output, then the ARexx interpreter is not running. The `RexxMast` command starts the interpreter, if it has not already done so, and shows to what extent ARexx is already running:

```
1.RAM Disk:> RexxMast
ARexx Version 1.15
Copyright © 1987 by William S. Hawes
All Rights Reserved
REXX server already active
```

If the line *'REXX server already active'* is missing in the output, then ARexx has not yet been loaded.

INFO **Line numbering**

To make command input easier to understand, we have labeled complete command lines in the following paragraphs with a preceding line number.

For example, here are two single-line command displays:

```
01   RX Open-RAM.rexx
02   RX "ADDRESS WORKBENCH NEWDRAWER
     '""RAM Disk:These lines still belong
     to the line labeled 02.""'"
```

ARexx: First steps

The typical way to execute ARexx commands is to write a script in a text file and execute this script. However, it is also possible to execute an ARexx command directly from the command line. To do this, open a Shell and type:

```
1.RAM Disk:> RX "SAY 'Hello world!'"
Hello world!
```

```
AmigaShell
1.SYSTEM:> RX "SAY 'Hello World!'"
Hello World!
1.SYSTEM:> RX 'SAY "Hello World!"'
Command returned 5/1: Program not found
1.SYSTEM:> RX "SAY '""Hello World!""'"
"Hello World!"
1.SYSTEM:> RX "SAY (10-5)/2"
2.5
1.SYSTEM:> RexxMast
ARexx Version 1.15
Copyright © 1987 by William S. Hawes
All Rights Reserved
REXX server already active
1.SYSTEM:>
```

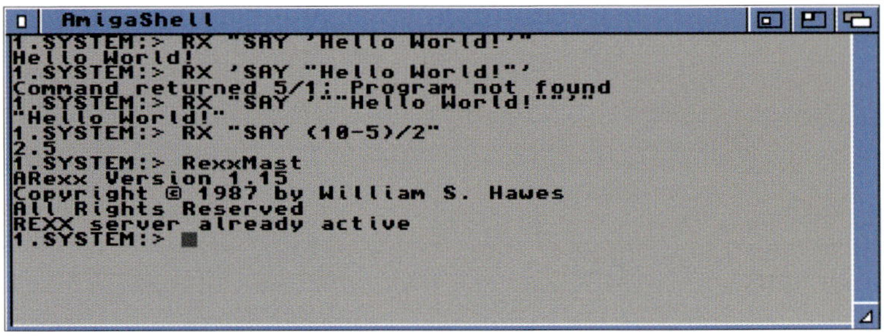

Hello world! with ARexx.

As you need both types of quotation marks (also known as inverted commas) in the first example, you may already have spotted a problem: where are the single quotation marks on the keyboard? On an English keyboard, it should be to the left of the Enter key, but on a German keyboard, for example, you will need the `[Alt]+[ä]` shortcut. Check *Tools > KeyShow* (see also section 4.7) to locate the position on your own keyboard.

Note: The order of the quotation marks is extremely important. Swapping the quotation marks would not work, as the Shell would otherwise pass the entire character string `SAY "Hello world!"'` to the RX command as one command, which ARexx would not find. This would lead to the error message *'Program not found'*.

In this way, you can not only output text, but you can also calculate (the result here is 2.5):

```
RX "SAY (10-5)/2"
```

This is far more powerful than the Shell command `Eval`, as ARexx supports numbers with decimal points, as well as dot-before-dash calculations and brackets.

INFO **Escaping**

Escaping refers to the marking of characters so that the Shell, ARexx or other programming language will use them as they are instead of evaluating them. A typical example is enclosing the words `"RAM Disk"` in quotes to make it clear that it is a single argument. Here, however, *RAM Disk* must be enclosed twice in quotes. Both ARexx and the Workbench evaluate the parameter. The single quotes tell ARexx that it is text that ARexx should not evaluate, i.e. no variable name and no formula. The double quotes tell the Workbench that it is a single argument and not two parameters separated by spaces. If the ARexx command is executed directly using the Shell command `RX`, the double quotes must also be written twice; in ARexx scripts, only once. The `RX` command also does not use the system functions of the *dos.library* to evaluate the command line, but contains its own routines for this purpose.

That is why it is recommended to use the `RX` command only for simple executions of ARexx commands and to write an ARexx script instead. Doing so, the double quotes are then omitted, and `'""RAM Disk:""'` becomes `'"RAM Disk:"'`.

It is important to pay attention to correct escaping while developing, as unintended and dangerous things can happen, especially when using file patterns.

Workbench command via ARexx

ARexx can also execute Workbench commands. For example, the following command creates a new drawer called *New directory* in RAM drive:

```
RX "ADDRESS WORKBENCH NEWDRAWER
  '""RAM Disk:New directory""'"
```

With the following command, the Workbench opens the window with the contents of the RAM Disk (read more about these ARexx commands below):

```
RX "ADDRESS WORKBENCH WINDOW WINDOWS
  '""RAM Disk:""' OPEN"
```

Shell commands via ARexx

You can also execute Shell commands with ARexx:

```
RX "ADDRESS COMMAND 'MakeDir
""RAM Disk:New Directory""'"
```

Here, the ARexx command ADDRESS is used to address the ARexx port of the Amiga Shell in order to execute Shell commands.

You can now use ARexx from a Shell by executing individual commands directly. But how about creating an ARexx script yourself?

An ARexx script is a simple text file that contains ARexx commands. To be clearly recognized by ARexx, it must start with an ARexx comment. Here is a simple example that also makes use of an ARexx command from the Workbench:

```
/* Open the window for the RAM Disk */
ADDRESS Workbench
WINDOW '"RAM Disk:"' OPEN
```

Simply write this small script in a text editor such as *TextEdit* and save it under the name *Open-RAM.rexx*.

You can save it to the RAM Disk for testing. If you want to keep it, save it to *REXX:*. This assignment points to the default directory for ARexx scripts. This is usually the *SYS:S* directory. Both directories have the advantage of being included in the command search path by default: you need only specify the name of the ARexx script, but not the path to the directory.

You can now easily start the script with the ARexx command RX:

```
RX Open-RAM.rexx
```

The Workbench opens the window with the contents of the RAM Disk. This is the same as double-clicking the RAM Disk icon with the mouse. When running an ARexx script with the standard filename extension *.rexx* via the Shell command RX, you can also omit the extension.

The first command, ADDRESS Workbench, is a built-in ARexx command that tells ARexx to pass unknown commands to the Workbench going forward. ARexx will then address the ARexx port of the Workbench. Every ARexx-enabled program has an

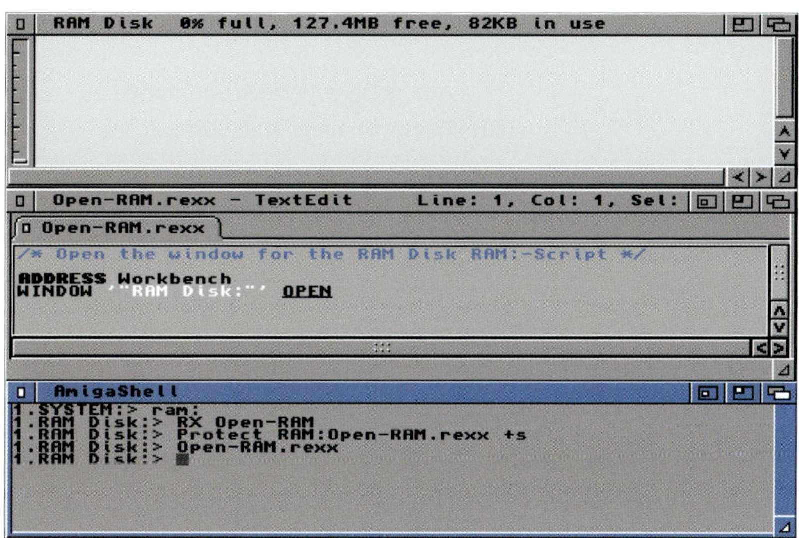

An ARexx script opens the RAM Disk.

ARexx port. ARexx can send commands to this port, and ARexx can receive responses from this port.

The second command, `WINDOW`, is provided by the Workbench. With the `OPEN` option, it instructs the Workbench to open the Workbench window for the specified path.

Simplified ARexx version

If it bothers you having to specify the `RX` command separately, you can also set the file attributes for the file *Open-RAM.rexx*, which marks a file as an AmigaDOS or ARexx script. For example:

```
Protect RAM:Open-RAM.rexx +s
```

You can then start the script just by entering its full filename:

```
Open-RAM.rexx
```

ARexx: Controlling the Workbench

The AmigaOS 3.2 Workbench offers a whole range of interesting ARexx commands. It is compatible with the Workbench from AmigaOS 3.9 and AmigaOS 4, allowing you to remotely control almost any action that you would otherwise perform using your mouse and keyboard.

TIP **Download instead of typing**
The WB-Tools from the author of this section on ARexx are an ARexx-based collection of extensions and comfort functions for the AmigaOS 3.9 Workbench that also work with AmigaOS 3.2. Download the archive: www.aminet.net/package/util/wb/WB-Tools

The ARexx interface of Workbench

The ARexx interface of the Workbench is divided into five main areas:

The `GETATTR` command allows you to obtain various information from Workbench, such as the Workbench version number, the position of a window or the type of an icon.

The `WINDOW` command opens, closes and changes Workbench windows. Certain window actions, such as minimizing and maximizing or bringing the window to the foreground, are also available via separate commands.

The `ICONS` command manipulates icons: they can be selected, deselected, moved and much more.

The `MENU` command allows you to execute any Workbench menu item as if the user had selected it, and to add new entries to the *Tools* menu.

There are also commands for certain Workbench actions, such as renaming files or displaying the information window. There are also special commands for locking the interface while an ARexx script is running, or for translating an error number to plain text.

For each of these areas, one or two examples are given below, with explanations. A complete description of Workbench's ARexx commands can be found in the *AmigaOS 3.2 reference manual* under *ARexx / Workbench's Rexx Port*.

A quick reference to the ARexx commands of AmigaOS 3.2 components

GETATTR command: I know something

The GETATTR command accepts the following parameters:

```
GETATTR [OBJECT] <object name> [NAME <name of the
    entry>] [STEM <name of the root variable>]
    [VAR <variable name>]
```

This sounds rather complicated at first, but is actually quite simple: GETATTR instructs Workbench to retrieve information on a specific object in the *Workbench database* and save it in an ARexx variable.

For example, the main object APPLICATION allows you to query the properties of Workbench itself, and might look like this:

```
/* Workbench information */
ADDRESS Workbench
OPTIONS RESULTS

/* Name of the ARexx port of the Workbench */
GETATTR APPLICATION.AREXX
SAY 'The Workbench can be addressed via the
    ARexx port "'RESULT'".'

/* Name of the font for WB icons */
GETATTR APPLICATION.FONT.ICON.NAME VAR font
SAY 'The Workbench uses the font "'font'" for'
SAY "icon names."
```

If you start this script in a Shell, you will receive the following information:

```
1.RAM Disk:> RX Workbench-information.rexx
The Workbench can be addressed via the ARexx port "WORKBENCH".
The Workbench uses the font "topaz.font" for icon titles.
```

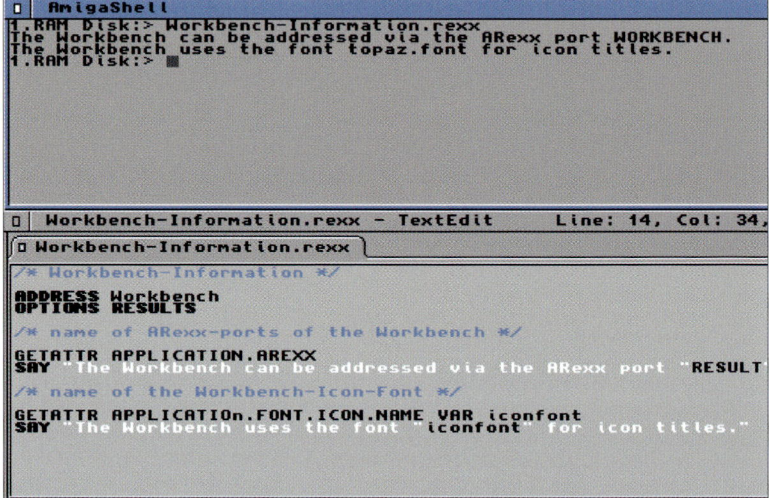

This script requests information from the Workbench

What's new about this script compared to the first example? The second command OPTIONS RESULTS instructs ARexx to receive results from other programs. Without this command, you would not be able to request any information from Workbench.

The two GETATTR commands query different properties of Workbench itself. With the first, the result is simply saved in the standard ARexx variable for results, i.e. the RESULT variable. The second explicitly specifies the variable in which the result is to be saved.

The following, slightly more advanced example immediately displays a list of all open Workbench windows and shows some information about the first icon in the *root* window, the main window of Workbench. This does not necessarily have to be the icon positioned at the top left.

```
/* Even more info */
/* Shows the names of all open WB windows */
ADDRESS Workbench
OPTIONS RESULTS
GETATTR WINDOWS STEM window
DO i = 0 TO window.count-1
   SAY window.i
END
SAY

/* Request name, position, size and type of the first icon in the WB main window */
GETATTR WINDOW.ICONS.ALL.0 NAME root STEM icon
SAY "Name: "icon.name
SAY "Position: X="icon.left "Y="icon.top
SAY "Size: "icon.width"x"icon.height
SAY "Type: "icon.type
```

This script also shows the use of ARexx root variables. These variables can combine several sub-variables. In this example, the window list is queried and stored in the root variable *window*. Here, *window.count* contains the number of windows, *window.0* contains the name of the first window, *window.1* the name of the second window, etc. The `DO` loop outputs these window names.

The second part of the script queries the properties of the first icon in the main window of Workbench. But how can this information be used? Some examples can be found in the following sections.

WINDOW command: Many, many windows

Workbench windows can be changed using the `WINDOW` command:

```
WINDOW [WINDOWS] <window name> ... <window name>
[OPEN|CLOSE] [SNAPSHOT] [ACTIVATE] [MIN|MAX]
[FRONT|BACK] [CYCLE PREVIOUS|NEXT]
```

You must specify the name or names of the windows on which Workbench is to perform an action. The name of a window is derived from the path to the directory in which the contents of the window are displayed. Typical names are *RAM Disk:*, *Workbench:Utilities* or *Work:Texts*, depending on the structure of your system.

In addition to the `WINDOW` command, there are also special commands that only apply a specific action to a window. For example, `ACTIVATEWINDOW` activates a specific window and `CHANGEWINDOW` changes the size of a window. The command reference contains other commands of this type.

Here are a couple of examples: a simple three-line command could, for example, close the *RAM Disk* window:

```
/* Close the window for the RAM Disk */
ADDRESS Workbench
WINDOW WINDOWS '"RAM Disk:"' CLOSE
```

TIP **Execution in the Shell**

You can try out such small commands directly in the Shell without writing a script:

```
rx "ADDRESS Workbench WINDOW
'""RAM:""' CLOSE"
```

Multiple commands can be separated from each other with semicolons.

The entire command must be enclosed in quotes so that `RX` does not try to start a script file instead. To ensure the double quotes in *RAM:* are recognized as such, they must be typed twice.

Together with `GETATTR`, all open windows in Workbench can be closed. The following script reads a list of all open windows in Workbench and closes all except the main one.

```
/* Close all windows */
ADDRESS Workbench
OPTIONS RESULTS

GETATTR WINDOWS STEM window

DO i = 0 TO window.count-1
   IF window.i~=="root" THEN DO
      WINDOW WINDOWS '"'window.i'"' CLOSE
   END
END
```

The main Workbench window remains open. (That said, it often cannot be closed anyway due to programs started from Workbench. Also, once Workbench has been closed, there is sometimes not much more you can do with an Amiga.)

Instead of closing all windows, you can also minimize them or bring them to the foreground. To do this, find the line with the `WINDOW` command and replace the `CLOSE` action with one of the following:

Action	**Function**
OPEN	opens window
CLOSE	closes window
SNAPSHOT	fixes window
ACTIVATE	activates window
MIN	reduces window to the minimum size
MAX	enlarges window to the maximum size
FRONT	puts window in the foreground
BACK	puts window in the background

The `WINDOW` command and the commands that execute special window operations also accept `ACTIVE` as an additional argument for the currently active window. However, the examples above does not use it as no Workbench window is active when starting an example from a Shell window.

However, the `ACTIVE` parameter is very useful if ARexx scripts are started directly in Workbench (see also the following *Menu command* and *Keyboard shortcuts* sections).

ICON command: Moving icons

The ICON command offers a whole range of options:

```
ICON [WINDOW] <window name> <icon name> ...
<icon name> [OPEN] [MAKEVISIBLE] [SELECT] [UNSELECT]
[UP <pixel>] [DOWN <pixel>] [LEFT <pixel]
[RIGHT <pixel>] [X <horizontal position>]
[Y <vertical position] [ACTIVATE UP|DOWN|LEFT|RIGHT]
[CYCLE PREVIOUS|NEXT] [MOVE IN|OUT]
```

With the ICON command, icons can be selected or deselected, moved, opened and much more. With the following script, for example, the *RAM Disk* icons goes on a journey:

```
/* Shift-RAM.rexx */
ADDRESS Workbench
increment=20
steps=3
SAY "Continue with Enter after each move!"

DO i=1 TO steps
   ICON WINDOW root '"RAM Disk"' RIGHT increment
   PULL
END

DO i=1 TO steps
   ICON WINDOW root '"RAM Disk"' DOWN increment
   PULL
END

DO i=1 TO steps
   ICON WINDOW root '"RAM Disk"' LEFT increment
   PULL
END

DO i=1 TO steps
   ICON WINDOW root '"RAM Disk"' UP increment
   PULL
END
```

What initially looks like a nice gimmick can be developed into a script using the GETATTR command, which organizes and fixes all icons in a directory.

You can also use the `ICON` command to select icons. The following script selects all the icons in the main Workbench window that start with the letter *a*, and deselects all the others:

```
/* Fussy */
ADDRESS Workbench
OPTIONS RESULTS
GETATTR WINDOW.ICONS.ALL.COUNT NAME root VAR amount
DO i=0 TO amount-1
  GETATTR WINDOW.ICONS.ALL.i NAME root STEM icon
  IF POS("a", icon.name)>0 THEN DO
     ICON WINDOW root '"'icon.name'"' SELECT
  END
  ELSE DO
    ICON WINDOW root '"'icon.name'"' UNSELECT
  END
END
```

This ARexx script first asks Workbench for the number of icons displayed in the main window and then asks for the name of each icon. If this name contains *a* lower-case *a*, the script instructs Workbench to select it, and if not, to deselect it.

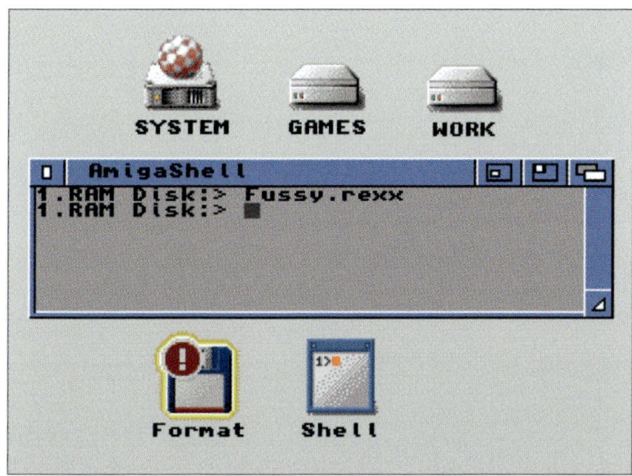

Selective: targeted icon selection

This script could be expanded into a useful search function. In a large window containing many icons that are not in the visible area of the window, you could add the `MAKEVISIBLE` parameter to scroll a specific icon into the visible area and then select it so that it immediately catches the eye with a GlowIcon due to its glow effect. However, the AmigaOS 3.2 Workbench already contains a built-in search function (see tip *Find content quickly* on page 350).

MENU command: à la carte menu

The ARexx interface of Workbench lets you select existing Workbench menu items. ARexx scripts can add their own menu items to the *Tools* menu. The MENU command does both.

When invoking menu items, you must specify the Workbench window on which the function should take effect. For example, this applies to the directory in which a new drawer is created using the menu function *Window > New drawer*.

The menu function to be executed is then specified. Workbench recognizes the following menu items:

When you select one of these menu items, Workbench does exactly what it would do if you had selected the menu item manually using the mouse or the matching key combination.

WORKBENCH MENU

Command	Action
WORKBENCH.BACKDROP	backdrop (Workbench as background)
WORKBENCH.EXECUTE	execute command
using WINDOW command	open volume
WORKBENCH.REDRAWALL	redraw all
WORKBENCH.UPDATEALL	update everything
WORKBENCH.LASTMESSAGE	show last message
WORKBENCH.ABOUT	show version and copyright
WORKBENCH.QUIT	quit (leave Workbench)

WINDOW MENU

Command	Action
WINDOW.NEWDRAWER	create new drawer
WINDOW.OPENPARENT	open parent (higher-level) drawer
WINDOW.CLOSE	close
WINDOW.UPDATE	update
WINDOW.SELECTCONTENTS	select contents
WINDOW.CLEARSELECTION	clear selection
WINDOW.CLEANUPBY.COLUMN	clean up contents by column
WINDOW.CLEANUPBY.NAME	clean up contents by names
WINDOW.CLEANUPBY.DATE	clean up contents by date

WINDOW.CLEANUPBY.SIZE	clean up contents by size
WINDOW.CLEANUPBY.TYPE	clean up contents by type
WINDOW.RESIZETOFIT	resize to fit (adjust window size)
WINDOW.SNAPSHOT.WINDOW	snapshot (fix) the window
WINDOW.SNAPSHOT.ALL	snapshot (fix) all
WINDOW.SHOW.ONLYICONS	show files with own icon only
WINDOW.SHOW.ALLFILES	show all files
WINDOW.VIEWBY.ICON	view contents by icons
WINDOW.VIEWBY.NAME	view contents by name
WINDOW.VIEWBY.DATE	view contents by date
WINDOW.VIEWBY.SIZE	view contents according to size
WINDOW.VIEWBY.TYPE	view contents by type
Shell command Find	seach with Find requester

ICON MENU

Command	Action
ICONS.OPEN	open
ICONS.COPY	copy
ICONS.RENAME	rename
ICONS.INFORMATION	show information
ICONS.SNAPSHOT	snapshot (fix position)
ICONS.UNSNAPSHOT	unsnapshot (release position)
ICONS.LEAVEOUT	leave out icon (put on WB screen)
ICONS.PUTAWAY	put away icon (put in drawer)
ICONS.DELETE	delete
ICONS.FORMATDISK	format disk
ICONS.EMPTYTRASH	empty trashcan

TOOLS MENU

Command	Action
TOOLS.RESETWB	reset Workbench

For example, WINDOW.NEWDRAWER opens the requester for creating a new drawer. The user is asked to enter a name for the drawer, and only when confirmed will the drawer be created. The NEWDRAWER command, on the other hand, creates a folder entirely without the user's intervention (see the *What else is possible* section on page 375).

The following example shows exactly how to do this. It opens the *RAM Disk* window that is so popular in these instructions and offers the user to create a drawer there:

```
/* Create drawer */

ADDRESS Workbench
WINDOW WINDOWS '"RAM Disk:"' OPEN
MENU WINDOW '"RAM Disk:"' INVOKE WINDOW.NEWDRAWER
```

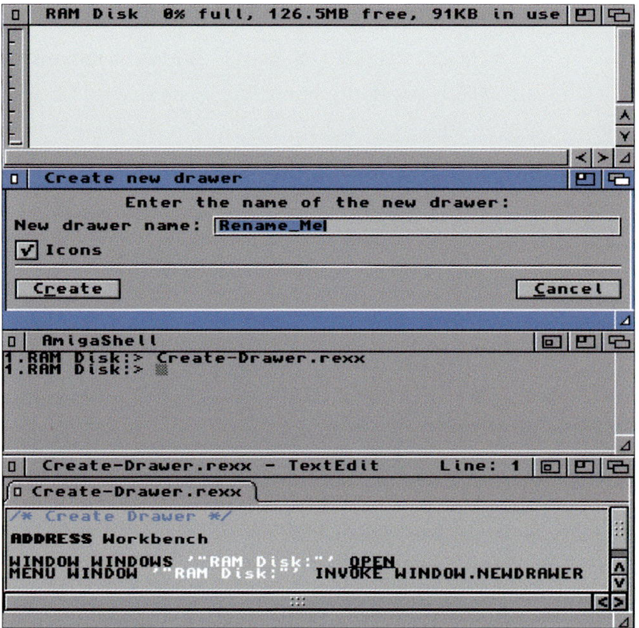

This script opens the RAM Disk window and a requester for creating a new drawer.

Another option would be to select certain icons with the `ICON` command and duplicate them with the menu item `ICONS.COPY`.

Even more interesting is the ability to add your own entries to the *Tools* menu in Workbench. To do this, give the menu item an internal name and a description of how it should appear in the *Tools* menu. You must specify what should happen when the menu item is invoked. You can also specify a keyboard shortcut.

The following script adds two functions to the *Tools* menu:

```
/* Workbench tools */

ADDRESS Workbench

MENU ADD NAME close TITLE '"Close all windows
"' CMD 'Close-all.rexx'
MENU ADD NAME openRAM TITLE '"Open RAM Disk"'
SHORTCUT '"."' CMD '"WINDOW ''"RAM Disk:"'' OPEN"'

SAY "Press Enter to remove the menus again"
PULL

MENU REMOVE NAME close
MENU REMOVE NAME openRAM
```

Important: Pay attention to the quoting in this script and also in the following script. There are indeed two single followed by two double quotation marks before *RAM Disk:*, and then, conversely, two double and two single quotation marks!

This script shows two ways to define a menu function: by either calling an external script or executing ARexx commands directly in a one-liner. In the latter case, pay attention to the quotes so that everything works. The second menu entry can be invoked with a key that is always used in conjunction with the right Amiga key, which is normally associated with menu items. Therefore, the shortcut `[R-Amiga]+[.]` will also open the window for the *RAM Disk*.

Press the Enter key in the Shell where the script is running to remove the menu items again. It is only necessary to inform Workbench about the internal names of the menu items.

Keyboard shortcuts

In addition to menus, keyboard shortcuts can also be defined. This works with the `KEYBOARD` command. The following script adds a keyboard control for the *RAM Disk* icon to Workbench. As long as the shortcuts are active, you can control Workbench with the arrow keys on the numeric keypad of the keyboard (except A600 owners, sorry). See the full script on the next page:

```
/* Workbench keyboard shortcuts */

ADDRESS Workbench

KEYBOARD ADD NAME left KEY '"NUMPAD 4"' CMD '"ICON WINDOW root ''""RAM Disk""'' LEFT 20"'

KEYBOARD ADD NAME up KEY '"NUMPAD 8"' CMD '"ICON WINDOW root ''""RAM Disk""'' UP 20"'

KEYBOARD ADD NAME right KEY '"NUMPAD 6"' CMD '"ICON WINDOW root ''""RAM Disk""'' RIGHT 20"'

KEYBOARD ADD NAME down KEY '"NUMPAD 2"' CMD '"ICON WINDOW root ''""RAM Disk""'' DOWN 20"'

SAY "You can now control the 'RAM Disk' icon"
SAY "with the numeric keypad ten keys after"
SAY "you have activated the Workbench window."
SAY "Press the Enter key to remove the"
SAY "keyboard shortcuts again."
PULL

KEYBOARD REMOVE NAME left
KEYBOARD REMOVE NAME up
KEYBOARD REMOVE NAME right
KEYBOARD REMOVE NAME down
```

As with the menus, each key combination has an internal name. The action to be executed is defined in the same way as for the MENU command. However, the definition of the key to be used is more flexible than with the menu definitions. In principle, you can specify any possible key combination. Some options are shown in the following two tables:

SHIFT KEYS (QUALIFIER)

Button	Function
CTRL	[Ctrl] key
SHIFT	any [Shift] key
LSHIFT	left [Shift] key
RSHIFT	right [Shift] key
ALT	any [Alt] key
LALT	left [Alt] key
RALT	right [Alt] key
NUMPAD	key on the numeric keypad

KEY NAMES

Key	Function
TAB	[Tab] key
F1-F10	function keys
BACKSPACE	[Backspace]
DEL	[Del] button
HELP	[Help] button
RETURN	[Enter] key
NUMPAD ENTER	[Enter] on the numeric keypad

Take care not to assign any key combinations that Workbench already uses. You should also avoid conflicts with global keyboard shortcuts.

What else is possible

In addition to the commands already described, there are other useful commands. For example, there are some commands that can be used to execute Workbench actions directly. DELETE deletes files, NEWDRAWER creates new directories and RENAME gives files a new name. In contrast to the ARexx-controlled execution of the corresponding Workbench menu items, the user will not be prompted. See the next page for an example script:

```
/* Action-in-RAM.rexx */

ADDRESS Workbench

WINDOW '"RAM Disk:"' OPEN

SAY "I am now creating a new drawer."
SAY "Continue with Enter."
PULL

NEWDRAWER '"RAM Disk:New"'

SAY "Now I am renaming the drawer."
SAY "Continue with Enter."
PULL

RENAME '"RAM Disk:New" "Renamed"'

SAY "And now it will be deleted ;-)"
SAY "Continue with Enter."
PULL

DELETE '"RAM Disk:Renamed"'
```

For all three commands, it is important that you specify an absolute path. The commands work independently of Workbench windows and therefore do not otherwise know on which drive and in which directory they should be active. Simply specifying *New* as the drawer name would not have been sufficient.

Two more commands are also important: the example scripts presented so far do not prevent the user from tinkering with Workbench while they are running. For example, a user could have simply deleted the drawer created in the previous example before the script continued to run. The RENAME and DELETE commands would then run into the void.

For this reason, it is important to lock the user interface of Workbench at critical moments and only release it again afterwards. The following example illustrates this procedure:

```
/* Locked */

ADDRESS Workbench

LOCKGUI

SAY "The Workbench interface is now locked."
SAY "Continue with Enter."
PULL

/* Critical actions can take place here */

UNLOCKGUI
```

TIP **Locking and unlocking the Workbench interface**

It is important to find a good balance here: it would be unfavorable if the script terminated with an error after locking the interface without unlocking the interface again. You can see the effect this would have if you send a cancel signal to the script with `[Ctrl]+[C]` before pressing the Enter key – the Workbench user interface will remain locked. Even running the script again will not unlock the interface, as `LOCKGUI` increments a counter. An additional `UNLOCKGUI` execution is required to set the counter to zero. The counter can take on negative values, so it is important not to run `UNLOCKGUI` too often. You can easily check this from the Shell with `RX "ADDRESS Workbench LOCKGUI"` and `RX "ADDRESS Workbench UNLOCKGUI"`. It is advisable to extend the Workbench function so that it remembers which script has locked the interface and automatically resets the counter when the script ends.

Workbench also lets you execute ARexx commands via the ARexx command RX:

```
/* Execute ARexx commands */

ADDRESS Workbench

RX CONSOLE CMD '"SAY 3*3"'

RX CMD 'Open-RAM.rexx'
```

With the CONSOLE argument, Workbench requests a console window that opens as soon as there is an output. Workbench then waits until the command or script has been processed, unless you specify the ASYNC option. The *Open-RAM.rexx* script must be located in the directory to which the *REXX:* assignment points. This is usually the *S* directory on the system drive.

Error handling

The previous examples did not deal with potential errors. In the event of an error, the scripts would simply have been canceled with an ARexx error message. However, ARexx and Workbench offer helpful functions for reacting to errors in a targeted manner:

```
/* Error handling */

ADDRESS Workbench
OPTIONS RESULTS
SIGNAL ON ERROR

WINDOW '"RAM Disk:doesnotexist"' OPEN

EXIT

error:

 SAY "The command returned a" RC "as response."
 SAY "This means that its execution has failed."
 SAY "Learn more about the WORKBENCH.LASTERROR variable:"
```

```
    SAY "The last error that occurred has the
    number:" WORKBENCH.LASTERROR
    FAULT WORKBENCH.LASTERROR
    SAY "This means:" RESULT

  RETURN
```

This script activates ARexx error handling with the sequence `SIGNAL ON ERROR`. In the event of an error, ARexx no longer simply terminates with an error message, but invokes the *error:* routine. Such error handling can also unlock the Workbench interface if it is locked. To do this, it is important to store the extent to which the script has locked the interface in a variable.

The ARexx script then attempts to open a Workbench window for a non-existent directory. As this technically does not work, the `WINDOW` command fails and reports an error with a return value not equal to 0. ARexx therefore jumps to the error handling routine. If the directory exists instead, then the script will open the drawer and there will be no error.

The error-handling routine first displays the return value of the `WINDOW` command stored in the `RC` variable (short for *return code*). The `WORKBENCH.LASTERROR` variable contains the AmigaDOS error number of the last error. This can then be translated into plain text using the Workbench command `FAULT`. The script will therefore output the following:

```
The command returned a 10 as response.
This means that its execution has failed.
Learn more about the WORKBENCH.LASTERROR variable:
The last error that occurred has the number: 205
This means: Object not found
```

You can also determine the plain text for an AmigaDOS error number using the `Fault` Shell command:

```
Fault 205
Fault 205: Object not found
```

ARexx: Controlling MultiView

In AmigaOS 3.2, MultiView also features an ARexx port, which allows for easy automation.

Functionality

MultiView's ARexx port gives the program greater scope for use. The somewhat rudimentary entry in chapter 9 of the AmigaOS 3.2 reference documentation, *ARexx Quick Reference*, under *MultiView's ARexx port*, is limited to a list of commands and options. The upcoming example shows how this works.

The script starts an instance of MultiView in the background with the help file for the `List` Shell command. To do this, it executes the Shell command `Run` via `ADDRESS COMMAND` (see *MultiView example*). The `PORTNAME` option sets the name of the ARexx port to *MVEXAMPLE.*, followed by a number. To allow the script to run multiple times, the `DO WHILE` loop determines a free port name at the beginning by appending the number in the *i* variable to *MVEXAMPLE.* in the *p* variable. A limit of 100 is set to avoid a potential infinite loop. It may be sufficient to execute the example script 100 times in parallel! The `SHOW('PORTS', p || i)` function in the `IF` query determines whether the port already exists. If it does not exist, which is checked by the non-operator ~, then the query exits the loop with `LEAVE`: a free ARexx port is found and the script will output it. If no ARexx port is specified, the program uses *MULTIVIEW.* followed by a number as the port name. Note that this is case-sensitive.

Additional note: it is possible, but unlikely, that another program reserves the port name in-between checking whether the port exists and MultiView assigning the port name.

TIP **ARexx port overview**
You can display a list of the currently available ARexx ports at any time in a Shell window with the command sequence `RX "SAY SHOW('PORTS')"`.

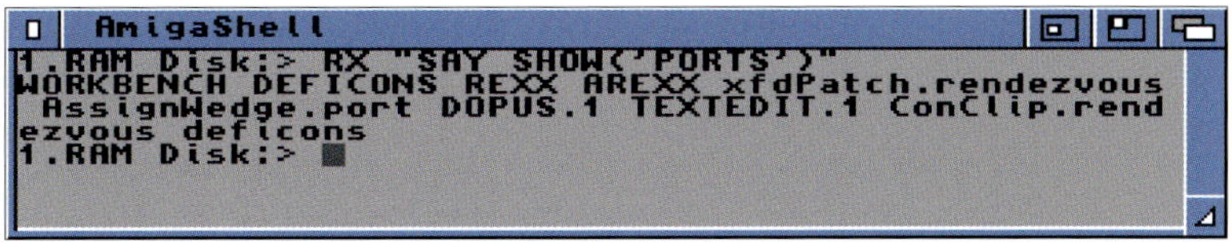

```
AmigaShell
1.RAM Disk:> RX "SAY SHOW('PORTS')"
WORKBENCH DEFICONS REXX AREXX xfdPatch.rendezvous
 AssignWedge.port DOPUS.1 TEXTEDIT.1 ConClip.rend
ezvous deficons
1.RAM Disk:>
```

Determining a list of existing ARexx ports at any time

MultiView example

```
/* MultiView example */

OPTIONS RESULTS

/* Search for free port */
i=1
p='MVEXAMPLE.'
DO WHILE i<=100
   IF ~ SHOW('PORTS', p || i) THEN LEAVE
   i=i+1
END
p=p || i

/* Start MultiView with determined port name */
ADDRESS COMMAND "Run Multiview
HELP:english/Sys/Commands/list.help PORTNAME" p
"WINDOWWIDTH 640 WINDOWHEIGHT 400"

SAY "Wait for ARexx port of Multiview..."
ADDRESS COMMAND "WaitForPort " || p
IF ~ SHOW('PORTS', p) THEN DO
   SAY "ARexx port not found. Exit program."
   EXIT
END
SAY 'ARexx port found: "'p'"'
SAY
ADDRESS VALUE p

GETFILEINFO

SAY 'MultiView has opened the file "'RESULT'".'
SAY "Next, open the help for Multiview ARexx port."
SAY "Please press Enter in the Shell window."
```

```
PULL
OPEN NAME '"HELP:english/Sys/Other/mvarexx.help"'
SAY "Move the Multiview window to the background."
SAY "Please press Enter."
PULL
WINDOWTOBACK
SAY "Bring the Multiview window to the front."
SAY "Please press Enter."
PULL
WINDOWTOFRONT
SAY "Please select some text in the MultiView window."
SAY "Then press Enter in the Shell window."
PULL
SAVEAS NAME '"RAM:Selected text.txt"'
SAY "Your selected text is in the file"
SAY '"Selected text.txt" on your RAM Disk.'
SAY
SAY "Please select a text in the Shell window or somewhere else and copy it"
SAY "to the clipboard with [Right Amiga] + [C]."
SAY "Please press Enter."
PULL
SAY
SAY "You have copied the text displayed in the MultiView window to the clipboard."
PASTE
SAY
SAY "Quit MultiView."
SAY "Please press Enter."
PULL
QUIT
```

The `WaitForPort` Shell command ensures that the script waits for the ARexx port of the MultiView instance that has just been started. In the test run, the time required for the Shell command to recognize the ARexx port ranged from several seconds to almost immediately. Without waiting, the ARexx command ADDRESS may fail, as MultiView has not yet been able to start and open the ARexx port by the time it is run. The VALUE option directs the ADDRESS command to assess the argument as an expression, rather than using the variable *p* as the port name.

This ARexx command now makes MultiView's ARexx commands available directly in the script. The rest of the script should be self-explanatory. It is important to note that both the SAVEAS command and the PASTE command remove the current selection in MultiView. It is therefore not possible to save a text selected in MultiView and open it again directly in MultiView without going through the saved file.

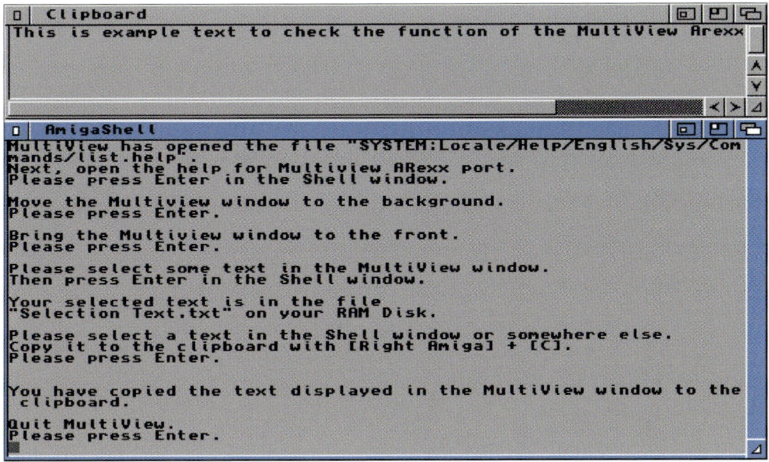

The script opens the content of the clipboard in MultiView.

The tables *File functions*, *Clipboard*, *Info retrieval* and *Window management* on the next page provide an overview of the options available. You can read more about this in the aforementioned reference documentation, which is opened by the script.

Executing OPEN or SAVEAS without specifying a filename with NAME or (for OPEN) the clipboard as the source opens a requester for file selection. The BEEPSCREEN command had no visible effect under FS-UAE with the UAE graphics driver, but briefly flashes the screen when using Amiga chipset graphics.

ARexx use of MultiView

FILE FUNCTIONS

Command	Function
OPEN NAME	opens the specified file
OPEN CLIPBOARD	opens the clipboard, unit selectable with CLIPUNIT
RELOAD	reloads the current document
SAVEAS NAME	saves the current document or selection to a file
PRINT	prints the current document or selection
QUIT	quits MultiView

CLIPBOARD

Command	Function
COPY	copies the current content or selection to the clipboard
PASTE	same as OPEN CLIPBOARD
CLEARSELECTED	removes the current selection

INFO RETRIEVAL

Command	Function
GETCURRENTDIR	path of the current document
GETFILEINFO	path and filename of the current document
GETOBJECTINFO	filename and information on the data type

WINDOW MANAGEMENT

Command	Function
MINIMUMSIZE	reduces window to minimum size
NORMALSIZE	sets window to normal size
MAXIMUMSIZE	enlarges window to maximum
WINDOWTOFRONT	window to front
WINDOWTOBACK	window to back
ACTIVATEWINDOW	activates window
SCREENTOFRONT	screen to front
SCREENTOBACK	screen to back
SCREEN	display on a screen? Yes with TRUE or No with FALSE
PUBSCREEN	name of the public screen
BEEPSCREEN	flash the screen

ARexx: Controlling TextEdit

The TextEdit program also offers an ARexx interface, as does AmigaOS's long-standing editor Ed.

Functionality

The ARexx port of TextEdit enables the loading and saving of files, as well as their editing. The port name corresponds to *TEXTEDIT.,* followed by the number of the TextEdit instance. Unlike MultiView, it is not possible to assign a different port name to the editor using an option such as `PORTNAME`. This makes it difficult to find the ARexx port of the correct TextEdit instance. It also does not seem to be possible to run an ARexx script directly from the editor. In this case, the script could receive the appropriate ARexx port directly from TextEdit.

One possibility, which the following example makes use of, is to see which instance has opened the desired file. The script starts TextEdit as a Shell command with the desired filename as an argument. As the exact name of the ARexx port is not known once TextEdit is started, the script waits one second using the Shell command `Wait` instead of waiting specifically until a port with a specified name appears (see *TextEdit* example below). One second is usually sufficient.

It then saves the names of all the ARexx ports found in the *ports* variable and queries all the ports with `TEXTEDIT` in their names for the appropriate filename. To do this, it uses `GETATTR PROJECT FILE` to determine the filename of the project without a path. The assignment with a path would be more complex, as *RAM:* can also be *RAM Disk:*.

TextEdit example

```
/* TextEdit example */

OPTIONS RESULTS

file="Test.txt"
ADDRESS COMMAND "Run TextEdit RAM: "file
ADDRESS COMMAND "Wait 1"

ports = SHOW('PORTS')
found = 0

```

```
DO n=1 to WORDS(ports)
   port=WORD(ports, n)
   IF POS("TEXTEDIT", port) > 0 THEN DO
      ADDRESS VALUE port
      GETATTR PROJECT FILE
      IF RESULT == file THEN DO
         found=1
         LEAVE
      END
   END
END

IF found=0 THEN DO
   SAY 'ARexx port of TextEdit with the file "'file'" not found.'
   SAY 'Exit script'
END

SAY 'ARexx port of TextEdit with the file "'file'": "'port'"' '0a'x

APICURSOR ON

SAY "Delete any existing text."
CALL Next

POSITION SOF
MARK ON
POSITION EOF
ERASE

SAY 'Add the text "Hello world!"'
CALL Next

TEXT "Hello world!" || '0a'x

SAY "Select the current line and copy it."
CALL Next

POSITION SOL
MARK ON
POSITION EOL
```

```
COPY
MARK OFF
/* Required with extra API cursor */
CURSOR DOWN
PASTE

SAY "Number the current line."
CALL Next

GETLINE
line=RESULT
GETCURSOR LINE
lnr=RESULT
newline=lnr+1": "line

/* Delete line */
POSITION SOL
MARK ON
POSITION EOL
ERASE

/* Replace with new text with line number */
TEXT newline

GETATTR PROJECT PATH
SAY 'Save text in "'RESULT || file'".'
CALL Next

SAVE
APICURSOR OFF
SAY "Quit TextEdit."
CALL Next

QUIT

EXIT

Next: PROCEDURE
   SAY "Continue with Enter,
   quit with Q and Enter."
   PULL input
   IF input == "q" | input == "Q" THEN DO
```

```
            EXIT
        END
    RETURN
```

If found, the script outputs the name of the port and activates the extra write marker for accessing TextEdit via the ARexx interface. The character string `'0a'x` inserts a line feed, eliminating the need for a single extra call to `SAY`.

As there may already be text in the file when the script is executed again, or for other reasons, it first deletes it. To do this, `POSITION SOF` sets the position of the cursor to the start of the file *(SOF)* and activates marker mode. The `POSITION EOF` command switches to the end of the file and `ERASE` deletes the selection. After each action, the script calls the *Next* procedure at the end of the script, which gives the user the opportunity to start the next step with `[Enter]` or end the script with `[q]` followed by `[Enter]`.

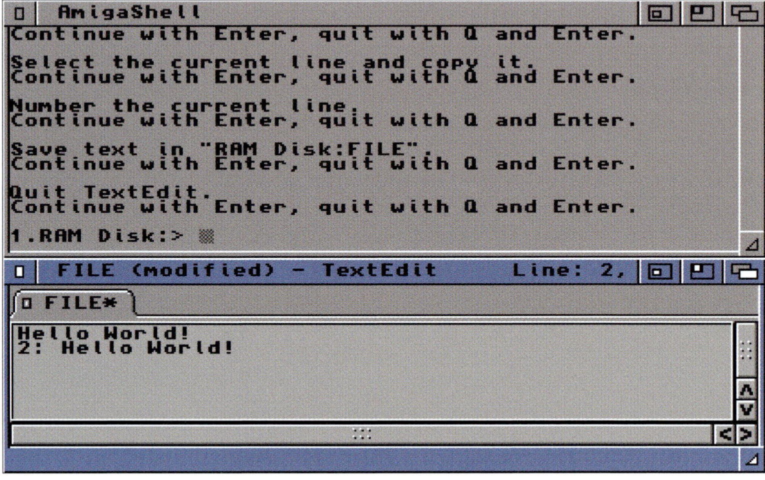

A remote-controlled TextEdit in action

The script inserts the text *Hello world!* using the TextEdit command TEXT. It then selects the current line, copies it to the clipboard and inserts it again. SOL and EOL are used instead of SOF and EOF. The *L* stands for the current *line*. To shift the text to a new line, CURSOR DOWN moves the cursor down. As the line is empty, provided the user has not entered anything in the meantime, the new text ends up at the beginning of the line. Here, the extra API cursor behaves differently to the normal cursor for the user, which does not require an extra call to CURSOR DOWN.

The next step uses GETCURSOR LINE to determine the current line number and GETLINE to determine the content of the current line in order to add a line number at the beginning of the line. By deleting the line and inserting the text with the line number, the line is given a line number at the beginning. Alternatively, it would be possible to insert the line number at the beginning of the line using the TEXT command without first determining the content of the line. However, the aim of the example was to show how a line can be changed almost arbitrarily using ARexx tools. The same is also possible with marked blocks using GETSELECTEDTEXT, whereby ARexx has a limit of 64 kilobytes for character strings.

At the end, the example saves the file in the RAM Disk and exits the editor. When testing this on AmigaOS 3.2.2.1, TextEdit crashed several times, especially when the example was called repeatedly without deleting the created text file first. Bug fixes may still be necessary here.

However, the possibilities are already promising. The tables *File functions*, *Selection functions, Edit text* and *Change position* on the following pages provide an overview. You can read more about this under *TextEdit's ARexx Port* in the *ARexx* chapter of the *AmigaOS 3.2 reference documentation.*

Calling OPEN or SAVEAS without specifying a filename with FILENAME or NAME opens a file requester window for selecting the file (see table *File functions*).

ARexx use of TextEdit

FILE FUNCTIONS

Command	Function
NEW	new empty text file
OPEN FILENAME	opens the specified file
SAVE	saves the current file
SAVEAS NAME	saves the current file under a different name
CLOSE	closes the current file without prompting with FORCE
QUIT	quits TextEdit
GETATTR PROJECT	determines the filename without path (FILE) or with path (FILENAME), the path (PATH), the file type (FILETYPE) or the changed status (CHANGED)

SELECTION FUNCTIONS

Command	Function
CUT	puts the selection in the clipboard and then cuts it out
COPY	copies the selection to the clipboard
PASTE	inserts at the cursor position and replaces the selected text if necessary
ERASE	deletes the selection, also works with DELETE
GETSELECTEDTEXT	returns the content of the selection, limitation to 64 kilobytes
GETLINE	returns the content of the current line

EDIT TEXT

Command	Function
TEXT	inserts the specified text and removes any selected text
UNDO	undoes the last change
REDO	redoes the last undone change
BEGINMULTICHANGE	begins the merging of several changes
END MULTICHANGE	executes several changes

CHANGE POSITION

Command	Function
GOTOLINE	moves the cursor to the specified line
GOTOCOLUMN	moves the cursor to the specified column
CURSOR	moves the cursor up (UP), down (DOWN), to the left (LEFT) or to the right (RIGHT)
LINE	moves the cursor up (negative number) or down the specified number of lines
COLUMN	moves the cursor the specified number of columns to the left (negative number) or to the right
GETCURSOR	determines the current line (LINE) or column (COLUMN)
PREVIOUS	moves the cursor to the beginning of the previous word (WORD), sentence (SENTENCE), paragraph (PARAGRAPH) or page (PAGE)
NEXT	moves the cursor to the beginning of the next word (WORD), sentence (SENTENCE), paragraph (PARAGRAPH) or page (PAGE)
POSITION	moves the cursor to the start (SOF) or end of the file (EOF), the start (SOL) or end of the line (EOL), the start (SOW) or end of the word (EOW), the start (EOV) or the end (SOV) of the current view
SETBOOKMARK	sets or deletes (OFF) a bookmark at the current position, switching is possible (TOGGLE)
GOTOBOOKMARK	go to the nth, the previous (PREVIOUS) or the next (NEXT) bookmark
LISTBOOTKMARKS	returns a list of bookmarks
CLEARBOOKMARKS	deletes all bookmarks
APICURSOR	extra cursor for access via ARexx on (ON) or off (OFF)

Next Steps

7

Welcome to this exciting chapter on upgrading your Amiga system! Here we will look at the range of hardware enhancements currently available as well as useful software that will enrich your Amiga experience. We will enter the realm of the internet and show you how to get your Amiga online and what web browsers are out there. And we will explain how to efficiently exchange data between your Amiga and PC. Get your Amiga ready for the modern era!

Internet access with the Amiga

Unlike AmigaOS 3.9, AmigaOS 3.2 does not have an integrated TCP/IP stack. This section will explain the means by which one may still gain access to the internet.

Prerequisites

Accessing the internet with AmigaOS 3.2 requires the installation of a network card (via cable or WiFi) and a so-called TCP/IP stack on the system.

On the hardware side, there are various PCMCIA, Zorro or serial and parallel network solutions available for the various Amiga models, which are explained in more detail in the *Amiga hardware* section (7.5).

Unlike AmigaOS 3.9, which contained an integrated TCP/IP stack called *Genesis* by default, AmigaOS 3.2 does not have its own TCP/IP stack. However, if you still own a copy of the original version of AmigaOS 3.9, you can also use Genesis in AmigaOS 3.2. An installed TCP/IP stack forms the software basis for using applications for the web, FTP, e-mail and other services. In this section, three TCP/IP stack solutions, Genesis, Miami and Roadshow, are discussed in detail.

TIP

IP address of the router (with Fritz!Box)

There are several ways to identify the required IP address of your network router. As an example, we will show you the method for the Fritz!Box, which is widely used in central Europe. Open a web browser such as Firefox on a device that is on the network (computer or mobile phone). Enter *fritz.box* in the address bar to get to the Fritz!Box login screen. Log in with your access data so that the Fritz user interface opens. Select the *Network* item under the *Home network* main menu. A list of all network connections will appear there. You can see the IP address from the Fritz!Box line, for example 192.168.100.1. Enter this IP as the DNS in the TCP/IP stack on the Amiga.

TIP **IP address of the router (with Windows shell)**
Alternatively, use the `[Windows]+[R]` keys on a Windows PC and enter `cmd` in the input field. Inside the Windows shell, simply type the command `ipconfig`. The *IPv4 address* entry shows the IP address of the router.

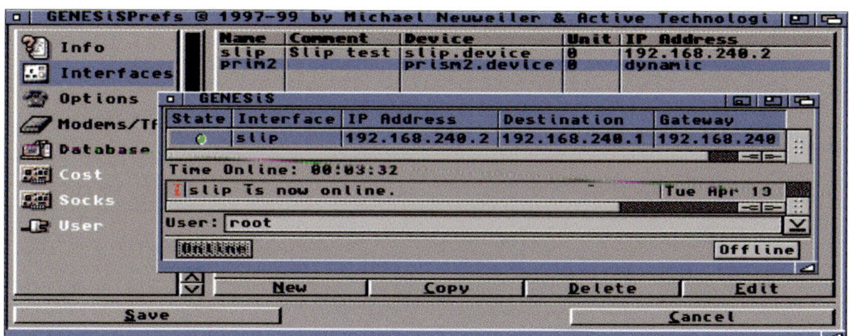

Genesis offers a user interface that makes setting up a network connection noticeably easier.

Genesis

AmigaOS 3.9 owners will have received the Genesis TCP/IP stack as part of the software bundle: you can use the tool from this bundle with AmigaOS 3.2. Alternatively, there is a demo version on Aminet. A prerequisite for using Genesis is the *MUI* interface system and the appropriate driver for your network solution.

Start the installation of Genesis via the installer on your hard disk in a directory of your choice.

If you have not already done so, copy the driver for your network card to the *Sys:Devs/Networks* directory. To use a WiFi card, the network SSID and password must also be stored in the driver. Detailed instructions can be found in the driver's documentation.

After restarting the Amiga, open *GenesisPrefs* in *the Genesis directory* on your hard drive. There, navigate to the *Interfaces* menu item and click the *New* button, to open a new window.

Assign a name for the interface in the *Interfaces* tab. If you use *DHCP* (*Dynamic Host Configuration Protocol*) on your router to automatically assign dynamic IP addresses to connected devices, set all options to *Dynamic*. Switch to the *Sana-II* tab, select *specify sana-II device* and the driver previously copied to *Sys:Devs/Networks*, e.g. the *cnet.device*.

In the last step, enter the IP of your router under the *Resolve* tab in the list of *domain name servers*.

Confirm the configuration and save all settings that you have made in *GenesisPrefs*.

Start the main program called *Genesis* and click the *online* button.

To quickly test whether you are online, type `ping google.com` in a Shell window. A response will indicate if the *DNS* (*Domain Name System*) is working and you are online.

Miami

Miami is a proven and user-friendly TCP/IP stack for the Amiga. Its popularity stems from its reliable performance and versatile configuration options.

First, you should install all Miami packages on your hard drive in a directory of your choice. Do not forget to place the corresponding driver for your network card in the *Sys:Devs/Networks* directory. To use a WiFi card, the network SSID and password must also be stored in the driver. Detailed instructions on this can be found in the driver documentation.

Restart the computer, open Miami and go to the settings. Click on *Interfaces* and select the *SANA II Ethernet* option under *Interface type*. Under *Driver*, select the network driver that you saved in *Sys:Devs/Networks*. If your network uses *DHCP*, make sure the settings under *Driver* are set to *DHCP*. In the next step, go to *Database* and switch to *DNS Servers* via the top button. Enter the IP address of your router as the DNS server.

Once all the settings have been made, save them. Press the *Online* button to start the connection.

To check whether you are online, open a Shell and type `MiamiPing google.com`. If you receive a response, the DNS is working and an internet connection to the Amiga has been established.

Roadshow

Roadshow is the only TCP/IP stack for the Amiga still being developed. This commercial program does not come with a graphical user interface and so is recommended only for experienced users. A separate user interface can be installed, but does not offer any configuration options.

To install Roadshow, use the installer to copy the software onto your hard disk. Make sure to install the correct processor version (CPU) of the *bsdsocket.library* for your Amiga. Copy the network card driver to the directory *Sys:Devs/Networks*.

Next, manually create a configuration file so that Roadshow can recognize the driver and other settings. The installer saves templates for many common network cards in the *Sys:Storage/NetInterfaces* directory. Copy the appropriate template to *Sys:Devs/NetInterfaces*.

Open this configuration file with a text editor such as *TextEdit*. Only a few settings will be relevant for most users. If you use *DHCP* in your router, these are the essential entries:

```
device=[NameOfDriver].device
unit=0
configure=dhcp
requiresinitdelay=no
```

Once you have saved the configuration file, you can go online. Open a Shell and enter the following command:

```
addnetinterface <name of the config. file>
```

If successful, you will receive a message in the Shell confirming the assigned IP address and DNS.

Although Roadshow requires manual setup, it provides a powerful and flexible solution for network configuration on Amiga systems and is particularly suitable for those who prefer optimized, script-based control.

TIP **Download links**

All links to the three TCP/IP stacks and necessary add-ons can be found bundled and continuously updated on the service website for this book: www.lookbehindyou.de/en/amigaos32book

Amiga on the World Wide Web

Despite lacking a modern browser, you can still surf the web with your classic Amiga. Daniel Reimann investigates how well this works in reality.

Purists and doubters will say that you should not and must not surf the World Wide Web with outdated browser technology. This is true insofar as the vast majority of websites today use CSS and HTML5 technologies, which no Amiga browser can currently process and probably never will, as the hardware requirements are not given so it doesn't make sense to implement it into an Amiga browser. There is also no Java support and very limited JavaScript support.

So why bother with browsers or the World Wide Web at all? There is an extensive, free software archive – Aminet – and several Amiga forums and news sites that can be visited without any restrictions. With a few tricks, you can even get the latest news on your Amiga.

The web browsers for the classic Amiga are two old favorites: AWeb and IBrowse.

AWeb

AWeb was originally included as a limited version with AmigaOS versions 3.5 and 3.9, and could be completely unlocked by purchasing the full version. In 2002, the original developer of AWeb, Yvon Rozijn, stopped the development and released the source code to the Amiga community for potential further development. In the same year, development of this open source version was resumed under the name *AWeb APL Lite*. The last public beta version dates back to 2007, but the archive was renewed in 2020. There was also an update to version 3.5.091 in 2023, which was compiled with the latest AmiSSL SDK (download: www.aminet.net/comm/www/aweb_3_5_091). This requires at least a 68020 processor and 3 MB Fast RAM. However, 4 MB RAM or more is recommended. Additionally, a specific iteration is available for 68000 processors, so even owners of an Amiga 500 or 2000 can give it a try.

AWeb requires the extended GUI toolkit *ClassAct*. However, since its successor, *Reaction*, is part of AmigaOS 3.2 by default, users do not have to do anything to acquire it.

IBrowse

IBrowse has always been a commercial software product. Originally developed by Stefan Burström and distributed by HiSoft, then later by IOSPIRIT, Oliver Roberts took over further development in 2008. The latest version 3.0a of IBrowse was only released at the end of 2023 after a lengthy development period. In addition to an improved HTML engine at its heart, there are revised prefs, improved GIF animation routines and other new features and optimizations.

You can download a demo version on the developer's homepage at www.ibrowse-dev.net/download.php. It is limited to 30 minutes of use and allows just two tabs, but is otherwise fully usable. The full version regularly costs €54.99, while an upgrade from versions 2.1 to 2.4 costs €29.99. As of July 2024, the software is available at a special launch price (€39.99 or €19.99).

IBrowse requires at least Kickstart 3.0, a 68020 processor, 8 MB Fast RAM and MUI 3.8, as well as AmiSSL 5.13 for secure connections. However, more memory and a faster processor are recommended for good performance.

In comparison: IBrowse vs. AWeb

Most websites today use secure, encrypted connections – the so-called *Hypertext Transfer Protocol Secure* (*HTTPS*). Both IBrowse and AWeb are generally capable of accessing such websites. IBrowse supports the current standard based on OpenSSL 3.0.5 (download: https://github.com/jens-maus/amissl/releases/tag/5.3), with the help of Amiga encryption software AmiSSL in version 5.3. The website of IBrowse developer Roberts also features customized AmiSSL in version 5.13, which was released at the end of 2023. AWeb, on the other hand, only supports AmiSSL 3, the last version of which, 3.6, was released in 2015 and is based on OpenSSL 0.9.7g.

In practice, it turns out that with AWeb you can only visit some encrypted websites without issue. However, for the most important Amiga website in terms of software, Aminet, it can be used without any problems.

If you want to test the browsers, you can install versions 5.3 and 3.6 of AmiSSL in parallel on one system. However, you should install the older version first to avoid any software conflicts.

These screenshots show the Aminet website as displayed by AWeb 3.5.09 and IBrowse 3.0a:

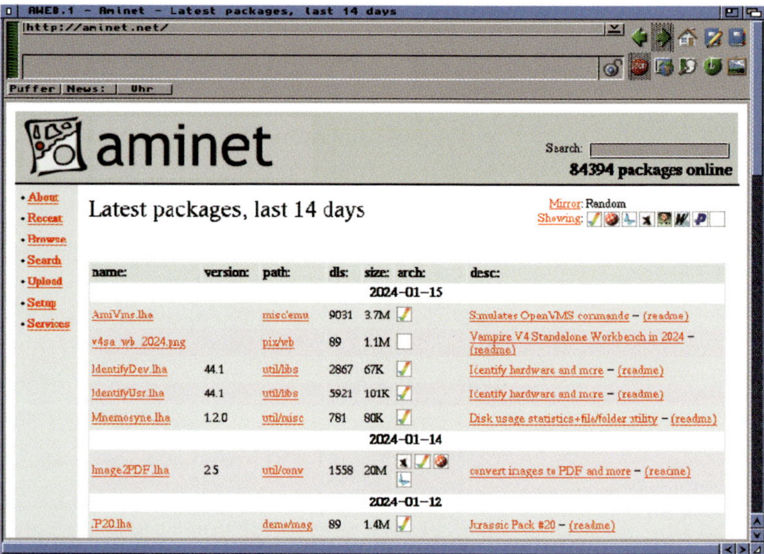

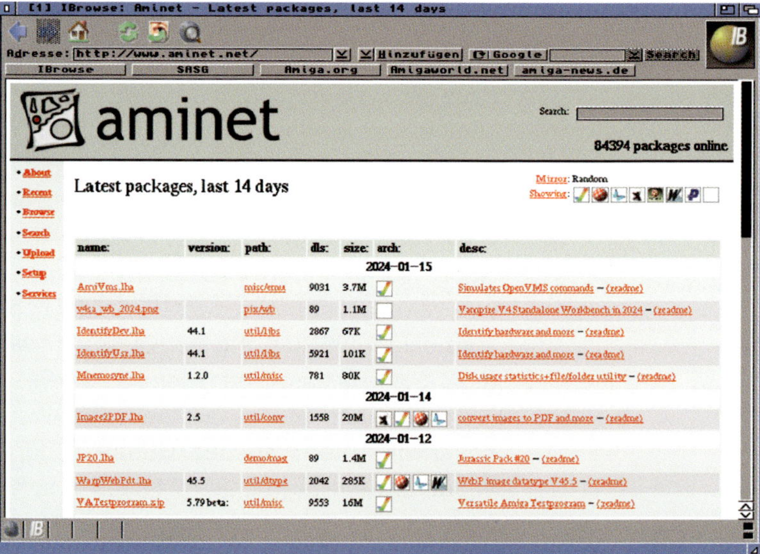

The Aminet homepage on AWeb (top) and IBrowse (bottom).

Website check

We have visited some Amiga-related websites with AWeb and IBrowse and determined whether they are accessible by either of them:

Website	URL	IBrowse	AWeb
Aminet	www.aminet.net	★	★
English Amiga Board	eab.abime.net	○	×
amiga.org	www.amiga.org	○	×
amigaworld.net	www.amigaworld.net	★	×
LemonAmiga	www.lemonamiga.com	○	×
GitHub	www.github.com	×	×
Amiga Addict	www.amiga-addict.com	○	×
amiga-news.de	www.amiga-news.de/en/	★	●

Legend
★ can be displayed without any problems
● shows a certificate error message, but this can be ignored
○ limited displayability
× not displayable

Web search with the Amiga

It can be assumed that the average Amiga user would like to be informed of developments in other fields not directly related to the Amiga, in addition to information about products and services that are: for example, through typical search engine queries, or by reading the news.

With IBrowse, Google is always successful. However, there is an alternative to Google that has been specially designed for retro computers that works perfectly with AWeb: *FrogFind!* (www.frogfind.com). *FrogFind!* displays results from the *DuckDuck Go* search engine and generates a greatly simplified version of the desired page when you click on a search result.

The Google news portal *68knews* (http://68k.news) has a similar concept: here, news items are displayed without menus, adverts, footers or anything else that is not part of the actual text body. The country from which you want to read the news, as well as the desired category, can be set in the menu at the top of the page. In many cases, IBrowse and AWeb can be used and display the contents without any significant problems.

Browser tip for adventurous Amiga users

In addition to the two browsers mentioned above, there is a third, more current candidate for AmigaOS 3.x: *Netsurf*. This browser is available free of charge. Its development commenced in 2007. Ports to AmigaOS 3 were made by developer Chris Young and are expressly to be regarded as test versions. The browser is continuously updated, most recently in June 2024, and can be downloaded from https://ci.netsurf-browser.org/builds/amigaos3/ or from Aminet. The *guigfx.library* and *AmiSSL 5.13* (both from Aminet), and 32 MB RAM on the hardware side are required.

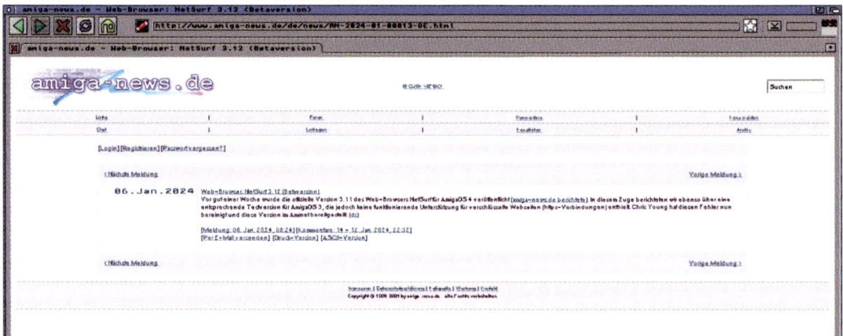

Not yet perfect, but on the right track: there are versions of the Netsurf web browser for Windows, Debian Linux, RISC OS and also AmigaOS 4.0 and AmigaOS 3.2.

More tools for Amiga surfers

AmiFTP is the leading FTP client (File Transfer Protocol) for the Amiga. This tool has a clear graphical user interface and all the key functions of an FTP client. A connection to a local or global FTP server can be quickly set up via an IP address with a login and password. Data can be transferred quickly and easily from or to the server using the file browser.

YAM (Yet Another Mailer) was one of the first e-mail clients on the Amiga and was the standard for a long time. Unfortunately, it has not been consistently developed since 2014, which is why modern functions such as IMAP and HTML display are missing. But if you can get by with POP3 and SMTP, you should definitely take a look.

Links for Amiga users

The internet is full of Amiga content. Here are some of the most essential Amiga-related websites, focusing on the English-speaking world:

News

Amiga-News.de/en/ – www.amiga-news.de/en/
news magazine about the Amiga, edited daily in English and German. Includes a forum. Running for over 25 years now.

Magazines

Amiga Addict – www.amiga-addict.com
UK Amiga print magazine, published every six weeks, available at newsagents in the UK or via subscription

Amiga Future – www.amigafuture.de
print magazine with six issues per year, German and English

Communities / discussion forums

amigaworld.net – www.amigaworld.net
English Amiga Board – eab.abime.net
amigans – www.amigans.net
amiga.org – www.amiga.org
These are the largest international communities with English discussion forums and additional services.

Knowledge

Amiga Wiki – www.amigawiki.com
extensive wiki on Amiga history and technology

TBBoAH – bigbookofamigahardware.com
The Big Book of Amiga Hardware, a comprehensive database of hardware with documentation and drivers

Workbench Nostalgia – www.gregdonner.org/workbench/
educational website to preserve the remarkable history of AmigaOS and Workbench in particular

Moby Games – www.mobygames.com
the world's largest software information database for computer and console games (of course, also for the Amiga)

Lemon Amiga – www.lemonamiga.com
an established database with details on 5000+ Amiga games

Retailers

AmigaStore.eu – www.amigastore.eu
Amiga retailer, distributor and developer (Spain)

Relec - www.relec.ch
Amiga retailer (Switzerland/France)

Amedia – www.amedia-computer.com
Amiga retailer (France)
Amiga on the Lake – amigaonthelake.com
Amiga retailer (USA)
RetroPassion – www.retropassion.co.uk
Amiga retailer and hardware service (UK)
Simulant – www.simulant.uk/shop/
Amiga and retro computer retailer (UK)
Sordan Electronics – www.sordan.ie
Amiga retailer and accessories manufacturer (Ireland)
GGS-Data – www.ggsdata.se
computer retailer (incl. Amiga) (Sweden)
Retro8BitShop – retro8bitshop.com
retro computer dealer (Netherlands)
Alinea Computer – www.amiga-shop.net
Amiga retailer, manufacturer, distributor (Germany)
DragonBox – www.dragonbox.de/en/
retro computer retailer and developer (Germany)
poly.play – www.polyplay.xyz
retro computer retailer, games publisher (Germany)
Archi-Tech – www.archi-tech.com.pl
Amiga retailer and hardware (Poland)
Retro Ready – www.retroready.one
Amiga and retro computer retailer (UK)
Amiga Kit – www.amigakit.com
Amiga retailer and developer (UK)
RetroKit – www.retrokit.com.au
Amiga retailer (Australia)

Software

Aminet – www.aminet.net
the complete package (in English): from games and applications to demos, everything is available here.
GitHub – www.github.com/search?q=amiga
open source platform for developers and users with software for all platforms, including AmigaOS
Hyperion Entertainment – hyperion-entertainment.com
developer of AmigaOS 3.2 and 4, as well as of various games
Amiga Forever – www.amigaforever.com
emulator package with pre-installed Amiga environments, legal Kickstart ROM files and historical material
WinUAE – www.winuae.net
powerful and customisable Amiga emulator for Windows

WHDLoad – www.whdload.de
software for the convenient hard drive installation of games and demos via the Workbench
Oliver Roberts – www.ibrowse-dev.net
developer of the web browser IBrowse and other tools
APC&TCP – www.apc-tcp.de
Amiga software publisher of tools such as CygnusEd and Roadshow, games such as ReshootR, and merchandising
AmiKit – www.amikit.amiga.sk
software bundle for enhancing emulated Amigas, PiStorms and Vampires

Hardware

Retro Games Ltd – www.retrogames.biz
developer of THEA500 Mini and other retro consoles
Elbox – www.elbox.com
hardware such as Mediator PCI boards
individual Computer – www.icomp.de
hardware such as the ACA, Keyrah or X-Surf; software-developer/support for P96 (formerly Picasso96)
A-Eon – www.a-eon.com
hardware such as the Prisma Megamix soundcard and the new X1000 and X5000 PowerPC Amigas
Amigaworld.de – www.amigaworld.de
hardware projects, instructions, workshops
Lotharek – www.lotharek.pl
Amiga expansions like the Tikus or Medusa
MNT - www.mntre.com
hardware such as the ZZ9000 and ZZ9000 AX
IrixLabs – www.irixlabs.com
hardware such as the SD Drive Z2, ZRAM 8 and ScanPlus
7-Bit – www.7-bit.pl
hardware such as the Wicher 1211 and Ryś MKII
A1200.net – www.a1200.net
replacement cases for Amiga 1200 and new keyboard caps
Checkmate – www.checkmate1500plus.com
manufacturer of Checkmate cases and modern displays
Tank Mouse – www.tank-mouse.com
new version of the Tank Mouse (the Amiga mouse)
Apollo Computer – www.apollo-computer.com
turbo cards and stand-alone computers, such as Vampire
Rastport – www.rastport.com
hardware developer, e.g. KA59 keyboard, Gayle-Fix etc.

Data exchange between Amiga and PC

On modern systems, file transfer between computers is typically done over a network. There are different ways of exchanging data between Amiga and Windows PCs – with or without network access. Here we present the most practical solutions for transferring files from one computer to another.

Via floppy drives with floppy disks and CrossDOS

The CrossDOS file system has been available on the Amiga since AmigaOS 2.1 (see sections 2.12 on *file systems* and 4.26 on *CrossDOS*). With CrossDOS you can read and write PC DOS disks in FAT format. However, DD floppy disks in FAT format only have a small storage capacity of 720 kilobytes. In addition, floppy disk drives can only be found in very old PCs. But if you still have a Windows-compatible PC with a floppy drive, you can use it to exchange data quickly and easily.

To activate CrossDOS on the Amiga, you only need to move the file *PC0*, the PC DOS device driver for the internal floppy drive, from the directory *SYS:Storage/DosDrivers* to *SYS:Devs/DosDrivers*. If another drive – usually an external drive – needs to be able to read and write PC floppy disks as well as Amiga floppy disks, then move the file *PC1* too. After double-clicking on the PC0 or PC1 drive icon, the device is mounted and can be used. As soon as you insert a DOS-formatted floppy disk into the drive, a PC floppy disk icon is displayed on the Workbench desktop.

You can now write data to and read data from the PC disk. Do not be alarmed by the fact that DF0: is still available, as the drive can be used for Amiga and PC floppy disks at the same time.

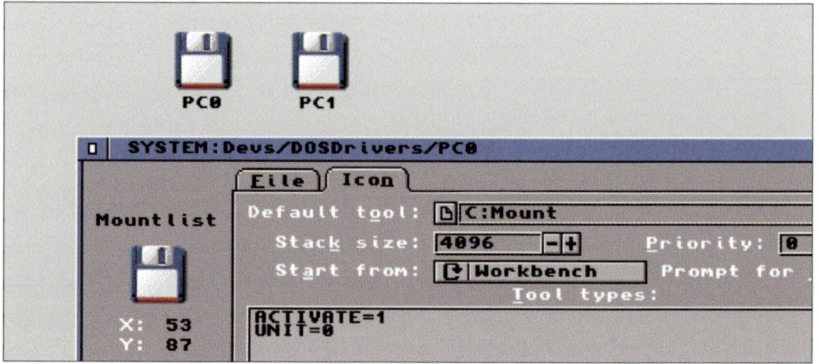

PC0 and PC1 DOSDrivers enable AmigaOS to read MS-DOS-disks.

Via Gotek drives with ADF files

Owners of Gotek drives (see section 7.5 on *hardware extensions*) can use them to exchange data with a PC (although this is not their intended purpose). There is one problem: the data must be in the ADF virtual disk format. ADF versions of Amiga games and programs, including new releases, are regularly available. These can simply be copied from the PC to a USB stick formatted in FAT mode and then read by the Gotek drive plugged to the Amiga. However, if you want to transfer data that is not yet available as ADF from an Amiga to the PC, you must copy it onto a floppy disk and convert the floppy disk to ADF format (or use an existing virtual floppy disk). Due to the natural limitations of the Amiga disk format, the maximum size of the data that can be placed on an ADF disk file is around 880 kilobytes.

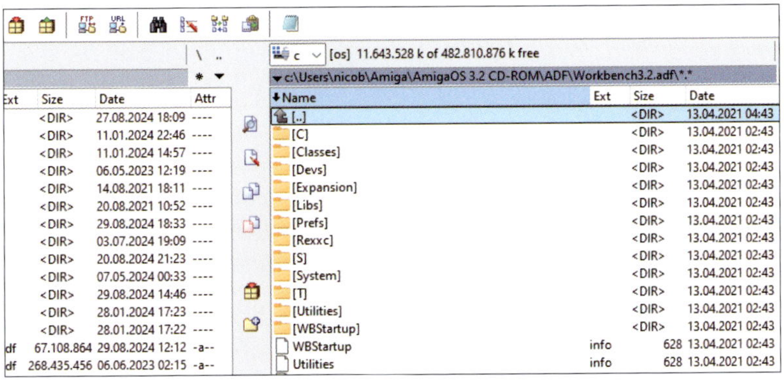

Windows file manager Total Commander with the AmigaDX plugin

On Windows PCs, you can use ADFs very easily with the reliable *Total Commander* file manager in combination with the *AmigaDX* plug-in, i.e. access the contents and copy files. Total Commander is shareware and is available in versions for all Windows systems between Windows 95 and 11. The current version of AmigaDX is available in 32-bit and 64-bit versions.

First download Total Commander (download: www.ghisler.com) and install it. Start Total Commander, open the settings via the menu *Configuration > Options*. In the settings window, switch to the *Plugins* section and click the top *Download* button. A Total Commander plug-in website will open in your system's web browser, which contains the *AmigaDX* entry. Download it by clicking on the green arrow. Alternatively, you can obtain the plug-in directly from the developer's website, in either 32-bit or 64-bit version (download: www.coderbug.rs/projects/amigadx).

Switch back to Total Commander and navigate to the directory in which you saved the downloaded plug-in. On Windows systems, this is typically the *Download* folder in the user directory. Double-click on the AmigaDX archive. Total Commander installs AmigaDX after your confirmation and links the file formats ADF, DMS, HDF and ADZ if desired. From now on, you can open these formats in Total Commander and edit them at file level.

Additional information on the ADF format, which AmigaOS has supported natively since version 3.2, can be found in section 2.11 on *ADF*.

Via IDE/SCSI adapters for CF/SD cards

If your Amiga is equipped with an IDE or SCSI controller, it may be possible to install a CF2IDE, SD2IDE or SCSI2SD adapter instead of a hard disk. With these adapters, CompactFlash, SecureDigital or microSD memory cards, respectively, can be set up and used like hard drives (see section 7.5 on *hardware expansions*). These memory card can be easily removed and accessed on a PC with a suitable card reader. There are even adapters that route the IDE interface outside the Amiga and make the memory cards easily accessible from the outside. This means the case does not have to be opened if the memory card needs to be changed.

The issue with this type of data exchange is that Windows PCs do not directly support the Amiga file system FFS. Therefore you need to install an emulation environment such as WinUAE to address the card as a drive and access the data. In section 1.3 you can learn more about the installation and use of WinUAE.

Via PCMCIA adapters for CF cards

A PCMCIA slot, which is required for this transfer method, is only available in the Amiga 600 and 1200 models. In addition, you will need a CompactFlash-to-PCMCIA adapter of type 1, or CF2PCMCIA for short. Type 2 variants are too thick for the PCMCIA slot in the Amiga. However, not all PCMCIA type 1 adapters and CF cards are compatible with the Amiga. For this reason, ensure you obtain these two items from an Amiga retailer you trust. This will ensure they have been tested on an Amiga and will work there. On the PC side, a CF card reader connected via USB is all you need for exchanging data.

This method allows the CF card to be used via the Amiga's PCMCIA port. You still need the driver for the CF card adapter. Download *cfd,* the device driver package for the PCMCIA adapter, from Aminet (download: www.aminet.net/package/driver/media/CFD133).

Some work is now required, but it will pay off in the end. Open the CFD LhA archive and unpack the contents onto the RAM Disk (for example). There are three files in the *RAM:CFD133/Devs* directory. Move the *compactflash.device* file to the *SYS:Devs* directory, then move the files *CF0* and *CF0.info to* the *SYS:Devs/DOSDrivers* directory. Rename *CF0* to *CFC* and *CF0.info* to *CFC.info*.

Open the *CFC* file with a text editor such as *TextEdit*. You need to make two important changes to the *FileSystem* and *DosType* lines. First, assign the specification `L:CrossDOSFileSystem` instead of `l:fat95` for *FileSystem*. Second, replace value `0x46415401` with `0x4D534800` for *DosType*. The two lines should look like this after the change:

```
FileSystem = L:CrossDOSFileSystem
DosType = 0x4D534800
```

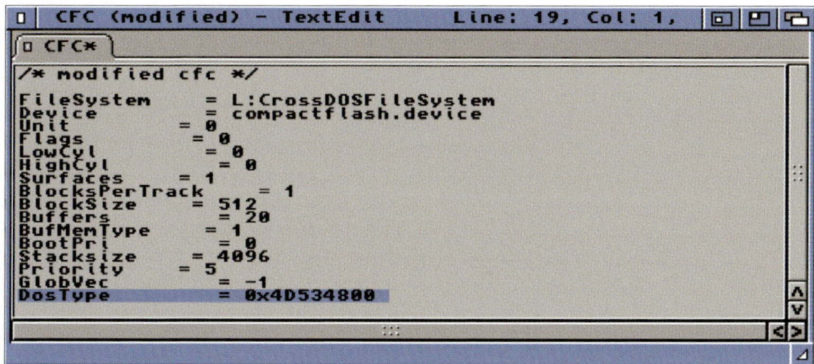

When modifiying the CFC file simply pay attention to the DosType value and FileSystem entry.

DosType0x4D534800is the DosType for a drive with a partition table. The second C in the name CFC defines the first partition on the drive. If there is a second partition on the drive, you would have to create a copy of *CFC* and *CFC.info* and name this *CFD* and *CFD.info* (and consecutively for further partitions, i.e. CFE, CFF, plus matching info files, etc).

Format the memory card in Windows using the FAT file system: insert the card into the card reader on the PC, right-click on the CF medium in Windows Explorer, select *Format* from the menu, choose the *FAT32* file system (alternatively FAT) in the format window and start formatting the card.

Once all these steps have been completed, a new drive icon should appear when the Amiga is booted up if a CF card is inserted into the CF2PCMCIA adapter. You have full read and write access to this drive and can easily exchange data between the two systems.

Please note, however, that you should never remove the card or the PCMCIA adapter while accessing the CF card, as there is a risk of losing data.

Via null modem cable

A simple way to communicate between the Amiga and PC is via serial port with a so-called null modem cable. However, this method has two big drawbacks: first, data transfer is very slow; and second, a serial port or USB-to-serial adapter is required on the PC, which is rare nowadays. Additionally, you must purchase a special null modem cable, which has a 25-pin D-sub socket at the end for the Amiga and a 9-pin D-sub socket for the PC. You can obtain the cable from any well-stocked Amiga retailer.

If you just want to exchange ADF files, you need the *Transdisk* software on the Amiga side. This is available on its own and is also distributed with the WinUAE emulator (download: www.stoeggl.com/amiga/index_de.html#soft or www.winuae.net/download/). On the Windows side, the *ADF-Sender* tool is needed (download: www.stoeggl.com/amiga/index_de.html#soft). Once the cable is connected, start these programs on the PC and the Amiga and you will be able to transfer ADF files.

If you want to transfer any kind of data – not just ADFs – between an Amiga and a PC, then Cloanto's specialist network software, *Amiga Explorer*, is the right solution for you. This is available independently and as part of the *Amiga Forever* software package. Amiga Explorer is commercial software, but a

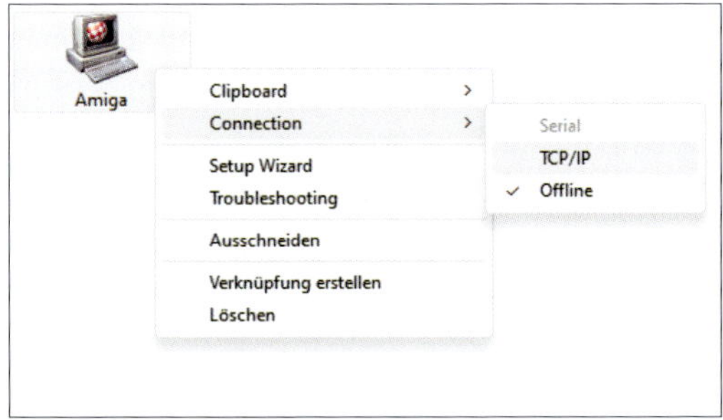

Amiga Explorer integrates the Amiga into the Windows network environment.

version of the program with some feature limitations can be obtained free of charge. Download your copy of Amiga Explorer (download: https://cdn.cloanto.com/pub/amigaforever/aesetup.exe or www.amigaforever.com/ae/) and install the software on your Windows PC. Connect the null modem cable to both computers and start them up. On the PC, you will see the *Amiga Explorer* icon on the desktop. Right-click on the icon and select *Properties* from the context menu. In the settings window, set the connection to *Serial*. You must also adjust the baud rates of the PC and Amiga. The decisive factor is how fast the serial interface in the Amiga works. On the A500 and A600, for example, a maximum of 57,600 baud is possible, on the A1200 or A4000 a full 115,200 baud can be reached. Experiment with the baud rate to see at which setting the transfer still works reliably. On the Amiga side, you can determine the baud rate in the *Serial* prefs (see section 3.15); on the PC side, this task can be done in the settings of Amiga Explorer. After changing the connection status in Amiga Explorer from *offline* to *serial*, you can use *Windows Explorer* to access all Amiga drives and even the Amiga's Kickstart ROM in a dedicated Amiga network area.

Via FTP network

The *File Transfer Protocol* (*FTP*), is a convenient way to transfer files between a server computer and a client computer on a local or global network. In order to transfer data via FTP, the Amiga must be made network-compatible with an ethernet card and a TCP/IP stack (see section 7.1 on *Internet*). In addition, an FTP client or server is required on the Amiga or PC. Put simply, an FTP client is an application that enables files to be uploaded to and downloaded from an FTP server, while the FTP server is the platform that stores these files and manages access to them. If the client is installed on the Amiga, then a server must be running on the PC (or vice versa).

On the Amiga, we recommend *AmiFTP* as the chosen client (www.aminet.net/package/comm/tcp/AmiFTP) and *rc-ftpd* as the chosen server (www.aminet.net/package/comm/tcp/rc-ftpd). On Windows, we recommend *FileZilla*, an all-in-one FTP solution with server and client functionality (www.filezilla-project.org).

First, install the FTP server on the PC or Amiga and set up the sharing of files or entire directories that you would like to use for the data exchange. Create a user with a login and password. When you start the server, an IP address is generated that identifies the server in the local network.

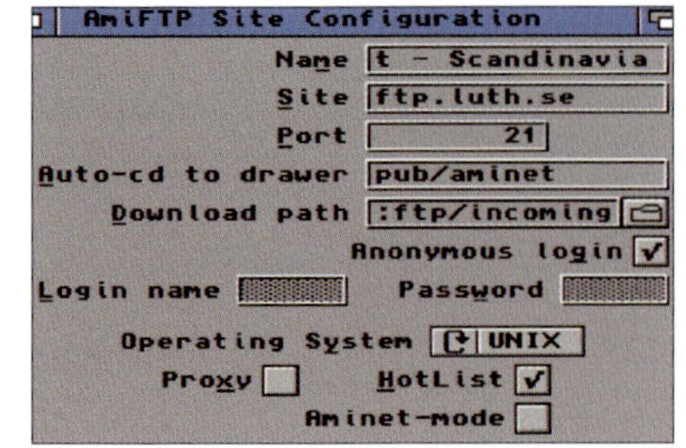

With little effort, AmiFTP allows you to connect to remote and local FTP servers.

In the newly installed client, create a new connection with the IP address of the server, the port (default is 21), and the login and password of the previously created user. You should now be able to connect to the server and copy the data in both directions using the FTP client's file manager.

Via Samba (SMB) network

The most convenient way to exchange data between an Amiga and a PC is arguably via the Samba network, which is based on the *Server Message Block Protocol* (*SMB*). SMB comes with Windows by default, so software only needs to be installed on a network-capable Amiga: namely, a TCP/IP stack for access to the network (see section 7.1 on *Internet*), and a suitable Samba client for access to the SMB server.

The Amiga client is a Shell program that is controlled via commands with parameters. It is more convenient to use it with a graphical user interface (GUI). You can use *smbfs* as a client on the Amiga (download: www.aminet.net/package/comm/tcp/smbfs-68k), with the matching GUI *SMBMounter* (download: www.aminet.net/package/comm/net/SMBMounter).

Samba on the Amiga using the smfbs client with the SMBMounter GUI

Before the client can be used, some setup is required. First, copy *smbfs* to any directory. Then, add the following line (with the correct path) to your *user-startup sequence* using TextEdit (see also section 6.2 on *user startup*):

```
Assign >NIL SAMBA: <path-to-smbfs-directory>
```

Restart your Amiga and install *SMBMounter* using its own installer. After successful installation, open SMBMounter and create a new connection. Click on *New* and the connection type *SMB*. Fill in all the fields in the requester:

SMB field	Contents
Name	name of the new connection, e.g. "PC connection"
Workgroup	name of the workgroup of the network, e.g. "workgroup"
Hostname	server name of the PC (without the share name)
Service	name of the share
Username	user name with which the share is accessed
Password	password for the user
Volume	name of the Samba drive as it should appear on the Amiga

When you are finished, confirm your entries by clicking *OK* and save the shares via the *Save all Mounts* menu item in the *Project* menu. Then select the newly created connection and click on the *Mount* button. The share you have just set up should appear as a drive icon on the Workbench. You can now use this network drive to read and write data of all kinds.

New hardware for the Amiga

Whether you need more speed, more memory or better graphics, there are a variety of expansions you can use to upgrade your Amiga. Find out about the most important accessories here.

The Amiga gained its popularity not only because of its operating system, which has now been updated to version 3.2, but also its special hardware, which set new standards at the time of its launch. It impressed not only with its high level of efficiency, but also its great expandability. This means that even after 25, 30 or more years, the computer can be easily customized to suit individual requirements.

Model variety

Before upgrading your Amiga, you need to ask yourself two simple questions. First, what application or software is the upgrade needed for? Usually the immediate need determines the upgrade, whether it is more memory, faster system speed, a modern data connection or better graphics performance. Second, which Amiga model is the expansion for? This dictates the type of connection for the expansion. The classic Amiga is available in three generations and a number of different models. It is important to know whether the expansion is to be used in an OCS, ECS or AGA generation model, and whether it is installed in a keyboard case or a big box case. Your motherboard revision and whether you already have any expansions installed can also play a role when choosing what to buy. Larger Amiga models offer plenty of room in spacious desktop or tower cases, and have additional expansion slots such as Zorro II or III, but no PCMCIA slot, which is reserved for the keyboard Amigas 600 and 1200.

On the page opposite you will find a list of Amiga models with accompanying chipset and case information. The latter refers to that which was originally provided from the factory by Commodore or Escom, not to any later modifications. As the A1000, CDTV and CD32 have limited expansion potential due to the size of their cases, these models will only be mentioned in passing in the following sections.

Model	Case	Chipset
Amiga 1000	desktop	OCS
Amiga 500	keyboard	OCS
Amiga 2000	desktop	OCS/ECS
CDTV	hifi	OCS
Amiga 500+	keyboard	ECS
Amiga 600	keyboard	ECS
Amiga 3000D	desktop	ECS
Amiga 3000T	tower	ECS
Amiga 1200	keyboard	AGA
Amiga 4000D	desktop	AGA
Amiga 4000T	tower	AGA
CD32	console	AGA

Memory expansion cards

Additional memory improves performance and multitasking in general, particularly when using multiple programs and processing large files.

Memory expansion cards enhance the Amiga with additional Chip or Fast RAM (see info box). Although there is no extra processor on board to boost processing power, the system is noticeably faster with a memory expansion card installed. This is because the software has more and faster memory at its disposal, and is therefore able to work faster. Most memory expansions cards increase the Fast RAM, as the Amiga can utilize a maximum of 2 MB Chip RAM. OCS and ECS Amigas have 512 KB or 1 MB Chip RAM and can be expanded with Chip RAM up to 2 MB. AGA Amigas, on the other hand, can only be expanded with Fast RAM, as they are already equipped with 2 MB Chip RAM out of the factory.

INFO **Chip RAM and Fast RAM**
Chip RAM memory can be accessed by the main processor and Amiga chipsets. As these accesses have to be synchronized, the data throughput is slower with Chip RAM than with Fast RAM. Fast RAM memory

can be accessed by the processor independently of the custom chips and is correspondingly faster. However, Fast RAM extensions can also relieve Chip RAM-hungry software that make intensive use of the Amiga chipsets.

Depending on the type, memory expansion cards can be installed in various places in the Amiga. Some models can be accommodated in the expansion port, others are given a piggy back in the processor socket or placed there as an intermediate layer, while a few are plugged into the Zorro II/III slot. Depending on the connection type, there are advantages and disadvantages, which are listed below.

Since AmigaOS 3.2 requires at least 2 MB RAM, we will not cover any memory expansion cards that equip the Amiga with less than 2 MB.

The A2048 memory expansion from iComp

Memory expansion cards for Amiga 500, 2000 and CDTV

The most popular expansion for the Amiga 500 was and still is the 512 KB memory expansion. As mentioned, this is not sufficient to use AmigaOS 3.2.

The *A2048* memory expansion from iComp is a 2 MB Chip RAM expansion for the A500 revision 8a or the A500+. The A500 revision 8a requires minor soldering work on the board, while the A500+ does not. In addition, the A2048 offers a clock port for an RTC module (battery-backed real-time clock).

The *Amiga 500 2 MB Chip RAM Module* from *Lotharek* is also a 2 MB Chip RAM expansion for the Amiga 500 in revision 8a. However, more extensive soldering work is required, which is why it is only recommended for users with soldering experience.

The *ACE2b* expansion from iComp is a 2 MB Chip RAM card for the Amiga 500 and 2000, and the CDTV. All A500 models up to revision 7, A2000 starting from revision 4.1 and the CDTV can be expanded with this card. The compatibility of the card and its ease of installation make this a good choice.

The *ZRAM 8* card from *IrixLabs* is specially developed for the Amiga 2000. However, it can also be used in other Zorro II Amigas. It offers up to 8 MB Fast RAM. As its memory is accessed via the slow Zorro II bus, the data throughput is considerably slower than with cards located directly on the processor bus.

Memory expansion cards for Amiga 600

The Amiga 600 has become increasingly popular in recent years due to its small size factor. Expansions for this model are correspondingly numerous, especially in the area of memory. When the Amiga 600 launched, there was a great deal of anger that Commodore had only equipped the computer with 1 MB of Chip RAM and had completely dispensed with Fast RAM. Chip RAM expansions can only be installed in the expansion slot in the bottom trapdoor. Fast RAM expansions, on the other hand, can only be installed on the processor via a PLCC socket.

The *PiggyBackNot v2* from *Archi-Tech* is a 1 MB Chip RAM card for the A600. It also features a socket for a battery-backed real-time clock, an expansion socket for the Indivision ECS, three clock ports and a battery holder for the clock.

The *eX601n* from *Lotharek* is almost identical to the PiggyBackNot v2, but only offers two clock ports.

The *A604n* from *iComp* is very similar to the previous cards. However, two aspects differentiate this model: the FastClockPort and the separate riser card slot. The fast clock port offers up to 60 per cent more performance, and the riser card slot means that the Subway USB card can be connected without a cable.

The *A6095* from *Archi-Tech* is a Fast RAM expansion for the A600 with up to 9.5 MB capacity – up to 8 MB can be used as Fast RAM, and 1.5 MB as Slow RAM. In the event of incompatibility, the Slow RAM can be used with the Fast RAM.

The *Wicher 608* from *7-Bit* is similar to the A6095, but offers a full 11 MB of Fast RAM and a MapRom function. The card is controlled with the supplied *WicherCfg* software.

The *A608mini* is the smallest Fast RAM memory expansion card for the A600 and offers up to 8 MB Fast RAM. It does have a PCMCIA-friendly mode, but in that case can only offer 4 MB of Fast RAM.

Memory expansion cards for Amiga 1200

The Amiga 1200 has remained one of the most popular Amiga models since it was introduced in 1992/93 and has a full 2 MB of Chip RAM as standard. Nevertheless, memory expansion cards were and still are popular, because Fast RAM was not available in the standard version. As a result, numerous expansion memory cards have come out since its release, with new developments still happening today. Memory expansions are installed in the processor expansion port of the Amiga 1200 in the bottom trapdoor, thus blocking the space for a turbo card. Due to their low price, they are nevertheless of interest to some users.

The *A1208* with 8 MB Fast Ram from *Archi-Tech* is a standard memory expansion card for the A1200 and is suitable for fans of pure AGA games. According to the Polish manufacturer, it can reach up to 2.92 MIPS.

The *Ex1T 11 MB* memory expansion from *Archi-Tech* adds up to 11 MB of Fast RAM as well as a socket for a battery-buffered real-time clock and a suitable battery compartment. PCMCIA compatibility is also provided if the memory is limited to 5.5 MB. With this additional Fast RAM, the Amiga 1200 performs noticeably faster.

The *Wicher 1211* expansion card from *7-Bit* equips the A1200 with 11 MB of Fast RAM like the Ex1T, but also offers an "onboard" SPI controller in addition to a MapRom and BootRom function. The SPI controller can be used to operate all kinds of additional expansions on the Amiga's fast processor bus, such as a network card or a microSD adapter for exchanging data.

The *ACA1211* expansion card from *iComp* offers 11.2 MB of memory and is especially compatible with PCMCIA cards. A special feature of this card is the *IDESpeeder*, which accelerates read access from the IDE port. It also offers a MapRom function and two clock ports. The second clock port can be used as a fast clock port.

Memory expansion cards for the CD32

Although it was designed as a games console, Commodore equipped the CD32 with an expansion interface, the so-called expansion port. Multifunctional expansions like the SX32/SX64 have been around for a while, but always command high prices.

Memory-only expansion cards were in short supply until two came along at once a few years ago. All modern expansions for the CD32 require what is known as a riser board for the expansions to be plugged into. Always check the compatibility of the expansion you are buying.

The *Wicher CD32* is a *7-bit* memory expansion that can be equipped with up to 11.5 MB Fast RAM via SIMM72 modules. It also features an IDE 2.5" hard drive connection and clock port. The product has been specially developed for gamers who want a basic Fast RAM expansion in conjunction with an IDE hard disk controller for the CD32.

The *Terrible Fire 328* is a memory card with 8 MB Fast RAM from *Steven Leary*. It also has a 2.5" IDE port for hard drives or CompactFlash cards from which it can be booted. It is cheaper than the Wicher and, unlike the competition, easy to obtain.

Memory expansion cards for Amiga 2000, 3000 and 4000

In the early days, there were no memory cards for Zorro Amigas like the Amiga 2000, Amiga 3000 and Amiga 4000. These computers were designed by Commodore's engineers to be high-end machines, either with high performance out of the box or with an accelerator card installed. The powerful A3000 and A4000 even came with a dedicated accelerator expansion port. However, most accelerator cards did not feature more than 128 MB of memory, so the Zorro slot was also used as a memory supply station. Zorro III delivers significantly better transfer rates than the Zorro II bus, though no miracles should be expected from Zorro III solutions either. As a result, you should always use the memory on an accelerator card where possible in order to achieve high throughput rates.

The *ZRAM 8* from *IrixLabs* is a Zorro II-compatible 16-bit 8 MB Fast RAM memory expansion that was specially developed for the Amiga 2000, though it can also be used with other Zorro II Amigas. The card features a jumper that lets the user configure it for 2, 4 or 8 MB of Fast RAM. This makes it possible to share the address space with other expansion cards that are mapped in the primary AutoConfig area.

The *BigRamPlus 2019 Edition 256 MB* was developed by *iComp* and runs exclusively in Zorro III Amigas. The card utilizes the full speed of the Zorro III and even offers 256 MB.

The *ZorRAM 128 MB* card was developed by *Amigakit*. Like the BigRamPlus, it only works in Zorro III Amigas. The additional 128 MB RAM can be used as Fast RAM.

Turbo cards (accelerator boards)

This is where real acceleration comes in: turbo cards give Amigas a genuine performance boost thanks to the use of enhanced and optimized processors from the Motorola 680x0 series.

Turbo – or accelerator – cards do more than just add memory to the Amiga, like the previously mentioned memory expansion cards. Instead, they feature a fast processor for additional computing power, along with additional onboard components, such as a fast IDE/SCSI interface or a CompactFlash connector. Some turbo cards even have a USB interface and their own graphics card or graphics output.

Turbo cards come in many different types and from a broad range of manufacturers: from the low-end to the super high-end, the market offers everything your heart desires. Only the Amiga 3000 and Amiga 4000 are currently being neglected: there is exactly one card available for these models currently. You may need to keep an eye on the solid second-hand market.

The low-end Amiga accelerator cards start with overclocked 68000 processors and end with high-clocked 68020 CPUs. The mid-range segment is represented by 68030 turbo cards from 25 to 50 MHz. The high-end segment is occupied by 68040 CPUs from 25 to 40 MHz and 68060 CPUs from 50 to 60 MHz. The super high-end range is made up of very modern accelerator cards with FPGA technology. These include Apollo Computer's accelerator cards (Vampire, Icedrake, etc.) and 68k emulation on the Raspberry Pi via PiStorm.

Turbo cards for Amiga 500 and 2000

Most of the original Amigas were equipped with a 512 KB memory expansion, while turbo cards were in short supply and rarely demanded by A500 owners. The Amiga 2000 was different, as it was designed as an upgradeable high-end first generation machine. In recent years, the trend for both the A500 and A2000 has been to increase performance. As a result, there are a number of attractive turbo cards on the market for both models, some of which are even compatible with each other.

The *Wicher 520EC* turbo card from *7-Bit* is compatible with the Amiga 500 and 500+ with a 68EC020 processor clocked at 25 MHz (up to 33 MHz is possible via overclocking), 11 MB Fast RAM

Turbo card BFG9060 from Matthias Heinrichs

(via fast SDRAM memory) and a 2.5" IDE port. The card's special feature is an SPI bus board with a network module and a microSD card slot that can be controlled with the supplied drivers.

The *Classic 520* from *Irix Labs* is the successor to the popular *HC 508 turbo card* for the Amiga 500/1000 and features a 68EC020 CPU with 28 MHz. With this, the card achieves speeds of 10 times a standard A500. But there is more: it has a 40-pin IDE connection and ports for CF and SD cards. 8 MB Fast RAM and 512 KB for a Kickstart round off the 520.

The *Terrible Fire 536* is a powerful turbo card for the A500/ A500+ or A2000. It offers a fully fledged Motorola 68030 processor (including MMU) with a 50 MHz clock rate and 64 MB RAM, as well as a 2.5" 44-pin IDE connector for hard disks and CF adapters. With a suitable CPU relocator adapter, this card is a perfect fit for the Amiga 500 and 2000.

The *ACA 500* from *iComp* is a special card in its class. At first glance the card looks weak: a 68EC000 processor with a 14 MHz clock speed and 2 MB RAM for the Amiga 500 is only twice the clock speed and four times the memory of the Amiga 500. But what really makes the ACA 500 stand out are its two bootable Compact Flash slots and, above all, its expansion slot. So if you own a 1220 or 1231/32 series accelerator card for the A1200, you can also plug it into the expansion port and get the full performance of that card.

The *Vampire v2 500* from *Apollo Computer* is a high-end turbo card with 128 MB RAM for the Amiga 500. The heart of the Vampire is an FPGA – simply put, a chip with a programmed integrated circuit – which is modeled on a 68k processor. According to measurements, this so-called 68080 is three to four times faster than the fastest 68060 ever released. The system also contains a graphics core known as SAGA, which enables the Amiga to display 24/32-bit true color resolutions and display them on a flat screen monitor via a digital HDMI output.

The *Apollo V4 Firebird* turbo card is related to the *Vampire 500* and also comes from *Apollo Computer*. Compared to the previous Vampire card, the performance of the V4 is significantly improved. The Firebird has 512 MB of Fast RAM, and a new FPGA chip enabling higher speeds. The card also has RTG graphics, two Fast IDE ports, USB for input devices, 100 Mbit network port and digital audio. Interestingly, the Amiga signal is looped through the card's HDMI port. This means that a Scandoubler is no longer needed when using this turbo card.

The *PiStorm 500* is actually just an adapter for the *Raspberry Pi* minicomputer, but together they become a super high-end turbo card. Acceleration is achieved by hardware emulation of the 68k processor. Multiple 68060 speeds are achieved. In addition, the microSD card can be accessed extremely quickly, making is useful as a fast hard drive replacement. The *PiStorm 500* can act as an RTG graphics card if required. Depending on which RaspberryPi is used, the PiStorm adds 0.5 to 1.9 GB extra Amiga Fast RAM. Since early 2024, any Amiga with the PiStorm solution also gives a fast network connection through WiFi.

Turbo cards for Amiga 600

The tiny Amiga 600 has become increasingly popular in recent years. This is more due to its compact size than its performance, which left a lot to be desired when it was launched. This shortcoming can be remedied with a turbo card.

The *xT 28 Mhz 11 MB* from *Archi-Tech is* one of the smallest turbo cards for the Amiga 600 and offers a MC68SEC000AA20 CPU with a 28 MHz clock rate and 11 MB RAM. This puts it in the lower end of performance, but it is cheap and good enough for fans of old games.

The *Furia* by *Lotharek* is an already legendary turbo card for the 600. It is priced in the mid-range and comes with a 68EC020 CPU running at 25 MHz, 9.5 MB RAM and a MapRom function. Due to the heat generated by the processor, it can only be used with a large heatsink or being active cooled by a fan.

The *A630* from *Archi-Tech* is a high-end turbo card for the Amiga 600 with 68030 processor (50 MHz clock, inc. MMU) and 64 MB or 128 MB Fast RAM memory. This makes it ideal for performance-hungry games, scene demos or applications on the 600. In the recently released revision 3, it also has a 68882 FPU.

The *PiStorm 600* is similar to the aforementioned *PiStorm 500*, except it was designed for use in the Amiga 600. The data and performance of the two models are similar.

The *Vampire v2 600* is very similar to the *Vampire v2 500*, albeit for the Amiga 600.

The *Apollo V4 Manticore* turbo card from *Apollo* Computer is similar to the *Apollo V4 Firebird* for the A500. The performance achieved is comparable.

Turbo cards for Amiga 1200

The Amiga 1200 was a milestone in the history of Commodore and the successor to the A500 and A600. Users could still be reasonably satisfied with its performance on launch, but just a few years later that performance was no longer up to date, leading to the first accelerator cards appearing on the market. The turbo cards from phase5's *Blizzard* series are legendary, but they have unfortunately not been available as new products for a while now and sell at high prices on the second-hand market. Fortunately, new manufacturers have stepped in to fill the gap.

The *ACA1221lc* from *iComp* is a small but capable turbo card and, with a 68EC020 CPU at 26 MHz and 16 MB RAM, is located in the low-end range. Active cooling and a good power supply unit are required if you want to overclock it beyond 26 MHz. The card is notable for its *IDESpeeder* technology, which allows read access to the internal IDE port to be accelerated.

The *ACA1234* is a mid-range turbo card from *iComp* for more demanding users. It is available in a range of clock speeds up to 50MHz and boasts a full 128MB of RAM to keep you happy. The card also has a MapRom function, *IDESpeeder* technology, a local CF card slot and a fast clock port.

The *Terrible Fire 1230* is a low-cost accelerator card developed by *Stephen Leary* and produced by various manufacturers. It features a Motorola 68030 processor at 50 MHz clock speed, an MMU unit, 128 MB RAM and a 2.5" 44-pin IDE port for hard disks and CF adapters.

The *Terrible Fire 1260* is a high-end turbo card with 128 MB RAM and a fast IDE controller. It is available with a range of 68060 CPUs clocked at 50 MHz and can be overclocked. The 68LC060 offers the best price/performance ratio, but the card does not have an FPU unit. Most gamers should be fine with this, as hardly any Amiga games require the FPU. If you need the FPU for applications or more modern software rendered 3D games, you should go for the more expensive revision 6, which features a fully fledged 68060 CPU.

Like the other PiStorms already mentioned, the *PiStorm32 Lite* is just an adapter for a *Raspberry Pi 3/4* that offers high-end processor acceleration and other hardware enhancements. In addition to RTG graphics output and fast access to the microSD card, WiFi can now be used with all PiStorm models. The PiStorm32 Lite is currently the flagship of the PiStorm series and offers unbeatable value for money.

The *Vampire v2 1200* from *Apollo Computer* is a high-end turbo card for the Amiga 1200 that is similar to the *Vampire v2* for the A500/600. The 1200 Vampire features an FPGA with Apollo core, with 24/32bit true color and a digital output (HDMI). Due to the better architecture of the A1200, the speeds are higher than those of the A500/600 Vampire. It also has a fast IDE port and a network section. For the latter, an additional ENC28J60 standard ethernet module is required.

The *Icedrake* turbo card from *Apollo Computer* is essentially a variant of the *Apollo V4 Firebird* for the Amiga 1200. The performance is higher than the A500/A600 version because this is a 32-bit system. The rest of the specifications are identical.

Turbo cards for Amiga 3000 and 4000

The “big” Amigas, as the A3000 and A4000 were always called, were Commodore's flagships. They were characterized not only by their performance, but also their expandability. For this reason, several manufacturers had turbo cards ready from a very early stage that were exclusively in the high price range and were the dream of many Amiga users. In fact, the prices for used Amiga 3000 and 4000 models are even higher today than they were at launch. As such, due to lower market penetration, there has been hardly any new hardware released for these systems.

The *BFG9060* from Matthias Heinrichs is the only new turbo card for the A3000 and A4000. This high-end card comes with fast 128 MB DMA Fast RAM and either a slightly slimmed-down 68LC060 or a fully fledged 68060 processor (50 MHz). Thanks to its modern architecture, the BFG also beats the popular CyberStorm from phase5, which is very rare on the second-hand market and can attract particular attention with its high memory throughput.

Turbo cards for the CD32

As mentioned, initially only multifunctional expansions were available for the CD32, as the device was designed to be a games console, not a fully fledged computer. However, an interesting turbo card for CD32 owners has been released that takes the console into new spheres: the *Terrible Fire 330* by *Steven Leary* – now the de facto accelerator board for the CD32. The card is available with 64 MB or 128 MB RAM and has a fully fledged 68030 processor at 50 MHz. In addition, a fast IDE controller for 2.5" hard disks or CF/SD cards is on board.

Scandoubler

CRT monitors have long been a thing of the past. The best way to connect your Amiga to a modern flat panel display is to use a scandoubler.

Amigas used to be connected to a television or RGB monitor with a horizontal frequency of 15 kHz and a vertical frequency of 50 Hz via the 23-pin video-out interface. The S-Video/Composite output was popular with users of AGA Amigas for this purpose. As many CRT monitors have since passed away, the Amiga video signal is now often output to flat screens. This requires a so-called flickerfixer/scandoubler, which allows the Amiga to display an image on modern TFT monitors or LED TVs using the internal graphics chipset. There is one exception: modern monitors or projectors equipped with a converter and their own S-Video/Composite or SCART input. With a scandoubler, the horizontal frequency can be doubled to 31.5 kHz and the vertical frequency can be raised to 60 Hz. With these values, the Amiga can be operated on VGA monitors as well as modern flat screens.

A flickerfixer also enables interlaced modes, e.g. hires interlaced, to be displayed without flickering. This feature was only useful for VGA monitors and is no longer necessary for TFT screens. As a result, only plain scandoublers are still available today.

Using the Amiga with a modern monitor is also possible at high resolutions with a graphics card. But even still, a scandoubler is often useful or even necessary. All Guru Meditation error messages, the boot menu and most games are output exclusively via the RGB output of the Amiga and not the graphics card port. Only a few solutions loop the signal from the Amiga through the graphics card so that no scandoubler is required (see the section on *graphics cards* from page 428).

Scandoublers (internal) for Amiga 500, 600, 2000 and 3000

The *Indivision ECS* from *iComp* is a scandoubler/flickerfixer veteran. It is already in its third generation (V3) for OCS and ECS Amigas, and a new version (V4) is already on its way. It is installed internally and converts the Amiga's signals into a VGA signal at 60 Hz or higher. If required, the frequency can be limited to 50 Hz for older monitors. In addition, the SuperHiRes resolutions of the ECS chipset can be used in full resolution. Last but not least, this Indivision also contains a Graffiti emulation function that allows to display 256 colors from 4096 simultaneously without the image being distorted by HAM artifacts. Note that its operation on an Amiga 600 requires one of the A603, A604 or A604n memory expansions, and modifications must be made to certain revisions of the A2000, 3000, 3000T and 1000.

The *ScanPlus ECS* from *IrixLabs* is a scandoubler for the Amiga 500 and 2000. This internal expansion supports so-called DPMS energy saving for PAL and NTSC screen modes via the OCS and ECS chipset and outputs the analogue signal at 60 Hz via a VGA port.

With the *RGB2HDMI* adapter, which is offered by various manufacturers in different versions, the RGB video signal can be converted into a digital HDMI signal on an Amiga 500 and 600 in conjunction with a *Raspberry Pi Zero* (1.2W). You will need the RGB2HDMI installed software on your Raspberry Pi and, depending on your model, either an HDMI cable or an additional mini to HDMI adapter.

The ScanPlus ECS scandoubler from IrixLabs

Scandoublers (internal) for Amiga 1200 and 4000

Like the *Indivision ECS*, the *Indivision AGA* is already in its third generation (MK3), but this version can only be used with AGA computers. It is the only internal scandoubler/flickerfixer equipped with an HDMI connector, allowing it to be plugged directly into modern televisions and monitors. The picture quality and adjustment options of the Indivision AGA MK3 are second to none, and it is currently the best solution for modern video output on the Amiga.

The *ScanPlus AGA* from *IrixLabs* is a scandoubler for the A1200 and A4000D. Like its brother, the ScanPlus ECS, it supports DPMS energy-saving PAL and NTSC modes. A variety of screen modes can be used via the VGA output: Multiscan, PAL, NTSC, DoublePAL, DoubleNTSC, Euro36, Euro72 and Super72.

External scan-doublers for any Amiga

The *D520* is an external video converter from *Schubert Hardware* that connects directly to the 23-pin connector of the Amiga. This makes it compatible with practically all Amiga moels. It converts the analogue Amiga video signal, whether PAL or NTSC, into a digital signal and outputs it via HDMI. In progressive video modes the D520 works as a scandoubler, and in interlace video modes as a flickerfixer. As a result, it achieves a very high picture quality and can be operated on TFTs, modern TVs and projectors without any problems. Right now, the D520 is sold out most of the time. Alinea Computer is due to produce a new batch of products that are expected to be available from autumn 2024.

The *Medusa* from *Lotharek* is an external scandoubler designed for retro computer systems in general, not just the Amiga. It comes in a high-quality metal case and supports RGB, RGBHS, Composite, S-Video, SCART, DB9 or VGA video inputs. DVI (analogue/digital) is available as a video output, which can output via HDMI with a DVI-to-HDMI adapter. The Medusa is compatible with PAL and NTSC and can play back some Super, Euro and DBL resolutions on the Amiga.

SCART/AV2HDMI converters connect devices with AV (CVBS) Composite video or SCART and R/L stereo audio to an HDMI screen. The A1200 and A600 only came with a Composite video connection, which is why all other Amiga models have to make do with the SCART2HDMI part. However, SCART/AV2HDMI converters are not suitable for demanding users as they cannot match the quality of a true scandoubler. They should be seen instead as an emergency solution if the Amiga is rarely used or several computers are in alternating use.

Graphics cards

A graphics card improves the system's graphics performance and allows higher resolutions to be used on the Workbench and other software.

At the time of launch, each Amiga model was renowned for its powerful graphics, and yet, relatively quickly, additional graphics cards were made for the Zorro Amiga, which were – and still are – often used in heavy-duty work situations. Games typically only ran on the internal chipset, but the Workbench and many programs benefited from graphics cards and related drivers. The Workbench and important graphics and video applications, 3D renderers, word processors or spreadsheet tools could be run in high resolution and in up to 24-bit color depth using a graphics card. Initially, proprietary drivers were required until two independent RTG (ReTargetable Graphics) standards, *CyberGraphX* and *Picasso96*, were established.

Picasso96 is still in use today. Its development is commercially driven by the license from iComp and today runs under the name *P96*. If you want to use the current drivers in version 3.3.3, you can licence them for a few euros online at iComp via the link https://icomp.de/shop-icomp/en/shop/product/p96-rtg-software-not-logged-in.html. The older version 2.2 of the Picasso96 drivers can be found on Aminet at www.aminet.net/package/driver/video/Picasso96. However, we strongly recommend using P96 in the new, greatly expanded and bug-fixed version.

Graphics cards for Zorro II and III

From the *Picasso* to the *Retina* to the *CyberVision*, numerous graphics cards for Zorro II and III (Z2 and Z3 for short) came onto the market in the 1990s. They are still very popular, but are only available on the second-hand market. However, some new products that are also worth a look:

The *VA2000* is an FPGA-based graphics card for Z2 and Z3 Amigas (2000, 3000, 4000) that can output high resolutions (up to 1280×720 pixels) and 8-, 16- or 32-bit color depth via DVI-D. It offers a hacker-friendly expansion slot for upgrades and user-specific modifications, and has a slot for microSD cards. The card is open source and can be produced by anyone with the appropriate skills, but it is also sold regularly by Amiga retailers.

The *ZZ9000* from *MNT* (Lukas F. Hartmann) is a graphics card – specifically, a multifunction card – for Zorro II or III Amigas. The successor to the *VA2000 graphics card*, it offers the functionality of a flickerfixer/scandoubler, a coprocessor to reduce load during computing operations (e.g. decoding JPG, MP3 etc.), a graphics card with 1 GB DDR3 RAM, a network card and USB interfaces. In terms of graphics, the ZZ9000 can offer a maximum resolution of 1920×1080 pixels (FullHD) with 8-bit (256 color "chunky"), and 16-bit or 32-bit color depth. Its strengths really come into their own with the faster Zorro III.
If you are looking for a current graphics card for Zorro slots, the ZZ9000 is the one for you.

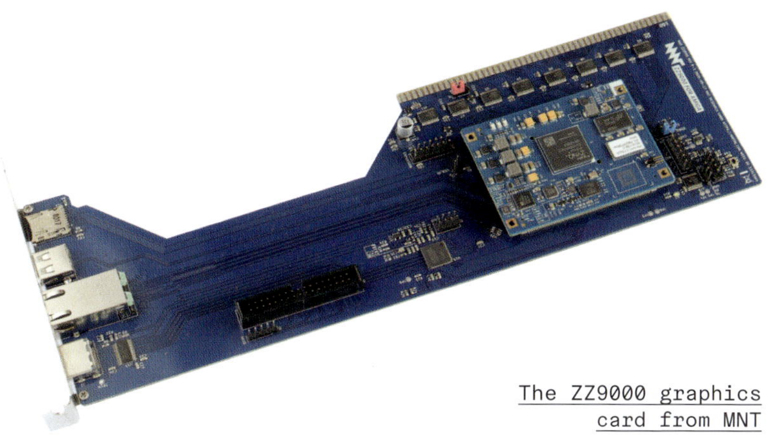

The ZZ9000 graphics card from MNT

Graphics cards for PCI boards

The different versions of the *Mediator* board from *Elbox* enable the Amiga to use popular PCI extensions from the PC world. New Mediator models are available for the A1200 in a tower, A3000D, A3000D in a tower, A4000D, A4000D in the tower and A4000T. All Mediator boards have varying numbers of PCI interfaces and some have additional Zorro interfaces. The big box Amiga variants usually have both types of ports and can be fitted with Zorro or PCI hardware as required. Drivers for all kinds of PCI solutions such as graphics cards or network cards are supplied by the manufacturer on a CD. Although many PCI cards are now only available second hand or from remaining stock, those who manage to get hold of one of these cards can raise the Amiga to a new level of performance. A range of Mediator PCI drivers are available for graphics cards: in addition to models from the powerful ATI *Radeon 9xxx* and 3dfx *Voodoo* series, graphics cards from S3 with *Virge* and *Trio chipsets* are also supported. The list at www.elbox.com/mediator_driver_guide.html shows all Mediator-compatible graphics cards.

Graphics cards in combination with turbo cards

The fastest and most modern solution for installing a graphics card into an Amiga is via a graphics card module integrated directly on a turbo card. This way, the graphics card and memory are connected directly to the processor bus, avoiding all technical bottlenecks. Detailed information on the accelerator cards listed here can be found in section 7.5.2.

The *Vampire 2* is a powerful turbo card for the Amiga 500, 600 and 1200. In addition to the 68k replica, an impressive graphics card component has been integrated into the FPGA part of the card. The Amiga can thus output up to 1280×720 pixel resolution in 60 Hz or FullHD (1920×1080) in 24 Hz via HDMI, each in 32-bit color depth. There is also integrated video acceleration. 3D support is still lacking, but the manufacturer says it's in the pipeline and will be added in future updates.

Firebird, *Icedrake* and *Manticore* are the latest turbo cards from *Apollo Computer*. Like the Vampire 2, they are based on their own SAGA system, but with more graphics card memory and higher performance available thanks to a faster FPGA. FullHD at high refresh rates in 32-bit color depth is no longer a problem. The graphics system also has a 3D unit with hardware texturing, Zbuffer and shading. The integrated flickerfixer/scandoubler loops the video signal of the Amiga directly through it.

The *PiStorm* is another high-performance accelerator card. In combination with a *Raspberry Pi 3* or *4*, graphics card output can be produced via the HDMI port. The *Picasso96* driver system is used with a special driver called *PiGfx*. The PiStorm an easoly achieve 24-bit true-color modes with FullHD resolution, but 3D and other acceleration modules are still missing.

Sound cards

The Amiga's Paula sound chip is legendary, but over the years, demand on the system's audio output has increased – sound cards can provide very good sound.

The audio quality of Paula was amazing, considering it was 8-bit sound. However, when MP3 became popular in the early 2000s, people wanted better quality and faster decoding. The first 16-bit sound cards for the Amiga, which connected via the Zorro interface or the clock port, came onto the market as early as the 1990s. Later, these cards were equipped with MPEG decoders and digital signal processors (DSP). At present, there is a very small selection of sound cards available for the Amiga.

Sound cards for Zorro II and III

Due to the empty market, used sound cards for Amigas with a Zorro interface are in high demand, especially the *Prelude*, *Toccata* or *Delfina*. The only new alternative is the *ZZ9000AX*: an optional sound module for the multifunctional *ZZ9000* expansion card (see details under *graphics cards*), which adds a high-quality sound unit with an ADAU1701 audio codec and a 28/56-bit DSP processor. The stereo output is 16-bit per channel at 48 kHz – equivalent to DAT quality – and the Paula audio signal can be mixed in and enhanced. Finally, the sound card has four RCA connectors for line inputs and outputs.

Sound cards for the clock port

Just like the Z2/Z3 sound cards, no new sound cards for the Amiga clock port are currently available. Recommended sound cards on the second-hand market are the *Delfina 1200*, *Delfina Flipper*, *Melody* and *Prelude*.

Sound card module AX for the ZZ9000 from MNT

Sound cards for PCI boards

Commercially available PCI sound cards based on either the 801 chip or the Soundblaster 128 can be used with the *Mediator* PCI boards mentioned in *the graphics card* section. A list of compatible sound cards can be found online at www.elbox.com/mediator_driver_guide.html.

Network cards

A network card or ethernet module is required to surf the internet – including Aminet – and for convenient data exchange in your own network.

Before the internet began its triumphal march, Amiga users were already visiting the legendary Bulletin Board Systems (BBS) with modems. As local networks became more popular, relevant connection solutions for the Amiga also came onto the market – initially only for the Zorro interface in large professional--use Amigas, but later also for private use. This was followed by products for the PCMCIA port of the Amiga 1200 and 600, as well as PCI cards for the Mediator PCI. In both cases, commercially available expansions, PCMCIA cards or PCI cards can be used with drivers.

Network cards for Zorro II and III

For Zorro Amigas, there is currently only one new solution available: the *X-Surf 100* from *iComp*, a 100 Mbit network card that can be operated on the Zorro II or III bus. It runs at full speed on the Zorro III, offering transfer rates of up to 1,600 KB/s. A TCP/IP stack and sufficient RAM is required.

Worth a mention is also the ZZ9000 (see graphics cards section). Additionally to its graphic part plus flicker fixer and more RAM (only with Zorro III), it features a modern Gigabit ethernet port.

Network cards for the PCMCIA port

The PCMCIA port of the Amiga 600 and 1200 offers an ideal interface for network cards that can be adapted from the PC. The network card needs to use a particular network chip that can be addressed by the existing drivers. One of these drivers is *cnet.device* (http://aminet.net/package/driver/net/cnetdevice), which supports most NE2000-compatible cards such as the

DFE-670TXD from *D-Link* or the FA410TX and FA411 from *NetGear*. There is also a driver called *3c589* (http://aminet.net/package/driver/net/3c589), which was developed for the integration of Etherlink III cards from *3Com*. The data throughput rate of these products is limited to 10 Mbit/s, which is good enough for fast and efficient data exchange.

The Wodem WiFi module from Alinea Computer

Network cards for the serial or parallel port

The *Wodem* from *Alinea Computer* connects the Amiga to a wireless network (WLAN) via the serial interface. It acts as a router that provides access to the internet using a TCP/IP stack. With a suitable turbo or interface card, transmission speeds of up to 115,200 bps are possible. Due to the limitations of the serial interface, the Amiga will not exactly go into a speed frenzy, but the data rate is sufficient for smaller downloads and for playing games over the internet.

The *Plipbox* is a network module based on the Arduino. This open source device connects to the internet using its own driver and TCP/IP stack. The advantage of the Plipbox over the Wodem is its higher speed, as the parallel interface achieves higher data rates. The disadvantage is that connection to a network is only possible via cable.

Network cards for PCI boards

Many commercially available PCI network cards based on the standard *RTL8139* chip can be plugged into *Mediator* PCI boards (see the *graphics cards* section in this chapter). For a list of compatible cards, see www.elbox.com/mediator_driver_guide.html.

USB cards

The Universal Serial Bus (USB) is the global technology standard for connecting computers and peripherals – the Amiga requires a USB card to use it.

Data sticks, hard drives, mice, gamepads, printers and many more – the majority of today's computer peripherals rely on the USB port. To make the Amiga compatible with USB, there are various USB expansion cards and drivers available for the Zorro interface, as a PCI card or for the clock port.

The Subway 2021 USB card

USB cards for Zorro II and III

The popular Highway and Deneb USB cards for Zorro Amigas were released in the early 2000s. They have not been available as new products for some time. The recent *Freeway Zorro* is the result of a hobby project by an Amiga user and is currently only available as a kit in an Amiga forum. It is compatible with the *Poseidon* driver system and fulfills all USB 1.1 and 2.0 specifications, including HiSpeed mode for high data throughput (for USB 2.0 devices). Up to three USB devices can be connected directly to the Freeway.

USB cards for the clock port

Amigas in keyboard cases can take advantage of the clock port to hook up a USB connector. This port is integrated as standard on the Amiga 1200, but must be retrofitted on the Amiga 600 and 500.

In addition to the Zorro version, the *Freeway* is also available in kit form for the clock port. Although this variant is somewhat slower than the Zorro model, it has similar specifications.

The *Subway 2021* from *Alinea Computer* is the modern successor to the popular *Subway USB* and provides up to four USB ports. It is compatible with the USB 1.1 and USB 2.0 specifications, but does not utilize HiSpeed mode. One shortcoming is the card's driver support, as the driver system used here is not *Poseidon*, but the newer *Anaiis*. New drivers for other USB devices are expected to be added over time.

USB cards for PCI boards

The *Spider II USB 2.0* is a modified PCI card for *Mediator* PCI boards, allowing the Amiga to be upgraded with up to four external and one internal USB interface. The Spider II has HiSpeed capability and, depending on the processor and IDE connection, can achieve almost full USB 2.0 speed.

CF and SD cards

CompactFlash (CF) and SecureDigital (SD) cards are reliable replacements for the noisy IDE and SCSI hard drives of yesteryear.

An IDE port comes as standard on the Amiga 4000, 1200 and 600 models, allowing for IDE devices of all classes. The two small Amigas rely on a 44-pin 2.5" connector, while the A4000 relies on a 40-pin 3.5" connector. There are very few new IDE devices on the market these days, but you can find some good alternatives that enable the use of modern storage media via the IDE port.

The CF-IDE adapter from amigaworld.de

CF-to-IDE solutions

Adapters that connect CompactFlash cards to the IDE interface have been around for many years, and cheap options from the Far East has flooded the market. Although Amigas are generally compatible with no-name adapters, compatibility, stability and mechanical problems often occur. This is why most Amiga retailers will offer higher-quality products tailored to the system.

One of the most well known and proven models is the buffered *CF-IDE adapter* from *amigaworld.de*. It was designed for the 44-pin 2.5" IDE port of the Amiga 600 and 1200, and provides a slot for a single CompactFlash hard drive replacement. It also loops through the IDE port to enable the connection of additional IDE devices. One special feature of this adapter is its buffering ability, which separates 24 IDE port signals from the rest of the system. This improves the signals and makes the system more stable compares with using CompactFlash adapters that are not optimized for the Amiga.

SD-to-IDE solutions

Like CF-to-IDE adapters, SD-to-IDE adapters have become a popular extension that can be used for replacing old hard drives with SD and microSD memory cards. Products are available for both 44-pin 2.5" and 40-pin 3.5" IDE interfaces. Various Chinese converters have proven to be reliable in this case. As the 2.5" versions are only supplied with a male connector, it is somewhat awkward to stow them in the Amiga case with an additional cable, especially as the connector must not touch any other part on the board. As such, IDE angle adapters with a female socket present a practical solution. As with CF adapters, you should choose a buffered version when buying an SD-to-IDE adapter, as these are more stable and reliable. The angle adapters are plugged into the IDE port of the Amiga and the SD/microSD converter is then installed in the socket at the upper end. Together, the components sit firmly and securely in the case.

SD-to-SCSI solutions

For many years, SCSI was the ultimate in high-end Amigas. The A3000 and A4000T have an onboard SCSI controller, and turbo cards for the A1200 and A4000 are also equipped with SCSI controllers. As SCSI devices are now almost impossible to find new, SD-to-SCSI adapters have been developed that adapt SCSI controllers with a SCSI II connection to an SD card. SD cards are then used as media which, in conjunction with fast controllers, can achieve a data rate of up to 20 MB per second. Well-known SD-to-SCSI controllers are *SCSI2SD* and *ZuluSCSI*.

SATA solutions

SSD technology can be used in the Amiga via a SATA port. To plug an SSD hard drive into the Amiga, all you need is a SATA-to-IDE adapter. This adapter is available for 2.5" and 3.5" hard disks and is simply plugged into the back of the SATA port and adapts to the 44 or 40 pins of the IDE port. In addition to adapters for SSD hard drives, hardware is also available for modern *mSATA SSDs*.

Gotek

A loud clacking floppy disk drive may exude charm, but the future belongs to the Gotek drive, a modern replacement.

The Amiga was designed for floppy disks from the very start. Even when the CD came along, floppy disks did not lose their relevance as booting from a floppy is uncomplicated and works without additional drivers. Over the years, however, more and more floppy drives have failed due to mechanical defects, and prices for replacement drives have risen continuously. So-called Gotek drives have since emerged as an alternative. A Gotek can be accessed by the Amiga just like a standard disk drive, except that the Gotek uses a USB stick as its storage medium. Floppy disks must be converted to and stored as ADF files on the USB stick so that the drive can access their date.

An internal Gotek drive with a rotary knob

For the Gotek to be accessible, certain files must also be present on the USB stick. What these specifically are depends on the firmware of the Gotek. Most retailers and suppliers install the *Flashfloppy* firmware as it has many features and is free of charge. This firmware requires the files *autoboot.hfe* and *hxcsdfe.cfg* on the stick.

Using a Gotek drive on the Amiga is very easy and convenient. A choice of internal and external solutions are available with different controls for selecting the ADF files, sometimes via two small buttons, sometimes via a large rotary knob.

Internal Goteks for Amiga 500, 600 and 1200

As an internal solution for smaller Amigas, many retailers offer Gotek hardware with a mounting frame that fits in place of the floppy disk drive. The frame is usually produced to a high standard using a 3D printer and even has an eject button so that the structural change is barely recognizable from the outside (although the button is just for aesthetic reasons and does not function). Gotek variants come with a 7-segment display or a high-quality OLED display. The display shows the active ADF or position of the ADF on the USB stick as a number. Nostalgia fans can even order an optional buzzer, the *Gotek Sound Module*, that emulates the click sound of the original floppy drive.

Internal Goteks for Amiga 2000, 3000 and 4000

The design factor of a Gotek is equivalent to that of a 3.5" floppy drive. This means that they can be installed in “large” Amigas without additional frames or brackets. These drives are currently available in black and grey, and the low-cost version comes with a 7-segment display while the expensive versions features an OLED display and rotary knob.

External Goteks

External Goteks are hard to find in ready-to-use condition. However, thanks to their mechanical and electrical compatibility, you can easily install a Gotek in an existing external 3.5" floppy drive case. A Gotek conversion kit is required for some drives. Please note that many games were designed to boot from the internal DF0 floppy drive. Therefore, if you want to start software from an external Gotek drive, you should purchase a boot selector (details on page 441).

Mice and mouse extensions

The Tank Mouse is legendary, but today, newer input devices can offer even more efficiency.

The nine-pin, trapezoidal DB9 connector was already in use in other home computers before the Amiga came along. Although the Amiga scored points with its precise Tank Mouse, even this is getting on in years with its ball system, and can be replaced with new hardware if necessary.

The new Tank Mouse by Lukas Remis

Tank Mouse

The wireless *Tank Mouse* emerged from a Kickstarter project. It can replace the original Amiga Tank Mouse and is available in classic beige and black colors. In addition to a USB connection, it also comes with an adapter to fit the Amiga's DB9 connector. Not only is the original Tank Mouse's cable gone, so is its ball: this new edition is an optical mouse with a resolution of 1,600 dpi. At first glance, unlike other modern computer mice, there is no scroll wheel – however, so as not to spoil the design, a sensor has been fitted between the two mouse buttons, enabling the user to scroll up and down just as you would with a haptic wheel. The look and behavior are very reminiscent of the original Amiga mouse.

Laser sensor conversion kit for Amiga mice

With the laser sensor conversion kit, you can convert your old Amiga mouse into an optical mouse with 8,500 dpi resolution using a small circuit board kit. Kits are available for the Tank Mouse, the A1200 mouse and the A4000 mouse. Installation is quick and easy and results in a mouse that works very precisely and smoothly.

Adapter from USB devices for DB9 connections

A USB interface card (see page 434) or a USB-to-DB9 adapter is required to operate USB input devices on the Amiga.

The *Tikus* is a USB mouse/joystick adapter for retro computers with a DB9 connection and works very well on the Amiga. The adapter supports USB mice with scroll wheels and up to three mouse buttons, as well as game controllers with up to six buttons.

The *Rys MK II* is another adapter for USB mice and game controllers. Mouse emulation comes with three definable tracking options. This allows the desired speed to be calibrated for connected devices. All settings are saved internally, so the device only needs to be configured once.

Other useful extensions

Small enhancements, like a battery backed-up real-time clock or a boot selector, make everyday Amiga life easier.

It is obvious that the Amiga originated in the 1980s – the system lacks many of today's common features. But it can be easily upgraded with specific extensions and spare parts.

Adapter

The *4-way clock port extension* adds three additional clock ports to the Amiga 1200. From revision G onwards, port 3 even comes as a fast clock port, which transfers data up to 40% faster. If you want to operate more than one clock port device on the Amiga 1200, this adapter is a must.

The *Gayle adapter* is also a useful purchase. It corrects the hardware error of the Gayle chip in the A1200, which causes some PCMCIA cards not to work after a system reset.

Real-time clock

Previously, the Amiga could usually only benefit from a battery-backed real-time clock if it had a turbo card installed. Today, however, so-called *RTC modules* (short for *real time clock*) enable all Amigas with a clock port to permanently store the time. These RTC modules are equipped with a button battery and are available in a wide variety of designs.

Terminator

If no hard drive is connected to the Amiga via the IDE port or there is no floppy drive, the boot process will be prolonged as the system, which expects these devices, searches for them. Therefore, to accelerate the boot process, these interfaces can be equipped with a so-called *terminator*. The devices are then no longer scanned and the boot process is significantly reduced. Terminators for all 2.5" and 3.5" IDE ports, as well as for the floppy port, are available from Amiga retailers for a small price.

Boot selector

Certain programs, often games, will only boot from the internal floppy drive DF0. In some cases, however, the boot process needs to take place from DF1, i.e. the first external floppy drive, or via an external Gotek drive (see page 437). For such situations, a *boot selector* is essential. This interface is installed internally. The desired boot drive can then be selected using a toggle switch.

Amiga 1200 Clockport Expander by Matthias Münch

Software must-haves

Thousands of software packages are available for the Amiga that can be useful additions to the system. These 15 tools are a perfect fit for the new AmigaOS 3.2.

Directory Opus

"DOpus" is the quasi-standard among file managers for the Amiga. It is the perfect solution for anyone who wants intuitive management of their files and folders, and improves productivity with extended functions and a customizable interface. The paid version 5 offers a wider range of functions – version 4 is free of charge. **[1]**

MUI

The "Magic User Interface" has revolutionized interaction with applications on the Amiga by providing a customizable and modern graphical user interface. A significant number of applications, especially older ones, are based on MUI, providing better looks and usability. **[2]**

WHDLoad

WHDLoad is the ultimate package for gaming on the Amiga, loading and enhancing games for use with the hard drive even if they were not intended for hard disk installation. It increases stability and reduces load times, making it an indispensable resource for any gaming enthusiast. **[3]**

Avalanche

This powerful archiving tool for LhA and other formats allows you to manage your archives in an efficient way. Avalanche features a simple user interface, the ability to edit archives, and support for compression and virus detection. One of many alternatives to this paid software is LhA Unpacker. **[4]**

VirusZ

Even today, nasty viruses like Saddam, Byte Bandit or LHA-Face are still circulating for the Amiga. As a comprehensive security tool, VirusZ (currently in version III 1.04ß), together with the external virus library Xvs.library, offers robust protection against viruses and malware. **[5]**

SnoopDos

SnoopDos is an advanced monitoring tool that provides insight into your Amiga's system activity. It is a valuable tool for advanced users who want to optimize the performance of their system and diagnose problems effectively. **[6]**

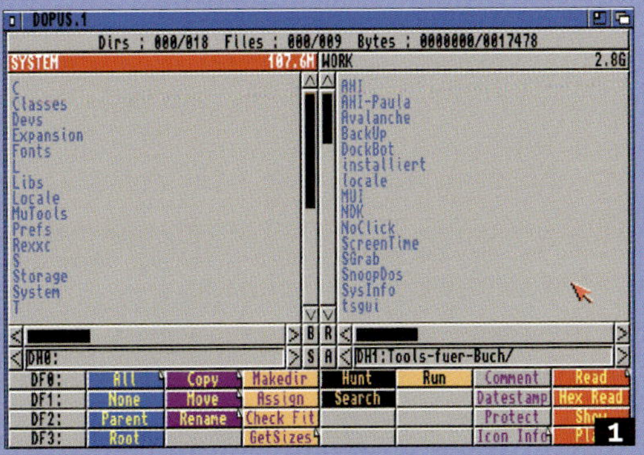

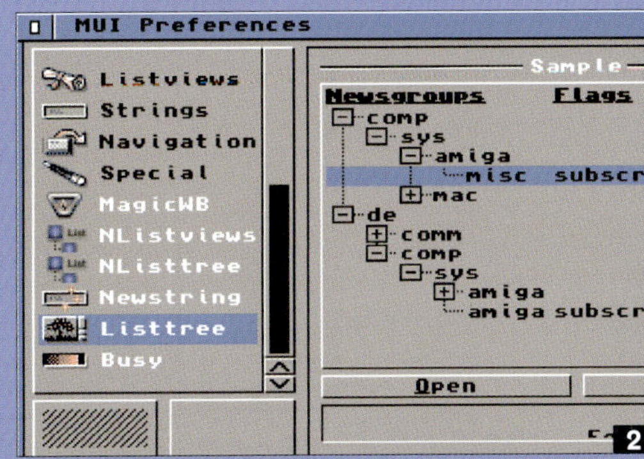

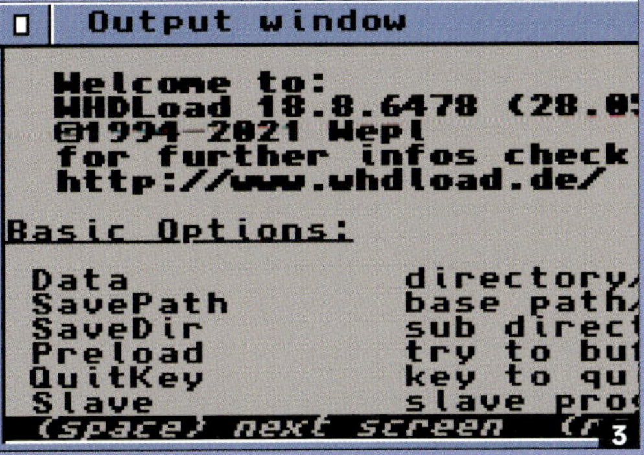

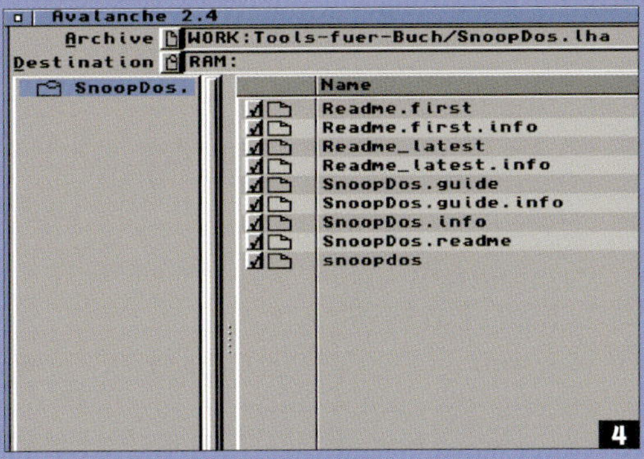

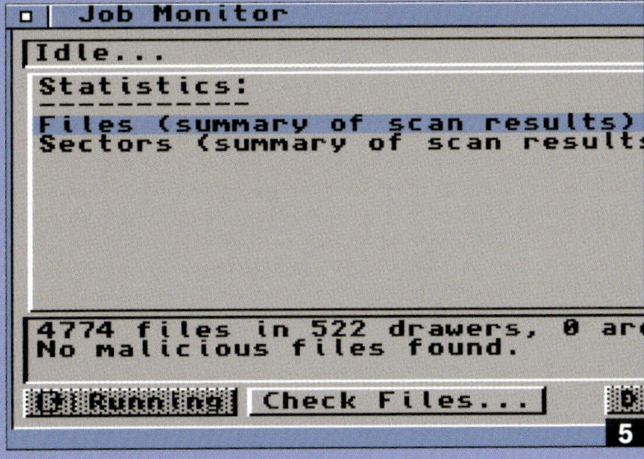

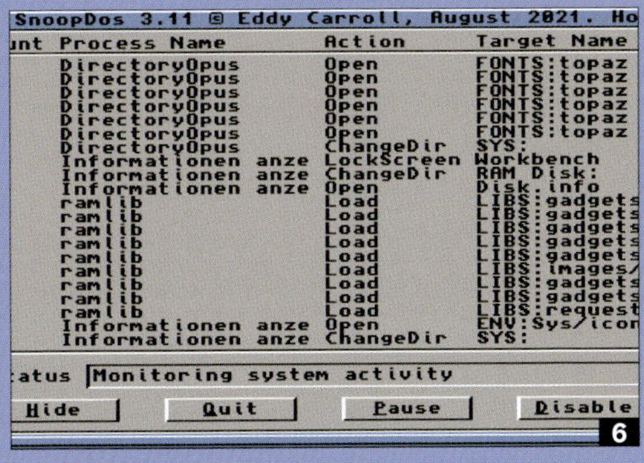

DOWNLOAD LINKS

Links to these tools, and other, are collected and updated on the service website for this book: **https://lookbehindyou.de/en/amigaos32book**

TSgui

TrackSaver GUI is intended to complement the new disk image support implemented in AmigaOS 3.2. Handling, creating and managing ADF images and even hard files (HDF) is made easy with this user-friendly tool. **[7]**

MagicMenu

MagicMenu is an extension of the Amiga's menu functions, with customizable navigation. For example, the menu appears where the cursor is when you right-click. This makes it faster and more intuitive to interact with the system. **[8]**

Dockbot

Dockbot is a good alternative to AmiDock, which was an essential part of AmigaOS 3.9. The versatile Start bar simplifies and speeds up access to frequently used programs and functions. It can be fully customized. **[9]**

SysInfo

SysInfo provides detailed insight into the specifications and performance of the Amiga. For example, it lists the chips and boards installed, as well as the libraries used in the system. It also benchmarks the Amiga's speed against that of other Amigas. **[10]**

ScreenTime

This commodity shows the time discreetly in the top right-hand corner of the Workbench menu bar. It is easy to adapt it to the screen style and comes with a calendar. **[11]**

P96

Graphics card users will be hard-pressed to do without P96 (ex-Picasso96), the commercial software that iComp continues to develop (currently 3.4.0). A graphics card driver package, it allows advanced graphics modes and higher resolutions. **[12]**

AHI

AHI provides a standardized audio interface for improved sound on the Amiga. It enables software to work with various audio hardware (including the Paula chip). **[13]**

SGrab

SGrab is an easy-to-use tool that lets you capture screens quickly and efficiently. It can capture entire screens as well as specific windows and even screen areas only. **[14]**

AmigaOS NDK

The AmigaOS Native Development Kit (NDK) is an essential toolkit for developers to create software for AmigaOS 3.2. It contains the latest include files, libraries and documentation required to develop applications and games, and improves compiler integration, among other things.

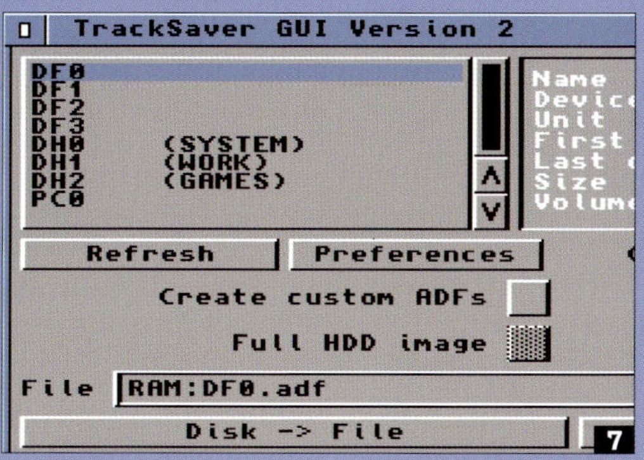
TrackSaver GUI Version 2
DF0
DF1
DF2
DF3
DH0 (SYSTEM)
DH1 (WORK)
DH2 (GAMES)
PC0
Refresh
Preferences
Create custom ADFs
Full HDD image
File RAM:DF0.adf
Disk -> File
7

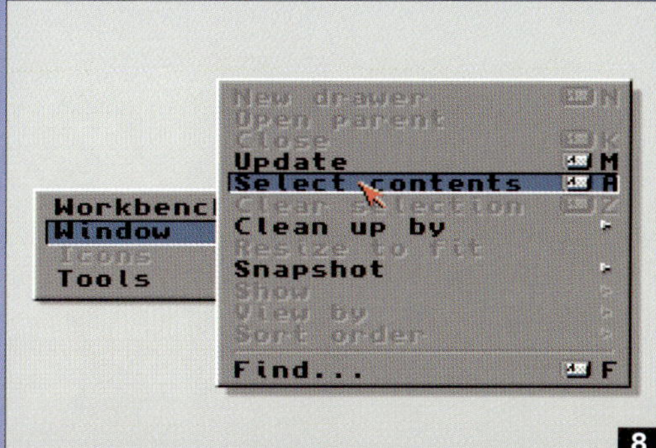
Workbench
Window
Tools
New drawer
Open parent
Close
Update
Select contents
Clean up by
Snapshot
Show
View by
Sort order
Find...
8

9

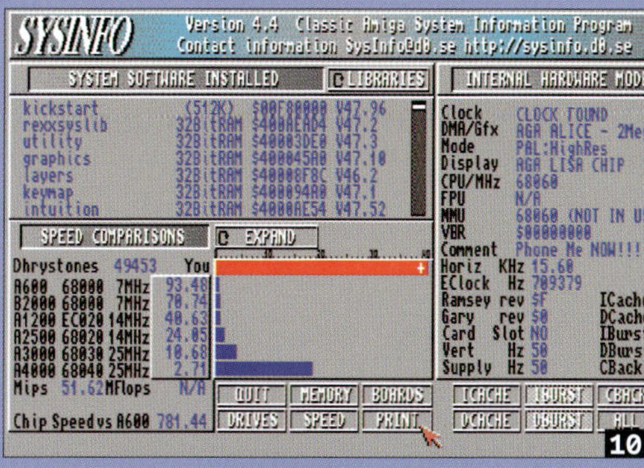
SYSINFO
Version 4.4 Classic Amiga System Information Program
SYSTEM SOFTWARE INSTALLED
LIBRARIES
SPEED COMPARISONS
EXPAND
QUIT
MEMORY
BOARDS
DRIVES
SPEED
PRINT
10

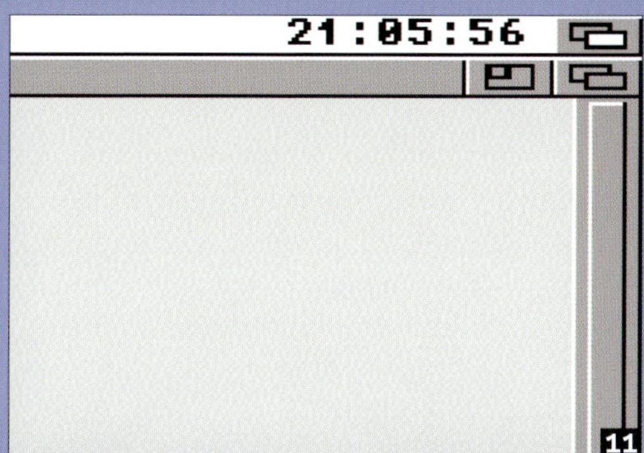
21:05:56
11

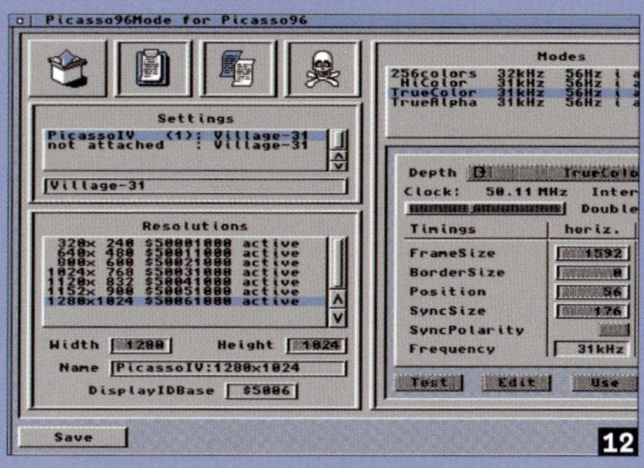
Picasso96Mode for Picasso96
Settings
Resolutions
Modes
Save
12

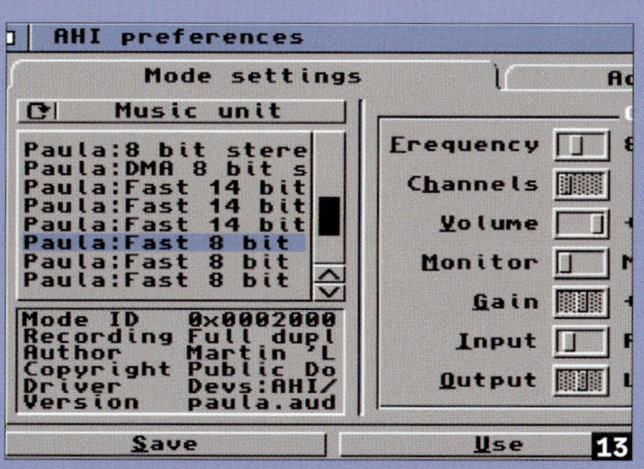
AHI preferences
Mode settings
Music unit
Paula:8 bit stere
Paula:DMA 8 bit s
Paula:Fast 14 bit
Paula:Fast 14 bit
Paula:Fast 14 bit
Paula:Fast 8 bit
Paula:Fast 8 bit
Paula:Fast 8 bit
Mode ID 0x0002000
Recording Full dupl
Author Martin 'L
Copyright Public Do
Driver Devs:AHI/
Version paula.aud
Frequency
Channels
Volume
Monitor
Gain
Input
Output
Save
Use
13

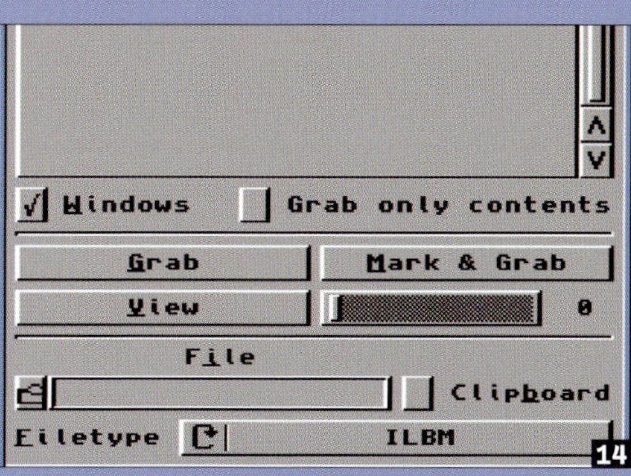
Windows
Grab only contents
Grab
Mark & Grab
View
0
File
Clipboard
Filetype
ILBM
14

Quick Reference

8

Discover some essential tips for using the Amiga in this Quick Reference chapter. Read our Frequently Asked Questions (FAQ) section for answers to common questions, suggested solutions, and to discover tips and tricks for setting up and using the device. Then, check out the large error messages overview to find out what is behind the various system codes, including the legendary Guru Meditation. Finally a glossary will deepen your knowledge with precise definitions of Amiga-specific terms. This final chapter is your personal guide to getting to grips with AmigaOS 3.2.

Frequently Asked Questions (FAQ)

There are a few common pitfalls that can trip users up when using AmigaOS 3.2, but there are also some tricks that can make life easier.

Preparation

What system requirements do I need to run AmigaOS 3.2?

The *minimum requirements* for AmigaOS 3.2 are an Amiga (native or emulated) with Kickstart 3.1, 10 MB hard disk space and 2 MB RAM (2.5 MB if no physical Kickstart ROM 3.2 is used). A drive (floppy disk, CD-ROM, Gotek or CF/SD memory card as a hard drive replacement) is required for installation and use.

A faster processor (68020 upwards), a Kickstart 3.2 ROM and 8 MB total memory (Chip RAM + Fast RAM) are *recommended*.

Ideally, you need a 68030 CPU or faster, an RTG graphics card, a total of 32 MB available memory, and a hard disk (or hard disk replacement) with 500 MB of free capacity.

My Amiga does not have a CD-ROM drive. How can I install AmigaOS 3.2?

Solution 1: The most convenient way is to buy an AmigaOS 3.2 installation CompactFlash or SecureDigital card from an Amiga retailer. With a compatible adapter connected to your IDE port, you can use such a card just like an installer CD. Later, you can make use of the CF/SD card as a hard disk, partition it and install the operating system on it. After installation, pay attention to the boot priority so that the partition on which the operating system was installed is loaded instead of the standard boot partition.

Solution 2: If you have access to another Amiga with a CD-ROM drive and a floppy disk drive, you can use it to write all the ADFs in the *ADF* directory of the CD to a DD floppy disk. Then insert the *Install3.2* disk into the Amiga's disk drive, boot the computer and start the installation from the disk.

Solution 3: You can install the system from ADFs copied to a USB stick using a Gotek. The Gotek should have the FlashFloppy firmware (download: https://github.com/keirf/flashfloppy/releases/tag/v3.40). On a computer with a CD drive, copy all the ADFs from the *ADF* directory of the CD to your USB stick and insert it into the Gotek drive. Select *Install3.2.adf* using the selector buttons or the rotary knob on the Gotek. The installation will start after a reset.

I have inserted the AmigaOS 3.2 CD into my CD-ROM drive, but the CD does not boot. What is the problem?

The Amiga cannot boot from CD without a driver. You will need to create a boot disk to boot from so that the CD-ROM drive can be mounted. If you are unable to create a boot disk, you can order one from a well-stocked Amiga dealer.

Do I need a new Kickstart ROM to use AmigaOS 3.2?

Not necessarily, but a new Kickstart ROM has two advantages. Firstly, the boot time is shortened as the new Kickstart does not have to be loaded into RAM during the first cold boot process. The typical reset after the first boot process, which will be familiar from AmigaOS 3.9, is therefore no longer necessary. Secondly, memory consumption is lower because the Kickstart can be loaded directly from the ROM chips and does not have to be copied into the main memory. Without ROM chips, the resources occupy 512 kilobytes in RAM.

Installation

What is the AmigaOS Preinstallation Environment that is displayed when booting from the OS 3.2 CD?

The *AmigaOS Preinstallation Environment* (*AmigaPE*) is a compact version of the operating system designed for the installation, setup and repair of AmigaOS installations. AmigaPE can only be found on the AmigaOS 3.2 CD, from where it can be booted directly. The use of AmigaPE is explained in section 1.5 on *Installation from CD-ROM*.

Can I use partitions larger than 4 GB?

Yes, the maximum partition size is 128 gigabytes. However, partitions should not be created this large, as the validation process can take a very long time, and AmigaOS requires more memory for the process. We recommend a maximum size of 1 GB for the system partition and 32 GB for other partitions.

How can I check whether AmigaOS 3.2 and the Kickstart ROM have been correctly installed?

Open a Shell and execute the `version` command. If a value of 47 or higher is displayed for Workbench and Kickstart, AmigaOS 3.2 and the Kickstart ROM have been correctly installed. You can simply click on *Workbench > About* in the Workbench menu.

Workbench

How many characters can I use when naming files, drawers and drives?

The new *FFS* file system allows for file, drawer and drive names of up to 31 characters. If the *Long Names* attribute is enabled via *HDToolBox* when setting up the partition, up to 107 characters are also possible. Pay attention to the value in the *Workbench Preferences*, as this limits the length of the filenames shown on the Workbench to 25 characters. Enter the desired maximum length in the *Icons* area under *Maximum Filename Length*.

I would like to move windows off the screen like in Windows. How does this work?

The Intuition library, which is responsible for the graphical user interface, offers new features, including the ability to drag windows beyond the edge of the screen. However, the function must be explicitly enabled with the option *Can Move Off-screen* in the *IControl Preferences*.

Where can I find more GlowIcons?

On the AmigaOS 3.2 CD you will find a large number of GlowIcon icons in the *GlowIcons-Collection* directory. Many more are available to download from Aminet and other websites for free.

How can I enter a Euro character on the keyboard?

The Euro character has not yet been implemented in AmigaOS 3.2. Support is expected in future updates. However, the Helvetica font contains a Euro character in sizes 13 and 15.

I would like to copy an icon from another drive, program or directory. How can I do this?

Use the Workbench info requester, which is technically based on RAWBInfo. Select the drive, drawer or program for which you would like to change the icon and choose *Information* from the *Icons* menu. The info requester will open. Drag and drop the desired new icon from the Workbench to the icon in the info requester. The icon in the info requester will take on the new look. Save the icon by clicking the *Save* button.

How can I use umlauts or characters with accents in filenames?

To use umlauts or other accented characters in file, drawer and drive names, enable the *International Mode* feature when setting up the partition via HDToolBox (i.e. while formatting the drive).

Shell

Why is Execute no longer located in the C directory?

The *Execute* command has been integrated into, and thus shares programming code with, the Shell, which saves space. However, the command is still fully functional and usable.

Is there no scroll bar for Shell windows?

The AmigaOS 3.2 Shell does not yet offer a scrollbar, but you can integrate it relatively easily with the alternative Shell *ViNCEd*. Details can be found in the section *Where is the scrollbar?* in the *Shell* chapter, including a do-it-yourself solution.

Tools

Is the AHI Audio System of any use to me if there is no sound card in my Amiga?

Yes. AHI is a standardized interface for audio hardware on the Amiga that makes it easy for all programs to support audio output. Tools such as the *AmigaAmp* MP3 player use AHI for sound output. AHI should therefore also be installed on systems without a sound card (i.e. with just the Paula custom chip).

What does it mean when an application reports an error message about a missing installer during installation?

Some applications use an alternative installer version. In this case, download the *Installer* from Aminet (download: www.aminet.net/package/util/misc/Installer-43_3) and copy the *Installer* file from the download archive to the *Sys:C* system directory. There is already a command file called *Install in this directory* – both installer versions can coexist.

How can I create an ADF containing my own content?

You can create an ADF file with your own data in AmigaOS 3.2 using the new Shell command `DaControl` (see page 287).

Performance and compatibility

During boot, the startup sequence stops and displays a warning about an incomplete installation. What is missing?

This can happen if you are using a 68040 or 68060 turbo card and have not yet installed the related CPU libraries. 68040/68060 systems in particular require these libraries in order to work reliably and with high performance. The 68030.library is not absolutely necessary, but recommended on 68030 systems. This is the only way to resolve all problems and ensure the system runs at full performance. Instructions for setting up the libraries can be found in section 1.6 on *Installing the CPU libraries.*

I have installed the Kickstart ROM 3.2 and want to load Workbench 3.1, but my system will not boot. Why is this?
In Kickstart 3.2, *icon.library* and *workbench.library* are not included and must be loaded. However, AmigaOS 3.1.4 and higher come with a useful function: when starting the system in Workbench 3.1, it will attempt to search for and find the required libraries for all connected drives, be they floppy disk, hard drive or RAM drive, and thus still manage to start. It's not a bug, it's a feature.

Hardware

My AmigaOS crashes occasionally, shows color screens when starting and does not run stably overall, even though I have made a fresh install. What should I do?
The cause is likely to be a hardware problem. Check whether the capacitors (electrolytic capacitors) of the Amiga have been replaced in the last 15 years. If not, then replacement is absolutely essential. Get a specialist to do the replacement and ensure the job is done professionally. The age of these components often causes hiccups with Amiga hardware. In certain circumstances, a different repair may be necessary if components have suffered additional damage over the years, but this is more rare.

The clock no longer works on my Amiga 2000 or 4000 and there are stability problems. What is the reason for this?
The battery in your Amiga may have died. Check the battery for the battery-backed real-time clock on your Amiga 2000 and 4000. Depending on its age, the battery may have corroded and damaged the motherboard by leaking battery acid. All old batteries in these Amiga models should be replaced immediately.

Registration

I would like to register my AmigaOS 3.2. Where can I find the registration number?
The registration number can be found on a sticker on the shrink wrap of the CD case. Some retailers also send the number digitally or include it on the invoice.

Help

I need help, or I have detailed questions about AmigaOS 3.2 or related topics.
Press the `[HELP]` button at any point on the Workbench to access the internal (English) help. The English FAQ for AmigaOS 3.2 can also be found online at http://aminet.net/docs/help/AmigaOS_3.2-FAQ.txt.

Error Codes

The Amiga is a stable system, no question about it. Yet system crashes and other undesirable anomalies do occasionally occur. Error codes of various kinds help to diagnose such issues – here is an overview.

Because the Amiga software developers have created a sophisticated system for identifying any errors that occur, most errors can be clearly determined by the error codes given and can therefore be rectified more easily.

The most significant error message is probably the mighty Guru Meditation. This red flashing rectangle is as feared by Amiga users as the blue screen is by Windows users. In addition, the Amiga can display error codes in the form of screen colors when booting the system. It also has a handy feature that displays the most common errors in info requesters, showing you the error codes at the DOS level.

Boot Error Codes (Screen Colors)

When booting the Amiga, one or more screen colors show the status of the system and any possible errors.

The following table lists the screen color error codes you can get while booting, along with their meaning. In addition to these error codes, which apply to all Amiga models, there are other color codes that can have different meanings depending on the model, components and chips.

Color error code	Error description
Red	Kickstart ROM is faulty
Blue	custom chip(s) is/are faulty
Green	Chip RAM memory is faulty
Light green	CIA (Complex Interface Adapter) chip is faulty
Yellow	an error occurred before the error monitoring tool (Guru) was executed

Software Failure. Press left mouse button to continue.
Error: 8000 0004 Task: 100293F8

Guru Meditation error codes

Notorious among Amiga owners is the Guru or Guru Meditation error. The red flashing, rectangular field at the top of the black screen is the Amiga's way of displaying serious internal errors.

If you encounter a Guru error message, often the only way out is to reset the Amiga by pressing the left mouse button. For more in-depth analyses, the so-called *ROMWack* can be started by pressing the *Delete key*. *ROMWack* is a simple debugger that is implemented in the operating system and can be viewed via a terminal in the serial port.

There are two types of error messages: recoverable and non-recoverable, depending on how critical they are. Non-recoverable alerts always require a restart, while recoverable alerts allow you to continue working with the Amiga, at least to a limited extent.

The numerical code inside the red box provides information on how the error occurred.

The error message is structured according to the following four-part pattern:

```
Error: SSGG EEEE Task: AAAAAAAA
```

SS specifies the affected subsystem.
GG specifies the general error description.
EEEE indicates the specific error.
AAAAAAAA indicates the memory address where the error occurred.

Available values for SS (subsystem)	
00	CPU exception
01	Exec.library
02	Graphics.library
03	Layers.library
04	Intuition.library
05	Maths Library
07	Dos.library
08	Ramlib.library
09	Icon.library
0A	Expansion.library
0B	Diskfont.library
10	Audio.device
11	Console.device
12	Gameport.device
13	Keyboard.device
14	Trackdisk.device
15	Timer.device
20	Cia.resource
21	Disk.resource
22	Misc.resource
30	Bootstrap
31	Workbench
32	Diskcopy
33	Gadtools
34	Utility.library
35	unknown

Available values for GG (general error description)	
00	Unspecified
01	Not enough memory
02	Couldn't make library
03	Can't open library
04	Can't open device
05	Can't open resource
06	I/O error
07	No signal
08	Bad parameters
09	Close library failed; usually too many closes
0A	Close device failed; or a mismatch

Available values for EEEE / subsystem Exec.library	
0001	68000 exception vector checksum (obs)
0002	Exec checksum bad (obs)
0003	Library checksum failure
0005	Corrupt memory list detected in FreeMem
0006	No memory for interrupt servers
0007	InitStruct() of an APTR source (obs)
0008	A semaphore is in an illegal state at Rem Semaphore()
0009	Freeing memory that is already free
000A	Illegal 68k exception taken (obs)
000B	Attempt to reuse active OIRequest
000C	Sanity check on memory list failed during AvailMem
000D	IO attempted on closed IORequest
000E	Stack appears to extend out of range
000F	Memory header not located. Usually an invalid address passed.
0010	An attempt was made to use the old message semaphores
00FF	A quick interrupt has happened to an uninitialized vector

Available values for EEEE / subsystem CPU Exceptions	
0002	Bus Error
0003	Addressing error
0004	Illegal instruction
0005	Division by zero
0006	CHK instruction
0007	TRAPV instruction
0008	Privilege violation
0009	Trace
000A	OpCode 1010
000B	OpCode 1111
000E	Stack frame format error
0018	Spurious interrupt error
0019-001F	Autovector Level 1 to 7 int error

Available values for EEEE / subsystem Intuition.library	
0001	Unknown gadget type
0002	Create port, no memory
0003	Item plane alloc, no memory
0004	Sub alloc, no memory

0005	Plane alloc, no memory
0006	Item box top <RelZero>
0007	Open screen, no memory
0008	Open screen, raster alloc, no memory
0009	Open sys screen, unknown type
000A	Add SW gadgets, no memory
000B	Open window, no memory
000C	Bad Stare Return entering intuition
000D	Bad message received by IDCMP
000E	Weird echo causing incomprehension
000F	Can't open console.device or Incompatible Shell and dos.library
0010	Intuition skipped obtaining a sem
0011	Intuition obtained a sem in bad order
0012	Intuition got updated, but a program called an old function

Available values for EEEE / subsystem Graphics.library	
0000	Graphics out of memory
0001	MonitorSpec alloc, no memory
0006	Long frame, no memory
0007	Short frame, no memory
0009	Text, no memory for TmpRas
000A	BltBitMap, no memory
000B	Regions, memory not available
0030	Make V Por, no memory
000C	(GFX New Error)
000D	(GFX Free Error)
1234	Emergency memory not available
0401	Unsupported font description used

Available values for EEEE / subsystem Workbench	
0000	No fonts
0001	Workbench (WB) bad startup Msg1
0002	WB bad startup Msg2
0003	WB bad IO Msg
0004	WB Init Potion Alloc Drawer
0005	WB Create WB Menus Create Menus1
0006	WB Create WB Menus Create Menus2
0007	WB layout WB Menus layout Menus2
0008	WB Add Tool Menu Item
000A	WB InitTimer

000B	WB Init Layer Demon
000C	WB Init WB Gels
000D	WB Init Screen and Windows1
000E	WB Init Screen and Windows2
000F	WB Init Screen and Windows3
0010	WBMAlloc

Available values for EEEE / subsystem Layers.library	
0000	Layers out of memory

Available values for EEEE / subsystem Expansion.library	
0001	Freed free memory

Available values for EEEE / subsystem Trackdisk.device	
0001	Calibrate: seek error
0002	Delay: error on timer wait

Available values for EEEE / subsystem Disk.resource	
0001	Get unit: already has a disk
0002	Interrupt: no active unit

Available values for EEEE / subsystem RamLib.library	
0001	Overlays are Illegal for library segments

Available values for EEEE / subsystem Console.device	
0001	Console can't open initial window

Available values for EEEE / subsystem Timer.device	
0001	Bad request
0002	Power supply: no 50/60 Hz ticks

Available values for EEEE / subsystem bootstrap	
0001	Boot code returned an error

Available values for EEEE / subsystem Dos.library	
0001	No memory at startup
0002	EndTask failure
0003	Qpkt failure
0004	Unexpected packet received
0005	Freevec failed

0006	Disk block sequence error
0007	Bitmap corrupt
0008	Key already free
0009	Invalid checksum
000A	Disk error
000B	Key out of range
000C	Bad overlay
000D	Invalid init packet for CLI/Shell
000E	A filehandle was closed more than once

Available values for EEEE / subsystem Alert Objects	
8001	ExecLib
8002	GraphicsLib
8003	LayersLib
8004	Intuition
8005	MathLib
8006	DOSLib
8008	RAMLib
8009	IconLib
800A	ExpansionLib
800B	DiskfontLib
800C	UtilityLib
800D	KeyMapLib
8010	AudioDev
8011	ConsoleDev
8012	GameportDev
8013	KeyboardDev
8014	TrackDiskDev
8015	TimerDev
8020	CIARsrc
8021	DiskRsrc
8022	Miscrsrc
8030	Bootstrap
8031	Workbench
8032	Diskcopy
8033	GadTools
8035	Unknown

AmigaDOS error messages

These error messages are issued by the system if a program or command fails to execute.

Error	Error message	Cause	Possible solution
103	Not enough memory available	The Amiga does not have enough memory to perform this operation. The memory may be fragmented.	Close all unnecessary applications. Enter the command again. If the error continues to occur, restart the system. If this problem occurs frequently, consider upgrading the system with more RAM.
105	Task table full	The CLI task list is full (limited to 20 tasks).	Close individual tasks and execute the command again
115	Bad number	The program expects a numerical argument.	Check the command format
116	Required argument missing	A required argument was not specified	Check the command format
117	Value after keyword missing	Keyword was specified without argument.	Check the command format
118	Wrong number of arguments	Too many or too few arguments	Check the command format
119	Unmatched quotes	The number of quotation marks must be even.	Place quotation marks at the beginning and end of the path or character string
120	Argument line is invalid or too long	The command line is incorrect or contains too many arguments.	Check the command format
121	File is not executable	Typing error in the command name, or the file is not a loadable (program or script) file.	Enter the filename again and make sure it is a program file. To execute a script, the s bit must be set or the EXECUTE command must be used.
122	Invalid resident library during load	The required library was found, but was not of the correct type. This may be caused by an old version of the library or the file is corrupt.	Replace the installed library with the original or an updated version

Error	Error message	Cause	Possible solution
202	Object is in use	The file or directory is already occupied by another application or is assigned elsewhere	Stop the application that is using the file or directory or cancel the assignment
203	Object already exists	There is already a directory or file with this name	Use a different name or delete the existing file/directory
204	Directory not found	AmigaDOS cannot find the specified directory	Check the directory name with the DIR command
205	Object not found	AmigaDOS cannot find the specified file or the specified device	Check the filename with the DIR command or the device name with INFO
206	Invalid window description	This error can occur when specifying the size for a Shell, ED or ICONX window	The window may be too large or too small, or you may have omitted an argument. This error can also occur with the NEWSHELL command if the name of a unit that is not a window is specified.
209	Packet request type unknown	You have requested an operation from a device handler that is not possible. For example, the console handler does not have the option of renaming something.	Search for the corresponding request in the request codes forwarded to the device handlers
210	Object name invalid	The filename contains an invalid character or is too long	Enter the name again and make sure that the characters and length are valid
211	Invalid object lock	The lock code was not recognized by the AmigaDOS call	This is a programming error
212	Object is not of required type	A directory name was specified for an operation instead of a filename (or vice versa)	Check the name and the command format
213	Disk is not validated	If a disk has just been inserted, the disk validation may not have finished. The disk may also be damaged.	If a disk has just been inserted, wait until the check is complete. This takes less than a minute for a floppy disk and a few minutes for a hard disk. However, if the disk is damaged, it cannot be validated. Try to read the files on this disk and copy them to another disk.

Error	Error message	Cause	Possible solution
214	Disk is write-protected	The disk is write-protected by protection bits, or the plastic protection tab on a floppy disk is in the write-protection position	Remove the disk, move the write-protection slider to the other position and reinsert the disk, or use another disk or use the LOCK OFF command
215	Rename across devices attempted	RENAME can be used to move a file from one directory to another, but not from one drive to another	Try to copy the file to the target drive using COPY. Then delete it from the source drive if necessary. RENAME can then be used.
216	Directory not empty	You have tried to delete a directory that still contains files or subdirectories	If you actually want to delete an entire directory, use the ALL option of the DELETE command
217	Too many levels	The directory nesting is too deep	Reorganize your directories or change directories one by one to reach the desired level
218	Device (or volume) is not mounted	If the device is a floppy disk, it has not been inserted into the drive. If it is a different device, it has not been mounted with the Mount command, or its name has been misspelled.	Insert the correct disk, mount the device, check that the device name is correct or correct the mount list/file or assign the device name accordingly
219	Seek error	An error occurred while processing a file	Make sure that SEEK is only executed within one file. Cross-file searches are not possible with SEEK.
220	Comment is too long	The comment is longer than the maximum permitted number of characters (79)	Shorten the comment
221	Disk is full	There is not enough free space on the disk to perform the requested operation	Delete some unnecessary files or directories, or use a different disk
222	Object is protected from deletion	The protection bit d (for "deletable") of the file or directory is clear	If you actually want to delete the file or directory, set the related d bit with PROTECT or use the FORCE option of the DELETE command

Error	Error message	Cause	Possible solution
223	File is write-protected	The protection bit w (for "writeable") of the file is clear	If you actually want to overwrite the file, set the related w bit with PROTECT
224	File is read-protected	The protection bit r (for "readable") of the file is clear	Use PROTECT to set the r bit of the file
225	Not a valid DOS disk	The disk in the drive is not an AmigaDOS disk, is not formatted or is damaged	Make sure you are using a correct and functional disk. Use a recovery tool with the disk to recover the data. If the disk is not formatted, do this with FORMAT.
226	No disk in drive	The disk is not inserted correctly in the specified drive	Insert the correct disk into the specified drive
232	No more entries in directory	The AmigaDOS call EXNEXT can ot find any further entries in the directory you are currently checking	Stop calling EXNEXT
233	Object is soft link	You have tried to perform an operation on a composite object ("soft link") that is not supported	None
235	Bad load file hunk	The loaded program is damaged	Load a new copy or the original program
241	Record lock collision	Another program is accessing the database	Try to access the database again
242	Record lock timeout	The database entry is blocked by another program	Try again, or exit the other program and then try again
303	Buffer overflow	This error occurs if a character string is too long for a name pattern	Shorten the character string
304	***Break	This error occurs if the program was stopped by pressing the keys [Ctrl] + [C]	None
305	File not executable	The protection bit e (for "executable") of the file is clear	Enter the filename again and make sure it is a program file. To execute a script, either the s bit must be set or the EXECUTE command must be used

Glossary

This short dictionary lists Amiga-specific technical terms that are used in the Amiga operating system and in Amiga software, as well as in this book and the original Commodore manuals.

A

AA (AGA)
→ *Advanced Graphics Architecture*

accelerator card
→ *turbo card*

action gadget
A gadget with plain text labelling in a window, the selection of which calls up an operation in this window. Common actions are *Save*, *Next* and *Cancel*.

active
Used with reference to the screen, the Shell window or the Workbench window in which entries can currently be made.

ADF (Amiga Disk File)
File format that saves disk images, including the file system, files and directories contained on the disk. ADF files are often used by Amiga emulators to run software virtually. AmigaOS supports virtual ADF disks as of version 3.2.

address
Unique identification number of a component (such as memory or a graphics card) in the computer or a peripheral device.

Advanced Graphics Architecture (AGA/AA)
A chipset built into the Amiga 1200, Amiga 4000 and CD32 that can display more colors simultaneously and improve system performance.

Agnus
A custom chip in the Amiga that is responsible for memory access management and for the coprocessors Copper and Blitter. Available in versions with support for 512 KB, 1 MB and 2 MB Chip RAM.

alias name
An alternative name for an AmigaDOS command or a character string that is defined by using the **Alias** command.

Alice
A custom chip in the Amiga 1200, 4000 and CD32 that offers extended graphics and memory functions. Successor to → *Agnus*.

Amber
A custom chip in Amiga 3000 models and on the A2320 Scandoubler card that acts as a specialized flickerfixer and scandoubler.

Amiga
Best computer in the world. Spanish for girlfriend.

AmigaDOS
The disk operating system (DOS) used in various Amiga models. It contains the most important functions of the computer.

AmigaOS
An operating system developed specifically for the Amiga. First released in 1985, it became famous for its advanced features, such as preemptive multitasking and a user-friendly interface. The operating system comprises two main components: the Kickstart ROM, which is loaded when the computer is started, and the Workbench, which contains the graphical user interface and system applications.

AppIcon
A special icon created and used by an application, also known simply as an icon.

AppWindow
The window of an application into which an icon can be dragged in order to load the related file into the application. The MultiView window and the Amiga file requester are examples of AppWindows.

application (app)
Software that has been developed for special purposes and can be executed, e.g. an internet browser or a text editor.

archive
1) A package that bundles one, several or many files, usually reduced in size by compression methods (LhA, ZIP, etc.). 2) The status or process of packing data into compressed archives or copying files to drives for backup purposes.

argument
Additional information, e.g. a filename, value or option that is added to a command and determines the exact action of that command.

argument passing
Specifying parameters in the command line for a program or command to be called up.

ASCII (American Standard Code for Information Interchange)
A standard for text representation in which characters are assigned standardized code numbers to enable data exchange between different types of computers.

aspect (aspect ratio)
The ratio of height to width for images.

Assembler
A software tool that converts assembly language code into machine code that a computer's processor can execute.

assign
Establishing a connection between a logical device name and a directory name using the *Assign* command. This allows programs that access the directory to use the logical device name. For example, the device name T: is normally assigned to the directory RAM:T.

Atari ST
→ *trashcan*

autoconfig
Autoconfig is a system for the automatic configuration of expansion cards and peripheral devices.

autoscroll
The automatic shifting of the screen display as soon as the mouse pointer reaches the edge of the visible area.

B

background process
A program that is launched by the Shell (CLI) using the RUN command and runs in the background so the user can perform other tasks in the Shell. Unlike a foreground process, which requires interactive user input and is executed in the foreground, a background process performs its tasks in the background without blocking the user interface or interfering with user activity.

backup (backup copy)
A copy of a file or entire drive on another drive for the purpose of preserving the data and restoring it after data loss or system relocation.

batch
→ *script*

baud rate
The speed at which data is transmitted, i.e. received or sent via a connection, measured in the number of signal changes per second and expressed in data bits per second – the higher, the faster.

big box Amiga
Amiga models in larger cases that offer space for additional expansion cards and peripherals. The larger design of the cases makes it possible to install more hardware components in the computer and thus expand the performance and functionality of the system. Typical big box Amigas are the Amiga 2000, 3000 and 4000 or the DraCo and MicroniK A4000.

binary
A number system that only uses the digits 0 and 1.

bit
A single binary digit (1 or 0) that represents the smallest unit of information.

bitplane
A memory area in RAM that contains graphic data for screens. Each bit in a bitplane controls a single pixel on the screen. The number of bitplanes determines the maximum number of colors that can be displayed simultaneously on the screen.

block (bytes)
A contiguous group of bytes (usually 512) that is treated as a single logical unit in RAM or on a permanent storage medium.

block (text)
A (content-wise) contiguous or marked section in a text file (e.g. IF block in a script, see section *ARexx*).

boolean
Means that only two different states are possible: on or off, true or false, yes or no, 0 or 1.

boot
Starting the system by reading the required data from a storage medium (e.g. hard disk or floppy disk), the boot disk, into the computer's memory. Compare → *reboot*.

bootable
Refers to a device from which the Amiga can be started (→ *boot*). A bootable disk requires a → *boot block*.

boot block
A special area on a disk that is automatically executed by AmigaDOS when the disk is inserted.

bridgeboard
An expansion card developed by Commodore, Golden Gate and other manufacturers that enables the Amiga to emulate the hardware of x86 PC-compatible computers.

brush
An IFF graphic file, usually a section of a full-format image.

buffer
A cache in RAM that is used for temporary data storage.

bug
→ *error*

bus
A communication system that transfers data between components within a computer or between computers. A popular bus system of the Amiga is → *Zorro*.

Buster
A custom chip in the Amiga that is responsible

for controlling memory access and address management. Buster allows access to additional memory and other extensions.

busy pointer
A stopwatch symbol that is displayed instead of the normal mouse pointer when the Workbench is running and will not accept any further input until a running process is finished.

byte
A memory unit consisting of eight bits that corresponds to a single character, for example.

C

cache (cache memory)
A temporary, i.e. short-term memory area with extremely fast access that increases system performance.

catalog
Files that contain the system and message texts in another (non-English) language in order to display them in the desired language in Workbench elements.

CD-ROM
Read-only memory on a silver disk on which around 650 MB of data can be stored.

Centronics
→ *parallel*

central processing unit
→ *processor*

character density
The number of characters per inch when printing in a horizontal direction. The unit is *cpi* (chars per inch).

character set
→ *font*

character string
→ *string*

checkbox
A selection field in which an option can be switched on or off. If the checkbox contains a tick, the option is activated.

chip
An electronic circuit in a small, black, rectangular case with connecting pins on the sides. Computers are made up of a large number of such chips.

Chip RAM
The part of the RAM accessed by the Amiga's special chipset. This memory can be used for graphic and audio data and is also referred to as graphic memory.

clear
1) Set a bit or an indicator to 0 (off), i.e. deactivate. Contrary to *Set*. 2) Delete contents of a screen or window display.

CLI (command line interface)
A way of communicating with the Amiga in which commands are entered with the keyboard. The CLI of the Amiga is the so-called → *Shell*.

click
Briefly pressing and releasing a mouse button. Unless otherwise specified, it typically involves the selection button (left mouse button).

clipboard
An area in memory that is used to temporarily store data such as text or graphics in order to transfer them between different programs.

clock port
A connection on the motherboard of the Amiga for the inclusion of a real-time clock (RTC), which continues to run on battery power even when the computer is switched off. The clock port can be used for other purposes, e.g. connecting extensions that provide additional functions such as Ethernet or USB.

close
The removal of a window from the display to close a drawer or program, or complete access to a data file.

close gadget
A gadget that is often (but not always) present, positioned in the top left-hand corner of a window that is used to close the window.

cold start
Turn on a switched off Amiga.

color correction
A print option that is selected via the graphic printer preset (PrinterGfx) to adjust the colors of a print output to the screen display.

command
An instruction to the Amiga to execute a task or achieve a certain result, executable for example via the Shell by text input or via the graphical user interface.

command line
The line into which commands and their corresponding arguments are entered. The term *command line* also refers to all information that is entered in this line.

command line buffer
A memory area that saves the last commands entered into a Shell so that they can be called up as required using the cursor keys without having to enter the command again.

command repeat
A function of the Shell to re-execute previously entered command lines using the cursor keys.

commodities
Small programs that run in the background of AmigaOS.

CompactFlash (CF)
A small form factor storage medium that was originally used in digital cameras and other mobile devices. It is robust, noiseless and has high storage capacities (from 4 GB to 512 GB). CF cards

can also be used as a drive and thus as a hard disk replacement in the Amiga via an adapter for the IDE interface.

console
A window that is used to input and output text, e.g. the Shell window.

control key shortcuts
A keyboard combination (shortcut) for executing a special function. It involves pressing the control key together with another key. Some functions of control key combinations are executed immediately after the shortcut is pressed, e.g. cancelling a process by pressing *Ctrl+C*. Some shortcuts, on the other hand, create an inversely displayed control character without any further immediate consequences.

controller
A hardware device, e.g. on a plug-in card that serves as an interface between the computer and a peripheral device (e.g. hard drive), e.g. SCSI or IDE controller for connecting a drive.

coprocessor
A separate processor chip that supports the main processor in certain tasks, such as floating point calculations or faster data transfers.

copy & paste
Copying a data block (text and/or graphic) and inserting this block at a different location.

CPU
→ *processor*

Ctrl
An important key on the Amiga keyboard, used as a → *qualifier.*

current directory
The current position in a directory structure. The directory used by AmigaDOS as the default working directory if no other directory is declared.

cursor
A cursor is a visual marker symbol – on the Amiga, a highlighted rectangle or vertical bar – that is displayed on the screen and indicates the current position or editing point in a text document or text gadget.

custom chips
Special chips i.e. integrated circuits developed for Amigas responsible for specific tasks such as graphics and sound processing, and play a key role in the Amiga's multimedia capabilities. Examples across the various Amiga generations include Agnus, Alice, Amber, Buster, Denise, Gary, Gayle, Lisa, Paula and Ramsey.

cycle gadget
A gadget that can be used to select one of several options. Only one option is displayed at a time and the next option becomes visible by selecting the gadget. The displayed option corresponds to the currently selected option.

cylinder
A technical, logical subdivision of a magnetic disk-based drive such as a hard disk or floppy disk. The 3.5-inch disks standardized on Amigas have 80 cylinders. A cylinder consists of superimposed tracks on several disk surfaces.

data
A collection of information.

daughterboard
An add-on board that plugs into the motherboard of an Amiga to provide additional functions or enhancements. These expansion cards are developed specifically for the Amiga and can have various functions, such as providing Zorro slots, video ports or additional memory. Available for certain big box Amigas only.

dead key
A key or key combination used to enter diacritical characters or accents over letters. By pressing the dead keys to the left and right of the number row on the keyboard (^, ' and `) in combination with a letter, various accented characters such as grave, acute or circumflex accents (for example à, á, â) can be created.

debugging
→ *troubleshooting*

default
A value or action that the system automatically accepts unless the user specifies otherwise.

default icon
A kind of pseudo icon, i.e. an icon that is displayed for an object for which no .info file is available when the menu item *Window > Show > All files* is selected.

default tool
A program specified in the information requester of a project icon. When the project icon is opened, the default tool is automatically loaded and started to edit the project.

delete
The removal of a file, buffer or other item in memory.

delimiter
A character or character string used in a text or data structure to separate or identify sections or elements, e.g. to mark the beginning and end of a character string. Examples of delimiters are commas, spaces, tabs, quotes or specially defined character strings.

Denise
A dedicated custom graphics chip in the Amiga that is responsible for displaying images, animations and graphic effects.

density
The number of print dots per inch. Many printers

support different print densities. Usually, the higher the density, the sharper and richer in contrast the print.

depth gadget
A gadget in the top right corner of a window or screen on the Amiga to bring it either to the foreground or background.

desktop Amiga
Amiga models in compact cases that feature a handy built-in keyboard and can be placed on the desk, but offer fewer options for internal expansions. Typical desktop Amigas are the Amiga 500, 600 and 1200.

destination
The device, directory or file that receives data during a read/write process.

device
A physical device such as a printer or floppy disk drive, or a software unit (logical device) such as CON: or NIL:. These devices serve as a source or destination for data, depending on how they are used in a system.

device driver
→ *handler*

device name
A system-wide, short name that designates a specific device. Device names in AmigaOS always end with a colon (:). Examples: DH1:, DF0:, PRT:.

device unit
→ *unit*

DF0:
Device designation for the first floppy drive, usually internal. Further floppy drives are labelled DF1:, DF2:, DF3: etc.

dialog window
→ *requester*

dir
→ *directory*

directory
The file system of an operating system, which comprises a subdivision that is used to store files and directories in an organized manner. On the Workbench, directories are represented by drawer icons.
→ *drawer*

disk
A storage medium for large amounts of data, often magnetic (floppy disks, hard drives), sometimes optical (laser discs).

disk drive
A storage device for writing and reading data on a storage disk (e.g. floppy disk, hard disk).

disk operating system
→ *DOS*

disk swap
Inserting different physical or virtual disks into the same drive, e.g. when installing programs with more than one disk or when copying a disk on a system with only one disk drive.

display
1) Showing a screen on the Workbench.
2) A monitor (screen) for video output.

display field
A rectangular box typically located under a scroll gadget or next to a cycle gadget that displays the current selection. A display field cannot be edited.

dithering
1) The creation of uniform color or greyscale shading by alternating pixel colors or densities. The PrinterGfx and PrinterPS preferences offer several setting options for the automatic dithering of printed graphics.
2) Creating the representation of a color by a pattern composed of other colors, e.g. violet by alternating red and blue pixels.

DMS (Disk Masher System)
An archiving format widely used on the Amiga with which the contents of floppy disks can be compressed and saved as single DMS files. Compressed DMS files can be extracted and restored using appropriate tools to restore the original disk contents. Emulators such as WinUAE also support DMS as a virtual disk.

double-click
Pressing the selection button (left mouse button) twice in quick succession.

DOS
The basic software of a computer that controls its basic read and write functions.

drag
Move an icon, window or screen across the Workbench by pointing to the object, holding the selection button down and moving the mouse.

drag select
Simultaneous selection of several icons by holding down the left mouse button and dragging a frame around them using the mouse. When the mouse button is released, all icons within this frame are highlighted and selected.

drawer
A section of a storage area on a drive. A drawer corresponds to an AmigaDOS directory. Sometimes also referred to as a *directory* or, outside the Amiga system, a *folder*.

drive
A storage unit, e.g. floppy disk or hard drive partition, which can be accessed after mounting.

drive name
The name of a drive (not to be confused with the device name). Renaming a disk changes the drive name, but not the device name. Examples: Hare: or Hedgehog:.

dump (graphic dump)
A printout of the image displayed on the screen.

E

ECS
→ *Extended Chip Set*

editor
A program for creating and editing certain file types, e.g. Prefs for system settings or TextEdit for text files.

emulation
Software that can imitate a computer on another computer. WinUAE, for example, can run Amiga programs and games on a Windows PC without requiring a real Amiga computer. The emulator reproduces the Amiga hardware and operating system so that Amiga software can run on it as if it had been executed on a real Amiga computer. In addition to WinUAE for Windows, there are many other emulation environments for a wide variety of platforms, e.g. vAmiga for Mac OS, FS-UAE for Linux, UAE4Droid for Android or Amiberry for Raspberry Pi.

environment variables
Environment variables (in ENV: and ENVARC:) are used to provide and save specific configuration data and settings for the operating system and for applications. These variables can contain various parameters, such as paths to directories, system settings or user preferences.

error (bug)
Generally a software or hardware error, or a fundamental technical malfunction. The first documented use of the term *bug* is by computer scientist Grace Hopper. In 1947, at a time when computers still consisted mainly of mechanical components, she found a fault in a computer and realized that a moth (bug) was stuck in a relay of the device and causing the error. Hopper removed the moth and noted in her diary: “First actual case of bug being found”.

error code
→ *return code*

escape sequence
A character sequence that begins with the escape character and triggers special functions when entered into the command line or printed as part of a character string. Escape sequences are normally used to change the font (or other settings) of a printer or console window.

expression
A written instruction that links a sequence of variables, fields or constants using arithmetic, comparative or logical operators.

execute
Execution of the instructions given in a command line, program or script file by the Amiga.

extended selection
The simultaneous selection of several icons by holding down the Shift key and selecting the icons with the mouse.

Extended Chip Set (ECS)
An improved version of the original Agnus and Denise custom chips of the original Amiga 1000/500/2000, used in the Amiga 600 and Amiga 3000, etc. The ECS offers additional screen modes (ECS modes) and extended graphical features. Many of the advantages of the ECS can only be used with version 2 of AmigaOS (or higher).

Extra Halfbrite (EHB)
A graphics mode that doubles the number of screen colors by providing an equivalent with halved brightness (intensity) for each existing color.

F

Fast RAM
Universal memory that is used by programs and data and usually works faster than Chip RAM.

field
The screen area in the background of the text under a Workbench icon. The color of this field can be changed using the Font preferences.

file
An organized collection of data that bears a name and is stored on a drive. It can be in any imaginable format, e.g. executable programs, texts, graphics or music.

file system
The system and software for organizing data, files and directories on a drive. The FFS (Fast File System) and the OFS (Old File System) are traditionally used on the Amiga.

flag
→ *protection bits*

flickerfixer
A flickerfixer is an add-on module that improves image output quality and expands the connection options for monitors. It *deinterlaces* the video output signal to create a flicker-free image on modern displays. → *Interlace*, → *Scandoubler*

floppy disk
A removable, magnetic storage medium, e.g. on the standard Amiga, a 3.5-inch floppy disk with a plastic cover. Since AmigaOS 3.2, also a virtual disk in ADF file format.

font (font set)
The specific design of a set of letters, special characters and numbers used for text display. The Amiga offers various predefined font sets that can be selected depending on the application and personal preferences. A font set defines the appearance of the letters and symbols, including their shape, thickness, proportions and style. Examples of font sets on the Amiga are Topaz and Helvetica. Each font can

be available in different sizes, which are specified in points, such as 9 point (pt).

format
Description of the correct syntax of AmigaDOS commands.

formatting
The preparation of a disk for use in the Amiga. Formatting deletes all data previously stored on this volume. This process creates a new file system structure that allows the Amiga to recognize the disk and store new data on it.

fragmentation
The scattering of related data in different locations on a drive or in the memory. Fragmentation can lead to a deterioration in system performance and software being unable to run.

function keys
Special keys labeled F1 to F10 at the top of the Amiga keyboard used to trigger certain predefined or customizable special functions.

G

gadget
A graphic element that appears in a window or screen and can be used to trigger a specific function with the mouse. Each gadget belongs to an individual type and has a function. Most gadgets appear to protrude slightly from the display and *sink* into the screen like a push-button when selected.

Gary
A custom chip in the Amiga that is responsible for various system functions such as keyboard and disk drive control.

gateway
An external connection between other computers, systems or networks.

Gayle
A custom chip in the Amiga 600 and 1200 that is responsible for controlling the hard disk and IDE interfaces, and regulates the connection of mass storage devices.

genlock
Abbreviation for *generator lock* or *generator locking*. A device in video production that enables the synchronization of image and sound signals from different video sources (e.g. TV set, video recorder) by creating a timing signal that determines the frame rate and picture synchronization for other connected devices. Genlocks have often been used for live broadcasts, picture-in-picture effects, or the integration of computer graphics or titles and subtitles into video content.

global
General: the global, comprehensive or system-wide scope or application of variables, configurations, services or networks. In relation to processes: valid in all processes. The opposite of *local*.

Gotek
A modern hardware alternative to the floppy drive that is based on USB technology and uses USB sticks instead of floppy disks to read Amiga disk format images (→ *ADF*). By using a Gotek on the Amiga, these virtual floppy disks in ADF format can be stored on a USB stick and loaded directly from the Gotek drive.

graphics memory
→ *Chip RAM*

GUI (graphical user interface)
The visual representation of an operating system or software that allows users to interact with the computer via graphical elements such as icons, menus, buttons and windows. A GUI facilitates user-friendliness and interaction with a computer, as text-based command line interfaces are largely dispensed with. The Workbench is the GUI for the Amiga.

H

HAM (Hold and Modify)
A special graphics mode of the Amiga that allows the full color palette of the Amiga to be displayed on the screen.

handler
Program files that act as intermediate instances between AmigaDOS and physical devices. These device drivers enable the communication and control of hardware devices by the operating system and are stored in the **L:** directory.

handshaking
An electronic or software-based protocol for handling serial communication between two computer devices.

hard disk
A magnetic, internal or external data storage device that is used for the permanent storage of data and offers a high read and write speed.

hard disk file (HDF)
A file type used by emulators such as WinUAE. It bundles data into one single archive and is recognized as a virtual hard disk.

HDD
Abbreviation for *Hard Disk Drive* → *hard disk*

HDMI (High-Definition Multimedia Interface)
A widely used interface for the high quality digital transmission of video and audio signals over a single cable, resulting in easy installation and improved audio and video performance. An additional HDMI adapter is required on the Amiga to convert the video and audio signal and transmit it via an output to an HDMI-compatible device such as a monitor or TV.

hexadecimal
A system for representing numbers and data that is often used in software development. It uses a base of 16, in contrast to the decimal system, which has a base of 10. In the hexadecimal system, the numbers 0 to 9 are represented normally, followed by the letters A to F, which represent the numbers 10 to 15. This system is often used in computer science and digital technology as it enables a compact representation of binary data.

hierarchical
In AmigaDOS the organization of directories is often referred to as a tree hierarchy. Directories in AmigaDOS can contain other directories (subdirectories) as well as files or a combination of both.

host
Usually a computer that is connected to other computers in a local or global network and provides services or resources. The host can be seen as the central hub through which other devices can access the network. It provides services such as file sharing, printing, database access or web hosting, and allows other devices to communicate with it and use its services.

hot key
A key or key combination that opens a hidden window in commodity programs.

hot spot
A pixel in a mouse pointer (usually the tip of an arrow or the intersection point of a crosshair) that must touch an object on the screen for it to be selected.

I

IC (integrated circuit)
→ *processor*

icon
A compact graphic that symbolizes elements such as a program, drive or drawer. Icons can be moved with the mouse and selected by double-clicking to interact with the elements they represent.

IFF (Interchange File Format)
A standardized file format that is mainly used on Amiga computers that was originally developed by Electronic Arts to enable the cross-platform exchange of data, especially multimedia content such as graphics, audio files and animations.

.info file
A file that contains, among other things, the image and position data of an icon.

initialize
Refers to the process in which an object, variable or system is brought to a defined initial state, e.g. formatting a drive or transmitting basic settings for a printer to ensure proper functionality.

input buffer
A memory area used to save incoming data via the serial interface.

interface
→ *port*

interlace
A display mode that doubles the vertical screen resolution in some Amiga screen modes and displays the image in two fields. By using interlace, more lines can be displayed on the screen, resulting in a sharper and more detailed image. However, it can lead to a flickering effect, particularly on modern flat screens, which can be remedied by using flickerfixers.

internal
Refers to a command that is integrated into the Shell of AmigaOS. This command is already present in the system and does not need to be loaded separately from a storage medium.

internet
A global computer network that enables data to be exchanged between connected computers. The internet enables the use of various services such as the World Wide Web and e-mail. In contrast to an intranet, which is restricted to certain user groups and is usually password-protected.

J

jumper
A small, black connector that can be plugged into various pins on a circuit board to configure hardware, for example to declare a floppy drive as DF0: or DF1:.

KB (kilobyte)
1024 bytes. Often abbreviated as K. (In contrast, a small k stands for exactly 1000, as in kg)

keyboard shortcut
A way of executing mouse actions or a command more quickly using the keyboard by pressing a single key or a key combination.

keymap
A file that defines the arrangement of characters on a keyboard and the function of each key. Each keyboard language supported by the system uses its own keyboard layout file.

keyword
A term recognized by an AmigaDOS command or in a parameter input to identify an argument or specify an option.

Kickstart
The ROM-based part of the Amiga operating system. It is a collection of firmware and operating system routines that are loaded when the Amiga is booted. Kickstart contains basic functions and drivers

required to run the Amiga system, including device management, the file system and the user interface. It provides the basic software platform on which Amiga applications can be run.

L

LhA
Abbreviation for *Lempel-Ziv-Huffman Archive*, a file format widely used on the Amiga. It is used to compress files on the Amiga, i.e. to *pack* and archive them. LhA is based on a combination of compression algorithms to save files in a space-saving manner. LhA-compressed archives can be extracted and restored using appropriate tools.

library
A collection of related functions and data that can be used by various programs. Libraries are located either in the ROM or usually in the *LIBS:* drawer.

Lisa
A custom chip that replaces Denise in AGA Amigas and is responsible for controlling sprites and bitplanes, among other things.

local
General: the scope or application of variables, configurations, services or networks that only apply on a single computer or in a limited network. In relation to processes: only valid in the current process. The opposite of *global*.

M

macro
A single command that represents a series of commands and is used to simplify frequently used command sequences. ARexx programs are often referred to as macros.

MB (megabyte)
1024 kilobytes (1,048,576 bytes). Often abbreviated as M or Meg. In some cases, MB can also mean a rounded 1,000 KB (1,024,000 bytes) or even exactly 1,000,000 bytes, e.g. when specifying hard drive capacities.

memory
The internal memory area in which data and programs are stored. The Amiga has Chip RAM (graphics memory), Fast RAM (normal memory) and ROM (read only memory). The size of the RAM (random access memory) is a significant factor affecting the number and size of programs that can be executed simultaneously on the Amiga. External drives such as hard disks or CD-ROMs are also referred to as mass storage.

menu
A displayed list of options that is called up by pressing the menu button (right mouse button). Commands for controlling a program can be selected from the menu.

menu bar
A list of command entries in the menu that appears at the top of the screen when the menu button is held down.

menu button
The right mouse button.

menu item
The individual options displayed in a menu. For example, *New drawer* is always the first menu item in the Workbench window menu.

microprocessor
→ *processor*

modem
A device that converts digital data into an analog format for transmission over telephone lines and converts analog signals back into digital data for reception and decoding. Modems can be operated on the serial port of the Amiga.

modular
AmigaOS is conceptually a modular and therefore very flexible and scalable operating system. It consists of clearly delimited, independent modules that fulfill different functions. Examples are the reloadable device drivers (→ *device*) and libraries (→ *library*).

monitor
A device for displaying the visual output of a computer. There are different types of monitors: old, analog CRT monitors (CRT with RGB support) and new, digital flat screens (LCD). Special accessories such as an HDMI adapter or interface are required to connect LCD monitors to the Amiga.

monospace
→ *non-proportional font*

motherboard
The main board of the computer on which the basic electronics and other hardware components, such as the processor, RAM, expansion cards and interfaces, are mounted. It is also the central element of the Amiga, connecting all components to each other and enabling communication between them.

mouse
A handy device for moving the mouse pointer on the screen and interacting with the Amiga. The mouse buttons are used to display menus and to select and move elements such as icons, windows and screens.

mouse acceleration
An option that can be set in the Input preferences that accelerates the movement of the mouse pointer in relation to the mouse movement. It enables a higher speed for larger movements, but at the expense of precision.

mouse pointer
→ *pointer*

multiscan
A special type of monitor that supports different deflection frequencies (screen modes).

multitasking
The special ability of AmigaOS to seemingly execute several tasks or processes simultaneously by dividing the computing time between them. This means that programs can run in parallel without influencing or blocking each other, for example calling up an internet page and executing a script in the background at the same time.

N

name pattern
AmigaDOS allows you to enter wildcards to search for files with common text patterns without having to enter the filenames individually.

non-proportional font
Also known as a monospace font, a character set with a fixed width (e.g. Topaz) in which each character takes up the same amount of space. A capital W, for example, does not take up any more space than a lowercase j.

O

offset
An offset to the left or right, or generally a distance (relative to another point).

open
Makes the selected object accessible for use. A tool can be opened by double-clicking on its icon or by selecting the *Open* menu item in the *Icons* menu. When a disk or drawer icon is opened, a window appears in which the contents of the disk or drawer are displayed. A program is started when a project or program icon is opened.

operating system (OS)
The software in the ROM or on a drive that controls the basic functions of the Amiga.
→ *AmigaOS*,
→ *AmigaDOS*.

overscan
The normally unused border area around a standard-sized screen. Use the Overscan preferences to expand your screen and utilize this area.

overwrite
Writing data to memory, file or disk by replacing the previous content at the storage location with new data.

P

parallel
An interface that transmits a complete byte (8 bits) during data transfer, in contrast to the serial interface, where single bits are transmitted. The Amiga has a parallel port (also referred to as Centronics), which is commonly used as a printer port.

parent
The window from which another window was opened. Also refers to the directory that contains the current directory.

parity
An error detection method in serial communication in which an additional bit is appended to data bytes.

partition
A storage area on a hard drive that is used to store data and is treated by the system as a separate volume.

paste
The process of inserting a copied content.

path
A character string consisting of a drive name and drawer names that describes the storage location of a file in the file system.

Paula
A dedicated custom sound chip that is responsible for audio output. Paula also controls the floppy drives and processes the serial port and joystick ports.

PCMCIA
Short for *Personal Computer Memory Card International Association*, a slot available in some Amiga models (1200, 600). It enables the connection of external PCMCIA expansions, which can offer various functions, such as network cards, CD-ROM drives or memory expansions.

peripherals
An external device connected to the Amiga, e.g. external drive, printer or monitor.

pictogram
→ *icon*

pitch
Character density for print output (cpi = characters per inch).

pixel
The individual dots of light that make up the Amiga's screen display. A pixel is the smallest unit of display information on a screen. The term is derived from *picture element*.

plane
→ *bitplane*

point (mouse)
Move and position the mouse pointer to point to a desired object to call it up (by double-clicking).

point (unit)
A unit of measurement for vertical font size. As a rule, it corresponds to 1/72 inch, which on the Amiga corresponds to one pixel on the screen.

pointer (mouse)
A small image on the screen (often in the form of an arrow or crosshair) that follows the movements of the mouse. The pointer can be used to select icons, symbols and other elements on the Workbench.

pointer (code)
In programs, refers to a specific type of variable that contains the address of another memory object.

port
Term for an interface connection. As a *message port*, it refers to a software interface that enables communication between two simultaneously running programs (ARexx). As an *SMTP port*, it describes the channel for sending e-mail communication between the user's mail program and the mail provider's system.

PostScript printer
A printer that can process text and graphic data in the *PostScript* page description language.

PowerPC (PPC)
A RISC-based microprocessor architecture developed jointly by IBM, Apple and Motorola. Stands for *Performance Optimization With Enhanced RISC Performance Computing*. The PowerPC architecture was used in various devices such as workstations and Macintosh computers, as well as some Amiga models, including the Amiga X1000 and X5000, as well as the Amiga 1200, 3000 and 4000 with Blizzard PPC or CyberStorm PPC turbo cards. PowerPC Amigas are not hardware compatible with the original 68k Amigas and require a special version of AmigaOS (version 4) that is optimized for the PPC architecture.

Preferences (Prefs)
A section of AmigaOS in which the central configuration of the system can be done with several Prefs editors, e.g. for screen, printer, pointer or icon behavior.

press and hold (button)
Hold down a mouse button or keyboard key while performing other actions (dragging the mouse, pressing an additional key, etc.).

printer driver
A program that allows for communication between Amiga and printer by converting data into a format that the printer can understand. The driver is fed data in standardized format (ASCII characters and ANSI escape sequences) from the Amiga and converts it into a format that the printer can process.

print-out
The output by a printer of data from a computer.

processor
The central unit of a computer, often referred to as the *brain*. This microprocessor chip is an integrated circuit (IC) that is mainly responsible for executing instructions in software. The term *central processing unit* is also sometimes used to describe the entire computer, as opposed to the peripherals.

processor slot
A slot on the Amiga's motherboard that is used to install processor expansion cards. These cards contain a processor and additional RAM memory that improve system performance. Such expansion slots can be found in various forms in almost all Amiga models.

program
A sequence of bundled instructions and commands that tell the Amiga how to perform specific tasks. Includes system tools, games and other software.

project
A file that serves as a storage location for data created or used by a program. Examples of projects are files created with a text editor or presentation program.

prompt
A message or gadget indicating that the Amiga is expecting a command input.

protection bits
A series of characteristics that can be saved for each file. Protection bits designate the file type and control the operations permitted for this file, such as reading, writing or deleting.

pure
The state of a command or program that can remain in memory. If a file is labeled as *pure*, it means that the protection bit p is set.

Q

qualifier
A key such as Shift, Ctrl, Amiga, Alt or CapsLock, that causes a different interpretation of the keyboard or mouse input by the Amiga at the same time or afterwards.

queue
A process sequence that resembles a queue in which a series of commands is processed sequentially, i.e. one after the other, for example from a script such as the *user-startup*.

R

radio button gadget
A round gadget next to an option in a list that is used to select a single option. Only one option can be selected from the list at a time.

RAM (random access memory)
The part of the Amiga's internal memory that can be used for data storage and to which the processor chip has direct access. Applications are loaded from disks into the RAM and occupy additional RAM for processing and storing data while the Amiga is switched on. Data in RAM is lost when the Amiga is restarted (rebooted) or turned off.

RAM Disk
An area of RAM memory that offers the functionality of a virtual drive. Because it contains no

mechanical elements, the RAM Disk is significantly faster than a physical drive.

Ramsey
A custom chip in the Amiga 3000 and 4000 (T) that takes over the function of the memory controller and is responsible for managing the main memory.

read
The process of retrieving stored information.

read only
The state of a disk in which its contents can only be displayed but not changed.

read/write
The contents of a drive in the *read/write* state can be read and also changed and saved.

real-time clock (RTC)
A real-time clock is a battery-operated (*battery-backed*) clock that is installed on the Amiga's motherboard, for example, and stores the current time and date. The RTC is important because it stores the time and date even when the computer is switched off and thus ensures that files and folders are and remain correctly dated.

reboot
→ *restart*

redirect
Redefining the default settings for the source or destination of the input or output of a command using the special characters < and >.

release
A specific software version, for example 3.2.2.1 for the current version of the AmigaOS.

reset
→ *restart*

resident
A program is resident if it has been permanently loaded into memory with the RESIDENT command in order to speed up its execution. Resident programs and commands are set up so that they do not have to be reloaded if they are executed repeatedly. Only pure files can be saved resident (→ *pure*).

requester
A window that requests user input and contains gadgets to select options and choose between continuing and cancelling the current operation. To close the requester, select one of the action gadgets displayed.

resolution
The number of pixels in a respective screen mode. The PAL high-res screen, for example, has a resolution of 640 horizontal by 256 vertical pixels.

restart (reboot)
You can reset the Amiga by simultaneously pressing the Ctrl key and the left and right Amiga keys. This resets the RAM memory, which has roughly the same effect as switching the power supply on and off. This process is also known as a warm start.

return code
A numeric value, variable or status message returned by AmigaDOS to indicate the success or failure of the execution of a command.

RGB (red-green-blue)
A color model, and the video signal based on it, that is used to display colors on screens and other digital devices by combining different intensities of the three primary colors. The standard Amiga output uses an analog RGB video mode.

Rigid Disk Block (RDB)
Compare → *root block*. The RDB contains geometry data and therefore the partition information of the drive.

ROM (read only memory)
Permanent memory that is preprogrammed with important system instructions and cannot be changed. User commands or program operations have no influence on the contents of the ROM.

root block
The area of a disk that contains the name of the disk, the root directory and information about its organization. If the root block is deleted, all data on the disk can no longer be retrieved and access to stored data becomes virtually impossible. This applies to different types of disks such as floppy disks or hard disks. See also → *Rigid Disk Block (RDB)*

root directory
The top directory in the hierarchy of a file system structure. It is the directory from which all other directories and files in the file system are derived and is created when a drive is formatted. In AmigaDOS, the root directory is specified with the drive name followed by a colon, e.g. DH0: (in Unix with /, in Windows with C:).

router
A device that controls data traffic between different networks by analysing packets and forwarding them to the correct destination, e.g. for connecting a home computer or computer network to the global internet.

RS-232
→ *serial interface*

save
Writing data or creating a copy.

scaling
Proportionally changing the size of a graphic to be displayed in an image editing program or a graphic for output on a printer. Scaling is possible in both directions: shrinking and enlarging. Not to be confused with zooming.

scandoubler
A scandoubler is an external device or hardware extension that *doubles* the vertical frequency of the image output from 15 kHz to 31 kHz so that modern monitors can display the image. The familiar flickering in interlace modes is retained. → *flickerfixer*

screen
The area of a display to which certain graphic properties apply, such as resolution or color depth. Screens are usually, but not always, as wide as the visible area. The Amiga allows several screens with different properties (public screens) to be opened and used simultaneously.

screen mode
A term for the parameter set that defines a screen, e.g. resolution and deflection frequency. An example of the high-res screen mode is 640×256 pixels.

script
A text file that contains a series of automatically executable AmigaDOS commands that are used together to perform a complex or repetitive task. Examples are the *startup-sequence* and *user-startup*, which are processed when the Amiga is started.

scroll
Moving the content through the visible area of a window or list.

scroll area
The shaded area in which the scroll bar can be dragged. You can click on the scroll area to move the scroll bar.

scroll arrows
Graphical icons in the form of arrows that are displayed in the user interface to enable content in windows or screens to be scrolled beyond the available display area.

scroll bar
A highlighted portion of the scroll area that is used to drag non-visible parts of a window to another position. The size of the scroll bar varies and indicates how much of the entire window is currently visible.

scroll gadget
A graphical element that allows the user to look through a list of options or move through the visible area of a window. A scroll gadget consists of a scroll list, a scroll area, scroll bar and scroll arrows.

scroll list
The options that appear in a scroll gadget. If the list is too large to be displayed in full in the scroll gadget, you can scroll through the list using the scroll bar or the scroll arrows.

search path
The list of directories (paths) that AmigaDOS scans when searching for a command. Directories can be deleted from or added to the list using the PATH command.

Secure Digital (SD)
A very small flash-based storage medium that is mainly used in mobile devices such as smartphones and digital cameras. SD cards and their modern variants (microSD) are robust and offer high transfer rates and low power consumption. They are available in various sizes and capacities and can also be used as a drive, and therefore as a hard disk replacement in the Amiga using an adapter for the IDE interface.

select
Select an element to be edited or opened by moving the mouse pointer over the element and simply clicking with the selection button.

selection box
A gadget from which one of several displayed elements can be selected. Often used for colors.

selection button
The left mouse button, used to select (mark) items.

serial port (RS-232)
An interface that transmits data bit by bit. In contrast to the parallel interface, which transmits complete bytes (8 bits) simultaneously. For example, modems or printers can be connected to the serial port of the Amiga, but the serial port can also be used to connect other Amigas or PCs for communication via a null modem cable.

set
Changing a bit or feature to the activated state (*on*). As opposed to *clear*.

Shell
A text-based input interface that can be used to send commands to the Amiga. The Shell is a console window that supports numerous special functions, for example command line repeatings, alias names and copy and paste operations. → *CLI*

shortcut
A key combination that provides quick access to a command, file, or application, reducing the steps needed to perform an action. See also → *control key shortcuts*

size gadget
A gadget that can appear in the bottom right-hand corner of a Workbench window and be used to enlarge or reduce a window.

slider gadget
A gadget that allows you to select a value by dragging a visual slider bar within the slider area. Changing values are displayed when the slider is moved.

slider value
A number that appears next to a slider gadget that indicates the currently selected value.

smoothing
An option in the PrinterGfx prefs that attempts to reduce the appearance of stepped or jagged lines in printouts.

snapshot
Saving the size and position of a window and/or the icons in it.

source
A device, drawer or file that provides data. When copying files from a CompactFlash (CF) card, for example, the CF card is referred to as the source medium.

SSD
A modern storage medium based on flash memory that is used in computers and other devices. Unlike conventional hard drives, an SSD has no moving parts and therefore offers greater speed, reliability and energy efficiency. SSDs are available in different sizes and capacities and are often used as an upgrade for older computers to improve their performance. Stands for *Solid State Drive*.

stack
An area of RAM memory reserved as temporary memory for applications.

standard
→ *default*

start
→ *boot*

startup-sequence
A script that is automatically executed when the Amiga is started and takes care of the configuration of hardware and directory systems.

stop bits
Additional bits that are appended during serial communication to indicate the end of a character.

streamer
A powerful if outdated mass storage device based on high-capacity magnetic tape cartridges, mainly used for backups and the general protection of large amounts of data. Rarely used today. Also known as tape streamer or tape drive.

Strg
Two keys on Windows keyboards that functionally correspond to the A-keys on an Amiga keyboards (relevant in emulators). Some keyboards use a Windows flag and menu symbol instead.

string
A coherent snippet of text characters that is treated as a unit.

string gadget
→ *text gadget*

subdirectory
A directory that is located within another directory and can be seen as a kind of *drawer within a drawer*.

submenu
A subordinate list for a higher-level menu item, e.g. the *Workbench > Window > Show* item with its submenu entries *Only icons* and *All files*. A branched submenu belonging to a menu item is identified by a right arrow symbol to the right of the entry. The use of submenus enables a hierarchical organization of options to provide a better overview.

Super Denise
A custom chip, used in the Amiga 3000 among others, that offers improved graphics functions and higher resolutions compared to the original Denise chip.

SYS
The name of the drive from which the Amiga is started. AmigaDOS assumes that the system files and directories are located there, unless they have been assigned to other folders/drives using the Assign command.

T

tape drive
→ *streamer*

Temp (T:/RAM:T)
A directory in RAM for storing files that are automatically deleted after a restart.

template
One way to display the correct syntax for an AmigaDOS or ARexx command. If you execute the command name with a following question mark (?) as the only argument (e.g. **makedir ?**), the template of the command is displayed.

text gadget
A gadget in which text information such as a filename or command can be entered. Such fields are used by many programs. One example is the text gadget inside the *Execute command* requester (*Workbench > Execute command*). Also called a *string gadget*.

threshold
A value in the PrinterGfx prefs that relates to color intensity. The threshold value specifies which colors are printed as black and which as white in black and white printing.

time stamp
The date and time assigned to a file. Typically the creation or modification date (or time) of the file or directory.

title bar
The top edge of a screen or window that normally displays the name of the screen or window. The appearance and content of the title bar can be customized using the Workbench prefs.

toggle
Switching between two states by repeatedly pressing a button. It is often used to switch a function on or off or to switch between different

displays or modes. Toggling allows users to change certain settings or views quickly and easily without having to perform additional steps.

tool
A program that creates or uses data, for example a text editor or image processor.

tool types
An optional parameter that can be entered in the information window of a program icon to control the behavior of the associated program. For example, if the SECONDS feature is specified in the information requester of the clock, the clock will display seconds when it is opened.

tracing
A function that can be used to trace and log the execution sequence of an ARexx program or the startup-sequence, for example. Tracing makes it possible to go through program code step by step and collect information about variables, functions and the program flow. It is helpful for troubleshooting, understanding program behavior and analysing problems.

track
Divides a disk into concentric circles. See also → *cylinder*.

Trashcan
A container for anything that is no longer needed.

troubleshooting
Finding and correcting errors (bugs) in software or hardware, also called *debugging*.

turbo card
An expansion card that can be installed in an Amiga to increase its performance. Depending on the type, the card can contain additional processor and memory resources that make the Amiga faster and expand its capabilities. Examples of turbo cards are CyberStorm, Blizzard, ACA or Viper.

tuning
Adding hardware to a system and adjusting hardware settings to optimise performance, energy efficiency or other aspects. One example is the overclocking of processors.

type ahead
A Shell function of AmigaOS that allows commands to be entered while the output of a previous command is still displayed.

UAE
→ *emulation*

unit
A physical or logical device, e.g. a serial interface, which can have several sub-units and is identified by a unit number.

Universal Serial Bus
The USB standard enables the convenient connection of external peripheral devices such as keyboards, mice or storage devices to a computer. USB offers fast data transfer, plug-and-play functionality and an integrated power supply for connected devices. Solutions for retrofitting USB exist for the Amiga (see sections *USB* and *data transfer*).

USB
→ *Universal Serial Bus*

user-startup
A system-defined, user-customizable file that is loaded and executed when AmigaOS is started. The file, which can be edited with a text editor, contains commands, scripts and configuration settings that are automatically executed when the system is started.

utility
Usually refers to small auxiliary programs in the operating system.

VGA (video graphics array)
Analog graphics standard for video output, widely used on PCs in the 80s and 90s.

VGA connection
Interface for the transmission of VGA signals. The interface was later replaced first by DVI, then by DisplayPort and HDMI. Today, there are still monitors and flat screens with a VGA port that can output an Amiga video signal via an adapter in the Amiga.

videoslot
A slot on the Amiga's motherboard (e.g. Amiga 2000, 4000) used for the installation of video editing and graphics expansion cards. These cards, such as the legendary *Video Toaster*, enable advanced video and graphics functions on the Amiga.

volume
→ *drive*

wait pointer
→ *busy pointer*

wildcard
A character that is used when searching or when checking character strings to leave space for different characters or patterns. Wildcards enable a flexible and extended search for matches in name patterns. The question mark (?), for example, stands for any single character.

window
A rectangular area that can hold or display information of various kinds. Each window has a title bar that defines it and can have various icons on the edge.

WinUAE
→ *emulation*

Workbench
The graphical user interface (GUI) of the Amiga.

write
The process of saving data into RAM or onto a drive.

write-enable
A protection state that allows data to be stored on a drive. A floppy disk is *write-accessible* or *read/write*-able if the hole in the corner of the disk is closed by the small plastic slider. A file or directory is write-enabled with the related w protection bit.

write-protect
A protection state that prevents data storage on a drive. A disk is write-protected if the opening in the corner of the disk is visible. A file or directory is write-protected with the related protection bit w cleared out.

Z

zoom gadget
A gadget that can appear in the top right-hand corner of a window. It allows you to switch between different window sizes. If the Shift key is pressed when clicking on the gadget, the window is enlarged to fill the screen.

Zorro
An interface system with which expansion cards, e.g. for graphics, audio or network, can be connected to the Amiga motherboard. The 16-bit Zorro II bus with supported bus mastering DMA and AutoConfig protocol for automatic address space allocation was introduced with the A2000. The A3000 and A4000 used Zorro III, an advanced 32-bit bus that required a full 32-bit CPU.

1

16 bit
16 bits refers to the number of bits in a data transmission or processing. It means that there are 16 bits in each data word. A bit is the smallest memory unit and can have the value 0 or 1. With 16 bits, 2 to the power of 16 (65536) different values can be represented. In the computer world, this is often associated with the representation of numbers or the memory size in a specific format. The higher the number of bits, the more information can be processed at the same time.

16-bit computer
A 16-bit computer like the Amiga 500 processes data in 16-bit units, allowing it to represent 65,536 values (2^16). This affects how it processes, stores and accesses data. Compared to an 8-bit system, a 16-bit system can handle larger numbers, perform more complex calculations and support a larger memory address space, increasing memory capacity.

32 bit
32 bits refers to the size of a data word in a computer system. It means that the computer processes data in units of 32 bits. This enables the representation of 2 to the power of 32 (approximately 4.3 billion) different values and supports larger numbers and more complex calculations compared to smaller data word sizes such as 16 bits.

68000 (68k)
A powerful, versatile 16-bit processor developed by Motorola, which is used in different Amiga variants, including 32-bit. The original 68000 was used in the first Amiga generation (A1000, A500, A2000). In later Amiga models, the more powerful 68020, 68LC020, 68030, 68040 and, in modified devices, 68060 processors were used.

Thank you!

Our special thanks go to the AmigaOS 3.2 developer team and beta tester team for their tireless commitment and support of this book project.

Many thanks to **Marcus Gerards** for his important coordination and support.

Sincere thanks to **Olaf Barthel** for his expert advice at all times.

A thousand thanks to **Camilla Boemann** for her valuable advice and beautiful foreword.

A big compliment and thank you to the attentive eyes in the specialist editorial team: **Rainer Müller**, **Thomas Klein**, **Mikhail Malyshev**, **Ignacio Gully** and **Per-Olof Yliniemi**.

Thanks to **Anton Preinsack**, **Sascha van Wahnem**, **Frank Greshake** and **Daniel Reimann** for their editorial contributions.

Many thanks to **Eric Schütz** for his helpful tips and ever-watchful eye.

Thanks to **Kymon Zonias** for providing Amigas for the Kickstart photos.

Special thanks to **Jürgen Haage** for his kind permission to use content and for the many years of friendly cooperation.

Author credits

Martin Steigerwald: 2.10, 2.12, 4.4, 4.14-4.21, 5.1-5.4, 6.1, 6.2, 6.5
Simon Neumann: 1.1-1.2, 2.5, 2.7, 3.3, 3.10, 3.14-3.15, 3.17, 3.19, 4.4, 4.13, 6.4, 7.1, 7.4, 7.5, 8.1
Nico Barbat: 1.3-1.7, 1.8, 2.1, 2.5, 2.11, 3.1-3.2, 3.4-3.9, 3.18, 3.20, 4.5, 4.12, 4.24-4.30, 4.32-4.34, 4.36, 4.38, 6.3, 7.6, 8.1, 8.2, 8.3
Sascha van Wahnem: 2.3, 2.4, 2.6, 2.8, 2.9, 3.21, 4.11
Anton Preinsack: 4.1-4.3, 4.6-4.10, 4.22, 4.23, 4.31, 4.35, 4.37
Frank Greshake: 1.8
Daniel Reimann: 7.2
Editorial: 0.X, 3.11-3.13, 3.16, 7.3, 8.4

Image credits

Photos: Simon Neumann; except: Holger Crome (p. 33, 36, 38), Torsten Hees (p. 28), PLAION (p. 68)
Cover image: Paul Kitching
Screenshots: editorial team (NBA, MS, SN)